Expanding the Palace of Torah

BRANDEIS SERIES ON JEWISH WOMEN

Shulamit Reinharz, General Editor
Joyce Antler, Associate Editor
Sylvia Barack Fishman, Associate Editor

The Brandeis Series on Jewish Women is an innovative book series created by The Hadassah-Brandeis Institute. BSJW publishes a wide range of books by and about Jewish women in diverse contexts and time periods, of interest to scholars, and for the educated public. The series fills a major gap in Jewish learning by focusing on the lives of Jewish women and Jewish gender studies.

EXPANDING THE PALACE OF TORAH

Orthodoxy and Feminism

◦ Tamar Ross ◦

Brandeis University Press

Waltham, Massachusetts

PUBLISHED BY UNIVERSITY PRESS OF NEW ENGLAND

HANOVER AND LONDON

BRANDEIS UNIVERSITY PRESS

Published by University Press of New England,
One Court Street, Lebanon, NH 03766
www.upne.com
© 2004 by Brandeis University Press
Printed in the United States of America

5 4 3 2

Library of Congress Cataloging-in-Publication Data
Ross, Tamar.
Expanding the palace of Torah : Orthodoxy and feminism / Tamar Ross.— 1st ed.
    p.   cm. — (Brandeis series on Jewish women)
Includes bibliographical references and index.
ISBN 1–58465–389–2 (cloth : alk. paper) — ISBN 1–58465–390–6 (pbk. : alk. paper)
1. Feminism—Religious aspects—Judaism. 2. Women in Judaism.
3. Orthodox Judaism. 4. Judaism—Doctrines. 5. Jewish law—Philosophy.
6. Jewish women—Religious life. 7. Women—Legal status, laws, etc. (Jewish law)
I. Title. II. Series.
BM729.W6R67 2004
296.8'32'082—dc22   2004000632

And in general, this is an important rule in the struggle of ideas: we should not immediately feel obliged to refute any idea that comes to contradict something in the Torah, but rather we should build the palace of Torah above it. In so doing we reach a more exalted level, and through this exaltation the ideas are clarified. And thereafter, when we are not pressured by anything, we can confidently also fight on the Torah's behalf.

—A. I. Kook, *Iggerot Hareayah* I, 163–164

Contents

Preface

One of the difficulties about a feminist view of things is that once you are deep into it, it is not only a radical transformer of everything, but also extremely compelling and apt to make you forget what things looked like from the other side. This may be why feminists are generally inclined to attribute all opposition to moral and intellectual shortcomings in their opponents. The feminist who can see the oppression of women in the trivia of every day life, in much the same way that the believer can see the hand of God in what to the atheist is the unremarkable course of nature, may also incline to the common religious view that since the truth is manifest, the fallen state of the heathen can be imputed only to Sin, or, in this case, to vested interests and conditioning.

However, the feminist way of looking at things is not at all manifest, and feminists must do their opponents the justice of recognizing this. Once we have done it, we may be more inclined to try to understand what it is which makes many people of good will resist the movement, and from that work out ways of making them more sympathetic. —JANET RADCLIFFE RICHARDS[1]

A Few Personal Remarks

I never used to think of myself as a feminist. Even today I am not totally comfortable with this label. My reservations begin with the obsessive preoccupation with gender that characterizes many of feminism's devotees (who seem to regard this as the ultimate yardstick by which all else is to be measured). I also resent feminism's ability to evoke a sense of alienation from a mainstream culture in which I have a great stake. Nevertheless, I believe that it is a revolutionary movement of tremendous importance and that it has much of value to teach us. In addition to feminism's direct message, there are lessons to be learned from the challenges that it poses to religious tradition. Religious believers ignore these at their own peril.

Having been born and raised in an Orthodox rabbinic family, I always had a strong sense of myself as a religious Jew. I was fortunate enough to have been daughter to a father who passionately loved books, learning, teaching, and me. Although he admired and respected independent women,

I think that his attitude toward Jewish feminism—to the extent that he had occasion to encounter it as such—was ambivalent: he was curious but also wary of the upheaval it appeared to augur for traditional Jewish life as he knew it. But as I was his only child until the age of twelve, he devoted a great deal of his personal time and effort to giving me the best Jewish education possible, and he let me know that he was proud of my knowledge. I was never made to feel that I must face any limits on that score.

This is not to say that I never experienced problems with being a Jewish woman. I did. Such problems had to do with feeling an outsider when men discussed Torah around the Sabbath dinner table and invoked arguments demonstrating Talmudic learning on a level beyond what even the private lessons with my father had given me. I admired and was envious of the sense of religious dedication and spiritual energy that these guests exuded. I also felt stabs of envy when they would describe the atmosphere in the *yeshivot* (academies) that they attended and their joy at the opportunity to meet with people whom they regarded as saintly and worthy of veneration. I found my- self frustrated and occasionally even humiliated at synagogue celebrations on Simhat Torah (marking the end of the yearly cycle of Torah reading), when all the lively dancing and festivities were concentrated on the men's side of the synagogue, and the only active participation expected of women was to push and squirm in order to get a view. My sense of insult was stronger yet at being made to feel a pariah at ultra-Orthodox social gather- ings where women were shoved out of sight.

My parents would have been surprised, however, to learn that one of the major factors that contributed indirectly to my feminist consciousness was a deliberate educational decision they made for me. Because they were both ardent lovers of Hebrew and determined that this should be my mother tongue, they chose to see to my Jewish education privately rather than send me to the yeshiva day school for girls that my father himself had founded. They considered this school unsuitable because it taught the sacred texts of tradition in an English-speaking environment. Thus it was that I received my general education in an ordinary United States public school—and began to sense a dissonance between women's passive role in Jewish religious life and the equality and opportunity that I encountered in the secular world. The segregated environment in which some of my religious women friends were educated appeared pale and impoverished in comparison. Nonetheless, these feelings were in the background and did not impose upon or jaundice my love and attachment to tradition in any major way.

After making *aliyah* (moving to Israel) as a young woman, I opted to study Jewish philosophy in an academic setting. Undoubtedly the greater part of my motivation lay in this field's being as close as I, as a woman, could get at the time to a formal grounding in higher-level study of sacred Jewish texts. My first introduction to feminism of the Jewish variety was upon publication of Blu Greenberg's *On Women and Judaism: A View from Tradition,*[2] which was also—to the best of my knowledge—the first book-length manifest written by an Orthodox feminist. I remember being disturbed by the book. Although I sympathized with many of the author's sentiments, I felt her attitude toward *halakhah* was too instrumentalist; she seemed to regard the halakhic process as a flexible means to achieve any goal one might choose. An insufficient appreciation for the fine points of halakhic deliberation from an *insider's* point of view meant that she had little chance of winning over the halakhic authorities she hoped to influence. In this sense, her point of view appeared somewhat removed from the more traditionalist religious environment steeped in Torah with which I identified and which I cherished. At the time, I wrote a review of her book expressing reservations to that effect,[3] and I appeared in several debates with her on the topic.

More compelling for me than the issue of feminism was the clash between Jewish tradition and modernity in general. At the Hebrew University of Jerusalem I was exposed to scientific study of Judaism—submitting texts to historical philological analysis—which brought the clash into sharp relief. Modernist issues such as the conflict between science and religion, the impact of sociology on claims of halakhic integrity, and historical development and the notion of divine revelation—these were the bread and butter of my intellectual life and my form of religious quest. During this period I discovered the writings of Rabbi Abraham Isaac Kook, the profound and saintly twentieth-century religious mystic. I felt that he was one of the few traditionalists whose avenue of response to these questions rose above the usual apologetics. These writings became a formative influence as I developed my own theology. The attempt to appropriate some of his ideas to contend with current problems that I was wrestling with became a major theme in my religious life.

My involvement as a teacher in the first post high-school program offering talmudic study for women in a yeshiva-like setting (then known as Beruria, and today as Midreshet Lindenbaum) also contributed to my lack of interest in feminist issues. Founded in Jerusalem in 1976 by Rabbi Chaim Brovender, Beruria pioneered the women's learning revolution that I shall discuss later. Here, in this little island of learning, where male rabbis and women cooperated to create an optimal Torah environment for women, I had no cause to feel oppressed. I had little doubt that I was participating in an exciting revolution, that its fruits were here to stay, and that it would only gain momentum as the years went by. But I felt no inclination to immerse myself in a movement called "feminism," whose interests were somewhat beyond my ken.

The initial push came with the first "Feminism and Orthodoxy" conference, which took place in New York in 1996. When Blu Greenberg, who was then in charge of organizing the conference, invited me to participate, I was rather reluctant because I really did not feel sufficiently identified with the group of women behind the event or their political concerns. I had nothing against the move to enhance the position of women in Jewish life, but my interests were more philosophical. I therefore told Blu that I would come only if I could speak about a more theoretical issue: the potential impact of feminism on Orthodox Jewish theology.[4] In other words, I was interested in using feminism as a handle on ideas that went beyond feminist concerns.

I was not prepared for the response that this topic evoked. The atmosphere at the talk was electric, and a flood of e-mails, telephone calls, letters, and lecture invitations ensued. Apparently, I had hit on a raw nerve in Orthodoxy: an issue everyone was struggling with but no one had properly articulated. I felt I had something unique to contribute and that I had a receptive audience.

An experience the following year stood in sharp contrast. I was invited to the Orthodox Forum, a closed meeting at Yeshiva University, the intellectual center of Modern Orthodoxy in the United States—an annual forum of handpicked invitees, rabbis, and academicians who formed part of the inner circle of this segment of Orthodoxy. The declared purpose was to discuss in a free and open atmosphere some of the burning current questions of Orthodoxy. Or so I thought. The theme of the conference that year was "human and societal influence on *halakhah*." I was asked to review the modern period and to use women's issues as a test case.

As an academician teaching in a university setting and in the intellectually open atmosphere established at Midreshet Lindenbaum, I expected to find the same spirit of inquiry at this forum. After all, it was a closed meeting. Surely the question of exposing "dirty laundry" was not an issue. I was entirely unprepared for the response my paper evoked. In it, I spelled out what I thought were some of the practical and theological challenges that feminism poses to the halakhic community. The paper was sent in advance to the conference participants, along with all the other papers to be discussed.

By the time I arrived at the conference I already had an intimation of the chilly reception awaiting me. Apparently the people who had invited me did not get what they had bargained for. Perhaps they relied on the opinions I expressed in my response to Blu Greenberg's book, an article that sat well with establishment positions. I do not think that my position has changed substantially in the intervening years, but in the wake of the first Feminism and Orthodoxy conference I was driven to read some feminist literature, and I was invited to develop a course on the topic of Orthodoxy and feminism for a new gender studies program at Bar-Ilan University. As a research fellow at the Shalom Hartman Institute in Jerusalem, I also benefited from participation in a workshop devoted to women's issues. All of these factors probably served to sharpen my feminist sensibilities on a theoretical level, influencing how I phrased the issues.

Before my talk a few people came up to me surreptitiously, whispering words of encouragement and telling me that they "admired my courage." What courage? I had no idea what they were talking about, but it did not bode well. It soon became obvious that members of the American Modern Orthodox establishment were not prepared to deal critically with the issues at hand. In the round of discussion after I presented an oral summary of the paper, the atmosphere was heavy and oppressive. The rabbis' faces were somber, and everyone was determined to be politically correct—that is, in terms of the establishment. Nearly everyone who asked for the floor began with a variant of "I am very disturbed by . . ." The only one who dared support not only my questions but even my answers (and brought a personal message of thanks from his wife for giving voice to exactly what she herself was feeling) was an Israeli academician unconnected with Yeshiva University and independent of establishment disapproval.

Although the forum customarily leads to a volume of the papers presented in a series devoted to this purpose, that year none was published. They dared not publish a book with my talk, which had crossed the bounds of rabbinic fiat, and they dared not publish without it. The article subsequently passed through so many hands informally that I hardly felt the need to publish it, but I did so eventually under other auspices.[5]

The present book is an outgrowth of that paper and the one prepared for the conference the year before, augmented by further material developed in teaching the course at Bar-Ilan and drawing on other articles that I have published. Writing this book has been important to me. In a sense, it has afforded me the opportunity to engage in an exercise of "theological housecleaning," forcing me to put in order a conglomeration of ideas that have been gestating for a long period of time. Feminism has merely provided the critical cause célèbre on which to center these thoughts.

The Threat of Feminism to Orthodoxy

What so troubled my interlocutors at Yeshiva University? What is it in feminism that Orthodoxy finds so threatening?

In 1982, in a short and little publicized article,[6] the influential Israeli thinker Yeshayahu Leibowitz declared that "the question of Women and Judaism is more crucial than all the political problems of the people and its state. Failure to deal with it seriously threatens the viability of the Judaism of Torah and Mitzvoth in the contemporary world."[7] I think that today, twenty years later, many people would concur; now more than ever they would regard the status of women in Jewish tradition as the greatest challenge to Torah Judaism. But, like Leibowitz himself, most Orthodox Jews today still see the problem as mainly a halakhic one; that is, in terms of the challenges posed to Orthodoxy on a practical level by the new role of

women in the Western world. To the extent that they view these challenges
as a religious problem, it is mainly because they perceive the women's revolution, in its struggle for equality, as drawing on influences foreign to the
hallowed practices of Judaism.

This struggle creates certain tensions, if not outright conflicts, with some
of the established norms of *halakhah* and tradition. When the demand arises
to find halakhic dispensation for women to learn Torah, don phylacteries
[*tefillin*], assume positions of religious leadership and authority, or extricate
themselves from failed marriages to husbands who won't grant a divorce,
the question usually raised is: To what extent can such demands for change
be legitimated from within the halakhic framework?

I believe, however, that this way of phrasing the challenge raised by the
women's revolution is shortsighted and mistaken. Granted, there is a difference of opinion among the halakhic authorities over how radical a break
with *halakhah* such changes entail. Granted also, women themselves are divided over how their struggle for legal and social equality in general society
will change the way they live out their daily Jewish lives. On this level, however, the problem could be viewed as a matter of simple negotiation: the
rabbinic authorities will give a little here, the women there, and peace will
be had. The real problem is rather that the threat of the women's revolution
is not limited to such practical issues; to understand it this way essentially
trivializes the challenges. Even some of the more positive and sympathetic
Orthodox treatments of women's newly defined needs[8] fail to take into account the full depth of the feminist critique, a critique highlighting several
aspects of the women's revolution that appear to be profoundly problematic
for the foundations of Jewish belief.

While Orthodox leaders have not yet spelled out for themselves the
broader implications of the women's revolution, I believe that some of them
have an intuitive sense of what is involved. Symptomatic of this is the highly
charged atmosphere that can accompany even the slightest suggestion of divergence from traditional ritual practice. The sheer energy of these responses, irrespective of their ideological orientation, is indication that the
feminist critique has honed in on an issue critical to contemporary Jewish
life. An outsider to traditional Judaism might understandably be perplexed
by the level of agitation and volatile rhetoric. Why not have a woman rather
than a man hold up the poles of a wedding canopy? And why shouldn't a
woman make the ceremonial blessing at her family's Sabbath meal over the
loaves of challah that she herself baked?

One reason for the disproportionately intense atmosphere surrounding
such discussions is the nature of the issue. Even the slightest symbolic
changes in ritual create a dissonance with primeval memories, associations,
and traditional patterns of worship that have nurtured the spiritual self-
image of Jewish women for centuries. For this reason, even an apparently
trivial question about a woman actively participating in a private family

ceremony is not easily relegated to a circumscribed category of issues that a simple legal technicality can resolve. The changes suggested often relate to moral sensibilities that are pivotal to human experience, touching upon religious attitudes and principles that define our total vision of ourselves, the nature of human sexuality, the family, and society at large.

What, then, is the cost of minimizing gender differences and destroying the cultural halos with which tradition has surrounded them, as against the gains of greater self-fulfillment, freedom of expression, and independence for the women concerned? Is there a specific feminine contribution to society that would be lost if taken outside the home and brought into the public arena? Conversely, are the Jewish people forfeiting half of their spiritual talents and energies by confining the religious activity of women to the domestic sphere? Does acceptance of women's changing status in society necessarily lead to other positions that are often associated with feminism but that appear to be unequivocally contraindicated by *halakhah,* such as acceptance of homosexuality or abortion on demand?

These are important questions, but the arguments around them, compelling as they may be, do not tell the complete story either. The history of *halakhah* provides other examples of deep ideological shifts on issues at the heart of Jewish spirituality and its moral sensibilities. I am thinking here of the attitude of Jews to non-Jews, the toleration of secularists by religious Jews, and the move from more ritualistic to more philosophical forms of worship. Even when such changes appear to take place gradually and imperceptibly, without much explicit ideological fanfare, the perceptive onlooker can discern a causal connection between halakhic change and shifting societal attitudes.

Compounding this difficulty in the case of women, however, is the urgency of the issue. The change in women's status in the general world is proceeding so rapidly (albeit more quickly in some countries than in others) that the sense of incongruence and anomaly experienced by some Orthodox women is extremely pressing. Critical problems are being raised that require immediate and global solution, as is evidenced most concretely in the case of the *agunah,* which will be discussed later on. Under the circumstances, the traditional caution displayed in most halakhic decision-making is often perceived as applying a bandage to a wound that requires major surgery.

It is precisely in the combination of these two factors—the charged nature of women's issues and their urgency—that we find the uniqueness of the women's question in Judaism. What we have here is an ideological enterprise of major proportions. Changing the fundamental halakhic status of women has profound implications for the entire system. In effect, it constitutes a major upheaval of some of the very foundations of Jewish tradition, as we have known it for centuries. For this reason, it inevitably leads to a cluster of broader second-order theological issues concerning the relationship between religious law and the values or ideals that it may be understood to embody. More profoundly it forces us to confront the relationship between the divine word and human interpretation and to ascertain the extent to which a religion based on the notion of a singular foundational revelation (the revelation at Sinai) can accommodate changes in the evolving moral sensibilities of its adherents. In this sense the women's issue can be said to constitute the test case par excellence of the ability of a two-thousand-year-old tradition to adjust to modern human and social realities without undermining its authority.

In the developing theory of the feminist movement, the problematic implications for Judaism of the change in women's status are being spelled out most explicitly. This may be why the very mention of feminism so often generates extreme anxiety and discomfort in Orthodox circles. Within mainstream Orthodoxy the term frequently conjures up a specter of nearly demonic proportions, as evidenced by the vehement objection to its inclusion in the title of the recent series of international conferences on feminism and Orthodoxy (and by the amount of casuistry concerning the order in which the two words were placed). Even some of the younger women who have palpably benefited from advances of previous generations of feminists prefer to dissociate themselves from this label and the cognitive, social, and emotional estrangement from established tradition that they sense it will create for them.

I contend that feminist thinking cannot be sidestepped, as it raises a new point of view with insights, values, and moral overtones that are, at least in part, intuitively persuasive for modern (and particularly postmodern) thinkers. These new perceptions constitute a genuine challenge to the traditional world-picture, one that sooner or later has to be acknowledged. This does not mean that Jewish traditionalists are obliged to accept the perceptions en masse or even partially. I do believe, however, that greater familiarity with the feminist critique will lead to the conclusion that response entails more than technical solutions to practical halakhic problems. For traditionalists, "recognizing the enemy" in a clear-eyed manner should be the first step in assessing what it is that Orthodoxy is confronting and in developing a reasoned and adequate response.

I believe that feminism need not be seen as a threat to traditional Judaism, and that Jewish tradition itself provides ways and means of dealing with the challenges. My optimism does not stem from a definitive picture of what these ways and means entail. It stems rather from a belief in belief itself, and the conviction that the true measure of belief lies in its ability to assimilate the lessons to be learned from whatever challenges it is destined to face. The challenges that feminism presents are challenges that carry within them the potential to enhance Judaism and make it more meaningful for all its believers, male and female alike. Only if halakhic Judaism is prepared to face the full implications of this apparent threat, however, with faith rather than fear, can it develop ways to adopt whatever in this movement is of genuine value and incorporate it into religious life. Filtered through the prism of tradition in a constructive manner, this social revolution has the potential to enhance rather than destroy the foundations of Torah, while deepening its relevancy for our time.

About This Book

Beyond a personal interest in clarifying my own thoughts, I had a number of audiences in mind as I wrote this book. The first group of readers are those who, like myself and my own close circle of students and friends, have been touched, disturbed, and excited by the challenges that feminism raises. These are people who have a great love for their tradition but seek to bridge the gap between its teachings with respect to women and the de facto position of women in the world we now live in. Beyond the practical question of finding some modus vivendi with the *halakhah,* they struggle for solutions to the deeper dissonance this gap creates—wondering whether it is in any way possible to make theological sense of it all.

In addition to this group, I hope to engage another type of traditionalist reader, more conservatively inclined. I would like to believe that beyond those who prefer to dismiss "so-called religious feminists" as a bunch of troublemakers, there are some traditionalists who would genuinely like to understand what all the fuss is about. These are people who are truly puzzled, sometimes asking themselves: What do these religious feminists want? They claim to be loyal Jews. Why then do they rebel against the word of God and a tradition that has served the Jewish people so well for two thousand years?

The third group that I invite to this discussion are Jewish and non-Jewish scholars and students of religion and of feminism at large. For them the Jewish example will serve as a test case for many of the broader issues raised by the confrontation between feminism and religion.

The diversity of the audience to which this book is addressed creates certain technical problems. Many of the names and concepts that I employ will be familiar to some of my readers. Others will require explanation to augment a more limited knowledge of Jewish texts and history or of general philosophy. Definitions of the Jewish terms will follow at least the first time that they are introduced. Regarding general philosophical concepts, I have tried (with limited success, I fear) to overcome the academician's propensity for professional jargon, and to provide at least minimal explanations. I have included copious notes and references to recent work that has been done on various topics discussed, particularly in Israel. Although much of it is written in Hebrew, I believe the English-language reader should be aware of its existence.

The book itself is divided into five parts. The first three correspond to stages in the development of feminism in the Jewish context, representing progressive incorporation of the feminist critique. The fourth part offers my own resolution of the Orthodox feminist's dilemma, while the fifth looks at current trends and speculates about the future.

The first stage consists of acknowledging that a problem exists. In the attempt to supply some of the background information necessary for appreciating this point, I begin chapter 1 with a survey of the history and tenets of feminism at large. I then proceed with an overview of Jewish law, how women fit into its hierarchies, and how this placement has affected their role in Jewish religious tradition. In briefly outlining various trends in feminist thought, I also introduce philosophical concepts that influenced its development. Inasmuch as some of these concepts are critical to understanding my reasoning later, I strongly urge readers of various stripes to peruse this chapter, so that we may start our discussion on common ground. The same may be said for central halakhic concepts and premises that figure prominently in subsequent discussions in the book. The chapter concludes with a description of the dilemma of the Orthodox woman today, resulting from the clash between basic assumptions of each system.

Chapter 2 opens with a brief historical account of what women thought of their situation, focusing upon some of the sources of their discontent. After tracing the development of Jewish feminism as an organized movement in the modern period, I continue with a survey and evaluation of various conservative responses to discrimination against women.

The second part of the book (chapters 3 through 6) describes what I define as the second stage of Jewish feminism: the attempt on the part of *halakhah*-abiding women to explore practical ways and means of improving their status in Judaism by working within the halakhic system. Chapter 3 reviews the objective and subjective constraints that various ideological, historical, and political factors have imposed upon this system over the ages.

Chapter 4 maps out the attempts of Modern Orthodoxy to provide viable solutions within such constraints, developing "meta-halakhic" theories that view *halakhah,* as it were, "from above." Fueling such efforts is the hope they will enable a comprehensive explanation of women's status in Jewish tradition and supply reliable and objective criteria for determining the validity of suggestions for change.

Chapter 5 assesses the adequacy of Modern Orthodoxy's meta-halakhic efforts. I begin with a comparison of the disparate responses of halakhic decisors to two seemingly parallel innovations in the lives of contemporary Orthodox women: the expansion of opportunities for advanced study of the sacred texts of tradition and the spread of women-only prayer groups. The discussion then extends to other anomalies that feature in halakhic decisions regarding women. The chapter ends with the skepticism of some Orthodox feminists as to whether any meta-halakhic theory is capable of maintaining legal consistency and freedom from bias.

The third part of the book (chapters 6 through 9) introduces a third stage of Jewish feminism. Feminists at this stage maintain that it does not suffice to work with the halakhic system as it stands, devising practical solutions on a piecemeal basis. They adopt a more radical approach, seeking to identify the deeper attitudinal reasons for the male-biased nature of the halakhic tradition. As described in chapter 6, some see the heart of the problem in unfortunate but extraneous sociological influences. Others view it as more inherent, stemming from the basically male-oriented imagery of monotheistic religion, which lends itself to a patriarchal social order. Both groups seek ways and means of restoring balance to the tradition without breaking continuity with it, by finding precedents and support for their feminist contentions in some aspect of the Jewish past.

Chapter 7 assesses various shortcomings of such revisionism, whether sociological or theological, as an appropriate response to the feminist critique. To my mind, these shortcomings provide sufficient grounds for traditionalist dismissal of this approach. The chapter culminates, however, with a more radical theological conclusion implied by third-stage feminism, one I regard as the heart of the feminist challenge to Orthodoxy and to monotheistic religion in general: that identification of an all-pervasive bias in Scripture poses a threat, in principle, to the notion of verbal, dictated revelation, upon which the entire authority of historic Judaism rests.

Chapter 8 reviews another track taken by third-stage feminism, one that focuses on the classical halakhic medium, but seeks to modify it by adopting a more proactive vision of law. This track is associated with a current postmodernist vogue in Anglo-American theory that finds support for this vision within Jewish tradition itself. I conclude that this approach holds some promise for feminists, but requires qualification.

The fourth part of the book (chapters 9 through 11) sets up what I regard as a more viable model, suggesting that continuity with tradition can be maintained by regarding the halakhic system as a living and dynamic organism that can only grow by positive acceptance and affirmation of its historical and intellectual legacy. Chapter 9 first develops this idea on the practical halakhic plane; that is, examining the role of interpretive traditions in constraining the freewheeling influence of postmodernist thinking on legal theory. I hope to demonstrate that precisely those women who are most affected by the clash between feminism and Orthodoxy are the ones with the greatest potential for resolving the problem.

Chapter 10 continues application of the more open-ended approach of tradition on a more theoretical plane. I regard this chapter as the spiritual heart of this book; it is here that I address the most penetrating level of the feminist critique. In articulating a theological position capable of incorporating a more sophisticated understanding of the mechanics of revelation alongside solid reaffirmation of its divine origins and claims upon halakhic commitment, I seek to break down the usual distinction between naturalistic, historic processes and claims of transcendence.

Chapter 11 anticipates some critical responses to this approach on the part of feminists and traditionalists. I respond briefly to their possible objections to a view of revelation that relies on a conflating of the divine and the human.

The fifth part, an epilogue, offers a qualified prognosis of developments and their contribution to Jewish life. It also suggests that our study of the meeting between feminism and Orthodoxy might provide a more general paradigm of interaction between long-standing traditions (even when not based on claims to divine authority) and the transformative power of interpretive revolutions in a manner that is beneficial to both.

Some Concluding Caveats

Because of the diverse nature of my audience, there are chapters that will appeal more to some readers, while others may find them redundant or a preaching to the converted. I expect that the bare bones of my analysis will appear radical to some of my traditionalist readers; indeed, I intend to take the feminist critique seriously to the extent of squarely acknowledging some of its claims and following them to their most extreme conclusions. For this reason many of these readers will take offense at much of what is included in the chapters that compose the first three parts of this book. On the other hand, after reading the concluding chapters, another segment of my readership may find my own suggestions disappointingly theoretical and vague. Although these suggestions may reveal some of my personal inclinations, they do not attempt definitive answers to such questions as "Should women marry early and have lots of children or dedicate years of their life to high-level study of Talmud?" and "Should women develop their own uniquely feminine spirituality or strive to replicate male forms of worship?" Worse yet, they may appear to the feminist purist as overwilling to compromise the feminist agenda.

I have already encountered the mix of responses I describe. After I delivered the address at the first Feminism and Orthodoxy conference that forms the theological core of this book (chapter 10), I was told that one of the non-Orthodox feminists who attended was quite pleased with what she regarded as its surprising audacity. The next year, however, when I was asked to address the practical issue of changing Orthodox ritual,[9] I delivered a traditionalist response that she considered a great letdown. In her view I had completely "climbed down the tree."

I, however, regard the two positions as part of one and the same piece. My aim in developing a Jewishly acceptable theological approach to feminism is, on the one hand, to achieve maximum intellectual integrity in the reading of canonized texts—without engaging in grotesque and morally obtuse postures of fundamentalism or unconvincing apologetics. This integrity involves admitting that, historically speaking, the Torah has both described and prescribed a patriarchal society. Disturbing as this may be, I believe that it need not be the end of the story and that Jewish tradition itself provides hope that an authentic understanding of Torah can accommodate what is, to all intents and purposes, an egalitarian ethos.

On the other hand, I *am* ideologically committed to the tradition as it stands as the basic grammar that governs the way that I relate to the world and my religious experience. To accept the tradition means to agree to speak in a certain way, to think in certain terms, to attribute to bottom-line formulas the formal status that tradition has always accorded them, and to articulate responses within their regulative constraints. The interpretations may change with the times; the formulas will remain the same. As R. Kook wrote (regarding the need to move beyond primitive understanding of the divinity of Scripture): "Torah from heaven is an example of all the generalities and particulars of beliefs, in the relationship between their articulation and their inner essence, the *latter* of which is the principle sought by faith."[10]

To be sure, the question "Is at all possible to distinguish between form and essence?" is real. It has been the subject of philosophical debate throughout the ages. It may well be that the residual influences of form on essence must always linger. Something of the irrational reverence for the past is preserved in the pomp and ceremony of the British monarchy, even though no subject of the United Kingdom regards this form of government as anything more than a medieval relic. In the same way, some remnant of the symbolic power of the language of Jewish tradition may be retained with regard to women's issues—even after having undergone so extensive a process of interpretation that the original meaning appears to have died the death of a thousand qualifications.

My response to this possibility is encapsulated in two of my favorite aphorisms from the philosophical writings of Ludwig Wittgenstein. The first:

> Tradition is not something a man can learn; not a thread he can pick up when he feels like it, any more than a man can choose his own ancestors. Someone lacking a tradition who would like to have one is like a man unhappily in love.[11]

But because simply having a tradition is not enough, we now turn to the second adage:

> An honest religious thinker is like a tightrope walker. He almost looks as though he were walking on nothing but air. His support is the slenderest imaginable. And yet it really is possible to walk on it.[12]

On occasion, to retain its identity, every generation must perform major acrobatics, stretching the past in order to create continuity with its present. The tightrope may not hold forever, but it is crucial that it be capable of at least temporarily bearing the weight of its burden safely.

To all my readers let me point out that the object of my enterprise is neither political nor practical. It is rather an attempt to understand the significance and ramifications of feminism to Judaism from a theological perspective. Perhaps part and parcel of the theological perspective that I adopt is
that there can be no definitive and final answer to many of the questions that
arise. Yet to the extent that ideas influence the course of everyday life, my
understanding may help traditionalists and feminists form some degree of
rapprochement between the ideas that seem to divide them. In this sense the
theological perspective may be a useful tool in formulating practical policy
as well.

Even in this limited sense, my work is not finished. It is just a beginning,
one that I expect will provoke a variety of detractors, critics, and embellish-
ers of a more constructive sort. I welcome all of these. If this book succeeds
in merely opening discussions or bringing discourse to new and more fruitful levels, it will have accomplished its task. I look forward to learning from
any discussion that may follow.

Acknowledgments

No book is ever strictly the product of one author. Certainly many people contributed to the making and completing of this one. It is now my pleasant task to acknowledge my debts to them and express gratitude for their support. First credit goes to the Ariel Rosen-Zvi Foundation, administered by the law faculty of Tel Aviv University, for their original grant. This grant generated the initial impetus for adapting into book form several articles I had written on the topic of women and Judaism. Other financial benefactors include the Hadassah International Research Institute on Jewish Women at Brandeis University, the Littauer Foundation, and various research grants from Bar-Ilan University. Special thanks go to Moshe Kaveh, president of Bar-Ilan University and Avi Sagi, head of the Mazor chair, for their efforts and support.

I was fortunate to have Nathan Aviezer and Charlotte Katzoff read selected chapters of a previous version of the manuscript and to have Stephen Benin, Yehudah Gellman, Chana Safrai, and Avivah Zornberg go through it in its entirety, benefiting from their general encouragement or more specific comments and suggestions. I am also obliged to several halakhic mentors with whom I consulted on various issues and points of technical detail that demand far more knowledge and expertise than I can claim; if my discussion is still misleading or mistaken, the responsibility for this is mine alone. Literary editors Laurie Fialkoff and Hannah Levinsky-Koevary volunteered to wade through a very rough first draft, offering their incisive criticisms and constructive advice. If the book now reads as a document intelligible to the ordinary layperson, offering down-to-earth applications of abstruse scholarly material, and a reasonably transparent structure, my readers have them to thank. Chaia Beckerman, my infinitely patient literary editor, helped me carry through their suggestions and hers, holding my hand while I committed the manuscript to radical surgery and to less major cosmetic face-liftings and gently prodding me out of the academic propensity for qualifying and hedging. Her professionalism and eagle eyes prevented many redundancies and inconsistencies.

   Most of all I would like to thank my life partner, Yaakov. Fueled by the unique amalgam of his Cambridge University background and Ponevez Yeshiva learning and its contribution to our joint intellectual odyssey, the story of our marriage has been a meeting of minds no less than of hearts, bodies, and souls. My world of ideas has been so nurtured by his that I find it difficult to determine where his ends and mine begins. The Talmud (BT *Ketubot* 62:b–63:a; *Nedarim* 50:a) relates that when Rabbi Akiva, flanked by a multitude of students, returned after twelve years of absence to his wife, who had supported his protracted Torah study by living in poverty, they tried to dismiss the unfamiliar woman who ran up to kiss the feet of their venerated rabbi. In a feminist take on his rebuke to them, I can only repeat to the reader, "What's mine and yours is his."

•PART I•

The First Stage:
Acknowledging the Problem

My discussion of the first level of confrontation between feminism and traditional Judaism takes note of some of the more obvious discrepancies and dissonances between two systems of thought. A few commonalities emerge (such as the lack of awareness of many adherents of each of these worldviews regarding the deeper tenets of their "faith," as well as a similar passion for righteousness). Nevertheless, even a rudimentary survey of feminist thought, followed by an introduction to Jewish law and its theoretical underpinnings, demonstrates what appears to be an insuperable gulf between the two movements in their methods of deriving and conceptualizing notions of morality and truth. The repercussions of this gulf are starkly illustrated when examining their applications to the formal and informal status of women in the classical canons of Jewish tradition in the light of feminist sensibilities.

In the second chapter I shall turn to some of the responses of Jewish women throughout the ages to their situation. "Acknowledging the problem"—a hallmark of first-stage feminism—emerges as less of a contemporary phenomenon than is often imagined. A survey of the reasoning of traditionalists who believe that the problem can and should be resolved by preserving the tradition intact (presented at some length) shows that interest in preserving the status quo is, similarly, not solely the province of men. Nevertheless, contemporary Jewish feminists raise serious doubts about the persuasiveness and viability of this response in the current cultural context and sociological reality.

CHAPTER 1

Feminism and the Halakhic Tradition

Introducing Feminist Theory

Many people think of feminism as a political movement with a practical agenda for advancing the cause of women and guaranteeing their rights to freedom, equality, and self-expression. Some regard it less sympathetically, as a skewed view of reality promoted by bitter women who view men as their natural enemies. Neither of these conceptions is accurate or up-to-date.

For the purposes of this book, I propose to understand the concept of feminism in its broadest possible sense—as a movement for the advancement of women's equality, viewpoints, and concerns. Such understanding may, or may not, involve egalitarianism or allegations regarding the deliberate oppression of women. Providing readers with a complete survey of feminism in accordance with this understanding is beyond the scope of this book. But I believe that before embarking on even the barest thumbnail sketch of feminism and its tenets, it is important to first dispel the notion that what we are dealing with is a monolithic ideology that can be easily stereotyped. Feminism is old, rich, and variegated enough to be spoken of as having a history with identifiable stages and trends (which are labeled in confusing and inconsistent ways). Feminism also has a future that is still developing and undetermined. Not all feminists think alike.[1]

The beginnings of feminism can be traced to the industrial revolution and the move to draw labor out of the home and into the public workplace. Its initial impact was felt among married, middle-class women, the first to find themselves left at home with little productive work to do. This development led Mary Wollstonecraft to write her best-selling book, *A Vindication of the Rights of Woman*,[2] in 1792. In it she stressed women's lack of equal opportunity to develop their powers of reason and thus achieve liberty and moral autonomy as independent decision-makers. The next century was witness to works such as *The Subjection of Women*,[3] written in 1869 by the philosopher John Stuart Mill, emphasizing the need of women to achieve economic and political independence as well. At this stage, feminism was still in its infancy, making first efforts to identify the nature and extent of women's discrimination and find ways to rectify this injustice.

The second, more practical stage of feminism as an organized movement began in the nineteenth century in Europe and North America. At this point feminism did indeed take the form of a political struggle for equal opportunities and rights for women and for the abolition of social, legal, and economic discrimination based on gender differences. One of the primary goals was to secure women's right to vote and to participate more fully in public affairs, as well as their freedom to own property and capital, to inherit, to keep money they earned, to attend college, to become professionally certified physicians, and to argue cases in court. This early wave of feminism in its more practical stage reached its peak at the beginning of the twentieth century and began fading out after women gained suffrage in the United States and in much of Europe after World War I.

In 1920, passage of the Nineteenth Amendment to the United States Constitution granted women the right to vote. For nearly forty years after, the feminist movement in the United States lay dormant, resurfacing only in the 1960s. Predicated on the understanding that women need economic as well as civil rights, the "women's liberation movement" strove to secure women opportunities equal to those of men in all areas of life. In her 1963 book *The Feminine Mystique*,[4] which became one of the classics of this stage of the movement, Betty Friedan also focused attention on the deeper ways in which women are more socially disadvantaged than men. Describing the frustrations of middle-class housewives who, despite having achieved the American dream (marriage, children, a home in the suburbs) after World War II, still suffered from "the problem that has no name," she attributed their dissatisfaction to the fact that their identities were defined in terms of their husbands. Friedan proposed interpersonal as well as political and legal solutions, recommending that women combine home and career in order to reach optimal fulfillment as human beings.

An important harbinger of the third, more theoretical stage in the history of feminism was the publication of French philosopher Simone de Beauvoir's classic, *The Second Sex*, which was to become one of the key texts of twentieth-century feminism.[5] First appearing in 1949, this work's comprehensive critique of the patriarchal structure at the base of Western culture was consonant with the existentialist philosophy of de Beauvoir's lifelong lover and intellectual partner, Jean-Paul Sartre. She built upon the notion that we, as human beings, create essential identities for ourselves only through exercising our freedom in conscious action—making choices and coming to decisions: "One is not born, but rather becomes, a woman . . . it is civilization as a whole that produces this creature which is described as feminine."[6] Though constructed culturally by a male-dominated society that views her as "Other," woman, like man, has no inherent essence. Thus, she need not continue to be what man has made her to be; she can refuse to internalize the male view of her as object. Woman can engage in positive action in society, and can redefine or abandon her roles as wife, mother, career woman, prostitute, or any other role Western civilization has relegated to her.

De Beauvoir's ideas were eventually developed and applied in various intellectual and social spheres, transforming feminism from a political movement to a more profound ideology. For de Beauvoir, women's liberation essentially meant celebrating and appropriating male norms; she deplored women's association with passivity and nature rather than cultural creativity, and rejected their reproductive functions as definition of their selfhood. For this reason, her critique—despite its striving to penetrate to the root causes of women's discrimination—can still be regarded as "liberal" feminism, which is generally associated with the second political stage.

Since de Beauvoir's time, the thinking generated by her more radical analysis of the sources of female oppression has passed through several transformations. Third-stage feminism today harbors an ideology marked by many differences of opinion. Uniting the thought of most third-stage feminists, however, is a new emphasis on the importance of preserving feminine uniqueness and appreciating the value of women's ways of thinking and behaving.

Nevertheless, the debate between liberal and radical feminists continues to this day. Social vision, practical politics, and critical theory intertwine in discussions revolving around three major feminist claims: (a) gender is a social construct; (b) gender is a tool of oppression; and (c) gender influences our processing of knowledge.

Gender as a social construct. One of feminism's primary objectives has been to challenge the widespread essentialist assumption (encapsulated in Freud's aphorism "Anatomy is destiny")[7] that differences between male and female are inherent. Developing ideas that already surfaced at the first stage of the feminist critique, second- and third-stage feminists seek to counteract what one might call a naive understanding of sex. Differences between men and women do not all derive exclusively and necessarily from given "essences": innate physiological or biological differences. Feminists argue that in speaking about the sources of difference between male and female, one must distinguish between sex (which they generally regard as a given) and gender (which they regard as an artificial cultural construct or institution learned through socialization).[8] Biological sex differences between male and female are much less significant than the similarities. It is human civilization that imposes a cultural halo upon these differences, in order to establish far more comprehensive distinctions in life patterns, ritual, dress, mating habits, nutrition, and role stratification. Social, legal, and religious pressures are then created to enforce conformance to the mores.

Within this feminist claim, there is still considerable debate regarding how and to what extent gender differences are socially constructed. At one end of the scale are the cultural (or gender) feminists, who still entertain a mild form of essentialism in regarding gender as a psychological or moral orientation that stems necessarily from a few sexual differences. Psychoanalytic feminist Nancy Chodorow,[9] for example, who grounds gender distinction on the differing early childhood experiences of little boys and girls, looks at the fact that mothers are generally the primary caregivers; boys must tear themselves away in order to achieve an independent sense of self, while girls can continue their sense of relationship and natural connectedness.

Alongside the cultural feminists are the Marxist (or political) feminists. Attributing a materialist basis to all social institutions, such feminists view gender distinctions more as a function of women's inferior social position, in which sex is only one determinant, alongside class, race, ethnicity, age, and other circumstantial factors.[10] These feminists point to the influence upon female gender identity of relegating woman to the home and keeping her out of the public domain.

As opposed to any variety of essentialism, the other end of the scale is represented by the entirely open-ended extreme of descriptive postmodernism. Feminists belonging to this camp regard our descriptions of both gender and sex as entirely determined by culture.[11] Only the linking of gender to reproduction leads us to conceive of merely two types of persons—man and woman—and to define these two categories as rigid and exclusionary. As Jane Flax, a political theorist and psychotherapist who writes on feminist theory, remarks:

> The actual content of being a man or woman and the rigidity of the categories themselves are highly variable across culture and time. . . . Everyone will agree that there are anatomical differences between men and women. . . . However, the mere existence of such anatomical differentiation is a descriptive fact. . . . There are many other aspects of our embodiedness that seem equally remarkable and interesting, for example, the incredible complexity of the structure and functioning of our brains, the extreme and relatively prolonged physical helplessness of the human neonate as compared to that of other (even related) species, or the fact that every one of us will die. It is also the case that physically male and female humans resemble each other in many more ways than we differ. Our similarities are even more striking if we compare humans to, say, toads or trees. So why ought the anatomical differences between male and female humans assume such significance in our sense of ourselves as persons? Why ought such complex human social meanings and structures be based on or justified by a relatively narrow range of anatomical differences?[12]

Flax implies that definitions of gender are capable of going in any direction. Beards or breasts and menstrual cycles do not on their own establish masculinity or femininity, and gender differences do not proceed automatically from sexual ones. Culture, not biology, is destiny.[13]

Gender as a tool of oppression. If gender differences are merely the result of culture, they are given to change. But feminists identified with all stages have regarded the exaggerated emphasis upon establishing gender differences as more than a matter of social expediency. Pointing to the political functions of emphasizing these differences, they link this process to a cultural history of oppression. As Wollstonecraft put it two centuries ago: "To account for and excuse the tyranny of man, many ingenious arguments have been brought forward to prove that the two sexes, in the acquirement of virtue, ought to aim at obtaining a very different character."[14]

Theoretically, perhaps, men and women could be different but equal. However, one similarity between all gender distinctions remains striking: one gender is usually the touchstone, the normal, the dominant, while the other is regarded as different, deviant, and subordinate. In most societies role differentiation in actual practice translates into differences in value, power, and prestige and the creation of unequal classes. "In Western society, 'man' is A, 'wo-man' is Not-A."[15] As anthropologist Margaret Mead noted, there are cultures in which men weave and women fish, and cultures in which women weave and men fish. But in either case, the work that women perform is valued less.[16] Male dominance does not relate only to the political and social sphere. It also spills over into the home and family, because "the personal is the political."[17]

Even in modern society, despite women entering the public arena, gender differentiation continues to construct women as a group to be the subordinates of men as a group and to protect male hegemony. The attributes ascribed to males (dominance, assertion, rationality, straightforwardness, interest in objective rules) and females (submissiveness, passivity, emotionalism, deviousness, interest in subjective relationships) may be the *result* of gender differentiation and the hierarchy of power it dictates, rather than its cause.[18] Most people, however, voluntarily go along with their societies' gender prescriptions, because these norms and expectations get built into their sense of worth and identity as human beings.

Most third-stage feminists challenge the project of liberal feminism, which, they charge, strives to solve the problem of women's oppression by eliminating gender differences entirely and converting women into "honorary men." This, they argue, would constitute a genuine loss for both men and women, forfeiting valuable qualities associated with the feminine gender. Thus, one camp, the radical-libertarian feminists, advocates the creation of an androgynous culture that resists dichotomies and avoids sweeping assertions about an essential nature of women and men. Instead, masculinity and femininity would be viewed as two poles of a continuum. Men would be permitted to explore their feminine dimensions and women their masculine ones. Nancy Chodorow,[19] for example, suggests that the problem of gender inequality should be solved by encouraging joint parenting, rather than leaving mothers chiefly responsible for the task. This would allow men to develop the emotional characteristics that they have been deprived of in their personal lives and would also allow valuable female input to complement male influence in the public domain. Radical-cultural feminists, on the other hand, insist upon the importance of creating women-centered societies with "breathing space" for women only. They stress the importance of feminist consciousness-raising, and the development of pride in uniquely female capacities. Biological motherhood and its attendant virtues of nurturing and caring are seen as a gift that women must guard and celebrate as a source of power.

Gender as a processor of knowledge. Some of the most far-reaching implications of third-stage feminism's understanding of gender as a tool of oppression stem from its discoveries about how gender influences the way that we acquire and organize knowledge. The initial discovery was simple recognition of the systematic exclusion of women from the primary centers of knowledge and authority. This recognition led to the political struggle of women for equal access to male centers of intellectual discourse, on male terms. But as women entered these arenas, which were constructed by and for men, they began to focus upon the male-oriented nature of their surroundings. At first, the realization of this androcentrism led feminists to push for women serving equally as objects of knowledge. Their issues, interests, and experiences gradually extended the accepted areas of research. However, in the process new questions arose that often challenged long-standing assumptions.

Women's struggle for equal access to knowledge and equal participation in the intellectual dialogue eventually led to the notion that their ways of knowing, and their methods of assimilating, defining, and evaluating what they learn, differ from those of men. Women's gender-determined biases influence not only the questions they ask, but also what they regard as legitimate evidence. Feminists have discerned male bias in the very norms that govern how we judge claims of knowledge: we glorify the goals of objectivity and rational justification and we sever reason from subjectivity. Even the "facts" of history, like the standards of "health" in medicine, "normalcy" in psychology, "morality" in law, "beauty" in the arts, and so on, are reflections of our prior subjective biases, born in a context influenced by gender. Indeed, the very polarization of genders—the tendency to dichotomize all of reality in terms of binary opposites—can be seen as a function of a male way of thinking.

All this notwithstanding, feminists still disagree about the extent to which such discoveries mandate a revision of classical epistemology. Some still accept the superiority and universal validity of conventional "male" rationalism, as de Beauvoir did, equating more intuitive and emotional ways of knowing with a narrow, unreliable and provincial view of reality. Others, however, object to the artificial distinction between reason and subjectivity cultivated by Western civilization. Their objection stems not only from political motives, but also from an understanding that this distinction has been used to devalue women and distance them from the centers of power.[20] They are also convinced that this distinction genuinely blocks both men and women from achieving full knowledge.

Supporters of feminine ways of knowing, generalizing from the influence of gender upon knowledge, call attention to the partiality of all knowledge. In response, they strive to construct a feminist theory of knowledge that incorporates a more nuanced and sophisticated understanding of the role of subjectivity in the cognitive process. This understanding is identified with the school of thought known as "standpoint theory." It posits that all knowledge is "situated"; that is, framed by the observer's prior values, expectations, and standards—which are themselves conditioned by the social group, culture, status, and gender to which the observer belongs. Both the subjects who know and the objects of their knowledge are necessarily interrelated and work upon each other within a broader context, rather than functioning as separate and distinct elements. Moreover, context influences the way in which they interrelate. Thus, for example, a rational and cautious person does not take the used-car salesman's arguments at face value.[21] Such skepticism, however, may well be an appropriate response to *any* form of persuasion or, for that matter, explanation.[22] Even when dishonesty or insincerity is not suspected, the possibility remains of arguments being advanced out of misguided judgment or a distorted sense of what is plausible.

To be sure, standpoint feminists are not the first to point out that prior interests and motivations may slant our thinking. Rather than aspiring to transcend subjectivity or situatedness, however (as did more traditional critics of bias) standpoint feminists prefer to acknowledge the essential role of these factors in cognition. As they understand it, without such tools for organizing reality, the process of knowledge could never take place.

Because it is impossible to speak of a sterile foundation of knowledge, clear of bias, an important corollary of feminist epistemology is that truth cannot be equated with an irreducibly self-evident reality. The male attempt to equate one point of view with objective truth by the appeal to pure reason is, on this understanding, just another way of privileging its partial knowledge and imposing it on everyone else. An illustration is seen in the history of midwifery in the Western world.[23] The knowledge of illiterate midwives, amassed by direct personal experience and by sharing information and stories of difficult births, was once as respected as that of male physicians. When professionally trained obstetricians, less attuned to women's interests, began to take over, it was not simply a triumph of men over women. It was the misplaced triumph of "propositional knowledge over practical knowledge."[24]

Standpoint feminists contend that true "objectivity," by contrast, is achieved by taking into account—or at least acknowledging—the existence of as many viewpoints as possible, setting them off against each other in order to arrive at some reasonably common ground. The more perspectives and experiences to which we relate empathetically as empirical sources of knowledge, the greater and more "objective" our understanding.

Some advocates of standpoint epistemology propose merging male and female ways of knowing to reflect an androgynous mode of cognition that is in fact common to both men and women.[25] Such merging would be accomplished by according equal weight to the feminine experience and the unique insights born of women's marginalization. It would acknowledge, for example, that because until this century women were generally deprived of the tools of literacy, they became in most cultures the natural healers, developing skills of empathy that were more valuable than following medical manuals and abstract rules.[26]

Other standpoint feminists regard marginalization itself as advantageous in terms of women's cognitive powers, sharpening their critique of the dominant male culture. These more extreme feminists argue for a theory of knowledge that would not have women's perceptions supplementing male epistemology, but rather replacing it. They maintain that the superiority of feminine perceptions—freer of bias and false values—is due at least in part to women's standpoint of distance from the centers of power and the inevitable epistemological distortions or blinkers that power creates.[27] According to this view, women, as physical and social producers of children, are grounded in material reality in ways that men are not. Thus, even if they are not so highly educated, women can generate valuable knowledge that is much more in touch with the everyday world and with interpersonal relations.

Radical feminism's relativization and subjectivization of knowledge joins forces with other postmodernist currents. The feminist contribution in this realm is simply its emphasis on the key role gender plays in structuring knowledge. Whether striving to supplement male ways of knowing or to replace them, feminist epistemology signifies the refusal of women to accept male categories of thought as the exclusive prism for viewing reality—a refusal not only for themselves but for humanity at large. Such an epistemology challenges the privileged status of some of the most basic assumptions of a culture perceived as predominantly male, and in so doing highlights the androcentric bias that has penetrated all areas of knowledge.

Some of the most influential work in the realm of delineating uniquely feminine ways of thinking has been in the area of morality.[28] Cultural feminist Carol Gilligan, in her influential work *In a Different Voice*,[29] charges that notions of women's moral inferiority are created when exclusively male standards for assessing moral behavior are applied unfairly. Similar claims have been made in the realms of history, psychology, philosophy, literature, and even the natural sciences, demonstrating how feminine categories of thought can have an impact on current ways of thinking and transform some of our most deeply ingrained assumptions.

More recently, one of the chief targets of the feminist critique has been the religious tradition of monotheism, with its emphasis on gender distinction at the heart of its symbols and myths.[30] Feminists regard these symbols and myths as potent tools of male domination, reflecting male interests and biases even in societies that are now largely secular. Understanding their argument in depth is critical and I shall return to probe it, as well as to evaluate the attempts at response. While feminists of all the monotheistic religions have raised the challenge, appreciating the particular implications for Jewish tradition, and the spectrum of response within this specialized frame of reference, requires a preliminary understanding of the basic principles that have influenced the Jewish way of life for generations. This entails an appreciation of the central role that rabbinic authority and the Jewish legal system played in the development of these principles.

Introducing the Rabbinic Tradition[31]

Established customs and oral interpretations of verses of the Torah (the five Books of Moses) undoubtedly existed from the earliest beginnings of the Torah's acceptance and spread. These unwritten traditions guided ritual practice in the sanctuaries and in the First Temple in Jerusalem, and served as a general basis for the maintenance of law and order. During the period of the Second Temple arguments between the Sadducees and Pharisees concerned the status of the oral traditions vis-à-vis text of the Torah itself. But when Pharisaic Judaism emerged as the dominant form of Jewish practice it became clear to all that Jewish life would continue to be massively shaped by the Jewish legal system which later on came to be known as the *halakhah*.

The foundations of the halakhic system as we know it today were initially transcribed by the talmudic sages in Palestine and Babylonia during the first five centuries of the Common Era. Their starting point was the widely accepted belief that the Torah is divine and that there is significance in every word and letter. These sages (known as "the Rabbis" with a capital R) inferred "mounds and mounds of laws"[32] from the biblical text, and added their own Rabbinic laws. This legal corpus became the basis of Jewish religious practice. As Michael Berger, author of a book on rabbinic authority, points out: "The authority of the Torah was mediated through *their* understanding of it—an understanding which seemed, at times, far from the plain simple meaning of the text."[33] The talmudic sages employed a unique method of exegesis known as *midrash*—focused on close reading of the style, particular vocabulary, and peculiarities of the narrative, and reconciling apparent contradictions and embellishing some of the Bible's more enigmatic statements. Because they were "aware of the distinction between the written text and their understanding of it," the Rabbis of the talmudic period "articulated a sophisticated notion known as the dual Torah—the Written Torah and the Oral Torah. The latter was a self-conscious, *contemporaneous* exposition of the former." Nevertheless, "the Rabbis considered both bodies of law to have been revealed, to varying degrees, at Sinai, rendering Rabbinic interpretation of the Torah as divinely grounded as the revealed letters themselves."[34]

The views and pronouncements of the Rabbis, which constitute the basis of what is defined as the oral tradition, were preserved in the Mishnah and in the Gemara, together making up the Talmud. The Mishnah, the first component of the oral tradition preserved in written form, sums up all the legal debates and decisions until the middle of the third century c.e. Several additional collections of material not included in the Mishnah but cited in the Gemara are known as *baraitot* (outside teachings). Of these, the work known as the Tosefta (literally, addition) has survived as an independent book.

The Gemara, the second component of the oral tradition, consists of the Palestinian and Babylonian Talmuds, whose printed editions include much of the text of the Mishnah. These are largely protocols of the more expansive and freewheeling discussions and comments on the Mishnah, which took place in the Jewish centers of learning until their final redaction. The range of this edited talmudic body of rabbinic opinion is diverse. It first and foremost engages in legal matters (*halakhah*), such as clarification of biblical law, resolution of disputes over differing rabbinic opinions or traditions, and legislation of new measures that would guarantee the continued observance of God's commandments. Another form of rabbinic influence is conveyed by nonlegal biblical exegesis (*aggadah*). Legends and anecdotes present an array of insights on human experience that hold a prominent position in Jewish religious life and consciousness. Closely tied to the category of *aggadah* are other statements on nonlegal matters, ranging from advice on how to act in a variety of social settings to home remedies for ailments, and homiletical accounts of historical events.

Although the Rabbis may initially have formulated their *halakhic* opinions as local judges of the Jewish communities of Palestine and Babylonia, these opinions achieved an added status within the academy, serving as material for continued study or as a guide to accepted practice. What began as "rabbinic authority" was transformed into the authority of a "text" and sanctified as an integral part of the hallowed tradition. Both procedurally and in terms of prestige, what rabbinic Judaism established provides the practicing Jew with the rock-bottom premises upon everything else is built. Any scholar cited in rabbinic literature from the talmudic period is, ipso facto, deemed to be of exceptional piety, extraordinary intellect, and impeccable character.[35] Admittedly, the extent to which the pronouncements of the Rabbis in nonlegal areas are binding has been hotly debated throughout the centuries, especially by Maimonides and his followers as against the French-German tradition of the Tosafists in the thirteenth century. Opinions range from regarding *aggadah* as mere allegory (the Maimonists) to a strict literalism (some of the *baalei tosafot*). But there is no question that in the halakhic realm the rulings of all those who bore the title of rabbi throughout the centuries are, to a great extent, merely derived from the authority of those talmudic rabbis who preceded them.

While *halakhah* is rooted in the pronouncements of these talmudic sages, accepted Jewish practice today has been further shaped by the history of its codification. The process commences from the decisions of the medieval scholars who applied talmudic opinions and continues down to the very recent handbooks on particular areas of the law, such as Sabbath observance or mourning practices. In other words, normative Jewish law is grounded not merely in the talmudic sages' authority, but in a more developed and historically evolving legal system that includes both widely accepted codes and the constant need to apply these codes to the contingencies of daily life. Contemporary sources of *halakhah* are always based on late medieval codes, which navigate among early medieval sources, these themselves being interpretations of talmudic sources. Thus it has come about that the Jewish community has always had recourse to a scholarly elite, well versed in Jewish law, who guided the laity in the practical application of *halakhah*. Whether the authority was the leading scholar in the academy or the officially appointed rabbi of the community, authority relationships with scholars or community rabbis developed as derivative of rabbinic authority and pervaded the structure of Jewish life.

Halakhic authorities in the Middle Ages and afterward were of two main types. Firstly there were the legal theoreticians, such as Rashi, the Tosafists, and other Rishonim (early commentators on the Babylonian Talmud), whose main activity was the exposition of the classical texts of the Talmud and other early rabbinic works. These theoreticians were known as the *mefarshim*, rabbinic commentators, and their writings formed the basis of their own and subsequent legal decisions, even when they did not primarily see themselves as producers of legal compendia. The opinions on practical legal matters of the second group of halakhic authorities, the *poskim* (decision-makers) were accepted because of their acknowledged expertise in this field. When direct guidance from the Talmud was not to be had, questions of law were addressed to the great legal luminaries, by correspondence. The accumulated answers of these world-renowned halakhic decisors constitute a vast body of literature known as *halakhic responsa*. From time to time responsa were collected, forming the basis for new compendia of the *halakhah*, in which both the new and older laws were classified and codified.

The process of responsa and subsequent codification continues down to the present day. Each contemporary legal community continues to study the responsa of its predecessors, analyzing them, sharpening them, and applying them to new situations. The most famous of these compendia of Jewish law is the gigantic *Mishneh Torah,* compiled by Maimonides in the twelfth century. Another and later compendium is the *Arba'ah Turim* of R. Jacob ben Asher (thirteenth–fourteenth century). An encyclopedic commentary on the *Turim* written by R. Joseph Caro in the sixteenth century formed the basis

of Caro's own summary compendium, the *Shulḥan Arukh*. Caro sought to
correlate the different opinions of earlier authorities which were sometimes
a reflection of differences in practice among various Jewish communities in
the diaspora that had developed in the course of time. While primarily reflecting the customary practice of Jewry living in Spain, North Africa, and
the Middle East, the *Shulḥan Arukh* offers a practical guide for a more generally uniform application of the *halakhah*. Supplemented by the annota-
tions of Caro's contemporary, R. Moses Isserles, which record the customs
of the Ashkenazic communities living in Eastern and Western Europe, the
Shulḥan Arukh has become widely accepted as the most authoritative summary of the *halakha* and a standard measure of Jewish piety.

Emerging clearly from this survey of the Jewish legal system as developed
by rabbinic Judaism is an authoritarian view. It is characterized by the ongoing process of canonizing legal precedent and by a universe of discourse that
considers new articulations as merely the interpretation or elaboration of
that which was already disclosed. This process is governed by a distinct
ranking of authority, whereby the greater one's distance in time from the
original revelation of God's word, the less weight one's words carry. Any innovation is constrained by deference to previous rulings and opinions.

Women's "place" in the halakhic system

Armed with this understanding of the rabbinic tradition, we now return to
examine the halakhic system that it developed in terms of the three aspects
of gender highlighted by feminist theory: gender as social construct, gender
as a tool of oppression, and gender as prism for processing knowledge.[36]
The basic principles of this system certainly do seem to corroborate the feminist critique of religion in full. Starting from the Bible's original statement
that "male and female He created them" (Gen. 1:27), the rabbinic tradition
appears to affirm and support the existence of two separate and clearly distinct genders in a hierarchical relationship. Just as God provided for light
and darkness, good and evil, heaven and earth, and holy and profane, the di-
chotomization of binary opposites extends to clearly discernible sexual differences in the human species. Feminist scholars disagree as to whether the
Bible itself is deeply committed to essentialist notions of hierarchy and *innate* male superiority or is simply complying with a social structure inherited from antiquity.[37] But irrespective of how we choose to interpret the
metaphysical significance of God's punishment of women ("and he shall rule
over thee" [Gen. 3:16]) in the wake of Eve's original sin, there is no denying
that women's subordinate status did receive concrete expression even in biblical times. Women's political and economic status is generally subordinate
to that of men. This is reflected in legal and even financial terms.[38]

More important, the Jewish concept of divine commandment encouraged
a vision of society that is based on obligations rather than rights. The biblical

God is likened to a king, and the realization of the community as a kingdom of God rests on the fact that each member of the community knows precisely who is obligated to do what and for whom. The development of this idea found its expression in the halakhic system; thus it came about that, although Judaism never adopted a caste order comparable in any way to that found in India, Jewish tradition—as opposed to contemporary liberal Western thought—definitely reflects a hierarchical view of society based on the degree of answerability to God's command. Various legal distinctions are drawn between the Jew and the non-Jew, between priests (*kohanim*) and "ordinary" members of Israel (*yisraelim*), and between free men and slaves in accordance with this principle. Undoubtedly one of the most cutting of these distinctions is that between men and women. In biblical law, women's status—while reflecting a clear social order—may not flow from systematic legislative thinking. By mishnaic times, however, women's subordinate position in the eyes of the law appears linked to the fact that men have greater obligations in the study of Torah and in performance of *mitzvot* (divine commandments; sing., *mitzvah*).[39]

Women's unequal obligation to perform mitzvot. A few rabbinic sources appear to have assumed that all the commandments were at the outset addressed only to men.[40] This would mandate examining each *mitzvah* seperately (scrutinizing the scriptural sources and the *midrash* that has accrued) in order to see whether it might apply to women as well. The established consensus of rabbinic law, however, is that all the negative commandments (prohibitions) of the Torah apply equally to men and women,[41] aside from those that are related to obvious biological differences (such as trimming the beard and sidelocks). Women are also obligated to carry out most of the positive *mitzvot* (divine commandments that involve taking action) that are prescribed for men, excepting those based on clearly physical distinctions (circumcision for men and the sacrifices at the Temple that a new mother must bring).

There are, however, other important distinctions between the legal obligations of men and women that are not biologically based. Halakhic compendiums will list such *mitzvot* as wearing fringes on any four-cornered garment (*tzitzit*),[42] donning phylacteries (*tefillin*) in the course of the morning prayer, and dwelling in a temporary booth (*sukkah*) and acquiring and blessing the "four species" (*arba minim*)—palm, myrtle, willow branches and citron—during the festival of Tabernacles (Sukkot), citing the reasons for the *mitzvah*. Thereafter they will deliberate whether or not women are exempt, for whatever given reason. In the course of such discussions, which display a more gender-based legislative bias, women's obligations usually appear as an addendum or as an exception to the male norm. Even including women in the religious obligations that apply on the holiday of Purim—commemorating an event with a female protagonist—necessitates a special argument: "They too were witness to that miracle."[43] The net result is that women are at times classified in halakhic literature together with other marginalized groups such as slaves, children, imbeciles, androgynes, hermaphrodites, and the deaf-mute[44]—either because they are excluded from certain *mitzvot* altogether or because they are merely exempt.

The Mishnah attempts to understand distinctions in the halakhic obligation of men and women that are not biologically based in terms of a neat legal-logical principle, establishing that women are generally exempt from the positive *mitzvot* that are "time-bound"—performed at a particular time of day or year.[45] However, the existence of so many exceptions to this principle[46] supports the suggestion that rather than governing as an a priori rule, this criterion probably developed as after-the-fact formulation of an existing socio-cultural reality.

As further examples will demonstrate, men's greater religious obligations, whether or not they are actually fulfilled, confer other legal privileges. By the same token, women's lesser obligations disenfranchise them in many areas. As in the case of other classes situated on the hierarchical scale,[47] difference in religious responsibility then serves as rationale for women's diminished valuation. Under certain circumstances, the legal repercussions are significant indeed. Because greater obligation to *mitzvot* is translated in halakhic terms as greater worth, the Mishnah rules that a man's right to life precedes that of a woman's in most life-threatening situations.[48] This consideration is explicitly stated in some sources as justification for the ruling that if a man and a woman are drowning, the man should be saved first.[49]

Of particular significance is also the fact that women are exempt (and according to the dominant traditional position, even deliberately distanced) from the central religious activity of studying Torah, despite the fact that this activity is not classified as time-bound.[50] As a result, although there is no ban in principle on women functioning as halakhic authorities (*poskot*),[51] in practice they have had no official part to play in the tradition's legislative and interpretive process.[52] Because of their lack of proficiency in the Oral Law, women have been virtually excluded from any participation in halakhic discussion and its formulation.

Restrictions upon women in the public domain. In the public domain, women are excluded from the right to hold any positions of authority. Women's exclusion from public office is formally derived from the Torah's reference to appointing a king with no mention of a queen,[53] which Maimonides applies by extension to all other offices of authority.[54] Women cannot serve as judges[55] or even bear witness in court.[56] Their activity in other roles of communal leadership and public ritual has also been circumscribed on strength of an assumption that the honor of the community (*kevod hatzibbur*) is compromised when women take on such functions[57] or out of considerations of modesty.

In modern times, such restrictions have been used as the basis in many Orthodox communities for banning women from participating on synagogue boards or from serving as principals in religious schools. Reluctance to place women in situations of authority over men extends, in some Hassidic circles, even to objection to their driving cars. In Israel, the religious injunction against female heads of state still prevents women in any of the ultra-Orthodox political parties from running for public office.[58] In 1969 this injunction also prompted the resignation of an ultra-Orthodox party from the government coalition after Golda Meir became prime minister.[59]

Women's dependent personal and family status. Although Jewish tradition has glorified the role of the woman in the home, women are accorded no greater halakhic status in the domestic realm. Men are the official heads of their families, leaving women with fewer independent rights or privileges. The *mitzvah* to "be fruitful and multiply" is, paradoxically, regarded as only the man's obligation.[60]

Legally, all responsibilities attendant upon the raising and educating of children are exclusively the obligation of the father.[61] Fathers and not mothers have complete custody of their offspring until they reach puberty.[62] Biblical law allows a father to marry off his daughter as a minor (before she reaches twelve years of age) without her assent.[63] Although the Talmud subsequently prohibits this practice and mandates delaying the betrothal until the daughter comes of age and agrees,[64] financial and social pressures encountered by Jews in medieval times prompted the revoking of this amendment.[65]

Women's subordinate status within the family is reflected in her financial standing as well. While alternative arrangements can be made, the general assumption is that all of a woman's earnings belong to her husband in exchange for his supporting her.[66] Men are normally the sole inheritors in property law, although the dowry is generally understood as a remedy for the exclusion of daughters from their father's inheritance.[67] Because a married woman may not use property even if it is her own without her husband's consent, she, like a slave, is not liable for damages.[68] The right of men to the return of their lost property precedes that of women.[69] By the same token, one must not accept large charitable donations from women— for fear that their having such sums at their disposal might indicate they were stolen.[70]

Inequality in marriage and divorce law. Nothing gives clearer expression to the subordinate status of women in the family than the original laws established by *halakhah* in the area of marriage and divorce. In legal terms, the institution of Jewish marriage is based upon a formal act effecting change of status (*kinyan*). Contemporary apologists make much of the fact that—unlike acquisition of a slave—*kinyan* in the context of marriage does not entail taking possession of the acquired object as property. The *kinyan* is merely a symbolic deed establishing *kiddushin,* whereby a man consecrates a woman as his wife, agrees to support her, and contractually acquires exclusive rights to conjugal relations with her—thereby forbidding her to all other men.[71] Although the woman's consent is required, however, only a man may effect *kinyan.* Moreover, in spite of the fact that over the generations monogamy has become the mandatory norm in almost all Jewish communities, the wife's rights to sexual exclusivity do not—to this day—carry the same halakhic weight.

Given that women in ancient times were usually given in marriage at the onset of puberty, the marital bond was not understood as a union of equals, but rather as a contract for passing responsibility for the woman from her father to her husband.[72] After marriage the woman's obligations toward her parents were taken by the Rabbis as overridden by her subjugation to her husband and her obligation to obey his authority[73]—another reflection of her lack of autonomy. Maimonides reinforces this understanding in stating that a wife should have the fear of her husband upon her, "and all her work should be done in accordance with his instruction; he should be in her eyes like a prince or a king who may act as he desires."[74]

Maimonides does prescribe parallel obligations for the husband, stating—in the name of the sages—that "a man should honor his wife more than himself," that "if he has money he should increase her portion," and that "he should not cast fear over her."[75] This could be taken as confirmation of the view that post-biblical *halakhah* represents a general trend toward improving women's status in marriage, initiating important protective measures for their benefit. According to biblical law, the husband's basic responsibilities toward his wife are not only to provide her with food and clothing, but also with the satisfaction of normal sexual needs.[76] While this prescription already constitutes recognition of women's independent needs and rights, post-biblical law establishes several other significant obligations, such as the husband's responsibility for his wife's medical care, burial, ransom from captivity, and sustenance even after his death so long as she and her children remained part of his household.[77] In addition, the marriage contract (*ketubah*), which was most likely introduced by postbiblical *halakhah,*[78] obliges the husband to pay a predetermined sum of money to his wife if he divorces her. This document served as a type of insurance policy protecting the woman in case of divorce, by guaranteeing her compensation for the dowry money she brought with her upon entering the marriage.

As against these obligations, the wife's responsibilities toward her husband in lieu of her daily sustenance, based entirely on rabbinical rulings (*takkanot hakhamim*), entail a complete array of domestic obligations of a more servile nature.[79] Although she may be absolved of some of these if she brings maid servants to the marriage, a wife is not released from the obligation to personally wash her husband's feet, prepare his cup of wine, and make his bed.[80] The medieval commentator Rashi understands this as a benevolent piece of rabbinic advice aimed at humanizing the institution of marriage and making wives beloved by their husbands.[81] Maimonides, on the other hand, formulates the matter more harshly, stating that any woman who shirks these responsibilities may be forced to comply, even by whipping.[82] No halakhic decisor nowadays would implement such advice in practice, yet traces of its influence upon conceptions of proper husband-wife relations are still evident in rabbinic responsa on the attitudinal level and in the approach of judges serving in the rabbinic courts.

Because it is the husband who enacts the marriage, by contractually acquiring the woman's services and thus making her his wife, he alone can initiate divorce.[83] This lack of symmetry is ostensibly redressed by the rabbinic ruling that even husbands, under most circumstances, require their wives' consent for release from marriage.[84] Further changes in the nature of the marital relationship accrued over the centuries, especially with the adoption of the ban on polygamy—instituted by Rabbenu Gershom, a leading tenth-century halakhic authority—by most Jewish communities.[85] Although in principle men may still remarry if they obtain the written agreement of one hundred rabbis, in practice this rarely happens. It happens all too frequently, however, that a man in a failed marriage denies his wife a writ of divorce (*get*) and thus prevents her from starting a new family. In our day this is the most common way in which a woman is consigned to being an *agunah*, an "anchored" woman.[86] If she does remarry without a proper *get*, generally after a civil marriage, Jewish law regards her as an adulteress. Any children from the new union will bear the religious stigma of *mamzerim* (halakhic bastards), prohibited from marrying most other Jews. This prospect is a far more powerful factor contributing to the disadvantaged status of women than the lack of ability to initiate divorce. No comparable threat hangs over the head of husbands who have extra-marital relations with other women. Children born to such a woman, provided she is unmarried and not forbidden to him for other reasons, will not be *mamzerim*.

The image of woman in Jewish tradition

While issues such as those surrounding the *agunah* have profound repercussions up to this day, many halakhic restrictions are abstract liabilities. They are buried in texts that few women see, and they have no impact on women's daily lives. For example, virtually no one today expects a wife to wash her husband's feet or even teaches her that such an expectation exists. Thus, the women in many fully observant families are unaware of the extent of their disadvantage in legal terms, believing it to be confined to ritual matters only. Moreover, such women often feel that there are considerable compensations for the limitations imposed by a strict division of gender roles. They may be relieved to be free of some of the obligations that their male relatives must carry out. They may enjoy the women-only spaces and times that are a by-product of gender stratification. And there is considerable justice to the claim that traditional Judaism, in viewing the home, rather than the synagogue as the center of religious life, has in many matters provided women with a status that is privileged over that of their counterparts in general society.[87]

Yet even when women are oblivious or indifferent to their disadvantaged legal status, a different sense of exclusion is not so easily dismissed. Once a contemporary Jewish woman gains competency in classic text study, she may discount as no longer operative such strictures as the list of wifely services. But a sense of her status as outsider in the traditional literature, whether acute or lurking only in the background of her consciousness and never achieving articulation, is not so easily avoided. Testimony to women's sense of exclusion as "the other" can already be gleaned from the titles of several classics of Jewish feminism, such as Rachel Adler's "The Jew Who Wasn't There: Halakhah and the Jewish Woman," Paula Hyman's "The Other Half: Women in the Jewish Tradition," or Judith Plaskow's "Standing Again at Sinai: Judaism from a Feminist Perspective," whose title is based on the observation that the most formative event in Jewish history, the Sinaitic revelation, by implication excludes women, by rendering them invisible in its account.[88] (Moses says to "the people, 'Be ready for the third day; do not go near a woman'" [Exod. 19:15].)

Both Plaskow and Adler dwell on the dissonance this exclusion creates with the women's sense that they *do* have a share in the revelatory experience.[89] At issue, as Plaskow acknowledges, is the danger of ritual impurity. While emission of semen in principle renders both man and his female partner as temporarily unfit to approach the sacred,[90] Plaskow's objection is that "at the central moment of Jewish history" it is only the men who are addressed by Moses as "the people." Taking exception to a biblical rendition of the revelatory experience as addressed only to males directly is for Plaskow and Adler not solely a matter of justice or historical accuracy; remembering is a very important part of Jewish ritual activity.[91] As Adler writes:

The woman hearing the Torah reading [on the festival of Shavuot, which celebrates the anniversary of the giving of the Torah at Sinai] is not there to study social organization in the ancient Middle East. If she were, she would accept as a given that in the culture under examination, women held an inferior status. That would have nothing to do with her. But (accepting Eliade's contention that every ritual is a re-enactment of a primary event), the woman's purpose in being present this Shavuot morning must be to re-enact through this reading the first covenant of her people. And because the text has excluded her, she is excluded again in this re-enactment and will be excluded over and over, year by year, every time she rises to hear this covenant read.[92]

There is no denying that in the body of the literary tradition the male is the representative Jew. Woman's role and value is defined and limited mainly by male interests and considerations. It is not only the Torah that generally addresses only males directly. In subsequent literature, women continue to be referred to as objects rather than subjects. Women are "they," to be regarded—as described by the sages—as "a people unto themselves."[93] A typical talmudic illustration of the multiple audience-exclusion of women, both subtle and explicit, is the statement: "A beautiful wife, a beautiful home, and beautiful vessels expand a person's spirit."[94] Regarded with even minimal feminist consciousness, this statement gives three causes for affront. First, the "person" (adam) here can only refer to a man. Second, the statement neglects mention of what might expand the mind of a woman, without the trace of an apology. Third, it unabashedly presents women in an instrumental fashion, on a par with other objects such as a house or vase.

Standard prayers are also phrased with reference to men only. The female pronoun appears only in brackets, if at all. This same androcentric bias also applies to all the classics of Jewish thought. Thus, women reading the traditional sources are likely to have the sense of eavesdropping on a male-only conversation.[95] Women's opinions do not figure in the discussion.

Because traditional Jewish sources are the record of males looking *out* and *upon* women, they invariably reflect male stereotyped conceptions of women, rather than women's understanding of themselves as individuals with priorities, rights, and interests of their own. Given that the classic image of woman in Jewish tradition is determined by rabbinic interpretation of biblical texts, her very essence is defined by men and on their terms. The net result is that Jewish women are culturally and religiously nurtured into acceptance of their prime function as "enablers."[96] Their merit accrues mainly in a vicarious way through the religious achievements of their husbands and sons. For example, the reward promised to women in the world to come (said to be more assured than that of the men) is merited because they send their sons to the synagogue to learn Torah and their husbands to the house of study to learn Mishnah and Gemara, and they wait for their husbands until they return from the house of study.[97]

The fact that woman's role is defined by men and perceived primarily in terms of male needs has also served to damage her image. A lowly view of women appears to be built into the very fabric of the Hebrew language. The late Rabbi Eliezer Berkovits (a prominent Modern Orthodox thinker of the twentieth century) cites[98] one of the earliest biblical statements about women, in the words of the prophet Jeremiah (51:30): "The mighty men of Babylon stopped waging war. They sit in fortresses. Their strength has left them. They have become like women." In other words, the use of the term "women" here is not just a reference to "the weaker sex"; it is a synonym for weakness. Another example cited by Berkovits is the midrashic play on the Hebrew word for son (ben), meaning to build (banah), thus conveying the notion that men are world-builders.[99] And, although the world cannot exist without both sexes, the birth of a male is regarded in the Talmud as an occasion for joy and special celebration, whereas the birth of a female is cause for anxiety.[100]

As a result of halakhic preoccupation with issues of modesty and ritual purity, women are often discussed in the classical sources in a one-sided manner, merely in terms of their sexual properties. In such contexts, they tend to appear either as threatening because of their unruly potential for sexual temptation or disgusting due to a lingering image of the uterus as "a place of rot."[101] In any case, detailed analyses of their virginity, bodily parts, and excretions contribute to undermining their dignity, especially when these analyses are codified in texts that have become standard study material in the religious education of young men. Although such material is the usual fare of legal discussion, the fact that it is conducted in men-only environments and not counterbalanced by more individualized accounts of women as persons encourages the occasional interpolation of chauvinistic and unflattering remarks.[102] Women are at times dismissed in talmudic discussion as frivolous,[103] lazy (and for this reason not to be relied upon for meticulous observance of *mitzvot*),[104] overtalkative,[105] and easily seduced.[106] With the passing of time, such judgments were supported by essentialist views phrased in the rhetoric of the Aristotelian tradition: women were seen as incomplete human beings functioning as "matter" in contrast to the more developed "form" of men. This hierarchic mode of thinking, which penetrated earlier Jewish sources and continued through medieval times,[107] is sometimes uncritically repeated even in later, more modern writing.

It is true that alongside derogatory remarks, there are many moving talmudic expressions of genuine love, esteem, gallantry, and appreciative regard for women. Many concern women in their role as wives: "He who has no wife lives without joy, without blessing, without the goodness of life [and finally] without life."[108] "He who loves his wife as himself and honors her more than herself—of him does the Torah say: 'And you will know that there is peace in your home, etc.'"[109] "Everything can be replaced; but for the wife of one's youth there is no replacement."[110] There are also many statements that refer to women's religious piety, emotional sensitivity, and practical wisdom.[111] One tradition attributes the Jewish people's meriting the Exodus to the piety of the Israelite women in Egypt.[112] For almost every offensive statement, another source can be cited to indicate the contrary.

But even when negative images of women are offset by others that extol their virtues, or by parallel statements regarding men's shortcomings,[113] they do not mitigate the fact that all of these judgments are pronounced by men. It is therefore not surprising that they necessarily reflect predominantly male interests and a masculine scale of values.

The Orthodox Dilemma

Any woman today who regards herself as a practicing Orthodox Jew must contend with her status in the halakhic system and its surrounding nonlegal tradition. As we have seen, the theological justification for this authoritative framework is based on two related assumptions. The first is that the Bible is of divine origin and therefore immutable, with every word and letter bearing divine significance. The second is that the Rabbis of the Talmud were its sole legitimate interpreters. Up until modern times, the majority of Jews affirmed their basic loyalty to the normative Jewish way of life and accepted its background assumptions, even if their personal practice fell short of the ideal. To be sure, observance was, for the most part, not a matter of personal preference or choice; it was simply a way of life imbibed from one's surroundings, beginning in earliest childhood. The approach was mimetic.[114] It is therefore appropriate to characterize pre-modern Jewish societies as "traditional." Practices were simply accepted without question. The internal cohesiveness of the Jewish community, coupled with the constant external pressures of a non-Jewish population intent on maintaining economic and social segregation (to varying degrees), essentially made fidelity to *halakhah* a given for most Jews, barring exceptional cases of conversion.

It was only in the nineteenth century that a massive challenge in the realm of ideology was staged against the halakhic tradition. The assault of biblical critics on the Written Law, and the attempt of some reformers to reject some elements or all of the Oral Law expounded by the sages of the Talmud, led to the birth of "Orthodoxy"—a Judaism that consciously embraces observance of *halakhah,* in the face of other options.[115] Despite the differences between various strains of Orthodoxy (some of which will be discussed in chapter 4), they do have—in ideological terms—a significant common denominator: their ongoing commitment to both the divinity of the Written Law and the authority of the Oral Law as developed by the talmudic Rabbis; they reject any major tampering with that tradition as it has evolved. Hence, Orthodox Jews are defined (even in their own eyes) by the degree to which they adhere to halakhic practice and remain engaged by a tradition that forms the basis of their commitment.

As George Santayana has so eloquently stated, the unique power of religious belief lies

in its special and surprising message and in the bias that revelation gives to life. The vistas it opens and the mysteries it propounds are another world to live in; and another world to live in—whether we expect ever to pass wholly over into it or no—is what we mean by having a religion.[116]

The fidelity of Orthodox Judaism to the rabbinic tradition allows it to continue functioning as a powerful counterculture, effectively impressing upon its adherents the notion that the ordinary commonsensical way of looking at the world cannot provide all that there is to see. Yet once exposed to the new possibilities that feminism intimates, the Orthodox Jew may well experience a new and heady sensation of discovery rivaling that provided by religion itself.

Feminism offers new ways of thinking that counter our deepest and most visceral sense of who we are. It highlights the contingency of male-female gender distinctions that have characterized the Jewish way of life over the centuries. Moreover, it suggests that the traditional images and roles that religion has designated to men and women may not be part of the fixed furniture of the universe. And it indicates that all sorts of deficiencies and injustices may have nonetheless been produced and perpetuated in the wake of such designations.

Most serious of all, feminist standpoint theory challenges the very notion of a privileged insight to truth—precisely what is implied by the bedrock status accorded to an exclusively male tradition of rabbinic interpretation. The adequacy and very divinity of the picture of reality that this tradition of interpretation propagates is called into question by feminist epistemology, with its challenges to the traditional notion of objectivity. In raising such challenges, feminism can be seen as undermining the deepest foundations upon which rabbinic Judaism—as an authoritarian system—depends for its survival.

Feminism is not going to disappear. Moreover, at this point in time it is a burning issue that cannot be ignored. It may be that some of the unsettling implications of feminism on the epistemological level have been grossly overrated, and that when the dust settles these will prove to have no more lasting impact than that left today by Marxist ideology. Nonetheless, as in the case of Marxism, the changing status of women in Western society will have exerted at least some residual influence on the social and cultural character of Western civilization. In terms of Jewish faith, this influence is already being felt on many levels: theological, institutional, and practical.

The desire to reconcile new insights with Judaism's venerated teachings motivates many a traditionalist's quest. At the same time, she may also be tempted to downplay the magnitude of the challenge. The first step is to acknowledge the problem.

CHAPTER 2

Sources of Discontent and the Conservative Response

A Brief History of Discontent on Gender Issues Throughout the Ages

It would be a mistake to assume that discomfort with women's status as defined by *halakhah* and the classic sources arose only in the twentieth century. Over the ages many leading rabbinic figures, attempting to overcome instances of blatant injustice to women and alleviate their suffering, have experienced genuine anguish over what they view as objective constraints of the law. This is particularly true with regard to *agunah* issues. In addition, the sources occasionally reveal a different type of unease on the part of women themselves, regarding some of the deeper implications of a hierarchical system that views them as second-class citizens with respect to basic privileges of religious worship.

A few rare testimonies of women's protest on this score were even included in the Talmud. I remember my first childhood confrontation with the famous talmudic anecdote about Beruria, the learned and pious wife of R. Meir, who chastised a "foolish Galilean" for asking her "Which is the road we take to Lod?" rather than "Which way to Lod?"[1] despite the sages' advice not to converse at length with a woman.[2] The phrasing of the story is terse, leaving a little girl much room to ponder upon the spirit in which the venerated Beruria had made her rebuke. Was she being earnest, facetious, bitter? Perhaps, as has been recently suggested, her reprimand expressed a sense of her own worth as a scholar.[3] According to this interpretation, Beruria implied that her questioner was wasting the time of a learned women on trivialities rather than using the opportunity to discuss matters of Torah with her, and so should have been more sparing with his words.

A more vivid expression of female protest is preserved in a tale about Yalta, the wife of the talmudic sage R. Nachman.[4] The trouble began when R. Nachman's guest Ulla refused to oblige his host and hand Yalta the customary cup of wine before the grace after meals. Quoting in his defense the biblical promise that God will bless "the fruit of your belly" (Deut. 7:13),

Ulla interpreted the use of the masculine gender to mean women's participation in the ceremony was inappropriate. In response, Yalta, in a fit of rage, went into the wine cellar and broke four hundred jars of wine.[5]

Legal responsa literature from the Middle Ages, in discussing marriage and divorce, property ownership, and inheritance, frequently reveals the frustrations that many women faced due to their restricted halakhic status. A recent scholarly study of the lives of Jewish women in medieval times has unearthed a few previously unknown instances of independence and protest.[6] If rabbinic authorities described as "pure and saintly" the Jewish women in Germany who sacrificed their lives to sanctify God's name in the riots of 1096, toward the middle of the thirteenth century we find a change of tone. Complaints are registered against "haughty and rebellious" troublemakers who attempt to challenge halakhic definitions of their legal position in the family and in the public domain and achieve greater social or religious privileges commensurate with their increased independence. For example, in Egypt and Byzantium at the end of the twelfth century, a considerable number of women protested immersion in the *mikveh* (the community's ritual bath), a rite of purification required after menstruation and childbirth. They preferred instead the heretical Karaite custom of merely pouring water over the body at home.[7] This protest should probably be understood more as a reflection of the influence of the Karaite movement on the Jewish community than as a protofeminist revolution. What was remarkable in this case nevertheless was the degree of self-confidence such women displayed and their ability to join ranks and organize to an extent that threatened the ability of the rabbis to stand against them.[8]

A different kind of rebellion was represented by women who insisted on assuming active roles in family religious ceremonies—for example, circumcising infant sons or performing ritual slaughter of animals—despite the explicit disapproval of halakhic authorities.[9] Rabbanit Brona, who continued wearing ritual *tzitzit* despite the objections of the Maharil (Rabbi Jacob Moses Moellin Segal, the acknowledged rabbinic leader of German Jewry in the fifteenth century) is a case in point. Even more interesting is his refusal to chastise her "for fear that she will not heed me."[10]

In modern times, objection to women's status originated in secularist circles. Early Yiddish and Hebrew writers of the modern Jewish Enlightenment movement (the *Haskalah*), described traditional religious life in their fiction. Their depiction of the unhappiness of women in the roles imposed upon them through arranged marriages, their limited education, and their lack of control over their own lives was another form of protest. The innovations of the Reform liberal movement in Germany in the 1820s, granting women equal rights and obligations mainly in the realm of synagogue ritual, have sometimes been credited as the first religious response to women's disenfranchisement. This interpretation may be misplaced, as the original motive for this form of egalitarianism was more likely the wish to make Jewish worship similar to that of the Gentiles. Nevertheless, such moves as abolishing the practice of separate seating in places of worship and including women in temple choirs eventually led to more far-reaching changes. With the establishment of Jewish women's organizations in Europe and the United States at the turn of the twentieth century, women themselves began to agitate for greater equality within the Jewish community.

Starting in the early 1970s, the women's liberation movement began to have a noticeable effect on the organized American Jewish community at large, as college-aged women and men began publicly objecting to the patriarchal character of communal institutions. The search for new values and ethnic identity brought many young people back to their Jewish roots. The establishment of communities of counterculture and New Age spirituality seekers (*havurot*) introduced creative modes of religious expression, geared toward taking women's needs into account and providing them with the opportunity for greater participation in public religious ritual. Gradually more mainstream Reform, Reconstructionist, and Conservative congregations in North America accepted the principle of mutual responsibility in public ritual, as did their counterparts abroad. This principle was introduced into the wedding ceremony as well, so that both husband and wife appear as active and equal participants.[11] Various national and international conferences were organized to address some of the major areas of Jewish feminist concern. Notable among these was an international conference entitled "Halakhah and the Jewish Woman," chaired by Penina Peli, which took place in 1986 in Jerusalem under the auspices of the Israeli Ministry of Justice. The ripple effect of such events influenced communal and religious institutions and led to increased prominence of women in positions of leadership. Educational opportunities for women grew dramatically, beginning with the primary school level and leading eventually to admission of women students to the rabbinical programs of the non-Orthodox denominations. By the early 1980s all of these denominations were ordaining women rabbis.

Alongside these developments, feminist scholarship began to emerge in the early 1980s. Female scholars influenced by de Beauvoir's writings applied her analysis of Western patriarchy to Judaism. Her notion of woman as the Other highlighted the role of men as both the subjects and the authors of classic Jewish texts. A veritable flood of literature followed in the wake of such scholarship, portraying the marginalization of women's interests and concerns in Jewish tradition.

Mainstream Orthodoxy for a long time managed to ignore or resist these developments, regarding them as fringe phenomena, of negligible relevance to normative Jewish observance. Over the past few decades, however, the feminist critique has penetrated Orthodox circles, first in the United States and other English-speaking countries, and more recently in Israel. As noted earlier, Blu Greenberg's book *On Women and Judaism,* written in a personal vein, was one of the first attempts to articulate feminist difficulties with Jewish tradition from an Orthodox perspective.[12] Some of the most notable formulations of the problem were voiced by a few American Orthodox rabbis sympathetic to women's concerns.[13]

What Do These So-Called Orthodox Feminists Want?

The first stages of Orthodox feminism, in the United States, were led by women affiliated with the more liberal end of the Orthodox spectrum, sociologically removed from the centers of Jewish learning, and characterized by a sense of estrangement and distance from the rabbinic establishment. Their major agenda was politically activist: setting out to solve problems Orthodox women faced when confronted with injustices and practical difficulties posed by their restricted legal status. The issue that angered them most was that of women seeking divorce from recalcitrant husbands.

The agunah problem. In previous generations, the plight of an *agunah,* a woman locked in marriage for lack of a *get* (bill of divorce), usually stemmed from her husband's disappearance due to war, the exigencies of travel, or desertion. In recent generations, however, this label often refers to any woman locked in formal marriage to a husband who refuses to release her from the relationship, under any terms or unless she pays him off. With the growing instability of marriage in modern times, the *agunah* has become an acute social problem. Religious courts regard the husband's financial extortion of the woman as almost a normal and inevitable step in divorce proceedings. Rabbinic authorities in previous generations often displayed great sympathy for *agunot,* bending over backward in order to find halakhic loopholes.[14] However, the increased dimensions of the problem today, compounded by practical difficulties involving current institutional politics (such as the perceived need to preserve a uniquely Orthodox line in the face of pressures to liberalize standards for the sake of interdenominational cooperation), have given rise to more conservative tendencies. Given these factors, the issue of the *agunot* has become one of the most volatile items on the political agenda of Jewish feminism.

Leadership and ritual in the public domain. Another area of growing concern has been the fact that current halakhic norms afford Jewish women little opportunity for meaningful participation in public religious ritual and other activities in the communal realm. Because modern Jewish life, especially in the diaspora, has transferred the weight of religious identification from the home and the study hall to the synagogue, women have increasingly viewed such constraints as depriving them of the opportunity for serious expression of their Jewish identity, as well as an affront to their dignity as full human beings.

The few *mitzvot* that have traditionally been regarded as women's unique preserve are closely connected to physical objects and tasks in the domestic arena, without any more distinctively spiritual counterbalances.[15]

Most Orthodox women have understood this phenomenon as the unintentional side effect of purely formal halakhic considerations. They accept the contention that it is only women's lesser formal obligation to *mitzvot,* in unfortunate combination with halakhic restraints in the public domain, that create undesirable situations of exclusion. For example, because only men are regarded as part of the ritual community (the *edah*), women are not counted as part of the quorum (*minyan*) of ten participants required for the performance of many (but not all) religious acts.[16] Women's lesser obligation in the performance of certain *mitzvot* also disqualifies their carrying them out on behalf of men; fulfillment of an obligation by proxy is a legitimate halakhic option, but only if the "proxy" has the same or higher obligation as the person designating him or her.[17] For this reason, Orthodox women do not lead recitation of the *zimmun* (invitation to say grace after meals) in mixed company as in theory all participants fulfill their obligation in saying grace through the leader, and a woman's obligation is arguably only rabbinical, while a man's is certainly biblical. This same difficulty bars women from serving as a leader of the prayer service (*shaliah tzibbur*). The principle of communal honor (*kevod hatzibbur*)[18] prevents women from being called up to the Torah (*aliyot laTorah*), or assuming formal positions of religious authority. Considerations of modesty restrict women's participation in other public rituals, barring them from praying in a mixed group without a physical barrier (*mehitzah*) between them and the men's section, where the central aspects of communal prayer take place.

Nevertheless Modern Orthodox feminists have sought to overcome these formal halakhic constraints, and to redress the feeling of marginalization in religious life that ensues, by creating conditions for greater involvement of women in synagogue ritual and communal affairs. In Israel, one of the historic milestones of Orthodox feminism was when the Israeli High Court of Justice in 1988 upheld the right of Leah Shakdiel to serve as an elected member of the local religious council in her hometown, Yeruham. Abroad, attention was focused more intensely on synagogue architecture. Orthodox feminists began pointing out that although women are encouraged to take on the *mitzvah* of prayer in the privacy of their homes, practical arrangements for their participation in Orthodox synagogues are usually not very welcoming. In many synagogues, the women's section is a balcony, hard to reach with strollers (or wheelchairs), and often accessed only via a separate back entrance for reasons of modesty. Moreover, at public functions outside the synagogue (at weddings or rallies, for example) it is assumed as a matter of course that women will not participate in communal prayer, and so the men congregate in areas where the required separation of the sexes is not feasible.

Orthodox feminists are offended by such assumptions. Women's exemption from the obligation to pray communally at fixed times of the day may have made sense when women's lives and timetables were drastically different than those of their male counterparts. The greater leeway that this exemption affords contemporary women in their daily routines as housewives and mothers may still be in order. But the fact that halakhically observant women in the workforce or at other public venues away from home are expected to stand around and gossip while their male colleagues engage in prayer is an anomaly that Orthodox feminists became unable to defend. While many observant women avoid praying at fixed times, either out of religious apathy or out of preference for less rigid avenues of relating to God, feminists increasingly felt that a less rigorous standard for women's participation in prayer, even if they are single or beyond their childbearing years, does little for the development of women's religious sensibilities. Women interested in more serious religious involvement began to demand arrangements enabling their inclusion beyond the customary synagogue attendance on Sabbath morning. Orthodox college students with egalitarian concerns began, in similar fashion, to call for the right of women to deliver Torah homilies (*divrei Torah*) at campus services and to serve in other positions of leadership centered around the synagogue.

Alongside their concern for enabling women's increased participation in positions of religious leadership and public ritual, Orthodox feminists found fault with the widespread practice of discouraging women from voluntarily performing those time-bound *mitzvot* that serve as the most tangible symbols of Jewish identity, perpetuating the traditional view that the *mitzvot* of *tefillin* and *tzitzit* are an exclusively male preserve.[19] They drew attention to the fact that even on the level of popular custom, Jewish tradition has not established outward signs of religious identification for women. Thus, for example, Orthodox women have no custom paralleling that of Orthodox men, who wear skullcaps throughout the day as an ongoing reminder of humility before God.[20] Indeed, although this is one of the customs that confers identity for the religiously observant male, the Orthodox public tends to label women of any denomination who appropriate it as "Conservative" or "Reform," equating this with "less religious."

Greater learning opportunities. Another cause promoted by Orthodox feminists has been greater equality in women's Jewish education.[21] It became clear that women's exemption from the obligation of *talmud Torah* also denied them involvement in serious text study, generally regarded by Jewish tradition as the most religiously significant spiritual activity.

A dramatic transformation in the education of Jewish girls and women had already begun in Kraków, Poland, prior to World War I, instigated by a woman. Enlisting the support of Rabbi Yisrael Meir Hacohen Kagan (better known as the Hafetz Hayim), Sarah Schenirer, a traditional Jewish seamstress by profession, founded what eventually became the Beth Jacob network of schools for women.[22] This network eventually spread to Israel, the United States, and other countries in the Diaspora, flourishing to the present day. As understood by the Beth Jacob system, however, the chief purpose of educating women is to enhance their effectiveness in their traditional role of wives and mother, within the changed modern context. Aside from vocational training that will allow women to supplement—or even take responsibility for—the family income, this demands more extensive knowledge of practical *halakhah,* and even the pursuit of other spiritual fare that is likely to deepen their religious devotion.[23] The type of education available to girls in Modern Orthodox day schools (some for girls only and some coed) took a somewhat different form, offering a well-rounded secular education, but usually limiting the curriculum and lowering standards for girls in Jewish studies. There were, however, exceptions.

A few of the Modern Orthodox institutions developed within the day school movement in the United States had already begun to provide their students with some rudimentary introduction to the world of the Oral Law in the 1950s. Concomitantly, a few high schools in Israel (most notably within the religious kibbutz movement) began enriching the program of religious studies for their female students.[24] A number of teachers' seminaries were also established, providing women some opportunity for attaining post– high-school levels of proficiency, mainly in the realm of biblical studies. But in the last quarter century, the call to equalize the education of boys and girls joined forces with a more significant revolution overtaking women's education on the post–high-school level, as will be discussed in chapter 5.

Political initiatives. In the United States, the Jewish Orthodox Feminist Alliance (JOFA) was established at the time of the first international conference of Orthodox feminists in 1996. Its Israeli parallel Kolech (meaning "your voice" in the Hebrew feminine) was established in 1998. The declared goals of both movements, in addition to the advancement of women's learning opportunities, include more practical and political objectives. Among these are the expansion of opportunities for women in the performance of *mitzvot;* calling the attention of the religious community and its leadership to the changes in the general status of women in the modern age; encouraging initiatives to find legal solutions to various issues that arise as a result of these changes; promoting appropriate adjustments in the educational curriculum of both males and females; and integrating women into public organizational settings. One of the more notable efforts on the part of these organizations is their work in conjunction with rabbinical authorities in developing and popularizing the use of prenuptial agreements to circumvent in the future the difficulties faced by today's *agunot.*[25]

The Conservative Response: Patriarchalists and Apologists

Given the litany of complaints and the limited scope of the solutions that have been forthcoming on the part of the official Orthodox establishment, an outside observer might wonder how traditional Judaism manages to defend the status quo. Yet conservative responses to the feminist critique continue to flourish,[26] and they still resonate with many Jews. These responses typically take one of two directions: affirmation of patriarchalism (accepting traditional norms as submission to God's will) or apologetics (aiming to dispel dissent as a misguided reaction to benign conventions).

Hierarchy as divine command. The former group of defenders (not all of them men) openly acknowledge women's subordinate status, but cannot justify pitting human values against divine command. Therefore, they believe that conformance—despite the discomfort—is a simple question of religious commitment and faith. Consulting psychologist and Yeshiva University professor Menachem Brayer, in defending the halakhic status of woman, lapses into this approach when he writes:

Mysterious are the ways of the Lord, and the finite intelligence of the human mortal cannot comprehend the Infinite wisdom of the Creator. The faithful and devoted child of God will not feel frustrated if some of the questions remain incomprehensible and enigmatic.[27]

Religious obligation does not always tally with human notions of justice. In this sense, argues Lisa Aiken,[28] author of several English-language books in defense of traditional Judaism, the less-privileged status of women is comparable to that of the Israelite who, irrespective of his merit, does not enjoy the privileges of the Levite or the priest.[29]

The "separate but equal" response. Some conservatives maintain that adherents of the patriarchalist position concede too much to their critics. It is by no means clear that the sources mandate a fixed and eternal hierarchy between the sexes. Utterly denying that the *halakhah* can be responsive to strongly felt human sensibilities is also religiously questionable. And it is difficult to accept the comparison of women's plight, which is manifested in every significant facet of their religious lives, with the lot of the Israelites whose lack of priestly privilege is a relatively minor concern. For these reasons a second, more mainstream, group of adherents of the faith accept (at least implicitly) some of the feminist critique's ground rules and assumptions. Not infrequently adopting feminist rhetoric and terminology, they deplore discrimination but maintain that tradition secures equality and justice through complementary roles for the sexes rather than by conferring identical rights and privileges. Others simply contend that the problem has been addressed. Religious educators, relying heavily on the advances made in recent years in the area of women's learning, tend to argue that any problem of discrimination that once existed has already been resolved.

The "separate but equal" argument, while reminiscent of the historical American defense of segregation between whites and blacks, usually assumes qualitative inborn differences between men and women—each possessing a different class of soul, each with a given task defined by God.[30] Feminists who view Judaism as patriarchal and discriminatory are said to operate under the mistaken influence of a "rights-oriented" society that teaches that "equal" means "same." Proponents of the conservative response enlist biological, psychological, and other evidence from beyond the halakhic tradition in order to defend the religious position.[31] Ancient regulations are made to appear as the natural counterparts of contemporary science and common sense in promoting a concept of equality based on complementary rather than identical roles.

Many apologists share the view that an alleged Western lack of appreciation for family values is the source of women's discontent.[32] Rabbi Mordechai Peron, former chief chaplain of the Israeli armed forces, militates in this vein against the corrupting influence of a "rights-oriented" society:

According to cultural and social trends in European thought, the establishment of a family unit is the product of a voluntary alliance between a man and woman. . . . this view regards marriage as an instrument for fulfilling legitimate social and biological needs, and . . . any attempt on the part of the state or the community to interfere engenders sharp criticism, appealing to the sanctified principles of individual liberty and autonomy in the personal domain. Such is not the case in Judaism. The Jewish religion regards marriage for the purpose of establishing a family unit as an absolute obligation, stemming from the divine command to "be fruitful and multiply." This *mitzvah* is imposed as a moral and religious challenge, within the more general framework of *mitzvot* and instructions of the Torah.[33]

There are others who still argue that a hierarchical political system is a more reliable guarantee of personal status than an egalitarian system of equal rights. Each member of the community is cognizant of the clearly defined obligations of his or her role. Rabbi A. I. Kook took this position in 1918, when elections were held for the first representative body of the new Jewish community in Palestine. Arguing against granting women the vote, R. Kook contended that, unlike their less fortunate gentile sisters governed by Western regimes, Jewish women have no need to hustle in the political marketplace for legislation that protects their equality in a formal, "mechanical" way. Their rights are secured by a legal system that regards the family as the sacred foundation for national life and enables women to fulfill their natural role within the family unit.[34]

R. Kook's position was not generally accepted, but variations of his argument appear in less reactionary form in contemporary formulations. Elaine M. Viders, Esq., participating in a right-wing website discussing issues of feminism and Judaism, attributes the modern American Jewish woman's discomfort with her religious heritage to "reluctance to leave the paradigm of entitlements for that of obligations.[35]

The support of essentialism

Justifying discrimination with arguments about men and women's different "essences" rather than on exclusively halakhic grounds precludes considering it as a response to a given social reality—and therefore as possibly subject to change. Once metaphysical differences are granted, opposing the halakhic order of things is tantamount to opposing the natural order of the universe. In earlier Jewish sources,[36] Aristotelian essentialism served to reinforce norms of discrimination and inequality between the sexes. It probably worsened the status quo because it encouraged the view that women are underdeveloped humans who require the subjugation and control of men, just as unruly "matter" requires the control and influence of "form."[37] Jewish mystics following the Neoplatonic tradition, however, gradually replaced this distinction favored by the medieval rationalists with a more value-free use of the concepts, whereby the passive obedience of "matter" serves a fairly benign function, enabling "form" to carry out its task.[38] Later thinkers ingeniously employ this understanding to harmonize apparently contradictory statements about women that appear in the Talmud. Attempts to ground women's inferior status on metaphysical differences between men and women occasionally evidence a tacit unease at the possible *impression* of divine injustice. In asserting harmony between halakhic norms and ontology, the apologists are responding to a demand for justification of laws that are intuitively problematic. Widespread blind obedience when rulings have ceased to reflect the current reality can no longer be assumed.

Such shifts of emphasis in the essentialist argument are not insignificant. Overtly the argument is still conservative, and the outside observer might be hard-pressed to discern the accommodation to new realities. Nevertheless, sometimes a softer rhetoric paves the way for new attitudes that diverge from the spirit if not from the letter of the hierarchical norm, sliding imperceptibly into the advocacy of "separate but equal."

Occasionally, modern apologists turn the rationale for the traditional distinction between men and women on its head: not by abandoning essentialist differences outright, but by idealizing women's nature. Rabbi Aaron Soloveitchik, who was the head of a leading American yeshiva, describes the need to curtail man's innate disposition toward excessive and abusive "grasping"; he contends that woman has an innate spiritual advantage in her capacity to "reach unto things and people through cultivation, work, dedication and perseverance," and he likens this innate advantage to that of the Levites over the members of all the other Israelite tribes.[39] Such rhetoric indicates the incorporation of new values and judgments, thereby showing some measure of assent to the very forces and sensibilities that the apologist

ostensibly resists. Although the apparent objective is to reinforce the rationale for existent halakhic practice, apologetics of this nature essentially
bespeak the beginning of a breakdown of the traditional picture. Given a
suitable social context, claims glorifying women's nature tend to lead to
more far-reaching halakhic accommodation that eventually gets translated
into actual practice. This process enables great respect and appreciation for
women and women's roles within the traditional framework.

The transformation of essentialist views: Three examples

Exemption from time-bound mitzvot. One significant example of this three-
tiered progression—from women as inferior, to separate but equal, to superior—can be discerned by looking at various justifications that have been offered for women's exemption from time-bound positive *mitzvot*. It is worth
noting that this Mishnaic exemption may not be an attempt to limit women's
participation in religious ritual, as exemption does not necessarily imply exclusion. Rather, it mitigates their subordinate position, by acknowledging
that women possess an independent status before God and can relate to Him
directly.[40] Only when women assumed a more active role in religious ritual
could there emerge an area to be circumscribed with exceptions.

The background assumptions about women articulated in post-Mishnaic
and medieval times were ahistorical and grimmer, but gained popular acceptance. Rabbi David ben Joseph Abudraham's commentary to the prayer
book (written in fourteenth-century Spain) explains that because woman
is subjugated to her husband and obligated to fulfill his needs, she is not in
full control of her time. Therefore, she is not free to offer it up in the service of God. Because women are, as it were, the servants of two masters,
God in His mercy took this into account and generously forfeited His
claims in the matter.

As women's status in society changed over the years, more palatable explanations were required for their exemption from certain *mitzvot*. Thus,
Rabbi Samson Raphael Hirsch (one of the most prominent founders of neo-
Orthodoxy in nineteenth-century Germany) set out to refute any connection
between the exemption and implications of women's inferiority. Women's
exemption from time-bound *mitzvot,* claims Hirsch, comes because tradition has already entrusted them with an enormously important convenantal
role in the development of the nation.

To be sure, Hirsch, like Abudraham, links the exemption to the nature or
the life situation of women, totally ignoring the possibility that *halakhah*
was born in a broader sociocultural context. And both commentators view
the *halakhah* as stemming from intrinsic-immanent considerations only.
They would deny the legitimacy of any approach that seemed ready to absorb and internalize values external to the law of the Chosen People. Nonetheless, while Abudraham focuses on the servility of women's lives, Hirsch

emphasizes their loyal nature as an invaluable source of spiritual strength. The notion of a unique women's spirituality is a thread in Jewish thought that builds upon the talmudic statement[41] that women will achieve greater reward in the world to come precisely on the strength of their devotion as enablers. Hirsch, elaborating upon the development of this idea by the sixteenth-century rabbinic leader, Judah Loew ben Bezalel (better known as the Maharal of Prague),[42] suggests that woman *requires* fewer formal obligations because she is capable of attaining ideal levels of virtue without the rigorous *mitzvah*-training assigned to men and the added assistance of symbolic reminders: "God's Torah takes it for granted that our women have greater fervor and more faithful enthusiasm for their God-serving calling, and that this calling runs less danger in their case than in that of men from the temptations which occur in the course of business and professional life."[43] Hirsch draws support for his understanding from an etymological analysis of Hebrew terms. The root of *zachar* (male) is related to the root meaning "memory." Hirsch takes this as indication that man's function is transmission: to receive the legacy of the past and pass it on to future generations. *Nekeva* (female) is related to the Hebrew term for "cavity," ostensibly establishing that woman's function is to attach to a man and accept his calling and position. But Hirsch then turns this passive, dependent quality into something considerably more positive:

just because the woman has not to acquire a calling and position for herself, she remains the nurse of all that is purely human in man. . . . The calling and position for which a man has to struggle are really nothing but the foundation on which he has to build his life's work, and carry out his own share in the general task of humanity. And there is a danger that he may completely lose himself in this struggle, that in striving to acquire the means he will lose sight of his real vocation and completely forget the great goal and his own task as a man, nay that he will sacrifice and subordinate to these efforts what is genuinely human in himself. This is an error which can almost be regarded as the key to all the mistakes made in history. It is then the woman who leads him back to what is truly human in him. The riddle of history is solved with the domination of woman, with the restriction of the man to the sphere of the genuinely human which has been placed under the care of the woman. It is the return of the citizen to the man.[44]

What is noteworthy in both passages is the subtle upgrade from an assertion of "separate but equal" to an implication that woman is superior.

Half a century later, Rabbi A. I. Kook and his son, Rabbi Zvi Yehuda Kook, also adopted a decidedly benign, if paternalistic, attitude toward women. Woman is entrusted with the important responsibility of managing the household and rearing the children because she is emotional, soft, endowed with worldly wisdom, introverted by nature, and more concerned with the personal. Man, who is more psychologically robust and practical, must be careful to protect her and show consideration for her delicate nature.[45] The younger Kook, like Rabbi Hirsch and unlike his father, takes pains to deny that any inferiority is implied by this role stratification.[46] Like

R. Hirsch, he turns to the Hebrew language to support his position. Because all the nouns for more abstract values, as well as the concept of divine teachings referred to in the word "Torah" are expressed in the feminine,[47] he too links women's exemption from time-bound *mitzvot* with their greater connectedness to the divine. This esteem for woman spills over into his halakhic reasoning. Although he repeats the view that women are also exempt from time-bound *mitzvot* in order to free them to attend to their domestic responsibilities, he supports their assuming the *mitzvot* voluntarily.[48] And if they recite the same blessing as men do, expressing gratitude for having been commanded to perform the act (. . . *asher kideshanu bemitzvotav vetzivanu*), he does not regard it as a blessing made in vain (*berakha levatala*).[49]

Thus the Mishnaic view establishing the ontological inferiority of women because of their lack of obligation in performing *mitzvot* runs full circle. Subsequent explanations would have it that women are exempted from time-bound *mitzvot* because the very nature of their constitution absolves them from the need to be made aware of the sanctity of time[50] or because they possess greater religious fervor and enthusiasm by nature and therefore require fewer devotional reminders.[51] Although the "separate but superior" argument maintains the halakhic status quo on a practical level, in terms of the spiritual self-image of women and the impact upon their social status there is a significant difference between a rationale such as Abudraham offers and later ones.

The blessing "shelo asani isha." A similar transformative process in traditional understandings of women's status can be discerned in the commentaries on the blessing thanking God for not having been created a woman. This blessing, prescribed for Jewish men to recite in the course of morning prayers, has been much maligned and has served as a popular focus for women's dissatisfaction in modern times. Initially the blessing quite likely reflected a perception of women as religiously underprivileged because they were not obliged to study Torah or perform all of the *mitzvot*. On this understanding, the blessing represents a man's expression of appreciation and gratitude for increased obligation, which also translates into awareness of their higher ontological status.[52] The Abudraham corroborates this understanding in stating that when women recite their version of the blessing—*she'asani kirtzono* (Blessed art thou, O Lord, who has made me according to His will)—they are performing *tzidduk hadin* (justifying, or making peace with one's "sentence").[53]

Some would have us believe that only contemporary feminists take offense at such a daily blessing. Yet it is not difficult to imagine that the reaction of Rebbetzin Rayna Batya, wife and granddaughter of prominent eighteenth- and nineteenth-century rabbis,[54] was shared by other pious women over the generations. In his memoirs, her nephew, Rabbi Barukh Epstein (author of the *Torah Temimah*) recalls:

How bitter was my aunt, that, as she would say from time to time, "every empty-headed ignorant man," every ignoramus who hardly knew the meaning of the words and who would not dare to cross her threshold without first obsequiously and humbly obtaining her permission, would not hesitate to boldly and arrogantly recite to her face the blessing of *shelo asani isha*. Moreover, upon his recitation of the blessing, she was obliged to answer "Amen." "And who can muster enough strength," she would conclude with great anguish, "to hear this eternal symbol of shame and embarrassment to women?"[55]

Rabbi A. I. Kook, in his twentieth-century commentary to the morning prayers, continues a tradition of essentialist justifications for this blessing. But although he still employs the medieval distinction between man as form and woman as matter, he downplays the negative tendencies of matter and emphasizes the aspect of complementarity: the receptive female, with her qualities of constancy and stability, keeps the more dynamic male drive on the "straight and narrow" path.[56] More recent explanations for the blessing, such as those developed by S. R. Hirsch and twentieth-century traditionalist rabbis such as Eli Munk and Aaron Soloveitchik, suggest that the different phrasing of the women's blessing comes to convey the more rarefied quality of female spirituality.[57] Most ingenuous and far-reaching is the interpretation offered by Rabbi Z. Y. Kook, suggesting that the male blessing reflects the relative and subjective perceptions of men's superiority in *this* world. In the world to come, men will not be able to make this blessing; they will recognize that women rather than men are closer to the divine.[58]

The creation of Eve. A third useful focus for examining the development of essentialist apologetics is found in the attempts to build an anthropology of men and women based on the story of the creation of Adam and Eve, with its account of the original sin.

Rabbi Isaac Abarbanel, the fourteenth-century biblical commentator, takes the Aristotelian tradition to an extreme, asserting that only the male, who was the ultimate purpose of creation, was created in the image of God.[59] Many other medieval thinkers understand woman being fashioned from Adam's rib (Gen. 2:22) to mean that her purpose is merely to serve man and ensure the propagation of the human species.[60]

Other commentators, more interested in asserting basic equality between men and women, draw upon the preceding and seemingly contradictory version of the Creation story, which depicts the original Adam as androgynous (Gen. 1:27). This common origin establishes, in their eyes, the absolute equality between the sexes, teaching that only the two together constitute full humanity. According to this view, moral deficiencies and the need for each to develop a fully independent nature became obvious only after the original sin that dictated a complementary division of labor.[61] In keeping with this idea, twentieth-century philosopher Emmanuel Levinas cites the talmudic opinion that the Hebrew term *tzella* (the part of Adam from which

Eve was created) refers to the first man's side and not his rib, thereby asserting once again absolute equality and symmetry of value between the sexes.[62]

Rabbi Z. Y. Kook, in a similar vein, takes pains to insist that although the division between male and female is imprinted on the physical and psychological nature of each sex, such differentiation does not involve a hierarchy of value. He finds clear indication of Eve's essential superiority and greater closeness to the divine in the account of her beginnings: While Adam was created directly from the inanimate coarseness of the earth and only afterward infused with the divine breath of life, Eve was created from a living body that already contained the spirit of God.[63]

Separate but superior in traditional mystical theology

Ideas stemming from the medieval mystic tradition of the Kabbalah, and its understanding of the metaphysical source of femininity, inform the reasoning of Z. Y. Kook and many others who adopt essentialist arguments ascribing women's halakhic status to their innate superiority. As a rule, kabbalistic thought maintains the hierarchical picture of the female below the male, with women embodying the constraining force of judgment (*din*) and men embodying unlimited bounty (*hessed*). Some Hassidic texts, however (particularly the writings of Chabad Hassidism), speak of a turning of the tables in the Messianic age. Their basis is a mystic principle that the more elevated and all-encompassing the source of any given spiritual or physical entity, the more it must be concealed in order later to be revealed.[64] Eventually, however, it will become evident to all that what now appears as lowly is in fact the more exalted. Cited in support of this are the words of the prophet (Jer. 31:21): "Female will encircle male."[65] According to at least one Hassidic source, *Esh Kodesh,* the merit of the biblical prophetess Miriam surpassed that of Moses, because her piety (as that of women in general) did not require commands imposed from without; rather, it emanated freely from her inner self. This outpouring of virtue is referred to as Miriam's wellspring. It is because Miriam's wellspring ceased when she died that Moses had to hit the rock in order to draw something out.[66] Another Hassidic source claims that Miriam managed to reach so elevated a spiritual state that hierarchical differences between femininity and masculinity were totally obliterated.[67]

Rabbi A. I. Kook also speaks of a utopian stage in history when the larger system of dualisms will be disrupted. All the binary principles that emanate, according to the Lurianic tradition of Kabbalah, from the primary male and female symbols of line and circle will be revealed as various stages of one harmonious continuum.[68] His allusions to an eventual reversal of sexual hierarchies are more explicitly tied to the situation of actual women in the teachings of his son, Rabbi Z. Y. Kook. In these teachings, as in those of other disciples of the elder Kook, a traditional understanding of the female as the embodiment of "the congregation of Israel" is employed as rationale for the special demands made of women for modesty. Just as the particularity of the Jewish people requires special insularity to preserve it so that it may embody the universal goals of humanity, so too does the female need protection from the aggression of male politics and the life of the marketplace. In maintaining her concealment, she faithfully reflects the more comprehensive holiness of the nation as a whole.

Separate but superior in contemporary feminine theology

Of particular interest is a new development in the appropriation of mystic theology to the case of women. For the first time, apologetics are being produced for women by women themselves.[69] A novel tone that these women introduce to their arguments derives from a number of factors. Most of them were not raised in religiously observant families, but joined a contemporary wave of return to tradition as a matter of deliberate choice, after fully experiencing the secular world. Some of them, involved in the outreach efforts of this *teshuvah* movement, are still in close contact with the secular world, attempting to attract the non-Orthodox to return to the fold. Because of their upbringing, these women are often quite familiar with the major arguments of the feminist critique. Their own counterideology utilizes some of the same central concepts and symbols, but it reverses their underlying values and conclusions in order to defend the Orthodox way of life.[70] Like the earlier essentialists mentioned above, they largely eschew legalistic reasoning and the virtues of unquestioning obedience to a higher authority. These arguments might appeal to women raised on a traditional and insular ideology, but returnees to tradition often seek a more spiritually meaningful rationale.

The female "converts" to Orthodoxy occasionally enlist feminist theory in order to prove that it is precisely the essentialism of tradition rather than nonessentialist notions of gender that empower women and grant them a more privileged status. Much of this genre of women-initiated apologetic focuses upon the three *mitzvot* that the Mishnah regards as a unique preserve of women (laxity in the observance of which is associated with the punishment of death in childbirth): *hafrashat hallah* (burning a bit of the dough before baking bread to commemorate the ancient priestly portion); *hadlakat haner* (lighting the Sabbath candles); and *niddah* (laws specific to married women, which involve immersion in a ritual bath after a period of sexual abstinence following menstruation).[71] The authors of this literature believe that when women enact the values and behaviors inherent in these *mitzvot,* the problems facing women in contemporary non-Orthodox society diminish. Their defense of the traditional image of woman as represented by these special *mitzvot* builds upon three motifs: the introverted or hidden nature of femininity (mirrored anatomically in the hidden state of her sexual organs); femininity as a paradigm for sanctification of the physical; and femininity as power.

The first motif, rather than criticizing women's separation from their husbands during their periods of ritual impurity, glorifies the laws of family purity.[72] The stigma of impurity traditionally attached to the female body and its emissions is transferred to the exposed realm of male activity: because the public sphere is described as less sacred and important, distancing women from the communal arena and political affairs enhances their worth.

The motif of femininity sanctifying the physical sees proud emphasis in the value that Judaism, in contrast to Christianity, places upon the human body. Confining women's *mitzvot* to the physical aspect of life is presented as a virtue rather than as one of the most damaging aspects of women's status in Judaism. Women, being closer to the natural and the physical, are considered better equipped to infuse the body and home with holiness. In mystical terms, their special *mitzvot* have greater influence upon the physical world than those of the male because these *mitzvot* have the power to elevate and transform the material. In baking the family *hallot*, lighting the Sabbath candles, and immersing in the *mikveh*, women sanctify the mundane.

When the Jewish woman recognizes the significance of all her actions within her home, she is able to perceive how the Jewish home can be considered a mini-Temple. Washing dishes, scrubbing floors or mending clothes all acquire a new dimension. When the Jewish woman knows she is coordinating a service of G-d within the realms of her own home, like the High Priest in the *Beis HaMikdash* (Temple), her joy is radiant, and the nature of her home is transformed. It becomes a great deal more than a physical building.[73]

In claiming that femininity means power, the female apologists assert unique methods of wielding influence despite (or precisely because of) women's public invisibility. The power held by modern, liberated woman is, by contrast, illusory and ultimately not fulfilling. The topic is often approached from a romantic perspective. The anonymity of women and its veil of silence is an art to be mastered, demanding special skills and yielding its own distinctive rewards. The laws of family purity are not oppressive, but an important strategy for marital health and emotional sustenance: when a wife is not always accessible to her husband, it enhances her attractiveness and ensures that she is never taken for granted. A measure of sweet yearning and erotic excitement is preserved in the sexual relationship, while leaving her time to attend to her own needs, rather than those of her husband. She need not insult her spouse when unwanted sexual contact does not fit her inbuilt biological rhythm, and this preserves a special spirit and harmony within the home. Thus women are afforded the ability to maintain a greater measure of control over their sexual lives.

It is not surprising that the rationale offered for laws of family purity (which are probably the most unintelligible to the modern mind) figures the most prominently in these writings and is by far the most detailed and sweeping in its ramifications. What surprised Jody Myers and Jane Litman, two Jewish feminists who researched this literature,[74] was that this writing often presents the special *mitzvot* of women, and especially the laws of family purity, as a paradigm for Jewish theology. The laws are understood to embody deep truths about the cosmic reality and God's relationship to it. The importance of observing them is defended not only because a traditional lifestyle within the home redresses the inadequacies of secular society, but also because these commandments have spiritual healing effects on the world. The system of family purity so reflects the divine that its very existence infuses the cosmos with harmony.

The women apologists also invest women's religious practice with metaphysical meaning by utilizing mystic symbolism that has previously been employed only by knowledgeable males. To this symbolism, the women apologists add their own original but monolithic theological interpretations. While their simplistic interpretations of a vastly diverse mystic legacy inadvertently reveal their relative lack of direct experience in the study of primary sources, a theology created independently by and for women is in the traditional world an unprecedented and bold phenomenon.[75] This new women's theology projects the social reality of the earthly world upon the divine reality above, in the fashion of male kabbalistic thought. But in the women's writing, the feminine aspect of God is now paramount. This derives from a kabbalistic view that earthly woman is the physical embodiment of the divine emanation (*sefira*) of *Malkhut,* which represents the feminine aspect of God. The lighting of the Sabbath candles—originating primarily in the mundane interest of creating conviviality around the Sabbath table—is now understood to reenact God's primordial creation of light.

By the same token, the rhythm of woman's sexual life becomes a metaphor for the process of divine creativity. It both reflects and has influence upon God's creative powers and enables a mystic merging with them. Just as the menstrual woman has fixed periods of separation from her husband, so does God have fixed periods of distance from the world that afford the opportunity to amass new creative powers.[76] This identification not only confirms the necessity of women's religious observance; it also affirms women's own sense of worth, by portraying God in their likeness.[77] If, within all forms of Jewish mysticism, menstrual impurity has been associated with demonic forces while semen became sacralized, now it is God as "female" who is the focus of purification and protection.[78]

As Myers and Littman point out, the type of Orthodox woman who identifies with this thinking stands in direct opposition to Orthodox feminists who advocate greater female participation in the communal sphere, promote Talmud study for women, and urge women to observe *mitzvot* that have been traditionally left to men. The mystic apologists are more deeply conservative in practice and pose less of a threat to the status quo. Nevertheless, a theology that strives to insinuate a female rationale in place of a religiosity whose forms are predominantly male-centered, and that elevates women's role in the home above men's activity in the communal realm, is in an important sense more radical and innovative than a theology that strives merely to give women an equal share in the religion as currently conceived. The popularity of this literature is an indication of how successful it is in addressing a genuinely felt need.

Evaluating the Conservative Response

I do not regard apologetics as a necessarily negative phenomenon. Apologetics are the very stuff of civilization, and if and when offered in good faith, they can assist in enabling the transition from one generation and mind-set to another.[79] The new rhetoric of essentialism makes a noble effort to incorporate higher moral insights while remaining loyal to practical tradition. Preserving a major part of tradition immune to change grants the system greater stability. In order for apologetics to work, however, they need to be convincing and what works for one generation or sociological setting may not work for another. While some women today are persuaded, others find the existing forms of conservative apologetics useless and even offensive.

Much of the appeal of the conservative approach to *halakhah* lies in its unequivocal message, impervious to surrounding circumstance and influence. The claim is that God's message continued to be preserved and passed on throughout the generations in this encapsulated form until the present age. Because proponents of this approach reject a historicist approach to religion, they tend to ignore signs of diversity within the tradition itself. But does contemporary talk of the Jewish family and woman's place within it truly tally with the model provided by our biblical forefathers and their concubines? Taking into account the radical fluctuations that such conceptions have undergone, might not these be more readily explained by considerations of social context than by conformance to some grand eternal plan?

In this connection, it is illuminating to discover how the transformation of essentialist views of women in Jewish tradition parallels similar shifts in Western thought. The justification of the traditional patriarchal family that proved most successful for about two thousand years of Western history held that men are superior to women by nature. This perception changed after the mid-seventeenth century, when the notion of the sentimental family started gaining popularity in European culture at large.[80] Philosophers of the eighteenth and nineteenth centuries, such as Rousseau, Kant, and Hegel, attributed to men and women different but complementary virtues. Wives, delicate and emotionally sensitive, were to be entrusted with keeping the family united, whereas the husband's special aptitudes as the strong and rational partner qualified him to act on the family's behalf in all matters affecting the outside world. The emergence of the new European family ideal, which placed much greater emphasis on romantic love, privacy, and intimacy between husband and wife as the expected norm, did not alter the traditional notion that the husband was the head of the family. Nevertheless, the whole of the patriarchal structure of the family was in practice placed under a new strain. For this reason, some writers on the subject see the sentimental family as significantly more egalitarian than the older traditional family.[81]

The similarity of this new line of thought to the type of apologetics developed by Rabbi S. R. Hirsch speaks for itself. It is easy to appreciate the appeal that the new European conception would have for Jewish apologists who seek explanations of the strict demarcation of gender roles established by *halakhah* that are more compatible with modern notions of justice. But it is also easy to understand how this new romanticism would lead a Jewish feminist with any degree of historical awareness to dismiss the idea that "separate but equal" is the timeless ideal of tradition. A sine qua non of any apologetic is certainly to admit that a lowly view of women reflects a real strand in the tradition and that an androcentric bias had its influence in the development of *halakhah*. Rachel Adler, one of the foremost spokeswomen of Jewish feminism, questions the honesty of the usual defense of women's status in tradition because its lyrical exegeses of selected *midrashim*, "however complimentary they may be, do not really reflect the way in which men are expected to behave toward women by Jewish law."[82]

The mystic attempt to defend women's status in the religious life by invoking feminine aspects of the divine also presents difficulties. The significance of women's monthly cycle as the embodiment of a metaphysical rhythm is only relevant to women who are not pregnant, yet the practical effect of the laws of family purity is to encourage continued pregnancies. And, Myers and Litman ask, how—if women's marital lives are to be identified with divine creativity—are we to understand sexual behavior "that cannot possibly result in pregnancy?"[83] The positive references to women's capacity for sanctifying the physical do not allow for any appreciation of women's sexual pleasure per se—a value that is recognized by the Torah itself.[84] And the claim that tradition enhances the power of women is undermined when such power depends upon the use of guile and other manipulative strategies of the underdog, rather than the normal exercise of authority. Even the relative control that observant women have over their sexual lives due to the laws of family purity still leaves ultimate authority with the male authorities who legislate and interpret the laws.[85]

Another major difficulty is that essentialist descriptions of women's nature just do not ring true for many women, especially those already uncomfortable with the contrast between the rigidly stratified gender roles demanded by tradition and their freedom of movement in their secular lives. In an age when the overpowering significance of essentialist views is being gradually demolished in general culture, it is difficult to accept that woman's natural calling lies exclusively in the domestic realm because of the unique metaphysical makeup of her soul. With the death of the myth of "women to the humanities and men to the natural sciences" in their secular reality, many observant women find it impossible to accept a halakhic ban on equal opportunities for learning sacred texts and on other activities of religious significance when that ban is grounded on essentialist claims. Adler rejected the "prepackaged orations" of rabbis "on the nobility of motherhood, the glory of childbirth, and modesty, the crown of Jewish womanhood" because they did not accept *her* as a person, and only set rigid stereotypes that define her by limiting the directions in which she might grow.[86]

Given these considerations, an increasing number of Orthodox women are finding that apologetics grounded upon absolute commitment to the existing status quo have limited problem-solving ability. As Debby Koren, a contemporary Orthodox feminist, has stated:

I can forgive the Rambam [for regarding men as superior to women]. He lived in Moslem society at a time when women really were not in the same position that men were. . . . But when a rabbi today tries to justify the reasoning [behind halakhic exclusion of women] with the same kind of apologetics, that's what I can't forgive. We can't try to sensitize the Rambam. But we can certainly attempt to open the eyes and hearts of our rabbis and teachers today. We can tell them that this hurts.[87]

Increasingly, the motif that dominates the mode of Orthodox women's relationship to their religious tradition is not the appeal to apologetics, but rather the wish to explore halakhic malleability within the existing system and the extent to which such malleability can be employed to take account of women's changed societal status and grant it suitable religious expression.

·PART II·

The Second Stage:
Working Within the System

The number of women who view themselves as traditional Jews, yet are uncomfortable with the role they see prescribed for themselves, is increasing. Unpersuaded by apologetics, these women find themselves at the second stage of the feminist critique, agitating for the situation to be rectified on a practical level to whatever degree possible. Given their loyalty to the halakhic tradition, the main question that concerns them is what—if anything—can be done to improve the legal status and image of women under the existing law. To avoid jeopardizing the notion of a just God or implying that His original message was wanting, they strive to engage the halakhic tradition from within.

This means attempting to determine how much impact external sociological factors have on the halakhic decision-making process. To what extent are halakhic authorities free to take such considerations into account? What role can and should such factors have in halakhic development? Is the halakhah in fact amenable to change? The history of Orthodox feminism is, in great measure, a history of exploring and testing the boundaries of the paths that halakhic authorities have followed in response to changing social situations and moral sensibilities.

Reflection on such questions in recent years has generated considerable discussion of a meta-halakhic nature on the part of both conservative and liberal segments of the Modern Orthodox community (paralleling developments in the school of Anglo-American legal theory known as legal positivism). Despite differences in the degree of importance relegated to formal and nonformal considerations, these meta-halakhic efforts share one feature: they all employ a distinction between an immutable and a contingent element in Jewish law. That is, one element of the law is regarded as emanating directly from God, explicitly conveying some form of absolute truth, while the other is regarded as given—in greater or lesser extent—to the arbitrariness and fallibility of human judgment. The common assumption of such discussion is that the halakhah *is a unified body of law governed by consistent principles and procedures. Once these are articulated, women can, in theory, themselves assess the extent to which suggestions for improving their lot are halakhically valid. It might also help them offer those involved in the decision-making process practical solutions that conform to procedural norms.*

Closer scrutiny in chapters 4 and 5 of the various meta-halakhic theories and analysis of their application in practice will reveal a more complicated picture. Even purportedly neutral constructs are (despite ideological protestations to the contrary) vulnerable to external influences and partisan interests. Because even religious law is not immune to the vicissitudes of shifting historical contingencies and human biases, it is doubtful whether any systematic theory of halakhah *can, on its own, provide satisfactory solutions for women who sense injustice within its confines.*

CHAPTER 3

Exploring Halakhic Malleability
and Its Limits

Halakhic Conservatism: Internal Considerations

The *halakhah,* like all legal systems, is inherently conservative. To preserve its integrity and stability, it must demonstrate continuity with its legal traditions. Another severe limitation to its malleability is theological. It shares this feature with other legal systems, such as that of Islam, that ascribe divine origins to their structural underpinnings. Any attempts at revision of such systems that extend too far beyond the procedural can be interpreted as questioning their perfection. For this reason, halakhic deliberation is (as noted in chapter 1) sometimes understood as limited merely to interpretation and the clarification of doubts that arise when the formulation of a particular ruling is brief and lacking in detail.

Moreover, despite the authority accorded to the scholarly elite throughout the generations, later authorities do not take the kind of innovative liberties that the talmudic sages availed themselves of in their development of the Oral Law. As Michael Berger concluded in his book *Rabbinic Authority,* "It is a gross over-simplification to state that the post-talmudic scholars did to the sages what the sages did to the Torah."[1] The nature of the legal activity of the later rabbis differs from that of the sages in terms of both substance and methodology.

Berger identifies three primary differences: First, no scholar after the sages revisited the primary text (the Pentateuch) in order to derive normative practice. Subsequent scholars, great as they were, were always in the position of interpreting the interpreters. The second difference is in the nature of the interpretation. The sages employed exegetical tools of *midrash* that allowed them inferences from the biblical text going far beyond what we would assume to be the plain and simple meaning. These interpretations often served as the basis for innovating laws of major significance that seem barely rooted (if at all) in the original source. The interpretive methods employed by post-talmudic scholars seeking the meaning of talmudic statements are, by contrast, much more circumscribed. Third, in many cases the

opinions registered in a talmudic discussion effectively exhaust the range of
views that can be legitimately maintained within the tradition. "Medieval or
even later interpretation can so limit the talmudic position as to leave open
the possibility of other decisions." However, as Berger states, "this is never
presented as a *rival* to the talmudic options; every scholar must deal first
with the positions staked out by the talmudic Sages."[2]

Even allowing for greater constraints in interpretive freedom, later authorities nevertheless still had at their disposal various halakhic mechanisms
that in principle allowed them considerable leeway for active and open legislative innovation. They had the authority to enact *horaot shaah* (ad hoc
rulings created under unique circumstances and therefore never taken as
precedents),[3] *takanot* (regulations motivated by socioreligious concerns),[4]
and *gezerot* (secondary positive or precautionary ordinances not based on
interpretation of previous sources but meant to distance the people from
biblically prohibited transgressions).[5] Although later *poskim* no longer allowed themselves the freedom available to the Rabbis in their use of *midrash,* they were still left with methods of interpretation based on textual arguments and rules of inference (such as context and logical flow), similar to
the strategies we use today to understand a text; because the line between
interpretation and innovation is never clear-cut, such methods still leave
considerable room for legislative creativity under the guise of simple interpretation. They also felt free to employ a method known as *sevara,* which in-
fers legal norms on the basis of nontextual considerations of natural reason
and common sense.

Beyond their own legislative initiatives and interpretive activity, authorities could also innovate by implementing or by sanctioning current popular
custom (*minhag*). This then sometimes served as a legitimate basis for promoting a particular interpretation or even fresh legislation. So long as popular religion functioned according to internalized religious standards that
were not governed exclusively by issues of convenience and self-interest, the
tradition of the people and their intuitive religious sensibilities were occasionally regarded as a bona fide element in halakhic deliberation and the
wellspring of living Torah, even when these were arrived at via methods independent of the fine points of *halakhah*.[6]

Nonetheless, the scope and availability of some of these mechanisms
have been severely curtailed in the course of time. Especially over the past
two centuries, various factors have reduced to a bare minimum the possibilities for overtly creative initiative on the part of the bearers of the Oral
Law. Some of these factors are attributable to objective historical and political circumstances. Others are more subjective and ideological. Their
combined effect has been to leave most attempts at negotiating the tension
between static rules and the dynamic flow of events concentrated in the
procedural realm.

Historical and Political Factors

The major objective constraint upon blatant innovation has been the gradual decentralization of Jewish communal authority. Up until the destruction of the Second Temple in 70 C.E. and even somewhat afterward, the High Court in Jerusalem, known as the Sanhedrin, served as the supreme judicial and legislative body in Judaism. A pale imitation of this institution continued to function in Yavneh up until the middle of the third century, evolving into the central seat of religious and political authority, initially for Palestinian Jewry and then for Jews worldwide. This substitute, however, never had the same clout as the original Sanhedrin, nor did a Diaspora-style version that existed for some time in Babylonia. Moreover, halakhic tradition required that each sage of the Sanhedrin be ordained by his teacher. This chain of official ordination (*semikhah*) was seen as going all the way back to when Moses ordained Joshua as the next leader of the Jewish people and the next link in the oral tradition. The chain continued up until the end of the talmudic period in the fourth or fifth century. While the term *semikhah* has since been applied to various forms of academic certification or rabbinic licensing, it no longer signifies unbroken continuity or transmission of oral traditions.

With the demise of formal institutions such as the Sanhedrin and the original line of *semikhah*, legal responsibility shifted during the Middle Ages to local rabbis or legal bodies and to world-renowned halakhic decisors and the accumulated responsa literature that their pronouncements generated. Those pronouncements were no longer deemed binding upon all Jews in quite the same way as the decisions of the Sanhedrin had been. But even when bereft of a central authority, so long as Jewish communities were still allowed complete judicial autonomy by the gentile governments under which they lived, the range of halakhic decision-making was still quite broad and included all aspects of civil law.

With the breakdown of Jewish autonomy in the Diaspora in the eighteenth century, however, and the restriction of the religious courts' jurisdiction in contemporary Israel, most rabbinical decision-making was restricted de facto to ritual matters such as prayer, observance of Sabbath and festivals, and *kashrut*. Matters affecting personal status, such as marriage and divorce, are still handled in Israel through the Rabbinical Courts. Outside of Israel the main halakhic function of pulpit rabbis and holders of rabbinic office is simply to disseminate information regarding existing halakhic practice. Actual decision-making—applying and adjusting the existing law to changing conditions—is reduced in most cases to a minimum. In Israel, official rabbis sometimes do even less than this, as the same legal summaries that serve the rabbis are equally accessible to any halakhically literate layperson.

A further consequence of the weakening of religious institutional authority in Jewish communal life is that the observance of Jewish law depends
increasingly on voluntary commitment. This weakening of halakhic mandate has been exacerbated by the spread of secularization. Both in Israel,
especially with the establishment of the courts of civil law in the modern
state, and in the Diaspora, rabbinic authority has had to contend not only
with the competition of secular legal bodies, but also with the fact that an
ever-increasing proportion of its constituency is not at all interested in
obeying its rules.

The process of secularization has tied the hands of rabbinic authority in
yet another manner, by limiting the feasibility of appeal to common practice
rather than texts as a source for legislative innovation. As the strain in-
creases between the real and the ideal of halakhic life, the *posek* is rendered
ever less free to follow the sages' advice to view the Jewish marketplace as a
reliable source for generating authentic halakhic norms.[7] Intensified ideological fragmentation, even within the halakhically observant community,
has limited the innovative power of contemporary legal authorities even further; there is no one authority who is generally accepted by all. For this reason, too, *poskim* today tend toward extreme conservatism. Any halakhic
authority contemplating innovation fears that his colleagues will term him a
rebellious elder (*zaken mamreh*). The spread of mass communication, which
exposes the decisions of the *posek* to the critique of an ever-broadening and
diversified audience, is another powerful factor curtailing the likelihood of
finding one halakhic authority who would be accepted by all. Such exposure
has made it virtually impossible for any individual or even group of individuals to achieve the breadth of consensus necessary to carry out significant
innovations even when these are intended only for a limited community
under specific circumstances. All these historical and political developments
have brought about a situation whereby *halakhah* is left to confront deep
ideological and societal shifts and the implications of new technological advances of the past two hundred years bereft of most of the usual tools available to a legal system. Thus it has come about that in the modern period
most halakhic deliberation consists of seeing whether a particular case is
covered by the accepted codes.

Remaining strategies of flexibility

Given these constraining factors, some believers may be forgiven for declaring that the very "miracle" of the *halakhah*'s continued survival as a
dynamic legal system is the greatest proof of its divine origin and religious
validity. In fact, however, even today there remains—in principle at least—
some degree of latitude for innovative legislation. Various strategies and
modes of legal circumvention that are still available can serve as powerful
tools in enabling deviation from established halakhic practice. Exploited

properly, they can relieve tensions and even provide long-term solutions to the conflicts that inevitably arise between existing law and the challenges of a changing social situation and its concomitant moral sensibilities. Even when these legal devices are applied on a very limited scale in the form of responsa to localized problems, broad general policies do eventually become established on the basis of more restricted precedents. Moreover, the application of such devices, under cover of the need to solve a practical problem, often serves the interests of a more radical shift in deeper ideological attitudes.[8] Described below are several examples of these devices as applied to women's issues. The hope of second-stage Orthodox feminists is that such precedents can provide the basis for similar applications to contemporary issues.

Reviving neglected practices. One form of adjustment open to Orthodox women who strive for minimal divergence from the law is appropriating for themselves religious practices that were never forbidden but were neglected for sociological rather than halakhic reasons. These practices include women leading the grace after meals (*birkat hamazon*), reciting the blessing over wine (*kiddush*) for themselves and others at ceremonial meals, or participating in the ritual ablution (*mayim aharonim*) that precedes the grace after meals.[9] Although such practices are sometimes at odds with current religious custom—and indeed the impetus for their adoption today might at times stem from forces that are not purely halakhic—their formal halakhic grounding is impeccable.

Increasing voluntary participation. Women taking on *mitzvot* from which they are formally exempt can be justified halakhically. The truth is that women since talmudic times have gradually taken upon themselves many of the *mitzvot* from which they are exempt and integrated them into their religious routines, with varying degrees of rabbinic encouragement, depending on the nature of the *mitzvah* involved, and—in the case of Ashkenazic women—reciting the blessings for these *mitzvot* as well.[10]

The main *mitzvah* adopted by women with universal approval is that of reciting the *Shema*, the prayer that affirms God's unity. Their regarding reproduction and child-rearing as a religiously significant endeavor, despite the fact that it is not formally their obligation, is also endorsed wholeheartedly. Women's appropriation of holiday *mitzvot*—hearing *shofar*,[11] dwelling in the *sukkah*, reciting a blessing over the *arba minim*, and counting the *omer* period between Passover and Shavuot—has also received varying degrees of approval and support. Though there were only occasionally women in the past who sought to extend this list, their numbers are increasing today. While wearing ritual items such as *tallit, tzitzit,* or *tefillin* has assumed the character of a last frontier, it would seem that such innovation in halakhic practice on the part of sincerely motivated women is not antithetical to halakhic values.[12]

Establishing context-related concepts. Existing norms can be interpreted flexibly on the strength of the argument that they employ halakhic definitions that are context– or situation-related and not absolute. One example is Rabbi Hayim David Halevi's explanation for the generally accepted decision that all women today should recline at the *seder* table, which runs counter to the original talmudic ruling that a woman "in the presence of her husband" does not recline unless she is "an important woman."[13] The criteria for an important woman[14] accord with the traditional explanation offered earlier by the Rashbam: normally a woman may not recline because "the fear of her husband is upon her, as she is subjugated to him."[15] Halevi, however, comments that "this is not true nowadays, as no woman is subjugated to her husband and the fear of him is not upon her. Therefore she must recline."[16]

More lenient definitions of modesty would also belong to this category. Considerations of context have been invoked to justify responsa permitting women to chant the Torah or blessings in the presence of men[17] or to sing as part of a group (joining in Sabbath songs together with men)[18] on strength of the argument that in these circumstances the danger of sexual temptation does not apply. Such considerations have also served as the basis for permitting women to deliver religious homilies (*divrei Torah*), and to work professionally or socialize in mixed company. By the same token, what seems to be a violation of the biblical injunction against women's assumption of authorative status (*serarah*) in the appointment of women as judges or public leaders in the state of Israel is justified with the argument that democratic acceptance of women's leadership does not fall under this category.[19] Although rabbinic authorities did not always regard the principle of communal honor (*kevod hatzibbur*) as relative to the society they lived in, establishing it now as context-based also opens up new halakhic possibilities. Today's favorable attitude toward women's religious study is another innovation that is sometimes based on the recognition that in order to remain religiously committed in the modern world, women need to acquire an independent knowledge of sources.[20]

Creatively exploiting halakhic lacunae and ambiguities. When the above measures do not suffice, another possibility is to exploit to the maximum any gaps or ambiguities that exist within the parameters of *halakhah*. This involves supporting new ideas that do not quite tally with traditional conventions or assumptions, without challenging the assumptions themselves head-on. This strategy is particularly useful for situations never anticipated in past halakhic deliberations, such as the advances of medical technology that enable childbearing without sexual relations. Thus, for example, some authorities condone wives of infertile husbands conceiving children through artificial insemination (particularly when the donors are non-Jews, as this prevents any chance of Jewish half-siblings unwittingly marrying each other when they grow up).[21] This strategy is also implemented to address issues of marriage and divorce. The use of prenuptial agreements, designed to lessen the power of recalcitrant husbands in the case of divorce proceedings,[22] is gaining popularity in Modern Orthodox circles. And women's testimony is now widely accepted in rabbinical courts under certain circumstances, not as formal testimony (*edut*) but as what is known as "appraisement" (*umdenah*).[23]

Invoking overarching nonformal considerations. In some cases authorities invoke overarching nonformal principles to support innovative rulings that appear to run counter to the explicit intent of traditional practices.[24] This strategy is a powerful tool for addressing "hard cases" when two existing rules come into conflict as the result of new circumstances, or when there are precedents supporting both sides of an argument.[25] What is involved here is the balancing of one halakhic rule against another by introducing a more overriding consideration. The *halakhah* contains a huge stock of such principles, which represent a variety of medical/scientific, sociological, economic, pragmatic, and ethical/psychological considerations. Some common examples include: monetary loss (*hefsed merubeh*), a changed natural or social reality (*nishtanu ha'ittim; shinnui hativ'iyot*); the danger of engendering hatred (*mishum eivah*), or of defiling the name of God (*hillul Hashem*). A particularly powerful consideration that falls under this category is the need to amend or abrogate even a biblical law under certain circumstances for the sake of upholding many other laws (*et laasot laShem heferu Toratekha*).[26]

Such principles do not apply in an all-or-nothing manner as do legal rules. A non-formal principle may unsuccessfully compete for control with various other principles in one "hard case," yet return to challenge those same principles in another. Thus in the question of when overarching considerations are to be invoked there is a great deal of leeway for subjective assessment. Sometimes, these considerations are brought to bear as counterarguments even in cases where the bottom line appears completely obvious on formal grounds, as in actual practice the technically correct ruling would lead to behavior that is counterintuitive morally. Occasionally instances arise where the application of existing *halakhah* would so offend all moral sensibilities that rabbinic authorities feel justified in resorting to even so vague a rationale as "the ways of the Torah are ways of peace" (*derakheha darkhei noam*) to sanction a different ruling.

It would seem, for example, on initial reading, that Jewish law discriminates between Jew and non-Jew in critical matters of life and death. While a Jewish physician is obliged to save a Jewish life, even when violating other Torah laws in the process, he is forbidden from violating laws for a non-Jew. In actual practice, however, a number of nonformal considerations were evoked over the ages to allow for treating a gentile patient as well. But even here, such considerations have been applied situationally and not universally.

The most cited principle is a pragmatic one: "because of enmity" (*mishum eivah*); in other words, legal dispensations are granted in order to prevent hatred between Jew and non-Jew, lest repercussions endanger other Jews. In some historical settings, considerations of a more positive nature than self-preservation have been invoked, such as "sanctification of God's name" (*kiddush Hashem*), or the creation of all human beings in the image of God.[27]

A relatively mild example of use of this strategy as applied to women's issues (which has nonetheless not been generally accepted by Orthodox communities) was the suggestion of Rabbi Aaron of Worms more than a century and a half ago:

It seems that we are forbidden to recite *shelo asani goy* [the blessing thanking God for not having been created a gentile] publicly [in the synagogue], because it will engender hatred [among the gentiles]. And as to reciting [aloud] *shelo asani isha* [thanking God for not having been created a woman]—how can we publicly insult someone (*malbin penei havero berabim*)!"[28]

Other innovations that are perceived as more problematic halakhically (or as more radical because they blatantly run counter to previous practice and ideology) may be justified after the fact (*bediavad*) on the basis of more pressing considerations of prudence. One example of this is R. Yehiel Weinberg's decision to condone the mixed singing of Sabbath songs at the family table, which he justifies not only in order to avoid unnecessary offense to women, but also out of the fear that such exclusion could drive women from the Torah community.[29] The Hafez Hayim's qualified sanction of women's formal study of Torah, accompanied by the halfhearted remark: "Better this form of frivolity (*tiflut*) than another,"[30] could be regarded as motivated by similar considerations.

Ignoring past halakhic stipulations. The most drastic option of all is to disregard past halakhic stipulations, relegating them to dead-letter status. This measure is not freely used or condoned, and it is generally not prompted by ideological tensions, but simply by the inapplicability of old norms in the context of new social settings. An example of this is the flagrant violation of the halakhically well-founded prohibition against unmarried men and *all* women, both married and unmarried, teaching young children. The intent is to avoid the teacher's socializing with parents coming to fetch their children, which would be considered immodest mingling of the sexes.[31] In his commentary on Maimonides' *Hilkhot Talmud Torah* where this prohibition is codified, R. Moshe Sternbuch, a contemporary authority who now serves as one of the leaders of an ultra-Orthodox community in Jerusalem, asks: Why is this *halakhah* ignored in such widespread fashion in our day? Could it be that it is the influence of the widespread mixing of the sexes in the modern marketplace? Although his query is voiced incredulously, the rhetorical suggestion is obviously the main answer.[32]

Ideological Influences

The existence of halakhic strategies such as those described above plays into the widespread perception that a solution can be found to almost every basic halakhic difficulty, given the proper institutional circumstances (that is, general consensus of opinion among a recognized community of major rabbinic authorities). A by-now notorious slogan first coined by Blu Greenberg—"Where there is a rabbinic will, there is a halakhic way"—is probably meant to express this faith in the halakhic system's ability to rise to the challenges of modernity. Nonetheless, the rather cavalier attitude to due process of law that this slogan seems to imply (omitting, as it does, any reference to limitations upon the nature of such solutions) has raised the ire of rabbinic authorities. Such an attitude continues to serve as a red flag; it ignores the fact that, beyond the objective political and historical constraints mentioned earlier, another more subjective and ideological factor is extremely influential in limiting the range of halakhic innovation: the perceptions of the halakhic decisor himself and of his community as to just how far he may legitimately take his interpretations.

Even the talmudic statements about rabbinic autonomy appear contradictory. Some seem to deny that the sages exhibited any autonomy and creativity as they interpreted the written Torah and in so doing developed the Oral Law. Thus we are told that "whatever a veteran student is destined to innovate was already told [by God] to Moses at Sinai." On the other hand we find statements that seem to indicate that God Himself learns Torah from the scholars of later generations.[33] It is a moot point whether these non-halakhic formulations are truly in conflict. If their purpose is to give a factual description of the nature of the Oral Law, they are indeed at odds. A more accurate way of understanding them, however (especially in light of the fact that divergent positions sometimes stem from the same source)[34] is to regard them as aggadic attempts to express or evoke certain attitudes to *halakhah*. Thus, the first statement comes to establish the absolute commitment required by the Oral Law, whereas the second stresses the sense of partnership and intimacy that sages felt with their Maker when explicating His Torah.[35] As mythic descriptions that were not intended to be taken literally, these formulations can exist side by side without contradiction. However, loyalty to the system, especially in times of perceived threat, appears to mandate tying on its ideological loincloths more tightly. It is at such times that we most often hear strident statements of faith dogmatically professing commitment to an eternal and unchanging Torah with exhaustively predefined parameters.[36]

The ideological constraints of Orthodoxy

The latest instance of this dynamic can be perceived in the sharply dogmatic turn that Orthodox Judaism has taken since the nineteenth century. Previous to this, as we have seen, premodern Jewish society was secure in its unquestioning acceptance of tradition as no less a primary source of authority than texts. The more relaxed, pragmatic, and nonideological religious climate that then prevailed still characterizes traditional Sephardic Jewish communities less affected by modernity.[37] In contrast, today's Orthodoxy represents a deliberate response both to a historicist approach, which views Judaism as shaped by external events and influences, and to the threat that the forces of modernity and its values have posed to the authority of *halakhah*.

Orthodox Judaism is not all of one ilk. Ultra-Orthodoxy (known in Israel today as *haredi*) stems initially from Hungary, but later absorbed the more popular sections of Eastern European, premodern, traditionalist communities, especially Hassidic ones, as well as some elements of the post–World War I Lithuanian yeshiva world that represented the main opposition to Hassidic spiritualism. Modern Orthodoxy (that variety of Orthodoxy with which ultra-Orthodoxy is nowadays usually contrasted) is also an umbrella term which covers at least three different historical components. The first of these is represented by the neo-Orthodoxy that originated in Germany in the nineteenth century and later formed the basis of the Modern Orthodoxy that developed in Western Europe, the United States, and other countries, including Israel. In its expanded form this later group adopted a slightly more flexible mode of religious commitment, which is at times based more on denominational allegiance than on rigorous personal observance, partly due to its relative absorption of various elements of modern life. A third component overlaps with the variety of traditionalism that developed in Lithuania and straddles both the ultra-Orthodox and Modern Orthodox worlds, thus forming a continuum between them.

Uniting all these groups, despite their differences, is the shift from traditionalism to modernity. The conscious, self-reflexive, conservative formulation of Judaism that constitutes Orthodoxy is—even in its antimodernist formulations—a uniquely modern phenomenon.[38] Precisely because of this shift, it has come about that, especially since the nineteenth century, Orthodox spokesmen have promoted a view of *halakhah* as a rigid and static system, impervious to outside influences and considerations. Thus we are typically told: "Normative Judaism teaches that Halakhah is not derived from any temporal 'worldview' or 'social situation' but expresses the transcendental worldview of the divine Lawgiver."[39] Because the *halakhah* is not bound to any contemporary ethos, it "possesses an enduring validity which, while applicable to changing circumstances, is not subject to change by lobbying or by the exertion of pressure in any guise or form. Nor may independently held convictions, however sincere, be allowed to influence our interpretation of Halakhah."[40] Both ultra-Orthodox Judaism and the various components of Modern Orthodoxy are united in their commitment to the preservation of halakhic integrity, alongside their acceptance of the basic tenets of rabbinic Judaism, but there are significant differences in the ways they ground this commitment. The differences have a direct bearing on the degree to which the possibility for halakhic change is acknowledged, and on the choice of halakhic devices utilized.

CHAPTER 4

The Meta-Halakhic Solutions
of Modern Orthodoxy

The Legal Realist Position of Ultra-Orthodoxy

The more traditional figures of ultra-Orthodoxy in the nineteenth century actually pursued the ambitious (and counterintuitive) strategy of claiming that *all* of rabbinic law (including exegesis, decrees, and even custom) was revealed together with the Written Torah at Sinai.[1] This renders the entire Talmud a record of *transmitted* divine law, direct and unadulterated from Moses at Sinai. Such a maximalist view runs counter not only to the historical consciousness of the nineteenth century but even to the testimony of the Talmud itself, which attributed legislative enactments to several rabbinic leaders of the first two centuries C.E. As Israeli historian Michael Silber declares in his study of ultra-Orthodoxy, this way of thinking, rather than representing continuity, is best described as the invention of a new, more potent tradition, whereby the past is "interpreted, shaped, filtered and recast to better serve the cause of traditionalism."[2] Stringency, as much as leniency, can be a deviation from mainstream tradition, and indeed, in order to preserve tradition uncompromised, sometimes the most conservative of authorities must employ methods that depart from what has been the accepted norm for generations. To take one example, halakhah throughout the ages ruled that prayer in accordance with the established ritual could be recited in any language.[3] But in reaction to assimilation and reformist tendencies in the nineteenth century, this leniency was abolished for public prayer.[4] Thus, despite its traditionalism, ultra-Orthodox ideology "is in fact not an unchanged and unchanging remnant of pre-modern, traditional Jewish society, but as much a child of modernity and change as any of its 'modern' rivals."[5]

The maximalist view of revelation was originally voiced only by the most extreme elements and eschewed by most learned traditionalists as oversimplified and, in some instances, simply false.[6] Nonetheless, at present it enjoys widespread support in more popular renditions of ultra-Orthodox ideology. This view obviously leaves little room for innovation, and opposition to change became the official banner of ultra-Orthodoxy. The essence of this extremely conservative approach to *halakhah* is epitomized in the slogan: "All innovation is forbidden by the Torah" (*Hadash assur min haTorah*), coined by Rabbi Moses Sofer (better known as the Hatam Sofer) in the early nineteenth century[7]—despite the fact that Sofer himself was a great innovator. On this understanding, Halakhic rulings are merely technical, rather than substantive responses, in specific cases, to the practical constraints that are thrust upon the community of believers by a changing and imperfect reality.[8]

In ultra-Orthodox circles, where the impact of modernity is fairly muted and the community continues unquestioningly to entrust halakhic decision-making to its rabbinic leaders, this view of *halakhah* continues on successfully. Little tension is experienced between theory and practice, because whatever adjustments deemed necessary are made by the established contemporary halakhic authorities, on the strength of their personal authority and judgment. The widespread traditionalist assumption is that the *posek* himself embodies "living Torah"; therefore, by definition he cannot err, and no matter what the values or understandings informing his decision may be, it *is* the law.[9] While the individual *posek* undoubtedly experiences constraints in interpreting the *halakhah,* decisions as to the relative weight given to the codified texts, versus consequentialist considerations or established practice, are ultimately a matter of his personal style and discretion. In this sense, the ultra-Orthodox position corresponds with legal realism, a theory of jurisprudence influential during the first half of the twentieth century, which maintains that law is determined not so much by the language of legal texts and enactments, but rather by the discretionary power of judges. The judges' decisions are "realistic" because they adapt the law to address social realities.

In actuality, entrusting *halakhah* to the personal discretion of the *posek* is no more than the continuation of a dominant tradition in Jewish law from talmudic times, encapsulated in the statement that "the *dayan* [judge] has no more than what his eyes can see."[10] According to contemporary legal scholar Bernard Jackson, who borrows terminology from Max Weber's typology of forms of authority, this preference for a more "charismatic" rather than legal-rational form of authority may even have its roots in the Bible.[11] Many talmudic deliberations seek the rationale for a given decision not in any guiding principle to be found in the text, but rather in principles that can be inferred from the sensibilities and practices of the rabbinic judge concerned.[12] This practice of relying on the judges' discretion, however, eventually proved controversial. Though accepted by the Babylonian Talmud, it appears to have been opposed by the Palestinian authorities and was never formally incorporated into the powers of the judiciary.[13] Nonetheless, current approaches to the *halakhah* that accord privileged status to the consensus of opinion among the generation's great Torah luminaries (*daat Torah shel gedolei hador*), regardless of how the consensus was reached, may be understood as lingering traces of this tradition.[14]

In principle, such a theory of law provides the judge with considerable leeway for making innovative decisions when necessary, despite a constricting ideological cover. In practice, however, given contemporary historical and political circumstances and the response of ultra-Orthodoxy to modernity, a *posek* of this camp is left with little room or impetus for global or substantive reform in today's halakhic reality. This constriction has led those segments of Orthodoxy that have been more deeply affected by modernity to formulate meta-halakhic theories that address their concerns.

The Torah and *Derekh Eretz* Distinction of Neo-Orthodoxy

The response of German neo-Orthodoxy to modernity differed from that of its ultra-Orthodox Hungarian counterpart. Neo-Orthodoxy held that the clamor for the reform of traditional Judaism could be adequately countered by strictly cultural and aesthetic responses. While accepting modernity in these external social aspects, the leaders of neo-Orthodoxy sought to adopt a line of defense that stood midway between accepting the notion of halakhic immutability and acknowledging or even celebrating some measure of innovative liberty. This solution was captured in their enthusiastic adoption of the rabbinic formula of "Torah with *derekh eretz.*"

The term *"derekh eretz"* (the way of the land) carries many connotations in the traditional literature.[15] In some contexts it clearly means "a livelihood"; in others it means the expectations we have on the basis of common human decency. In nineteenth century neo-Orthodox circles it was interpreted as referring to the conditions of modern enlightenment, the idea being that the Torah could be observed in such a setting no less than in ghetto conditions. The religious leaders of the German variety of Orthodoxy deemed fundamentally authoritative only that which was patently divine, granting that this did not necessarily include all of the aggadic material and customs of later ages. They therefore maintained that meticulous observance of Jewish practices and customs was possible, even within the context of the accepted culture of the surrounding non-Jewish environment. Alongside this liberalism, however, the neo-Orthodox authorities refused to allow for the possibility that rabbinic exegesis represented anything other than a loyal reflection of the Pentateuch's simple meaning. Much of the energy of Orthodox German scholarship was devoted to examining carefully the grammar of the original Hebrew text and to other lexical issues, in order to demonstrate that the sages' interpretations were actually the accurate expression of the text's plain sense, if only one understood the subtle nuances of the language. In other words, the oral tradition merely unpacked and explicated what was implicit in the written text; it certainly did not veer from its original intent, which was one and the same for all time.

Although such a sharply dichotomized understanding of *halakhah,* differentiating clearly between the divine and the human, does not have much basis in traditional sources, it could rely on a distinction made by Maimonides in the introduction to his commentary on the Mishnah. Maimonides juxtaposes the law transmitted to Moses at Sinai (*halakhah leMoshe meSinai*), representing unequivocal truth not given to debate, and the rest of the Oral Law, representing contingent truths given to the arbitrary rulings of the majority. Whatever Maimonides' motives for drawing this distinction,[16] such a two-tiered view of *halakhah* held great appeal for neo-Orthodoxy. If one area of *halakhah* remains transcendent, impervious to outside influence and personal bias, the believer can view halakhic practice as more than a self-serving activity responding to human needs. If, at the same time, at least one area of the law is pliable and given to context-bound considerations, it allows the halakhic community much greater freedom of movement than does a rigid ultra-Orthodox ideology that limits all prospective change to questions of practical application. With this understanding, religious observance need not be regarded as a premodern form of ghetto existence. On the contrary, it may easily be adjusted to modern circumstances, so long as the essence of Torah remains intact.[17]

The Positivist Formulations of Modern Orthodoxy

German neo-Orthodoxy's initial distinction between the form and content of Torah was appropriated and developed further by more modern segments of the Orthodox population. As a result, considerable effort has been expended in recent years on attempts to articulate the precise nature of *halakhah* and the halakhic process. These efforts have taken the form of several meta-halakhic ideologies ("philosophies of *halakhah*"). Common to all is a tendency to posit one element of law as fixed and eternal and to characterize another element as more responsive to its surroundings and given to change. The difference between the ideologies lies in their conceptions of the nature and scope of the fixed element. This difference also has some influence upon the range of strategies to be employed within that area still left open to judicial discretion.[18]

Broadly speaking, the new meta-halakhic efforts on the part of Modern Orthodoxy bear some affinity to legal positivism, a philosophy of jurisprudence that has been bandied about in the past few decades in Anglo-American legal writings. What characterizes the positivist approach is that it "posits" the source of law in authoritative social institutions (such as monarchies, parliaments, and courts). Originally formulated for the express purpose of *rejecting* a notion of law derived from abstract principles, such as universal morality, natural law, or divine command,[19] its application to a religious context can therefore only be understood in a figurative sense.

Nevertheless, what is common to positivism in either context is opposition to the approach of legal realism, which invests the ultimate authority of the law in the person of the judge and his subjective assessments of law's outcome in practice. Like their secular counterparts who view law as issuing from a known and predetermined set of standards, the "positivists" of Modern Orthodoxy prefer to ground *halakhah* on the proper application of a closed and static system of rules, conceptual categories, and/or values implicit in the codified sources. Law's content is determined only with reference to the mode of thinking and precedents shaped by these given criteria. What such an approach comes to deny is that law may have reference to any extraneous claims, agendas, or questions of substance beyond its predefined parameters, thereby serving as an instrument to independently determined principles or goals. Its overall function is reactive, referring only to already existent standards and formulating its norms within their bounds.

The interest of Modern Orthodoxy in viewing *halakhah* in terms of legal theory is symptomatic of a more general wish to move away from the legal realism of tradition. Diverting the weight of authority in halakhic deliberation from the persona of the individual *posek* to more theoretically prescribed grounding responds to a cluster of conflicting contemporary needs. Reliance on codified sources arguably serves the same conservative function that essentialism does for apologetics; basing halakhic decisions on what appear to be more objective considerations, rather than on the subjective judgement of the *posek,* implies greater credibility. But the appeal to texts also caters to more liberal interests. Beyond the general reluctance of Modern Orthodoxy to rely upon charisma-based authority, the shift of focus to predefined precedent indicates the alienation from more traditionalist halakhic authorities that some members of this community experience. The disparity they perceive between the norms of the typical Modern Orthodox community and the life experiences and sensibilities of these leaders also contributes to their desire to "open the books" for themselves.

Formalist and Nonformalist Positivism

While all the positivist formulations of Modern Orthodoxy adopt the distinction between fixed and contingent elements of *halakhah,* they define these elements differently. Two broad categories can be identified here: formalist and nonformalist approaches. Although the twin concepts of positivism and formalism are often conflated in legal theory, so that positivism is assumed to include formalism, they can and—for our purposes—should be separated. When positivism is understood in this narrower sense, it refers merely to a theory regarding law's *essential grounding,* whereas the terminology of formalism and nonformalism refers to theories regarding law's *nature* and its *process of deliberation.*[20]

For the formalist, then, law consists of a hierarchy of well-defined rules and concepts. The main duty of the judge is to apply the relevant rules and principles to the case at hand, and the correct outcome should be generally predictable and clear-cut. Subjective judgment comes into play only in the unusual case of legal lacunae, gaps in the authoritative texts, in which case the judge relies on less specific principles, public policy considerations, and standards that are outside or beyond the law. Room for leeway and innovation exists principally with respect to those questions that do not fall into the clearly defined categories of the law. In such cases nonformal considerations of context and moral principles can be applied.

A nonformalist approach, by contrast, does not define the nature of law technically, merely in terms of clear-cut rules and legal concepts. Alongside these elements are ideological principles, ethical standards, policy considerations, and even political theories, all of which are also stated explicitly or embedded in between the lines of the primary legal sources. Because the law incorporates an ultimate purpose (a *telos* or an ideal vision of the individual and society), its scope is more comprehensive when fashioned in accordance with these more general precepts, blurring the distinction between legal prescription and moral ideal. Legal considerations as prescribed in the codified sources are seen as far-reaching, touching upon vital areas of moral concern. There are no legal lacunae, because when there is no relevant rule the broader principles apply.

Ostensibly, a nonformalist view leaves *less* room for autonomous decision-making because of the all-encompassing nature of its legal *telos*. However, moral ideals, even when spelled out in a divine text, are by nature more elusive and subject to interpretation than are rules. Moreover, to the extent that a nonformalist moves beyond a monolithic, ahistoric view of tradition, he or she must also allow for the possibility that even the formulation of law in terms of comprehensive principles may have incorporated passing or changing norms. This allows much leeway for considerations of context in the weighing of arguments. If, for the formalist, the room for judicial discretion lies in the areas *not covered* by law and its formal prescriptions, for the nonformalist it lies in the application of those general principles *within* the law in a manner that realizes their purpose to perfection.

The difference between formalism and nonformalism in Jewish terms, then, involves how they relate to the stock of overarching principles loosely related by tradition to halakhic procedure and to variable considerations of context. Formalism would regard such principles and considerations as extralegal, while nonformalism would consider them as part and parcel of the guidelines that govern halakhic procedure.[21]

It perhaps will be useful to offer a practical example, illustrating how the adoption of one approach versus the other might make a difference in practical halakhic decision-making. The accepted understanding until fairly recently has been that the *halakhah* requires married women to cover their hair.[22] Indeed, in some circles this practice has become a litmus test of a woman's faithfulness to halakhic dictates.[23] Women in the past fulfilled this obligation by wearing kerchiefs and headcoverings of various sorts. Ever since the widespread manufacture of fashionable wigs, many observant Jews have accepted this as a viable alternative.[24] Do wigs satisfy the halakhic requirement? The formalist might say that a woman can technically fulfill her obligation with any cover other than her own hair. For a nonformalist, conflicting issues of modesty versus considerations of livelihood and the need to "pass" in a secular or gentile workplace may also enter the balance.[25]

Formal positivism in the tradition of Brisk

One of the chief sources for a more formal approach to halakhic jurisprudence lies in the text-based method of study established in Mitnaggedic circles of Lithuania. This tendency, which began with a premodern authority, the Gaon of Vilna, was reinforced in new ways generations later by the analytic school of learning (*lomdus*) initiated by Rabbi Hayim Soloveitchik of Brisk. The dominant force even today in those *yeshivot* continuing the Lithuanian tradition, this method places great emphasis on rigorous analysis of the classical sources, downplaying the role of popular custom, imagined consequences, or extralegal moral implications as the ultimate determinant of *halakhah*.

According to the school of Brisk, *halakhah* is embodied and shaped by abstract legal concepts. The cohesiveness of this system is answerable only to its own internal logic and procedural rules. Through these, concrete *halakhah* is gleaned. Relying on their understanding that *halakhah* is a self-contained, internally consistent system, followers of the "Brisker method" strive to explain the differences between various decisions and reveal the logic that stands behind them. Such a view does not preclude halakhic creativity. On a theoretical level, the talmudic scholar may display great virtuosity in the attempt to reconstruct the conceptual structure lying behind the rules and uncover the roots of precedent. On the normative level, however, as all halakhic activity is conducted only in terms of the conceptual logic of the system, jurisprudence is limited to local questions of practical application. The halakhic decisor may sometimes leap back to the Gemara in order to correct mistaken interpretations engendered by later *poskim;* ideally, however, his conclusions are unaffected by real-world considerations and consequences and do not relate to broad matters of ideology and substance.

The Soloveitchik school: Formalist distinctions between "pure halakhah" and public policy. The Briskian version of formalistic positivism has become the accepted approach within the ranks of Modern Orthodoxy in the United States, owing to the powerful influence of the late Rabbi Joseph B. Soloveitchik (a grandson of R. Hayim), who is reverentially referred to in these circles as "the Rav." If at the hands of his grandfather, the aim of the Brisk approach was only to elucidate the *halakhah* itself, the Rav expanded it into a more full-blown philosophy that addresses the connection between *halakhah* and religious experience in general.[26] This philosophy consists of a unique amalgam of "the Brisker Method" and modern existentialism on the one hand, and on the other, neo-Kantian philosophy, which regards science as the product of a humanly formed system of categories. Influenced by the approach of Herman Cohen (who explicated Judaism on the basis of his interpretation of Kant), the Rav understood the abstract concepts of Brisk as ideal categories that serve as a methodological tool for approaching and accessing the inner spiritual reality that *halakhah* is meant to render concrete. As in mathematics, these categories have a priori status. Their definitions are absolute, eternal, and not to be equated with historic, ideological, or moral interpretations that have accrued to them. Nor do they come to serve any value external to themselves. In subjugating himself to the norms of *halakhah*, "Halakhic Man" (the title of the Rav's famous essay on this topic)[27] discovers and internalizes the ideal values and principles that are embedded in its structure and realizes them to the best of his ability in the imperfect universe he inhabits.

The Rav's objective was mainly phenomenological, describing the way the existing halakhic system ideally functions in mediating the religious experience. Under the more stringent interpretation of some of his disciples, however, this theory became normative and prescriptive; the absolute directive for conducting the religious life.[28] They portrayed the validity of any religious act and experience as determined *only* by formal halakhic categories. As phrased by Soloveitchik's nephew, Rabbi Moshe Meiselman, "*Halakhah* stands prior to all religious concepts and is the only source for their cognition."[29] The Rav's son, Professor Haym Soloveitchik, writes:

> If law is conceived of as religious law must be, as a revelation of the divine will, then any attempt to align that will with human wants, any attempt to have reality control rather than to be itself controlled by the divine norm, is an act of blasphemy and is inconceivable to a God-fearing man.[30]

The independent experience of the worshiper is irrelevant as a criterion for assessing the validity of religious ritual. The spiritual ambition of every Jew is succinctly encapsulated in the charge of the Mishnah: "Void your will before the will of God" (*batel retzonkha mipnei retzono*) (Ethics of the Fathers 2:4). This injunction is understood not only in the sense of suppressing one's ego or personal interests on a normative or ideological level, but also in terms of internalizing halakhic categories as the exclusive method of cultivating a Torah personality more thoroughly permeated by Torah ideals.

Within the ranks of the Soloveitchik school, however, disciples differ as to how far the influence of ideal halakhic categories extends. A maximalist position views the scope of formal *halakhah* as all-encompassing, acknowledging the possibility of legal lacunae only with regard to questions of application and not with regard to substance. Ideally, every action, decision, judgment, and evaluation, even the more general attitudes appropriated by a Torah Jew, is subjected to the prism of the internal, metahistorical conceptual categories for ultimate validation and justification. Such a position represents little more than a return, with the addition of a more sophisticated philosophical rationale, to classic ultra-Orthodox ideology, which limits the entire range of halakhic deliberation exclusively to questions of application. Attributing the substance of *halakhah* exclusively to ideal categories rather than to the personal authority of the *posek* is simply a more powerful tool for defending the observance of current halakhic norms as they stand. In this sense, the concept of ideal halakhic categories functions in a manner akin to the essentialism of conservative apologetics.

Against this maximalist position regarding the one-way influence of *halakhah* upon the real world, however, "softer" applications of the formalist ideology abound. Each appropriates some form of distinction between the fixed and the more contingent aspects of halakhic deliberation, which is usually expressed in terms of "pure" *halakhah* versus public policy. "Pure" *halakhah,* according to all, refers to issues that must indeed be decided on the basis of purely formal and objective considerations derived from the *halakhah* itself, yielding unequivocal answers of "permissible" or "forbidden." Rulings on such issues are not elastic or open to debate. By contrast, questions of public policy—those involving educational, communal, or political considerations—even when relating to the law, belong to a discretionary gray area not governed by formal criteria. Here the individual *posek* is free to supplement the law by exercise of personal discretion.[31]

The nonformalist critique of formalism

A formalist approach to *halakhah* that distinguishes in this manner between pure *halakhah* and public policy undoubtedly carries certain religious advantages. A system that retains a fixed element of law that is measured only in accordance with its own clearly defined internal rules and conceptual framework holds greater promise of transcending the vagaries and limitations of subjective human judgment and self-interest. In the eyes of its opponents, however, it also carries serious drawbacks. The major drawback is to their mind a spiritual one: blindness to the possibility that the *halakhah* expresses a worldview and values that lie beyond its details. The religious life, they contend, cannot be reduced to mechanical jurisprudence and obedience to mere technicalities. It must be infused with a significance and moral pathos that transcends its formal requirements; with values such as making the world a better place to live in (*tikkun olam*), cultivating a proper ethical-moral-religious-intellectual disposition, inducing the unique emotions and existential rhythms of intimacy with God.

Because opponents of halakhic formalism consider *halakhah* a teleological system, bearing values leading to a purposeful ultimate destiny, they refuse to relegate to the areas of technical application, public policy, or legal lacunae (even when broadly conceived) any discretionary issues involving principles that are spiritually meaningful. Substantive rather than formal issues must compose the fixed element in *halakhah* and constitute its backbone, they insist. This is not to say that formal legalities have no place. All things being equal, the *halakhah* will be determined in accordance with its well-established regulations. But when blind conformance to such norms obstructs realization of the *halakhah*'s ultimate *telos,* the hierarchy of formal rules and precedents should be reassessed so as to allow for the realization of the higher principles they are meant to reflect.

Rabbi Berkowits's nonformalist distinctions: Torah-taught and Torah-tolerated ideals. One example of a nonformal application of positivism that takes responsiveness to human sensibilities into account was proposed by the late Rabbi Eliezer Berkovits. Rabbi Berkovits saw himself following in the footsteps of Maimonides in his belief that the Torah expresses a spiritual vision yet to be realized.[32] Implicit in the Torah is a set of ethical values that were not fully revealed to Moses, but that can be gleaned from the text on the basis of human reason and social experience. These values serve as our guides in the interpretation of texts and in the application of the formal mechanisms of *halakhah*. For this reason, the legitimacy of the *halakhah* is not to be measured only by the degree to which it conforms with previous rulings and a priori principles. Rather, Torah must be understood as a series of provisional enactments gradually leading toward the realization of an ideal society. *Halakhah,* then, is instrumental in actualizing certain values or achieving certain social ends implied in an overall *telos.* Its mission goes beyond implementation of its own formal logic. While its rulings change as society changes, its purposes remain constant.

On the strength of this understanding of Torah, Rabbi Berkovits creates a distinction between authentic, eternal Torah principles and transient norms that the Torah tolerated because they prevailed at the time of its revelation. Even when ideal moral perceptions or other implicit principles of the Torah have not yet been fully translated into halakhic norms, they are what grant us today the energy and legitimacy for change. Change represents the fulfillment of the *halakhah,* even when it poses obvious tension with some of the normative practices of the past.

Formalism and Nonformalism as Keys to Halakhic Adjudication

Both the formalists and the nonformalists nourish the hope that in elaborating their respective methods of distinguishing between fixed and flexible aspects of the *halakhah,* they can provide clear, internally consistent, and reliable guidelines for determining legal options, while not closing the door completely to halakhic viability. A widespread belief is that formalist considerations are more trustworthy in that they preserve a higher degree of halakhic objectivity. For this reason, they are regarded as the hallmark of the halakhic purist. Modern Orthodox groups with a more liberal orientation generally favor nonformalist approaches, as they appear open to greater interpretation. Yet closer examination of how these theories work in practice with respect to women's issues yields a more ambiguous picture.

While all formalists deviating from a maximalist position agree that in areas of public policy the halakhic decisor is free to respond to human needs and shifting societal realities in a manner independent of formal halakhic categories, they may still differ significantly in their understandings of just how pliable the public policy decisions of the *posek* really are. Rabbi Saul Berman, for example, has suggested that because the opinions of halakhic experts regarding discretionary matters are not offered authoritatively, but rather in a spirit of persuasion, the experts may have cause to rethink their position if the community they address is not persuaded.[33] Other formalists posit a stronger influence of halakhic categories even in the determination of issues that are by nature more sensitive to context and extralegal considerations. Although they too acknowledge some form of distinction between pure *halakhah* and public policy, they maintain that even with regard to public policy, clear-cut rights and wrongs are still involved and discretionary latitude curtailed to a minimum.

Assumptions regarding the liberal character of nonformalism can similarly be refuted. Despite the discretionary nature of all-encompassing nonformal principles, the degree of flexibility that a nonformalist displays depends chiefly on how these principles are defined and applied. One overriding principle common to nonformalists and formalists alike is the general commitment to perpetuate Torah and guarantee the future of halakhic performance. Such a principle leaves much leeway for the personal predilections of the *posek* and can therefore generally be pressed into the services of either leniency or constraint, irrespective of his professed meta-halakhic orientation.

Because of the extent to which interpretive slack allows other powerful factors to come into play, halakhic outcomes may be far less predictable and argument-dependent than what the meta-halakhic theoreticians would have us believe. In the final analysis, women may discover that what keeps *halakhah* going is something more rich-blooded than the *posek's* assent to certain narrowly construed positivist claims.

CHAPTER 5

Does Positivism Work?

The Modern Orthodox discussion of meta-halakhic policy has yielded a wealth of rulings on women's issues. As in all areas of the law, sustained and detailed argumentation is generally regarded as critical in determining how to decide recurring questions as well as in determining the fate of new suggestions. Close scrutiny of the degree to which such argumentation is affected by its professed meta-halakhic orientation affords us the opportunity of assessing how effective meta-halakhic policy really is in pinpointing precisely the areas of halakhic malleability. Viewing how various strategies are employed even within such areas as tools of halakhic constraint with respect to women's issues will then lead us to questions regarding the suitability of the halakhic medium in general as a tool for addressing the needs of contemporary Orthodox women.

In assessing the adequacy of meta-halakhic theory as a response to women's concerns, two issues in particular come to the fore. The first refers to a quiet but powerful revolution that has taken place in Jewish women's learning in recent years. The second is the innovation of women-only prayer groups.

The Women's Learning Revolution

As was already noted in chapter 2, a few of the educational institutions established by Modern Orthodoxy began to provide their female students with a rudimentary introduction to the world of the Oral Law back in the 1950s. However, no educational settings existed paralleling the post–high-school-level *yeshivot* in which many young men continued their study of the Oral Law as a matter of course. The last few decades, however, have seen an explosion of interest on the part of Modern Orthodox women in intense study of Jewish sources, a phenomenon following upon the spiritual euphoria induced by the Israeli Six-Day War and the religious revival movement of "returnees" (*baalei teshuvah*) that developed in its wake.

What was unique in the learning revolution instituted by Modern Orthodox women in the following decade was not simply the level of literacy they
sought, but also its subject matter and institutional setting. The women involved were not content with what had come to be regarded as the "softer"
areas of Jewish study (Bible, *aggadah,* Jewish thought, and the pietistic writings of the *musar* [morality] teachers). These had come to be accepted as legitimate fare for women, because they could still be construed as enhancing
their ability to function as enablers. What the initial pioneers of the new
learning revolution now sought was the real "meat" of in-depth halakhic erudition. Moreover, while a few alternative possibilities for approaching
study of the Oral Law had begun to open up for women in teacher training
seminaries or university settings, these women preferred a rarefied spiritual
atmosphere akin to that of a men's yeshiva. This meant replication of the
same institutional methods of study: the Torah study hall (*bet midrash*), the
appointment of a spiritual guide (*mashgiah ruhani*) and head of the academy
(*rosh metivta*) as role models, *havruta*-style learning emphasizing independent study with learning partners, and all the experiential associations of
joint prayer and celebration of Sabbath and festivals. Such learning is not
achievement-oriented; the study is conducted without exams, grades, and
other external measures of success. The goal is the learning itself, which is
conducted "for its own sake" (*lishmah*) rather than for any practical benefit.[1]

In 1976, Midreshet Lindenbaum (then known as Michlelet Beruria, or
simply as Brovender's, after the name of its founder) in Jerusalem launched
the first program for women in which study of the Oral Law figured as the
main component. Its initial year began with four university students from
the United States who had come to Israel for the express purpose of gaining
greater proficiency in Jewish sources. Since then the institution has expanded significantly, housing educational programs for women of various
ages from Israel and the Diaspora. It includes a program that combines military service with religious studies, paralleling what are known in Israel as
hesder yeshivot for male soldiers. More significant, at least twenty more
such institutions have developed in Israel in its wake.[2] Several of these are
designed to cater to students from abroad (in the United States it has become a matter of course for both male and female graduates of religious
high schools to invest at least a year of post–high-school study in Israel).
Study of the Oral Law has become a routine element in some of the study
programs established for women in the Diaspora as well, most notably in
the Drisha Institute for women, founded in New York in 1985.

The Proliferation of Women's Prayer Groups

At the time that the women's learning revolution began to develop in Israel,
the quest of Orthodox women for greater participation in religious life gave

rise to a parallel phenomenon: the formation of women-only groups that convene for the purpose of worship. These gatherings, more popularly known as women's *tefillah* groups, have mushroomed in Modern Orthodox communities around the world since the 1970s, reflecting the need experienced by some Orthodox women to participate more actively in the service, in a manner prohibited to them in the presence of men.

Unlike women's institutional study of the Oral Law, women convening on their own for prayer is not unprecedented. Even in medieval times there is evidence of women holding their own prayer meetings.[3] In modern times, many educational frameworks for religious girls, including schools and summer camps affiliated with ultra-Orthodox circles, include female group prayer as part of their daily routine. The innovation of the *tefillah* groups lies simply in the preference of women for conducting prayers on their own even when they have the option of joining the service conducted by men (such as on the Sabbath). Of particular appeal is the opportunity to be called up to or read from the Torah scroll, practices that do not figure in weekday school prayers.[4]

Positivist Responses to Women's Learning and Prayer Groups: A Survey

There is no denying that both advanced women's learning and the spread of women's prayer groups represent a break with dominant interpretive traditions of the past. Also common to both is that they were instituted from the "bottom up"—via the grassroots initiatives of women themselves, in an effort to resolve dissatisfying aspects of their current situation—rather than beginning with the official approval and orchestration of the religious male establishment. The most significant feature they share is the dissonance they create with established halakhic practice and the upsetting ideological implications born in their wake.

Although the original struggle of Modern Orthodox women for greater learning opportunities was not consciously motivated by a wish to challenge the halakhic status quo in terms of gender roles, or to develop new feminine ways of thinking that challenge existing norms, initially the halakhic establishment resisted, with only a few maverick male sympathizers aiding and abetting the new feminine zeal for learning. These mentors, mainly disciples of Rabbi Joseph Soloveitchik, no doubt drew moral sustenance from the positive attitude of "the Rav" himself to women's learning. R. Soloveitchik was responsible for establishing one of the first Jewish day schools in the United States to foster the principle of an identical religious studies curriculum for girls and boys,[5] even forgoing any halakhic requirement of segregating the sexes in separate classrooms for this purpose.[6] He also demonstrated his belief in the importance of women's learning by delivering the opening *sheur*

(Torah lecture) in the Bet Midrash established in Stern College—the women's division of Yeshiva University—in 1978. Nevertheless, at that time the phenomenon of women wishing to devote themselves to full-time study of Torah after the fashion of men was regarded even in Yeshiva University circles with great reserve. Some of the earlier graduates of Midreshet Lindenbaum who returned to study at Stern College were made to feel that they were ruining their prospects for marriage by championing the cause of women's learning.

Despite the initial suspicion surrounding the revolutionary character of yeshiva-style institutions of higher study for women, the deep visceral reactions of sacrilege originally evoked by the sight of a woman poring over a tome of Talmud are being overcome fairly quickly. By now (perhaps overoptimistically) many regard the struggle of Modern Orthodox women for equal learning opportunities as a battle that has been won in all but the most diehard reactionary circles. Women's desire for higher levels of learning is generally encouraged, out of an appreciation of the importance of greater understanding of the values and implications of faith, in the face of challenges from the "outside" world of modernity. The greater erudition of women is tolerated to varying degrees even when it crosses the border between Written and Oral Law. So long as it is understood as strengthening women's identification with the existing structure, it is not regarded as radical or threatening.

Women's prayer groups, however, have won the support of only a handful of Orthodox rabbis. The reaction of most has ranged from suspicion to virulent opposition.[7] The declaration of Rabbi Moshe Tendler, a prominent rabbi associated with Yeshiva University, is revealing: "I'm prepared to divide my *bet midrash* in half. My synagogue—never." Orthodox women should know that in synagogue, "they're welcome guests, but they're guests. Their presence is not required. That's not their role, to modify the service so that they can participate more fully."[8] Beyond such responses, the spread of the groups has triggered an animated round of meta-halakhic discussion on this particular issue. While some of the discussion is generated by the wish to locate those open-ended aspects of *halakhah* that would support the women's innovation, it has also been fueled by the increasingly sophisticated expositions of a conservative opposition. Much of the argument has focused explicitly upon the nature and limits of public policy, an issue indigenous to a formalist approach.

Contrasting the responses on the part of the halakhic establishment to women's learning versus women's prayer groups is instructive, as is a look at the repercussions for other related issues. Moreover, the exercise stands to teach us something about the adequacy of meta-halakhic theories in general in providing reliable criteria for evaluating solutions to new halakhic dilemmas. We shall begin with offshoots of Rabbi Soloveitchik's formalist approach, and their varying distinctions between "pure *halakhah*" and public policy, gradually proceeding to more flexible views that distinguish between the fixed and contingent elements of *halakhah* on other grounds.

Rabbi Twersky's equation of public policy with permanent halakhic values.
The opposition to women's prayer groups of Rabbi Mayer Twersky, a grandson of Rabbi Joseph B. Soloveitchik, stems from a more stringent approach
to questions of public policy. Rabbi Twersky sets out with a maximalist view
regarding the range of influence of *halakhah*'s ideal categories. In addition
to halakhic practices, which are "concrete, particularized commandments
governing our actions," these categories also embody axiological principles,
which serve as the *halakhah*'s driving spirit—its *elan* or *telos,* which nur-
tures the halakhic personality.[9] Twersky is willing to adopt the terminology
of the formalists in distinguishing between halakhic practices and those abstract imperatives that govern religious values and attitudinal (*hashkafic*)
concerns, by referring to the latter as public policy. But because he regards
even such values and concerns as integral to the system, this maximalism
leads him very close to a nonformalist position.

Twersky's difference with the nonformalists, as well as with less stringent
formalists, is his understanding that even the abstract principles of *halakhah*
are already incorporated completely in the existing halakhic norms. Such
principles are stipulated either in the form of broad imperatives that constitute separate *mitzvot* (as in the injunction to be holy; Lev. 19:2), or as integrated with concrete particulars in the same *mitzvah* (as in the obligation to
inwardness in prayer).[10] This renders even those injunctions that are defined
as public policy as absolutely mandatory and immutable. The *halakhah*
emerges in this view as an absolutely self-validating system that is fully delineated in the sources, and therefore impervious to the vicissitudes of the
real world and current human sensibilities. Even a violation pertaining to a
question of public policy—although distinguishable from a technical infrac-
tion, which is always labeled as "forbidden" (*assur*)—is categorically wrong
and culpable.[11]

Rabbi Twersky applies his understanding of public policy to the issue of
women's prayer groups by invoking Rabbi Soloveitchik's understanding of
prayer as an inner experience (or, as the sages describe it, as a service of the
heart). This inwardness, Twersky argues, is antithetical to the desire for active participation and leadership. Women's *tefillah* groups thus violate the
very essence of prayer. Even if the women concerned take great pains to
conform to all the practical halakhic constraints, the groups cannot be
granted legitimacy.

*Rabbi Meiselman's equation of public policy with the application of perma-
nent halakhic principles.* Rabbi Moshe Meiselman, R. Soloveitchik's
nephew, invokes another conservative version of the formalist position to
justify opposition to women's *tefillah* groups. In contrast to Twersky's opposition, Meiselman's opposition focuses not on their violation of the *telos* of
prayer, but rather on their inattention to the more formal requirements of
halakhic worship. Because *halakhah* is not the expression of spirituality, but

its very definition, any attempt to find external meaning in halakhic behavior is mistaken at the outset, and smacks of idolatry.[12] He charges modern women who wish to intensify their religious experience by "introducing new rituals," preferring to adopt for themselves forms of worship that were specifically designated for a male *minyan,* with contempt of *halakhah.* Pagan rites allow the expression of beliefs and opinions by means of ritual activity, so that the focus of the activity remains with the worshiper. But halakhic acts begin and end with the divine command, and only this lends the acts their significance.

Paradoxically, this understanding is almost directly contradictory to Rabbi Twersky's. While Twersky describes prayer as an inward experience that does not sit well with extroverted ceremonialism, Meiselman contends the opposite: that women who prefer to express their spirituality outside the normative social form of organized communal prayer are performing a meaningless act:

Although a woman cannot participate in the formation of a *minyan,* when she does pray with one her prayer is elevated to the status of *tefillah betzibbur* [i.e., communal prayer]. One who chooses not to pray with a *minyan* makes a statement that he or she cares not whether God listens or does not listen to his or her prayer. It goes without saying that such a person has missed the essence of prayer and is obviously not motivated by proper religious intent.[13]

Unlike Rabbi Twersky, Rabbi Meiselman does speak of a variable contextual element in that aspect of *halakhah* that he terms "public policy." However, his understanding of public policy (involving attention to the possible impact a particular ruling could have on the Jewish community), does not touch upon the general meaning and purpose of *halakhah,* but only upon the tactics of its dissemination. Social circumstances raise only pragmatic and tactical questions. For example: if an errant act does not warrant halakhic severity, and if parts of the community may be unwilling to heed a ban, when should the demands of the *halakhah* be disclosed and in how much detail? At stake is the culpability of the transgressors—which is less if they are acting in ignorance. Meiselman's classification of women's prayer groups as a public policy issue (attributing his view, as does Twersky, to "the Rav" himself) thus reduces the issue to the advisability of publicizing a halakhic ruling against them.[14] The ruling itself is "pure" *halakhah* and not a public policy issue at all.

Although Twersky and Meiselman articulated their respective meta-halakhic theories specifically with regard to the issue of women's prayer groups, both have voiced their opinions elsewhere about women's learning as well. In this case they are somehow prepared to waive the rigidity of their maximalism and the weight of rabbinic consensus for centuries, and to view the issue contextually. As Twersky writes in an article dedicated to his uncle's memory, "Torah intuition" and "reasoning" may at times transcend facile classification and defy superficial stereotyping.

The *halakhah* prohibiting Torah study for women is not indiscriminate or all-encompassing . . . the prohibition of teaching Torah she-Ba'al Peh [Oral Law] to women relates to optional study. If ever circumstances dictate that study of Torah she-Ba'al Peh is necessary to provide a firm foundation for faith, such study becomes obligatory and obviously lies beyond the pale of any prohibition. Undoubtedly, the Rav's prescription was more far-reaching than that of the Hafetz Hayim and others. But the difference in magnitude should not obscure their fundamental agreement: intuitively, it is clear that the guidelines of the Talmud in Masekhet Sotah [opposing women's Torah study] were never intended for our epoch.[15]

Similarly, in a chapter entitled "Torah Knowledge for Women," in his book *Jewish Woman in Jewish Law,* Meiselman admits that "the sages were cautious" about permitting women to venture into areas of learning not directly concerned with performance of their mandatory tasks. Nevertheless, he contends: "No authorities ever meant to justify the perverse modern-day situation in which women are allowed to become sophisticatedly conversant with all cultures other than their own."[16] Here Meiselman too is prepared to regard the context of a new social reality as sufficient cause for relaxing prohibitions on women engaging in a *mitzvah* specifically designated for men.

In expressing their support of women's learning, Meiselman and Twersky appear to echo the position of their venerated uncle and grandfather. Whatever interpretation we choose to apply to the Rav's reticence regarding women's innovations in the realm of ritual, he was—as already noted—undoubtedly a pioneer when it came to educational policy for Modern Orthodox women. Yet in the eyes of their more liberal critics, who may be characterized by varying degrees of attachment to Rabbi Soloveitchik and his circle of influence at Yeshiva University, the categorical attitude of Rabbis Twersky and Meiselman against women's prayer groups may be a true reflection of the Rav's personal views, but it is only a *possible* (rather than necessary) consequence of his meta-halakhic position. Although not critical to the discussion on a purely theoretical level, the meta-halakhic debate regarding the role and nature of public policy in *halakhah* often becomes embroiled at this point in a more general controversy regarding the precise nature of the Rav's spiritual legacy.[17]

The Frimer brothers' equation of public policy with the area of individual discretion. More liberal views on the issue of women's prayer groups among formalists of the Soloveitchik school are made possible by understanding the distinction between "pure" *halakhah* and its technical application more loosely, and broadening the vision of what public policy issues entail.

Exemplifying this approach is a monumental article on women's prayer groups by Aryeh and Dov Frimer in *Tradition* (a publication of Orthodox Judaism closely affiliated with Yeshiva University circles).[18] After exhaustively reviewing the various positions pro and con, the brothers conclude that a halakhic authority is fully entitled to forbid ostensibly permissible actions, but some are misrepresenting their rulings; what is being judged in this case is a public policy issue, and not pure *halakhah*. Public policy, by their definition, does not refer to predetermined and fixed principles, leading to clear and unequivocal conclusions, but rather to questions that are more subjective and context-related. The authors advise that stringency in the resolution of such questions be avoided if possible, recommending persuasion as preferable to a categorical ban.[19]

Given the caveats, the article suggests that even if women's voluntary acceptance of rituals bears no intrinsic halakhic value from a formal point of view, it might also be evaluated on the basis of nonformal considerations. These encompass not only strictly political factors such as the repercussions for the community (which might find itself torn over the issue); the self-image of the community in the face of "competition" from the Conservative and Reform movements; or the willingness of the women to uphold a ban. Nonformal considerations could also include the spiritual satisfaction and enhanced sense of involvement with *halakhah* that some women gain from independently conducting their own communal prayers.

Although the Frimer brothers do not take their argument further, they imply that such considerations might be applied in like manner to other women's issues. Under certain circumstances it might be advisable to condone voluntary acceptance by women of additional religious activities that were always the preserve of men, when such acceptance can be construed as serving the interests of Torah. This position has certainly been adopted by other formalists who, like the Frimers, have less totalitarian conceptions regarding the scope of "pure" *halakhah*. The compelling reasons that many *poskim* now offer for women's religious learning (such as the centrality of textual study in the Jewish religious experience; the beneficial influence it has on one's entire involvement in the Torah; and the enhancing of women's effectiveness in their traditional roles as wives and mothers)[20] are not self-contained arguments derived from formal considerations within the halakhic system. They rely, rather, on the type of nonformal considerations that are generally reserved for those areas that are left to the discretion of subjective judgment and the consideration of various contingent factors beyond the scope of "pure" *halakhah*.

Professor Leibowitz's expanded concept of diavad. Another variation on the formalistic approach is that of Yeshayahu Leibowitz. While Leibowitz never functioned as a halakhic authority, he did develop a meta-halakhic approach that has been influential in certain Modern Orthodox circles in Israel. Instead of distinguishing between pure *halakhah* derived from fixed conceptual categories and more contingent *halakhah* based on subjective public policy concerns, the two categories he contrasts are *lekhathila* (a priori) and *bediavad* (ex post facto).[21] In Leibowitz's usage, *lekhathila* can be roughly understood as referring to constitutive law (between God and man) and *bediavad* as referring to regulative (social) legislation.

As in the Brisk approach, Leibowitz regards the a priori aspect of *halakhah*, which is text-based and theocentric, as immutable and eternally binding. Any anthropocentric or moral justification offered for *lekhathila* commands he terms idolatrous. As in Brisk, Leibowitz holds on to the model of subjugation and denial of self-interest in this area as the definitive mode of religious worship. The ex post facto aspect, however, relates to the entire range of social legislation. Marriage, divorce, government, and contract law all exist independently of the Torah; *halakhah* merely provides the detailed forms such regulation takes for Jews. Such *bediavad* legislation reflects or is even shaped by adjustment to changing natural or sociological conditions. Halakhic questions in this realm are not decided on the basis of text (because no text in the past could have possibly anticipated them) but rely rather on human judgment, and bear no intrinsic religious significance.

The distinction that Leibowitz makes between immutable text-based law and regulative legislation based on changing social concerns may sound like the pure *halakhah* versus public policy distinction of the Frimer brothers, but the difference is not merely semantic. Leibowitz's division between the two categories is much more extreme. The strength of his objection to any attempt to base the immutable aspects of *halakhah* on human perceptions of reality impels him to classify numerous halakhot—all those which to his mind derive from outdated conceptions regarding the nature of women—as belonging to a relatively broad category that is colored by changing circumstances and not eternally binding. Leibowitz's approach on this score, then, is much more open to flexible interpretations of existing norms than that of other formalists, based on an understanding that some established halakhic definitions (and not merely public policy questions) are context- or situation-related and not absolute. As a result, he has no compunctions, for example, in calling for correctives in *halakhah* in all those areas that discriminate against women in the name of modesty, such as social separation of the sexes, certain limitations on women's style of dress, and restrictions on their participation in public life, army service, government, and courts of law. In this he treads the same path as other *poskim* (most of whom do not share his formalism) who also adopt lenient definitions and contextual considerations when addressing women's issues.

As against his liberal definition of the contingent aspect of *halakhah*, however, Leibowitz goes to even greater lengths of formalism than Brisk in protecting the immutability of *lehatkhila* legislation, emptying it of extrinsic meaning.[22] Whereas Rabbi Soloveitchik views *halakhah* as grounded on permanent ontological principles (the way things really are), Leibowitz shuns such claims. He rejects any grounding for the fixed commands of Torah beyond the humanly initiated decision to accept the Torah as God's dictate and to observe its *mitzvot* for this reason only.[23] Here Leibowitz distances the halakhist even more emphatically from the possibility of picking and choosing what values may be introduced to the system. In applying these meta-halakhic notions to women's issues, Leibowitz adopts a position similar to that of Rabbi Meiselman, asserting that women's voluntary assumption of *mitzvot* that were relegated to men (such as *tzitzit, tefillin,* and dwelling in the *sukkah*) is "pseudo-religion," a type of "sport" totally devoid of religious meaning.[24]

Interestingly enough, Leibowitz omits mention of the wish of some women to pray communally. Granted, he wrote before the rise of women's prayer groups as a halakhic issue; nonetheless, the omission is still surprising, as many women—irrespective of women's prayer groups—do prefer to attend synagogue services, regarding this as a religious virtue. Yet Leibowitz does make an explicit exception of *talmud Torah,* maintaining that despite its classification as a *lekhathila mitzvah* from which women are exempt, it must now be incumbent upon them no less than upon men. In addition to its ritual significance as a *mitzvah,* he argues, learning Torah provides indispensable access to the Jewish heritage and all its attendant spiritual values, in an age when these are no longer a male preserve.[25]

Rabbi Berkovits's application of Torah-true ideals. In his book *Jewish Women in Time and Torah,*[26] Berkovits, like Leibowitz, applies the distinction he develops between Torah-true and Torah-tolerated ideals specifically to questions relating to women's status in *halakhah.* Evaluating the need for halakhic change, Berkovits describes the status of women in *halakhah* as passing through two different levels. Women's status in the Torah was largely defined in terms of the social and economic conditions of an early society and mirrored what could be observed in the non-Jewish cultures of the time. It was a condition tolerated by the Torah, but not instituted by Torah teaching and Torah values. In the second phase, woman's value and dignity were increasingly recognized. Taught and refined by Torah ideals, this change represents the authentic halakhic ethic and even led to halakhic innovations that stemmed from concern for the rights and welfare of women.

Unfortunately the transformation of women's status from an early unavoidable and Torah-tolerated condition to the true ideal prescribed by Torah teaching was never fully realized as a historical reality. The two value systems have continued side by side for centuries. Yet, if a developing *halakhah* is the vehicle for realizing an implicit moral vision in Torah, the need for rethinking halakhic rulings regarding women's status is not to be viewed merely in terms of solving practical problems or responding to passing social forces. Such rulings must also be viewed as *moral* issues, which involves applying value considerations and ethical principles implicit to the world of Torah.

Berkovits's notion that much of women's current status in *halakhah* is expression of a primitive morality that the Torah had to tolerate temporarily for pragmatic reasons but did not in fact condone, extends further than Leibowitz's less value-laden assumption: that their status simply reflected women's status in general society. Where precedent and formal reasoning do not suffice, Rabbi Berkovits sometimes promotes practical solutions that on the surface appear similar to the creative innovations of those formalists who feel free to rely upon the leeway provided by current halakhic lacunae. His justification for such innovations is different. With his more teleological approach to *halakhah* (viewing it as developing toward a larger purpose), it seems he is prepared to go further than the formalists in interpreting some of the established norms of *halakhah* as context-bound. He is open to challenging these norms on strength of the appeal to more general principles that are not fully delineated. Moreover, unlike the formalists, he regards these overarching principles as part and parcel of "pure" *halakhah*, and not just as guidelines to be applied judiciously to the more fluid questions of public policy.

Thus, Rabbi Berkovits's teleological view of *halakhah* allows him to include considerations beyond the formal in his halakhic assessment of women's prayer groups. In addressing this issue, he takes into account women's own views about which acts have religious value for them. His argument for supporting them begins with a formal consideration; he enlists the fact that women do not legally constitute a quorum for communal prayer in order to suggest (in direct opposition to Rabbi Meiselman) that there is no halakhic advantage to their individual prayers in the presence of a male quorum over conducting prayers for themselves. He then adds, however, that because the prayer experience in a women's service is more meaningful to them than participating in communal services from which they feel excluded, it may even be halakhically superior, for it may bring them nearer to the experience of Jewish unity that was intended by Torah.[27]

Berkovits's nonformalist approach extends to other women's issues as well. In his eyes, the acceptance of women's testimony in the courts does more than help solve the problem of *agunot*. It reflects deeper issues, such as the extent of women's responsibility for ensuring social justice in the world. Beyond public policy, allowing women the vote is a statement about the halakhic conception of woman: that she can act autonomously in both the family structure and in the public domain. Whether to consider three women in the presence of men a quorum and thus grant one the privilege of inviting others to say grace after meals (*zimmun*)—apart from the technical consideration of hierarchy of obligation (rabbinical rather than biblical)—is not merely a question of modesty and social propriety; it is a question of women's personal humanity and dignity (*kvod habriyot*).[28]

Berkovits cites with approval the decision of his teacher, Rabbi Yehiel Yaakov Weinberg, who in the early part of the twentieth century defended *bat mitzvah* celebrations for girls. Despite superficial similarities to Christian confirmation ceremonies, Weinberg permitted the practice because prohibiting it would constitute a serious affront to their sense of human dignity.[29] Berkovits's justification for the acceptance of women's testimony in rabbinical courts,[30] or their appointment to public office,[31] is also context-related: they have already achieved the Torah ideal in general society. To circumvent the problem of recalcitrant husbands who won't grant divorces, he relies upon precedents provided by rabbinic authorities of previous generations, calling for the reinstitution of conditional marriage contracts.[32] In the case of a woman who is already an *agunah*, he again relies on precedent in sanctioning retroactive nullification of the marriage agreement.[33] These recommendations, despite the fact that they overthrow more established halakhic norms, were made on the strength of overarching halakhic principles such as preventing the desecration of God's name (*hillul hashem*) and protecting the dignity of the daughters of Israel. With regard to the question of women's learning, Berkovits is unequivocal: the rabbinic view discouraging women's study

was a completely time-conditioned, midrashic interpretation. . . . With the comprehensive education they receive, present-day girls and women . . . should study Torah comprehensively and in depth, so that they may integrate their secular knowledge into a Torah-taught world-view of meanings and values.[34]

Rabbi Berman's distinction between legal objectives and their by-products. In his classic article, "The Status of Women in Halakhic Judaism," Saul Berman combines elements of a formalist view with an even looser version of the teleological approach offered by Berkovits.[35] He describes *halakhah* as a status-oriented legal system whose basic laws protect social interests through assigning roles and classes with differing responsibilities toward each other. Once this protection is assured, those laws may be modified to ensure the highest possible level of individual rights consonant with the desired social goals. That pattern is reversed in a modern, contract-oriented legal system; its basic laws are those that assure the rights of individuals, and they are then modified or limited only to the extent necessary to secure certain basic social interests.

Rabbi Berman seeks to avoid the temptation of the apologist to employ some neat formulation that would provide a comprehensive key to women's halakhic status. Nevertheless, he does discern a certain broad pattern in the tradition: the social interest of centering women almost exclusively in the home and protecting family stability. Berman recognizes that this has created several serious areas of discontent for women, particularly in the realm of marriage and divorce and in the perception of women as relegated by nature to a service role. On the strength of his assumption that many of the problematic elements in women's status today are mere side effects of a legal system based on the conferral of status, he concludes that if the limitations on women no longer serve any positive purpose and may ultimately interfere with attaining the central social goal, "it is the unavoidable responsibility of religious leaders to do all within their power to eliminate these detrimental side effects."[36]

Writing in 1973, before either women's prayer groups or the learning revolution had made their mark on Modern Orthodoxy, Rabbi Berman, in his classic article "The Status of Women in Halakhic Judaism" does not address these issues. Despite doubt as to whether the initiative of a small number of religious women who had begun donning *tallit* and *tefillin* daily would become widespread, he acknowledges precedent for it in *halakhah*. He recognizes that in appropriating such practices for themselves some women have discovered a vital source of religious expression and strength. Like Berkovits, he also encourages women to develop in a creative fashion whatever additional forms of expression they find conducive to their religious growth, within that discretionary realm of *halakhah* that is responsive to sociological considerations. As for the advancement of women's learning, Berman now sponsors a study program for the training of female religious leaders, alongside a similar program for men.

Anomalies and inconsistencies

Even this cursory survey of Modern Orthodox attempts to identify reliable criteria for deciding women's issues, on the basis of a comprehensive theory of *halakhah* that distinguishes between fixed and contingent aspects of *halakhah,* reveals them insufficient as explanations of current halakhic policy.

Regarding the practical conclusions of conservatively inclined formalists, such as Rabbis Twersky and Meiselman, who define the fixed element of *halakhah* as almost total: is there really a difference in formal principle between allowing women to form their own prayer groups and allowing them to study Torah? Extending the question further, is there a formal difference that can be invoked to explain banning women's prayer groups, while allowing women to assume the obligations of hearing the *shofar* and sitting in the *sukkah*? Similarly, can a formal principle explain the willingness of the rabbis in talmudic times to allow women to lay their weight on a sacrificial animal in order to grant them "spiritual pleasure" (*nahat ruah*),[37] as opposed to the objection of many contemporary rabbis to passing them a Torah scroll to kiss in the synagogue? Such anomalies can only lead to the conclusion that considerations beyond the ken acknowledged by a position of stringent formalism do play a determining role in the decisions. The claim that virtually all of the *halakhah* falls under the rubric of a formalism that precludes discretionary considerations (and allows no room for additional goals or agendas) is overstated.

As opposed to the stringent formalists, more moderate Soloveitchikians, such as the Frimer brothers, prefer to justify halakhic inconsistencies by relegating them all to a more broadly defined area of public policy that leaves room for flexible decision-making. However, the decision as to what is "pure" *halakhah* and what is public policy itself seems a matter of public policy, socially conditioned and bound up with the biases of those who determine it. How laws are classified is very much a matter of the eyes of the beholder. Although Aryeh Frimer has characterized more blatantly instrumentalist approaches to *halakhah* than his own as intellectually dishonest ("determining the location of the bull's eye only after shooting their arrows"),[38] what he has not realized is that the very determination of what the bull's eye *is* can be characterized as a discretionary matter. A case in point is Rabbi Meiselman's employing a definition of public worship to prohibit women's prayer groups in principle, whereas Twersky defines this ban, though absolute, as a matter of public policy. The ultimate irrelevance of such classifications is further demonstrated by Berkovits's presenting as a basis of leniency the technical argument of women's formal exemption, while Meiselman uses this same argument to opposite effect.

Despite his more stringent formalism, Leibowitz's interest—like that of the Frimers—is to expand upon the halakhic status quo regarding women rather than preserve it intact. Nevertheless, similar flaws of tendentiousness can be detected in his artificial attempt to distinguish between a category of *diavad* and *lekhathila*. First, it does not match the use of these terms in the halakhic literature.[39] Moreover, viewing issues of modesty (and perhaps also issues surrounding women's status in public life) simply as determined by social circumstances snags him in several contradictions in terms of his own definitions. A halakhic responsiveness to contingent social conditions may indeed be evident in limitations on women's dress, their right to positions of authority, and their participation in public life (all of which in Leibowitz's opinion are after-the-fact considerations). But is it really possible to distinguish between this responsiveness and a theocentric imperviousness to social conditions in other areas, such as sexual taboos (*arayot*) and family purity laws (which he relegates to the a priori realm of *lekhathila*)? No historian or religious anthropologist would find it difficult to claim that limitations of the latter sort also bear the influence of customary practices of the time.[40]

As for the issue of women's Torah study, it is as problematic for Leibowitz as it is for Meiselman to categorize the obligation to study Torah as a public policy issue, rather than as a clear-cut obligation belonging to that fixed and eternal element of *halakhah* that knows no outside considerations. And if this anomaly is explained by distinguishing between two senses of *talmud Torah* (study for the sake of the *mitzvah* as opposed to study for the sake of its fringe spiritual benefits),[41] could not this same distinction be applied (as indeed it is applied by implication in Berkovits's discussions) with regard to prayer?

A similar charge of subjective bias can be made against Berkovits, who claims to find support in the halakhic corpus for a contemporary moral vision and uses this as the yardstick for change. Fathoming the divine purpose is an extremely speculative affair. When seeking in past precedent a reflection of our current moral sensibilities, there is always the danger of wishful thinking. So if the formalists' distinctions between "pure" *halakhah* and its variable elements—all of which would confirm their interest in maintaining the status quo—are suspiciously tendentious, the nonformal, teleological camp's selective discovery in the Torah of affirmation for twentieth-century views is all the more suspect. Are present notions of God's intentions really the only criterion for deciding when to rely on original texts and when to accept them with the accretion of two thousand years of interpretation? Assuming an alternative preconception, is there not at least as much basis in the interpretive tradition for the nonformalist to classify organized Torah study for women as a violation of the *elan* of *halakhah* as it has been understood for generations? Indeed, this is what Twersky does with respect to women-only prayer groups.

An example of this type of bias—even as he urges his colleagues against falling into this trap—is highlighted in the impassioned plea of Joel Wolowelsky, a more liberally inclined Modern Orthodox educator sympathetic to women's wish to recite the mourner's prayer (*kaddish*) in a men's *minyan*. Objection to women reciting the prayer persists in most Orthodox communities, despite known precedents for this practice in Lithuania (where some communities even allowed bereaved women to briefly enter the men's section). Wolowelsky argues:

Women have the same psychological response to death as men. Why should they not be offered the same traditional tools for responding? But such reasoning plays only a small role in the traditional assessment of this issue. Psychological insights must flow from the realities of *halakhah,* not conversely. The question of women saying *kaddish* must be addressed through the sources and logic of *halakhah,* and not through current formulations of its ethos.[42]

The problem with this argument is the proposition that there are "sources and logic of *halakhah*" that are capable of leading to halakhic realities and psychological insights without the mediation of current formulations of the halakhic ethos. Wolowelsky assumes that taken on their own, these sources and logic are on the women's side in this matter, but a *posek* who holds a different view of women's nature might understand the sources and their logical applications differently.

Even Rabbi Berman's minimalist theory—that the guiding principle in *halakhot* concerning women is the social interest in relegating responsibility for the family mainly to them, and most of the undesirable side effects of this principle are simply inadvertent—does not suffice as explanation for the discrepancies in rulings regarding women's issues. As we saw in chapter 2, the desire to protect women's special role in the home is indeed cited often as the reason for the exemption of women from the time-bound *mitzvot*. Berman stops short of viewing these by-products of the social principle as directly cultivated by the religious system as a whole—a conclusion with which not all feminists agree.[43] If allowing women to devote themselves to their important duties at home is truly the rationale behind women's unique halakhic status, they ask, how are we to explain the talmudic exemption of women from the *mitzvot* to be fruitful and multiply or to educate their children?[44]

In sum, the interpretive play allowed for by any meta-halakhic theory leads one to believe that the dressing up of contingent causes with a legal rationale is something that only comes after the fact. While there may be good reasons for distinguishing between the issue of women's Torah study and that of women-only prayer groups, positivist theories regarding distinctions between fixed and contingent elements in the *halakhah* are not their likeliest source. One more plausible explanation might be the fact that women's *tefillah* groups were initiated in the Diaspora, where synagogue affiliation serves much more as a focal point of Jewish identity (but for this reason also invests considerable authority in the rabbi in charge). The learning revolution, by contrast, began and is still centered primarily in Israel, where the existence of an educated laity allows more room for grassroots initiative that does not necessarily seek the approbation of the official establishment. Orthodox Diaspora initiatives are also particularly constrained by the need to accentuate symbolic differences between themselves and rival denominations. While greater egalitarianism in Orthodox prayer format would constitute a breach of this constraint, greater dedication on the part of women to traditional Torah study would not, as non-Orthodox movements present no competition on this front.

Another reason may be that on the immediately experiential and symbolic levels, the vision of women taking an active part in public worship may be more powerfully upsetting than the sight of women studying in their own *bet midrash*. As Orthodox feminist Tova Hartman Halbertal has suggested, "I wonder whether it might be the sudden strangeness of seeing women in a group, led by a *hazzanit* (prayer leader), women. . . . chanting a tune that only men have sung?"[45] That women opt for their own services even when the option of joining the men is available is also significant. Perhaps for this reason, the impetus for women-only prayer groups emerges as the product of a more consciously feminist impulse—indicating a sense of something missing for the women in the normal service. On Hartman Halbertal's understanding, acquiescing to women's *tefillah* groups may be tantamount to an admission that tradition has not wholly defined women's needs, and to a declaration on their part that "we can get to God on our own, without the mediation of men. Our congregating has religious significance."[46]

A third reason for greater toleration for women's study may be that their learning satisfies, at least for the moment, a more universally felt need of the women themselves; therefore it cannot be resisted. It has also managed to persist long enough to convince halakhic authorities—rightly or wrongly—that this is an innovation that can be co-opted to advantage by the existing system for the benefit of Torah even as defined by prevailing norms. Indeed, in the more conservative element of the Orthodox community, the

heightened zeal for learning has translated into strong ideological identification with the ideal of Torah learning for men, and a willingness to support it
with great devotion. Women graduates of the Beth Jacob schools routinely
take on the role of "superwomen." In addition to raising large families, and
studying for themselves whenever possible, they also assume most of their
families' financial burdens, teaching, tending stores, working in banks, and
increasingly, learning high-tech skills, in order to allow their husbands to
continue learning full-time. Under the circumstances, one rabbi officiating at
ultra-Orthodox weddings has expressed doubt whether he can, in good
faith, repeat the formula of the traditional marriage contract, in which the
groom undertakes to provide for his wife and family. Yet, despite the blatant
break with tradition that this represents,[47] no massive rabbinic outcry has
been registered against the reversal of halakhically prescribed gender roles
effected by *this* outcome of women's learning!

Similar allegations of inconsistency in the use of meta-halakhic theory
may be applied to a much broader array of women's issues. The multitude of
interpretive options allowed for by the varieties of formalism and nonformalism gives cause for skepticism regarding the adequacy of any meta-
halakhic theory of legal positivism as a tool for addressing women's concerns. The fact that even within the accepted definitions of any particular
theory, the distinctions between fixed and contingent law are often applied
in an arbitrary and inconsistent manner merely intensifies such doubts. The
disparity between the various ways such distinctions are drawn indicates
that all systematic explanations of halakhic process are artificial constructs
unequal to the task of providing a consistent explanation for present rulings. Neither do they fulfill their promise as a reliable guide for assessing the
halakhic viability of new proposals or interpretations, while still preserving
some basic core of the law free of contingencies and subjective bias. Close
examination of rulings based on distinctions between one element of *halakhah* that is immutable and another that is sociologically determined, and
therefore open to change, reveals that such distinctions can be used tenden-
tiously in order to support positions that were arrived at by independent
means, and do not reveal the true forces at work.

Strategies for protecting the status quo

Meta-halakhic theory may indeed make a practical difference to the *form*
that halakhic rulings on women's issues take. It can determine which area of
the *halakhah*—if any—is amenable to the deliberate application of those
strategies and modes of legal circumvention provided by halakhic tradition,
and which is hypothetically closed to discussion. Whether or not the final
outcome of such distinctions leaves *any* area of the law free of contingency
and subject bias is another matter. This point is illustrated again and again in
a lively electronic forum known as the WTN (Women's Tefillah Network),

which was first founded as a support group for Orthodox women engaged in their own prayer groups. Because discussions on this listserve often branch out into learned analyses of halakhic issues concerning women, the forum was once dubbed by one of its participants—with some measure of justice—the "virtual Talmud" of women. What emerges from its "pages" is that just as there are halakhic strategies that hold promise of opening up new possibilities for women, so are there other strategies that can be used to protect the status quo. Moreover, it is not within the power of any meta-halakhic theory per se to limit the choice. The strategies include:

Inconsistent application of exclusionary textual readings. Aside from a few cases that explicitly stipulate "man or woman," most of the laws of the Torah are phrased in the masculine. The Talmud nevertheless establishes that the Torah regards men and women as equally culpable for all transgressions of biblical law.[48] However, the same rabbinic literature contains many instances in which the sages are more exacting in their reading, concluding from the use of the masculine gender that given verses do not apply to women. Thus, for example, the basis for defining a congregation (*edah*) as ten or more *men* is the fact that in the Torah both the community of Korah (Num. 16–17) and desert spies sent to spy out the land of Canaan (Num. 14:27) were called *edah* and both groups numbered men only.[49] For this reason, women are excluded from the quorum of ten that requires the recitation of certain blessings for the sanctification of God's name (*devarim shebikedushah*). Nonetheless, women may be counted as part of a quorum of ten for the purpose of obligating someone to sanctify God's name through martyrdom.[50] This appears paradoxical to say the least. Another example of an exclusionary reading of the scriptural text bearing tremendous cultural repercussions is the traditional explanation for the ban on women studying Torah. Here again the Talmud[51] bases its exclusionary ruling on a biblical phrase: "and you shall teach these to your sons" (Deut. 11:19), inferring that daughters were not included. The same type of reading is applied to verses of another biblical passage (Lev., chapter 1) as the basis for women's exclusion from any ritual activity in the Temple.[52] The term "citizen of Israel" (*ezrakh*) provides additional illustration of the arbitrary way such verses are interpreted: in the case of the obligation to dwell in a *sukkah*, this term is taken as excluding women, whereas in other instances it is understood as including them.[53]

The most incredible example of an exclusionary reading of the biblical text pertains to the highly valued *mitzvah* of reproduction. For obvious biological reasons one would expect this commandment to be considered the special preserve of women, yet the general consensus of the *poskim* is that it does not apply to them.[54] The fact that the biblical injunction to "be fruitful and multiply" is phrased in the plural compounds the difficulty. Talmudic discussion already queries the basis for this discrimination.[55] The several justifications that are offered there and in subsequent halakhic literature are not entirely convincing.[56] If the immutable element of *halakhah* is indeed determined by purely formal considerations, how are we to explain the apparent arbitrariness of these textual interpretations? The anomalies belie explanations of women's status in *halakhah* as simply the technical working out of abstract formal considerations.

As noted in chapter one, the explanation most frequently offered for variant readings of laws written in the male gender is the principle of women's exclusion from all positive *mitzvot* that are time-bound.[57] The Talmud itself, however, already struggles at length with the adequacy of this principle[58] when there are so many exceptions to this rule.[59] The prevalence of these leads the talmudic sage R. Yohanan to declare that one cannot rely on such principles at all, even when a careful list of exceptions comes to confirm the existence of a general rule.[60] The notion of a fixed and untouchable element of the *halakhah* governed by consistent and comprehensive rules stemming from the texts themselves just does not seem to apply.

Arbitrary application of nonformal exclusionary principles. When precedent or formal considerations and rules of procedure do not provide adequate basis for women's exclusion, additional considerations are often brought to bear. These considerations belong to the same stock of overarching nonformal principles that has occasionally been mined in order to increase options for women, but they can serve to achieve the opposite effect. The nonformalist may regard such principles an integral part of the law itself, while the formalist will believe they are meant to guide the law on questions of public policy. Either way, these considerations are more effective as exclusionary measures than the formal notion of time-bound commandments, which women may still decide to take on voluntarily. They bar women from areas that have become men's preserve, even when this exclusion is not warranted by straightforward legal considerations.

One example is the long-established exclusion of women from positions of authority. As we have seen in chapter 1, Maimonides grounds this exclusion on the biblical verse that speaks of appointing a king and not a queen,[61] despite significant biblical precedent for the acceptance of a woman as judge or queen. Such an aberration demands explanation.[62] One abiding apologetic that we encountered earlier lauds the woman's place in the home. Another suggests that women's emotional nature renders them both more vulnerable and unreliable and thus less suitable for such activities. In addition, the claim that women's appearance in public compromises their modesty is brought to bear. A further principle introduced in connection with public ritual as already noted is that of *kevod hatzibbur.*[63]

Two similar exclusionary principles that are enlisted to support strictures on female participation in essentially permitted halakhic activities are *zila milta* (an impropriety or disgrace of usual standards) and *ein havrutan na'ah* ("their company is unbecoming").[64] *Zila milta* is invoked to justify discouraging women from reciting the ceremonial blessing over wine (*kiddush*) on behalf of men (thus fulfilling the men's obligation), or on their own behalf in the presence of men (even under conditions where this may be halakhically preferable).[65] *Ein havrutan na'ah* is used to support prohibiting women from being counted as part of the required quorum of three entitled to invite recitation of blessings after the meal (*zimmun*).

Other nonformal considerations are brought to bear with regard to women who wish to take upon themselves the *mitzvah* of *tefillin*, usually thought of as a time-bound commandment.[66] The wish to take on this *mitzvah* has generally met with a vehement resistance and hostility that is not easily explained on formal grounds, since other initiatives on the part of women to taking on time-bound mitzvot have earned them approval. The arguments that are introduced to support this exclusion and to discourage women from voluntarily taking on the *mitzvah* reveal a double standard of scrupulousness for men and women.

Chief among the more offensive and less widely known principles that are invoked here concerns women's relationship to their bodies; that is, their supposed lack of attention to personal hygiene.[67] Since the *mitzvah* of *tefillin* deals with matters of holiness, one is obliged when performing it to take great care that the body is clean. The allegation that women don't know how to keep themselves clean raises almost as many hoots of protest among feminists as the talmudic statement that women are lazy. (The latter charge, brought as justification for not relying upon women to perform the pre-Passover ritual of checking that one's home is free of forbidden leaven [*bedikat hametz*], adds insult to injury, as women are invariably landed with the heaviest burdens of pre-Passover cleaning). The reference to cleanliness in the written sources primarily concerns flatulence. Given that the danger of this is no greater in the case of women, the special disqualification of women makes little sense.[68] One of the major arguments brought in defense of stringency nevertheless is that since it is so difficult to maintain the high level of bodily cleanliness required for *tefillin,* only those who are actually obligated to do so should risk failing this standard. This argument, however, may also be rebutted.[69]

Excessive scrutiny of women's motivation. Another objection raised to women wearing *tallit* or *tzitzit* (and occasionally also to their donning of *tefillin*) is the suspicion of religious exhibitionism (*mishum yoharah*).[70] This objection merges with a more general consideration of motivation, by now an established standard for measuring the danger to the integrity of the *halakhah* posed by women's assuming male forms of worship. If a *posek* believes that the motives for proposing any innovation are not purely halakhic, this is regarded as sufficient basis for a ban, even if the innovation is technically permissible. The reasoning is that initiatives for women's increased ritual participation must flow from the realities of *halakhah,* and not vice versa.

Both Rabbi Meiselman[71] and the Frimer brothers[72] tell of an Orthodox woman in Boston who asked her local rabbi for permission to wear a *tallit* in synagogue. Because this was a major departure from accepted custom, the rabbi expressed hesitation and recommended that she turn to Rabbi Soloveitchik for approval. R. Soloveitchik suggested that she proceed gradually, by first wearing the prayer shawl without ritual fringes for a period of three months, and then report back to him. Upon her return, she told R. Soloveitchik that the trial period had been the most inspiring experience of her life, and she was ready to proceed further. But R. Soloveitchik's response was to point out to her that wearing a *tallit* without *tsitsit* is halakhically meaningless. He concluded that her sense of religious euphoria was generated by something other than the religiously authentic element of *mitzvah.* Consequently, he forbade her to wear a true *tallit,* concluding that this would be a misuse of *mitzvot* for a purpose other than the service of God.[73]

The popularity of the *mishum yoharah* argument in recent years, despite its rather weak exclusionary power (tacitly admitting that there is no other genuine basis for such exclusion), is fair indication of the challenge that *poskim* currently perceive in the face of a rapidly shifting social milieu vulnerable to extra-halakhic influences. As Rabbi David Bleich, a prominent halakhic expositor of Modern Orthodoxy, writes in another context: "It is the pretense of seeking halakhic authenticity and the distortion of sources in order to arrive at preconceived conclusions which is particularly offensive."[74]

In practice, however, distinctions between the sincere wish for greater participation in religious observance and less noble considerations cannot readily be drawn. In modern times, the very wish for a more active role in *mitzvot* may already be the subconscious influence of feminist attitudes and new self-images. On the other hand, the fresh interest of women in halakhic rigor may be traceable to Rabbi Soloveitchik's notion of objectified *halakhah,* which has made its impact upon the sensibilities of religiously observant women and men alike. Another factor is a new confrontation with textual sources, resulting from the breakdown of the mimetic tradition of premodern times in which conduct was governed more by cultural expectation than consultation of codes. Haym Soloveitchik, son of the Rav, describes the modern believer's quest for a "perfect fit" between behavior and the prescriptions of *halakhah,* contending that "faultless congruence between conception and performance" has become the hallmark of contemporary Orthodoxy, in the effort to reassert its difference from the surrounding culture.[75]

Returning to the Bostonian would-be *tallit*-wearer, women confronting it have not only commented on the story's narrowly legalistic definition of authentic religious worship, but have also wondered what the Rav's response would have been if the woman had been disappointed with her three-month trial. Would he have then advised her to wear a halakhically kosher *tallit?* As he was one of the first leaders of Modern Orthodoxy to insist upon higher education for women, R. Soloveitchik cannot be suspected of disrespect to women or their intellectual capabilities. Yet his response in this case shows a particular woman, in her innocence, placed in an invidious situation in which no answer would have been acceptable.[76]

A woman whose notions of religiosity are derived from the logic of the codified texts, unmediated by the filter of lived tradition, may well be led to fresh conclusions that fly in the face of traditionally accepted norms. Such a woman might in all sincerity be convinced that donning *tefillin* (considered more radical and problematic than *tallit*) is the most reasonable consequence of her voluntary commitment to recite the prayer of *Shema,* which prescribes that God's words be a mark on the arm and forehead. This line of reasoning is arguably far more compelling, despite its novelty for women, than is abstinence simply because the practice was unheard-of in earlier generations. Without the conditioning of the generations of women who found their spirituality in the running of their homes and rearing of their children, such a woman may genuinely believe in the halakhic superiority of her consistent stance. There are no easy distinctions between context-free halakhic zeal and the incorporation of ideals foreign to Judaism under the pretext of religious fervor.

Application of double standards. In contrast to the stringent scrutiny of women's motivation, attitudes toward men's motivation to perform *mitzvot* are more relaxed, and even lackadaisical. As in the case of *tefillin* and the questioning of women's ability to maintain a *guf naki* in that context, this double standard of scrupulousness with regard to motivation is sometimes justified on formal grounds: Since men are obligated to perform certain *mitzvot,* their motivation (or lack of it) is beside the point. But since women are not obligated, more exacting standards are called for. Sometimes the challenge is phrased as a rhetorical question: "Have women already complied so completely with all the obligations that are clearly incumbent upon them that they must look for more?" Often the yardstick is women's compliance with norms of modesty in dress or with standards of charity, which by its very nature knows no bounds. Even when it is offered in a spirit of religious earnestness and sincere halakhic commitment, feminists recoil from this schoolmarmish approach to the spiritual life as an inconclusive checklist of routine preliminaries to be ticked off before one gets to the real prize. They also take issue with having the legitimate forms of their spiritual expression circumscribed to a feminine stereotype defined by men, who see modesty and voluntary good works as its chief components. But even when complying with an essentially male configuring of the initial ground rules, indications of a double standard remain.

First, there is a traditional principle of valuing performance of *mitzvot,* irrespective of motive. While greater merit is indeed attributed to a person who is obliged to perform a *mitzvah* and does so (*gadol hametzuveh veoseh*), voluntary performance is also deemed praiseworthy. In this connection women are no different than other classes of population that seek full participation in the life of *mitzvot* despite their lesser obligation. They may take their cue, for example, from sympathetic accounts in the sources of pious men who, despite physical limitation that exempted them from the requirement to perform certain *mitzvot,* nevertheless strove to continue doing so.[77] And, indeed, although women are not obliged to observe *mitzvot* such as *tzitzit, tefillin, sukkah,* or the study of Torah, the classical halakhic sources establish that if they do so voluntarily, they merit reward.[78] Thus we see that voluntary acceptance of such acts qualifies as more than "merely a type of sport," as Leibowitz put it,[79] and is not devoid of religious significance.

Second, there is the traditional notion that ulterior motives are acceptable because they lead to pure ones (*mitokh shelo lishmah ba lishmah*). Often unworthy motivation is tolerated, in hope that the very practice of *mitzvot,* even for the wrong reasons, will eventually lead to performance for its own sake. Rabbi Twersky discredits women's prayer groups because the pomp and ceremony of their convening contradicts the essence of prayer, but are *men* impervious to considerations of ceremony? Their usual synagogue service, replete with its array of honors carefully distributed according to rank and prestige, is, if anything, more liable on this account.

Male-oriented considerations of halakhic integrity, denominational politics, and communal identity. A more contemporary justification for halakhic discrimination between men and women is the specter of secularism or other threats to halakhic authority. This threat translates into extreme regard for the integrity of the halakhic system as it stands, particularly in the realm of synagogue ritual. The conservatives feel a need to set themselves off from other less halakhic groups within the Jewish community or from the world at large. At issue for the *posek* is not simply his own community, but other, more extreme, communities from which he would not want to cut himself (or his followers) off.

The argument that the integrity of the halakhic system demands unswerving maintenance of the status quo is tremendously powerful; it can, in principle, be used against virtually any relaxation of accepted practice. Going one step further, some *poskim* regard the prohibition of even what has been permitted as preferable to "tinkering with tradition" (despite the recognition of other authorities that this might well encourage transgressing what is forbidden). Thus, for example, Rabbi Moshe Eisemann, the spiritual guide (*mashgiah*) of Ner Yisrael Yeshiva, declaring his opposition to women making use of the water passed around for ritual rinsing of fingers at the end of the meal (*mayim aharonim*), asks: "Why not just tell the truth . . . [and] make a powerful statement that we refuse to tinker with our traditions, that we want our daughters, as far as possible, to be like our mothers and like their mothers before them?"[80]

Such appeals to tradition and the importance of preserving continuity with the customs of the past[81] are not persuasive to women who have developed a more independent self-image. When that past itself was formulated completely in terms of male terms and interests, or—at best—only in terms of men's conceptions of what is good and proper for women, the justice of the demand is called into question.

Although they may share some of the conservative interests of the male authorities who are doing the deciding, the feminists' scale of priorities is often at odds with that of the *poskim*. Because women traditionally have been the excluded class, maintaining the integrity of the tradition means perpetuation of their exclusion. Because they are not at the helm, their interests are often the first to be sacrificed, in the interest of emphasizing religious differences between the community of the faithful and the outsiders.[82]

Disillusion with Second-Stage Feminism

The introduction of so many exclusionary principles and considerations in the effort to discourage women from voluntarily assuming extra *mitzvot* or to discourage their greater participation in the more public aspects of religious life raises many questions. The more moderate second-stage feminists suffice with the notion that no one theory can ever sufficiently explain the halakhic status of women. They may find it preferable to compile a list of factors, each a partial explanation for women's unique status in *halakhah*. Partial explanations testify to the ups and downs in the status of women, the status of certain *mitzvot,* and the nature of women and of *mitzvot* as conceived by the commentators and halakhic decisors over the generations.

Viewed from this combination of internal and external perspectives, *halakhah* is an unwieldy body that is not governed by one legitimate methodology or homogeneous moral vision that endured two thousand years. Nor were its rulings translated uniformly in all their details by consistent adherence to precedent or one systematic master plan. Sometimes its rulings are a deliberate expression of moral principles; sometimes they represent the working out of its own internal grammar. Sometimes, however, they are the reflection of passing sociological conceptions, parading under the cloak of eternal verities. Thus formal explanations for women's exclusion are often brought simply in order to provide legal corroboration for what has already become commonly accepted practice.

For second-stage Jewish feminists, there is no denying that each generation saw things differently than did the previous generation, and found itself limited by precedent. Continuity was maintained thanks to the fact that rabbinic exegetical ingenuity knows no limits.[83] The early rabbinic mind was never inhibited by formal legalities, and the hermeneutic activity of the great rabbis throughout the ages consisted of a reconstruction of the past in light of their present social reality and spiritual needs. Not every halakhic change could be justified formally by the appeal to logic. Neither did accurate reconstruction of textual or historical precedent always play a critical role. The technical details bore some constitutive influence, but did not necessarily function in every case in accordance with a unified and predetermined scheme. The decisive factor, so it is claimed, was always the contemporary world of the *posek,* and the interpretive tools that he brought with him to the text.

Some moderates regard the rather amorphous and unpredictable character of *halakhah* as its most admirable feature. Those who seek integrity and credibility by flattening out the *halakhah* into some uniform mode of artificial neatness trivialize its vibrancy as a living organism and run the risk of encouraging mediocre thinking where imagination is called for. Indeed, Modern Orthodox Jews often cite the *halakhah*'s pluralism, reflecting the open-ended aspect of God's word, as its greatest virtue.[84] Contradictions are the life blood allowing any progressive system to grow.

Other feminist critics have come to reject this sympathy for halakhic anomalies and inconsistencies. Sensitive to the way that power relations regulate the production of legal discourse and practice, these more radical critics problematize women's halakhic status as a whole, abandoning the effort to formulate more nuanced explanations of halakhic development. This line of thinking is strongly influenced by the revolutionary methods of social analysis introduced by the French postmodern philosopher, Michel Foucault, who managed to turn many a conventional insight on its head.[85] Foucault reveals the darker underside of social practices, and he demonstrates how the subjectification of humans is not part of the ready-made order of things but rather is reconstructed by power relations. In similar fashion, feminist critics of the *halakhah* conclude that it was the desire to banish women from male centers of power and prestige, rather than the wish to preserve the family for the benefit of society at large, that nurtured the original interest in distancing women from key areas of religious life.

Grim versions of this view are fueled by academic studies that attribute the rabbinic exclusion of women from the obligation to have children to a primeval male jealousy and fear of women's reproductive powers, and men's need to compensate for their natural inability by acquiring ultimate control over this privilege.[86] The exaggerated emphasis on essential differences between men and women in Jewish tradition is ascribed to similar motives, as is the obsessive preoccupation of *halakhah* with the sexual temptations that could arise from social intermingling. Fear of sexual temptation is now understood not as the *cause* for separation of the sexes, but as the *result* of men's interest in establishing exclusive privileges of hegemony. This artificially blown-up emphasis is then pressed into the service of male interests, by setting up a universe of discourse based on the necessity for extreme precaution against the negative influence of female seduction.

The newfound proficiency that women have gained by independently reading halakhic sources extends this suspicion to present-day decision-making as well. When "after-the-fact" rationalizations for women's exclusion from certain religious practices are no longer relevant under prevailing social conditions, pious concern for preserving halakhic integrity may also be accompanied by less honorable motives. In a critical analysis of the Meiselman-Twersky opposition to women's prayer groups, Tova Hartman Halbertal notes the unusually volatile rhetoric accompanying their objections, in which the women concerned are described as "silly" and "deceitful," and their activities as "eliciting contempt."[87]

What can it be that elicits this response—the harshness, the virtual violence of the language, the coaching of the arguments in terms of disdain, derision, contempt, assimilationism? What is it that gets at the core of their being? . . . Why are the motives of the women involved under suspicion, not only their behavior—their motives? . . . [Women] are being caricatured by adjectives and definitions that are not theirs. . . . If we don't understand the extremity of this, we can't understand what is going on.

Official explanations for prohibitions appear—at least in part—as an unconscious defense against the threat that women's audacity poses to traditional male authority. As Orthodox feminist Rochelle Millen confesses: "Going over these sources always leaves me with a sense of amazement over how many legal contortions are created in order to withhold religious autonomy from women, so that women may participate only in a manner that leaves them dependent upon men."[88] Hartman Halbertal also notes the fear of halakhic authorities that women, in their newfound independence, will be led to a wholesale examination of their place in the halakhic world and find it wanting.

This fear is seen, for example, in the widespread contemporary objection to women reciting the mourner's prayer in synagogue. A few halakhic authorities have quite frankly admitted that the practice is permissible[89] and (as we saw earlier in this chapter) precedented; the opposition of these authorities is grounded exclusively on the danger they perceive: that it could either weaken allegiance to existing Jewish customs[90] or encourage more radical egalitarianism, thereby inciting a major revolution against of a way of life as it has been known and cherished for centuries.[91] Similar considerations are invoked in opposing the right of women to recite some or all of the seven blessings that are part of the marriage service (for fear that this would lead to demands for mixed seating in public prayer)[92] or in opposing women's readings of the Book of Esther on Purim (for fear that the permissibility of women's constituting a quorum for this activity would be applied to women's prayer groups, according them the formal status of a male *min-*

yan).[93] Even Rabbi Twersky's objection to women's prayer groups, ostensibly grounded on the notion of prayer as an essentially inward experience, relies on this slippery slope argument: such groups, he says, "*nolens volens* lead to the *inevitable* conclusion that the Torah has, God forbid, shortchanged women."[94] Hartman Halbertal sees this as the real motive behind his puzzling appeal to what is basically a weak argument (the notion of prayer as an essentially private experience); obviously the importance of inwardness could just as easily be used to delegitimize other forms of organized prayer as well.

Such fears may indeed be corroborated by recent developments since the voicing of Twersky's original objections. A small number of communities in the United States and Israel that consider themselves Orthodox (including one that Hartman Halbertal helped to found) have implemented more egalitarian forms of worship in the synagogue. These include the practice of calling women up to the Torah and allowing them to lead those portions of the service that are not halakhically defined as prayer, such as the set of hymns welcoming the advent of Sabbath. They rely on minority opinions that halakhic problems with men hearing women sing do not apply to synagogue worship.[95] These practices go beyond the renegade conventions of those liberal congregations that run the divider between men and women down the center of the synagogue (instead of seating women in back of a partition or in the balcony) and, in a few cases, sponsor separate women's Torah readings on synagogue grounds. The new groups rely heavily on arguments in favor of women's Torah reading that are compiled in a weighty article authored by Jerusalem resident Mendel Shapiro, an ordained rabbi of Yeshiva University and alumnus of its law school. Shapiro presents an array of sources and arguments to substantiate the claim that this practice does not constitute a halakhic difficulty in our day and "is at the very least a legitimate halakhic option."[96] He contends that the only grounds for objection is the principle of "the honor of the community" (*kevod hatzibbur*).[97] As we have seen, this refers to the implication that damage to the community's good name would be caused by relying on the services of women and thereby giving the impression that there are not enough men competent to read Torah. Shapiro argues that (a) it is possible to forgo this principle when a community does not view women's reading as damaging its honor, and (b) the concept does not apply in any case in an age where the ability to read is common.

The issue of women's *aliyot* is particularly interesting when compared to that of women's prayer groups. In terms of the traditional narrative of women's place in public ritual, calling both women and men to the Torah at the regular synagogue service is arguably a far more radical breakdown of established gender distinctions, introducing an unfamiliar form of egalitarianism. On the other hand, in formal terms, this practice evades the main fault that formalists of the maximalist variety have found with women-only prayer groups; namely, the creation of "pseudoceremonies" lacking the required quorum of ten men. At the fourth international conference of feminism and Orthodoxy, Rabbi Daniel Sperber, Bar-Ilan University professor of Talmud, defended this position in nonformal terms, arguing that in our day the overarching principle of *kevod haberiyot* (human dignity) surely takes precedence over that of *kevod hatzibbur*.[98] This method of addressing women's desire for more active participation in the service also avoids splintering the community into gendered enclaves (the main reason why the women's groups tend to meet only monthly or on special occasions). In this sense, women-only prayer groups may be serving merely as the temporary training ground for revival of an ancient and more inclusive practice of calling women to the Torah.[99]

The Insufficiency of the Practical Halakhic Approach

Dwelling on the most extreme examples, feminists sometimes evince an intolerance toward the explanations and self-understandings of the halakhic establishment that borders on complete cynicism. When a legal ruling is not an inevitable conclusion of the conceptual architecture of *halakhah,* these critics of the *halakhah* emphasize its contingency. Beyond that, they are also led to undermine the ruling by exposing the political function that it serves in perpetuating women's subjugation. Do the authorities' reservations about women's increased participation in ritual stem, they ask, merely from the wish to protect women from unavoidable God-given limitations?

The predilection of halakhic authorities for implausible justifications of their legal activity emerges as no more than another strategy for preserving the familiarity and comfort of what has traditionally always functioned as an exclusive "men's club."[100] Employment of judicial discretion to fill in gaps where the law is unclear may seem legitimate and even innocuous. However, even the most saintly, well-intentioned, and dedicated of *poskim* operate no less than anyone else in accordance with their own class and gender biases, and they have no less natural a stake in perpetuating a status quo that is right and proper in these terms. In the eyes of many feminists, the negative consequences are not at all mitigated by the possibility that the *poskim* may be totally unaware of the influence of their biases because they are unused to viewing their actions from a critical, external perspective.

Charges of this sort raise doubts regarding the efficacy of second-stage feminism. Because of its vulnerability to misuse by the prevailing male establishment, the halakhic medium on its own is not a useful enough tool for improving the status of women. Says Hartman Halbertal, "Often we assume that the sole task of women is to find a legal precedent. We assume that such discoveries will have contemporary practical consequences."[101] But such efforts may be insufficient. The objections being raised to women's *tefillah* groups and other attempts on the part of women to develop "a self-definition that expands to the spirit of their Judaism" are not primarily halakhic or even intellectual but rather "have to do with how women and women's spirituality are viewed."[102] As the issue is more often than not a feminist and not a halakhic one, the deeper reasons for women's exclusion must also be understood and addressed.

Although the bulk of attention, especially among the more traditionally oriented, is still concentrated upon the practical ramifications of women's unequal status in *halakhah*, other energies are now being directed to more penetrating and theoretical issues characterizing third-stage feminism. As in the feminist movement at large, Jewish feminists who reach this level of the feminist critique no longer approve of proceeding merely by way of the struggle to create equal opportunities for women and their spiritual expression, in accordance with current norms, standards, and procedures. Because of the built-in limitations of the halakhic system and its vulnerability to misuse when operating under the influence of the prevailing gender biases of the male establishment, the practical halakhic approach is ineffective on its own.

·PART III·

The Third Stage:
Revamping the System

At the third level of the feminist critique, ameliorating the status of Jewish women is not merely a matter of exploring how halakhah *can be creatively adjusted to address their concerns. It is also not just a matter of eradicating bigotry on an individual or localized basis. Removing all traces of oppression of women from Judaism involves locating and revising the more deepseated structures of patriarchy that operate in a moral space behind the halakhic scene and are ultimately responsible for its generally androcentric orientation. The fundamental presuppositions of a legal system that regards women as Other—and reveals traces of an overriding fear of their sexuality—must be addressed. The attempt to do so can be divided into three tracks: sociological, theological, and halakhic. In the first chapter of this section, I focus upon representatives of the first two tracks, such as Cynthia Ozick and Judith Plaskow, describing some of the techniques that they, as well as their non-Jewish counterparts employ.*

In the following chapter I evaluate these two tracks and elaborate upon historic, pragmatic, and theological reasons for finding them wanting. I then turn to a more profound theological issue that third-stage feminism raises: divine revelation, which I regard as the most penetrating challenge that feminism poses to Orthodoxy, and one that Orthodox thinking has yet to address.

Another form of third-stage feminism—as represented in the writing of Rachel Adler, who pursues a proactive halakhic track—is described in chapter 8. Adler's suggestions are more appealing to the traditionalist because of her appreciation of the centrality of the halakhic medium to Jewish spirituality. Nevertheless, as is the case with Plaskow and other more radical third-stage feminists, her general rejection of the rabbinic tradition's authoritative assumptions and how they are understood within the established community of halakhic practitioners renders her approach incapable of engaging this tradition on its own terms. Moreover, it fails to address the major theological concern raised when undermining traditional claims to be in concert with a transcendent divine will—a challenge I shall take up in part IV.

CHAPTER 6

Sociological and Historical Revisionism

The Sociological Track

The milder third-stage level of response to women's subordinate status in Jewish tradition, which I shall label sociological revisionism, could be regarded as a position midway between second-stage feminism and a more radical approach. Its relatively benign explanation for women's subordinate status in Jewish tradition points to contingent sociological factors that have more to do with the cultural context in which the religion developed than with any of its inherent principles. Whenever women's general status in society improved, their halakhic responsibilities and privileges expanded accordingly. Scholarly studies trace a connection between women's increased participation in the economic world and the improvement in their halakhic standing.[1] Therefore, what is required beyond halakhic tinkering is to distinguish between the essence of Judaism and the influence of dispensable cultural influences.

The need for sharp distinctions is clearly stated by Orthodox feminist Judith Antonelli, in the introduction to her feminist commentary to the Torah:

misogyny and male supremacy are not inherently "Jewish"; that is, not endemic to *Judaism*. This does not deny, however, that misogyny and male supremacy have entered Jewish *culture* as a sociological phenomenon. Just as this book refutes feminist anti-Judaism, so too does it seek to separate Torah (divine law) from men's sexism, which is an unfortunate and all-too-widespread part of Jewish sociology.[2]

Feminists adopting the sociological approach find comfort in the claim that the inferior status of women is not an essential feature of Judaism. In this case, they argue, we are not bound by religious mandate to perpetuate discriminatory arrangements. In her classic article, "Notes on Asking the Right Question," Cynthia Ozick asserts: "The status of women is, in any Jewish context, by no means a 'theological' question. It is a sociological fact, and that is a much lighter load to carry."[3]

To support her thesis, Ozick compares the Jewish and Christian versions of Eve's sin. Although both paint "a nasty portrait of the First Woman," in the Jewish view, once Adam and Eve are banished as equals from paradise, "that is pretty much that. The human race continues, under realistic—i.e., non-paradisic—conditions. You can take Eve out of Scripture and the nature of divinity continues as before: I-am-that-I-am." In contrast, the Christian scheme has Eve's sin leading to Adam's fall—without which there would be "no need for Redemption, no Crucified Christ and no Vicarious Atonement"; thus, "if you take Eve out of Scripture, Christianity itself vanishes." In general, Ozick maintains, Judaism never placed great stock in theology. It would be entirely misplaced to blame negative attitudes to women on the male imagery that traditional texts employ to describe the nature of God.

The link with restorativism[4]

Ozick's argument notwithstanding, it is worth noting that there is no Jewish monopoly on sociological revisionism. Representatives of this approach can be found among all the monotheistic traditions. In addition to their common interest in distinguishing between sociology and theological "essence," feminist revisionists of all three religions try to state their argument in affirmative terms. As a rule, they are not satisfied with the minimalist premise that hierarchical views of women are not essential to the religious tradition. They prefer to view modern notions of equality as an outgrowth and enhancement of their tradition, rather than as a new and foreign value. They highlight whatever nonpatriarchal motifs can already be found within the monotheistic mold, even when these appear only implicitly or as a minority view. As a result, sacred texts emerge as more complex and equivocal than they appear on the surface and are therefore capable of providing authentic precedents for present norms.

Protestants belonging to the school of liberation theology contend that their tradition started out as egalitarian, in opposition to the surrounding rabbinic culture[5] and assumed its sexist character only with the influx of foreign influences extraneous to the system. Many claim that Jesus originally strove to reform the androcentric nature of the Old Testament, alongside his general aim of eradicating class differences between rich and poor, masters and slaves.[6] Moslems too distinguish between the original authentic tradition and subsequent corruption or deviation from its spirit. Islamic feminist scholars such as Leila Ahmed and Aziza al-Hibri argue that early Islam brought a great improvement in the status of women, given the extreme patriarchal practices that prevailed in the Middle East. Under Mohammad's egalitarian rule, women joined men in prayer and were called upon to testify to God's unity and to Mohammed being His prophet. These scholars see the status of women in Islam deteriorating only after Islam's widespread exposure to Western culture in the wake of Mohammad's conquests.[7]

With respect to Judaism, Blu Greenberg similarly asserts:

True, the original impulse for [seeking dissolution of the hierarchical model in the religious life] derives from feminism, but even if such a movement hadn't evolved, I still would like to think that a creative pondering of the ideals of Torah Judaism might lead to the same conclusions. Thus, the central concern of these observations has to do with organic, internal changes, changes in our private Jewish lives, unmediated by society, quotas, alternative action, and the like—changes based on intrinsic Jewish values and brought about because the halakhic way of life calls them forth.[8]

This restorativist dimension clearly serves Greenberg's wish to avoid a break with the historic past. It also satisfies her religious need to assert a Jewish view of justice that would actively support modern egalitarian notions rather than merely accommodate them by default.

Even Ozick, who—in contrast to Greenberg—admits that she cannot find in the Torah any reference, implicit or otherwise, to the ultimate egalitarian ideal of feminism, does not attribute this lapse solely to sociology. In calling for a corrective "eleventh commandment" ("Thou shalt not lessen the humanity of women!"), she too feels compelled to peg it on the general biblical exhortation to justice and on rabbinic Judaism's subsequent efforts gradually to ameliorate women's status.[9]

This restorativist move in a sense supplements the positivist response of Modern Orthodoxy in the meta-halakhic realm. To the extent that they follow the restorativist track, third-stage feminists also seek some link with what the tradition already "posits." Their innovation is simply in widening the net. Rather than seeking precedent exclusively in established *halakhah*, other less obvious sources of authority are sought from within the tradition.

Historical restorativism

The restorative move in monotheistic religions is generally conducted on two levels. The first involves engaging in revisionist history: unearthing concrete evidence of forgotten practices of the faith community before its ideal standards became "sullied" and mining classic texts for hints of more egalitarian practices. Much research has focused upon uncovering women's "lost history," reconstructing the religious experiences of women over the ages and whatever vestiges of spiritual creativity that can be attributed to them.[10]

Restorativists all agree that only the infiltration of foreign, negative notions of sex and womankind corrupted expression of the authentic religious ideal. There is no consensus, however, as to when this occurred.[11] The differences of opinion reflect differing views about the precise nature of the corruption and what could undo it. As a rule, the further back the restorativist feels she must go in order to find grounds for reinstating the ideal, the greater the entanglement she perceives between tradition and patriarchy, and the more radical the remedy she prescribes.

The idealizing of rabbinic Judaism. Some Jewish restorativists view rabbinic Judaism as congenial to feminist ways of thinking, to the extent that it rejects Hellenism's sharp dichotomy between spirit (as represented by the male) and matter (as represented by the female). Daniel Boyarin cites the rabbinic preference for *midrash,* a literary form that embraces the physical and the concrete, as opposed to Greek allegory, which uses physicality merely as a metaphor pointing to a more abstract and universal reality.[12] He views rabbinic Judaism as predominantly sexist, but he attributes its rejection of the imperialist warrior to the traditional Jewish veneration of the nonaggressive, almost effeminate Diaspora image of the male Torah scholar.[13] In his eyes, at least one crucial distortion of authentic Judaism occurred only with the transformation of gender roles effected by "macho" Zionist ideology.

Others locate the deterioration of women's status in Judaism in the passing from the talmudic to the medieval period, another assessment that enables a favorable view of rabbinic Judaism. Judith Hauptman regards the rabbinic period as essentially initiating a gradual process of repair of women's inferior sociological status.[14] Hauptman takes issue with Jacob Neusner, who until very recently saw the rabbinic attitude to women uncritically reflecting the misogynist norms of the surrounding culture.[15] The Mishnah and Talmud may still be androcentric, she asserts, but the rabbis took many measures to improve the lot of women over that which prevailed in the Bible.[16] This change is reflected, for example, in the rabbinic attributing of impurity to males as well as females under certain conditions. Hauptman also finds encouragement in talmudic evidence of communal women's experiences, indicating that women in this period were not completely isolated from each other in their private domestic environments. In the Mishnah, she points out, we often find women "baking bread together, lending each other pots and pans, and gossiping," as well as conducting business in their homes or in the marketplace. They also appear in rabbinic courts as litigants and as active participants in weddings and funerals.[17] To this one might add significant aggadic statements of concern for women. A *midrash* that takes the trouble to emphasize the inclusion of women in the covenant can also be viewed as an important attempt to correct the exclusionary nature of the original biblical account of the revelation at Sinai.[18] If the gradual move toward egalitarianism never succeeded, Hauptman maintains that this is not because of Jewish constraints, but rather the influence of conflicting tendencies in the surrounding Roman culture.

Looking back to biblical precedent. Others view the rabbinic period in its entirety as an unfortunate veering from biblical precedent. While Israeli biblical scholar Amnon Shapiro admits that the Bible is not a feminist manifesto, he finds in it important trends qualifying its generally patriarchal orientation. These lie mainly in the religious sphere, where equality of the women as subjects before God is emphasized. Biblical women participate alongside men in the sealing of national covenants and on occasions of their renewal. They reveal personal initiative in decisions relating to the survival of their relatives or the nation, at times maneuvering seeming positions of weakness to their advantage. Blurred as these themes are, Shapiro sees in them the basis for spiritual renewal today.[19]

Theodore Friedman, former president of the Conservative movement's Rabbinical Assembly, similarly argues that women in the biblical era still actively participated in every aspect of social life: political, economic, and religious. Like Shapiro, he points to the fact that women were expected to attend the great religious assemblies. They accompanied their husbands on pilgrimages to the Sanctuary and prayed there. They participated in song and dance alongside the men when greeting victorious warriors returning home from war. Women consulted the prophet on Sabbaths and festivals. Mention of biblical prophetesses is unaccompanied by comment on gender or apologetics. Several references are made to females who bear the status of "wise woman." Such women are portrayed as particularly gifted in their powers of speech and persuasion, and appear to engage in what today would be called diplomatic missions.[20]

Friedman claims that the only explicitly misogynist view of women that appears in the Bible is in Ecclesiastes. Biblical scholars date this book somewhere in the Hellenistic period, and find in it a strong Greek influence.[21] This would corroborate the widespread view that the marginalization of women's voices grew in direct proportion to Greek dualism's penetration of Jewish thought. He contends that only in talmudic times are women distanced from public view. Only then do we learn that their public exposure is to be regarded as an affront to their dignity and that their main function is the rearing of children.[22]

Beyond issues of social position, a radical shift between the biblical and talmudic periods is gleaned from what males say about females—moving from unreflective acceptance of a hierarchical social order to justification of gender inequality by an ideology of male superiority. American biblical scholar Tikva Frymer-Kensky draws support for this opinion from recent scholarly studies that attribute essentialist views of gender in the Bible to later sources.[23]

Exegetical restorativism: New ways of learning Torah

In addition to highlighting textual and historical precedents that support their ideal, feminists interested in restorativism concentrate their efforts on reinterpretation of the Bible. The search for early alternative models has led them to develop new ways and methods to study religious texts that are more fruitful for women, or at least generate insights more helpful to their interests. Similar strategies have been developed by their Christian and Islamic counterparts.[24]

Golden thread methodology: Depatriarchalizing the Bible. One technique employs what the post-Christian feminist theologian Daphne Hampson has termed *golden thread methodology.*[25] It looks at holy texts that have become overlaid with sexist interpretations and purports to find underlying messages that could be read as supportive of women's interests. The claim is that the sexist overlay was able to develop either because the original texts did not apply their message specifically to the reality at hand, or because the texts themselves speak in more than one voice. Judith Antonelli's feminist commentary on the Torah[26] provides one example of an extensive Jewish effort to depatriarchalize the Bible, implying that a good restorativist reading entails simply peeling off the centuries of androcentric interpretation that have accrued to the original text.

Some Jewish feminists who adopt this approach have benefited from the work of Christian biblical scholar and feminist theologian Phyllis Trible.[27] Trible acknowledges the male bias of Christian tradition but denies that the biblical texts themselves are misogynist, arguing that even the more flagrantly biased ones can be read differently. Because the texts are often ambiguous, how they are understood depends much on the prior assumptions of the reader. By paying attention to two conflicting viewpoints in the same story, Trible exposes a complex interplay of voices, whereby the less patriarchal one is divine. She understands biblical tales of horrifying female abuse (which she terms *texts of terror*), such as the concubine of Gibeah, as subtle lessons designed to illustrate how ill-treatment of women reflects the degenerating morality of the social order. Thus, she concludes, interpreters have patriarchalized many biblical texts by projecting their androcentric cultural bias onto them; when correctly understood, the texts actually foster the liberation of women. Trible has presented her readers with fresh readings of many texts heretofore held up as paradigmatic for displaying male biases, including the story of Adam and Eve.

The privileging of egalitarian views over other voices in the tradition, on the basis of a depatriarchalized reading of foundational texts, is favored by Moslem feminists as well. For example, they draw confirmation for the legitimacy of egalitarian notions from the creation story of the Koran, by claiming that the original text does not describe Eve as being fashioned from Adam's rib and thus subordinate to him. According to this view, it is only in later Islamic interpretations that reflect Jewish and Christian influence that the rib theme begins to surface.[28]

Multiple thread methodology: Reconstructing the voices of protest. Another means of maintaining continuity with the past is by highlighting shreds of evidence militating against a motif that is decidedly not golden. Operating on a historical level, this highlighting is accomplished quite straightforwardly by ferreting out evidence of women's activity that has been relegated to oblivion. Sometimes this ferreting involves relying upon *midrash* to fill in the gaps of women's lost history, reading stories of Sarah's reactions to the sacrifice of Isaac or Miriam's role in the desert in between the lines of the terse biblical text. On an exegetical level, however, the methodology involves the use of more sophisticated tools of analysis to uncover whatever traces of moral discomfort with an exclusively male hegemony can be found, even when these protests are admittedly only minority opinions. The assistance of interdisciplinary techniques is often enlisted, enabling a more nuanced reading through the simultaneous lessons of literary analysis, psychoanalytic method, source criticism, and feminist theory.

Thus, for example, feminist Israeli Bible scholar Ilana Pardes[29] focuses attention on the muted account of women's roles and upon various subplots and narratives, rather than on the main theme of a story. She also looks at subtle intratextual connections (viewing one text as critical commentary or antithetical supplement to another). This re-viewing serves to reconstruct traces of motifs challenging the patriarchal oppression of women. In like manner Daniel Boyarin approaches aggadic accounts of women in talmudic literature not merely as legendary kernels of biographical-historical truth, nor as purely fictional signifiers of values within the culture; rather, they are also a literary medium adopted in order to convey political and ideological attitudes. On this understanding, the inclusion of these aggadic narratives can sometimes be interpreted as the vehicle for a suppressed counterpoint to challenge the assumptions and values of a predominantly male culture.[30] Such subversive readings help locate otherwise unrecognized forces within this literary medium that express empathy with women and rising opposition to a predominantly androcentric hegemony.[31] Following the chronological development of such protests can reveal changing cultural attitudes.[32]

This method of reading the sources engages Jewish tradition with a suppressed voice that careful feminist re-readings of Torah and of *halakhah* are gradually uncovering. Restorativists see, for example, a counterpoint filtering through mystic *midrash* that link the souls of Tamar and Ruth, implying approval for their farsighted breaking of norms, which ensured the seed of the Messiah.[33] Or they hear a "second voice" in the many tales strewn throughout the Gemara of women challenging men in the *bet midrash*, pitching family loyalties above the scholarly idealization of temporary abstention from family life for the sake of "exile to a place of Torah," [34] or valuing genuine piety and spontaneous acts of charity over formal conformance to rules or blind subservience to authority.[35] In this manner, an underlying intent more supportive of women's current attitudes and interests is reconstructed.

One of the unique features of multiple thread exegesis is its ability to proclaim its ideological interest frankly. Rather than claim objectivity, some restorativists adopting this method attest to their political agenda in seeking out precisely those little-known themes from the past that can serve as models for the present and future.[36]

Ethical a priori methodology,[37] *or the principle of charity.* A third method of maintaining continuity with the past is to assume that there are certain ethical standards that it is inconceivable for God to deny. Proponents tend to exercise what philosopher W. V. O. Quine has dubbed "the principle of charity"[38] when reading traditional texts, privileging whatever interpretation gives the text the "benefit of the doubt." If, for example, someone tells us that he feels both well and not well, we do not conclude that he is speaking nonsense, but rather that he means to say that sometimes he feels well and sometimes not, or that he has mixed feelings.[39] When confronted with a divine text, we shall assume not that it is unwittingly contradictory, but that it is perfect in every way; therefore we shall be justified in assuming that its deeper intent was to uphold the highest a priori standards of morality, even when the plain meaning of the text does not explicitly support this reading.

A sample of this is found in Ozick's statement that the Oral Law is "the first to inform us" that a precept honoring the humanity of women is "implicit though absent."[40] Her justification for adding "Thou shalt not lessen the humanity of women" to the Decalogue is the conviction that "halakha is founded on and incorporates scriptural aspirations toward decency of daily conduct and the holiness of the ordinary." As she also notes, "a deep halakhic premise is that the individual's well-being is enhanced, through reasoning compassion, by the communal good."[41] Even if the Torah does not directly come out against the prevailing practices of its time, its larger moral vision must surely call for its message of justice to be fully extended to women.

The Theological Track

While revisionists opt for a sociological explanation of the patriarchal aspects of religion, other critics have come to adopt a radical and less benign understanding. The futility of distinguishing between sociological and essential features of *halakhah* is here extended to sociological versus essential features of religion at large. The critics argue that such distinctions overlook the fact that in religious traditions sociology tends to get objectified as absolute truth. Because our perception of God is the grand canvas upon which we generally project our understanding of reality, they continue, it is religious *belief* and not sociology that lies at the heart of the problem. Feminists adopting this line are characterized by a more thoroughgoing skepticism regarding any approach that relies on divorcing the negative aspects of religion from its inherent features. Whatever the origins of these aspects, the sociological eventually becomes the theological.[42] To this extent at least, patriarchy gets bound up with the very core of monotheistic belief.

Feminists who criticize religion at this level concentrate on exposing the internal connections they discover between the monotheistic conception of God and male ways of thinking. To the extent that monotheism places men at the center, then the world it constructs in order to make sense of human experience is also a world imbued with a male perspective. The entire shape of the religion, its image of God and His relationship to creation, and its perception of reality reflect the hopes, needs, and fears of men living in a patriarchal framework. Its basic paradigms are specially designed to suit the male psyche.

What are the specifically male thought structures featured in monotheism that are presumed inherently antithetical to the feminine perspective, and inimical to women's interests? First of all, underlying these structures is the concept of God as transcendent. In monotheism, God's unity is bound up with His self-sufficiency and preeminence over any other being. God existed before creation, and brought it into existence ex nihilo as something extraneous to Himself. In this act of creation He was not obliged to take anything outside of Himself into account. He was free, autonomous, not bound by any law. God continues to stand over and above creation as its exclusive master. Because He is omniscient and all-powerful, his position vis-à-vis the world is analogous to that of the grand ruler, king, judge, warrior, victorious conqueror. He is the object of totally unqualified respect. In other words He is nothing other than the fulfillment of a male's wildest dreams, but for a woman—as Daphne Hampson has put it—"What a nightmare!"[43]

The feminist critique contends that this basic concept of divine transcendence embodies a whole cluster of distinctively masculine perceptions, that are threaded into the very fabric of monotheistic belief. The notion of God as transcendent, for example, leads to the idea that holiness lies only in that which is totally exalted and separate. It also requires that our knowledge of God be conducted via a deliberately initiated revelatory event, whereby He stands opposite us and speaks in the name of an objective truth that is external to our natural experience. Many feminists interpret this aspect of monotheism as predicated upon a sense of separate selfhood that is typical of men's self-regard. To transcend, after all, is to separate from. And to yearn for transcendence presupposes a separable self.[44] Women, on the other hand, neither require nor desire the type of disengagement that transcendence promises, possessing as they do a sense of a "soluble" self, defined within and by reference to a web of immanent relationships.[45]

All the monotheistic religions are "historic," in the sense that they hold one particular period or event in their collective memory as more revelatory of God than others. Reference must always be made to that period or event as the ultimate source through which God is supremely known, demanding absolute obedience. It is the ideal archetypal model for the present and the future, against which any new suggestion or insight must be measured. Thus, as Daphne Hampson points out, the ordination of women by the church is not rejected because of current considerations, but rather because of the fact that Jesus did not appoint his mother, or any other woman, to the priesthood.[46] If the Vatican ever finds grounds for dispensation, this will invariably be effected on the strength of some past precedent. This exclusiveness is not only vertical in time, but also horizontal—excluding the legitimacy of any alternative revelation on the part of rival religions and their faith experiences. Christian feminist theologian Mary Daly has coined the term "methodolatry" in order to describe this practice of granting divine authority to a method that not only dictates what answers are to be given, but also what questions are to be asked.[47] When the choice of problems to be discussed is determined by the method, instead of the method determined by the problem, believers are prevented from raising questions never asked before and from being illumined by ideas that do not fit into the known categories. And because this past history has been overwhelmingly defined by a male perspective, deifying the basic assumptions of the method in effect renders women as irrelevant, and their voice is silenced.

The main path to be taken in approaching the God of monotheism is a covenant between two unequal partners. Although this option is offered by the divine ruler to His human subjects in a spirit of charity, they are also threatened with punishment should they refuse to comply. The pact between the two partners is phrased in legal terms of rights and obligations. Religious ritual is concentrated upon a system of laws imposed from above and religious success is measured by how obedient we are to these norms. Another means of overcoming the vast distance dividing God from His human subjects is appeasing Him with sacrifices. It is not surprising, claim the feminists, that the binding of Isaac was assumed as a central symbol of patriarchal religion, in that it once again confirms God as a supreme authority who is capable of abusing humanity with cruel and unreasonable demands in order to satisfy Him and provide proof of absolute loyalty.[48] A related notion, the mystic demand for self-denial and annihilation, also suits the self-image of the male. Lacking a more fluid image of his identity, the male finds no other means of overcoming the boundaries of his impermeable selfhood.

Radical feminists adopting the theological track argue that fixing our vision of reality exclusively on one particular picture does an injustice to both religion and women. From the point of view of religious doctrine: if the object of religious belief is an infinite God, then the tendency of the ordinary monotheist to picture God only as male is a type of idolatry. We are used to thinking of idol worship as bound up with images of wood and stone. But limited mental images can be even more dangerous precisely because their pernicious influence is not so readily discerned.[49] From the point of view of women, binding worship exclusively to male-oriented monotheistic conceptions also leads to the marginalizing of female forms of spirituality. It is hard to imagine, say feminists, that women (or even men living under another social regime) would describe God in estranging terms of dominion and authority, or talk about their relationship with Him in terms of law, coercion, sacrifice, fear, and submissiveness. Thus it comes about that half of the population in Western civilization is excluded from the process of conceptualizing the divine in their terms and prevented from giving expression to the manner in which they experience spirituality.

Perhaps the most damning criticism of all is that the monotheistic notion of God has had a pernicious influence upon relations between men and women on the anthropological level. Feminists are fond of relying here on the insights of anthropologist Clifford Geertz,[50] who points to the constructive function of religious language. Religion does not merely create a certain social pattern, it also represents it and grants it legitimacy. Religious symbols reflect the moral character and sensibilities of the people who employ them, and structure their world. They are both models *of* and models *for* human behavior and the social order. It is for this reason that rulers have traditionally made use of religious beliefs to fortify their positions and divide power inequitably.

The point made regarding the anthropological repercussions of monotheism is that *this* particular image of God is responsible for the gendered view of reality that has dominated Western culture. The very conception of God as the transcendent "Other" creates the blueprint for hierarchical structures and sharp definitions, whereby the essence of any given entity can be defined only against something else. As God is conceived as transcendent by a creation that is separate from Him, so the rest of the world is understood as a hierarchy of separate creatures. As God relates to humans, so humans relate to the levels of being under them—through dominion and control. Thus is created a model of dictatorship and dependency, and the distinction between the "insiders" (who resemble each other) and the "outsiders" (the others). If men stand as weak and sinful before the all-powerful and perfect God, so is earthly woman seen by male eyes. As God is capable of displaying absolute authority and irrationality in His relationship to His male "wife" (granting him a son and then demanding that son as sacrifice), so the abusive and capricious husband behaves toward his wife.[51] Demonstrations of love and mercy on the part of the husband come to educate the wife, to induce her to fulfill her duty and be all that the male wishes of her. Independent of him, her existence has no meaning.

The function for men of certain religious artifacts is to reinforce symbolically the notion that man is to God as woman is to man. One study suggests that *tefillin, tzitzit,* and the adornment of *mitzvot* in general parallel customary women's ornaments in ancient times and serve to dramatize man's unique relationship with God and the wish to win Him over and please Him.[52] Another study suggests that the disquiet and deeper visceral reactions of traditionalists to women wrapping themselves in *tallit* and *tefillin* may be understood in terms of the erotic associations embedded in these rituals. Such women transform the original significance of the associations, usurping the relationship between men and God that these *mitzvot* imply and breaking the traditional hierarchical relationship between men and women that they are meant to reflect and enforce.[53]

The harsh assumptions of an integral connection between monotheism and patriarchal structures have led some feminists to conclude that the

Jewish religion's specifically patriarchal character is no mere accident, adopted under the influence of the surrounding culture. In their eyes, it is precisely the Jewish paradigm that is responsible for the basic social model that eventually spread and influenced Christianity and Islam.[54] Such allegations have on occasion born a discernible anti-Semitic streak.[55] But even without taking conclusions to such extremes, the net result of this theological critique is that monotheism appears as a powerful tool of patriarchy that can be used against women on metaphysical grounds. For this reason, no diet of religious reform can suffice with recipes for improving women's sociological status. What is really required to effect equality for women in the religious tradition is to revamp its theological basis, liberating it entirely of its predominantly male orientation. Replacing this orientation requires a profound paradigm shift to a new nonauthoritarian model of spirituality, founded upon a relational rather than a hierarchical view of reality and other selves. This view would allow for heterogeneity and pluralism, for living in harmony with the universe rather than in accordance with artificially contrived acts and outworn dogmas that speak to us no longer.

Third-stage feminism of this more radical variety has led a few of its proponents, especially those who were raised in the Christian tradition, to conclude that the lack of congruence between the world they inhabit and the concept of God that they have inherited has reached the breaking point. In their eyes monotheism can no longer sustain the feminist critique. New forms of religion must be explored. But as to the proper source of inspiration for these forms, the feminists disagree.

Neo-paganist restorativism

One theological response to the feminist critique of religion, which we may label *pre-monotheistic,* may also be regarded as restorativist to a degree. More moderate restorativists, as we saw, rely on the argument that patriarchy is merely a sociological overlay of the original monotheism. Premonotheistic restorativists, by contrast, regarding patriarchy as intrinsic to monotheism, seek to revive an ideal that by their claim existed in a prior age.

Psychoanalytic theory speaks of the wish to return to a pre-Oedipal stage in the development of personality, a stage that preceded separation from the mother. Similarly, neopaganism strives for the return to a natural nonhierarchical state of affairs, before the appearance of the jealous God of monotheism. Some view the very establishment of social institutions as the source of patriarchy, and turn to a pre-historic age when families and social structures as we now know them did not exist. Thus Adrienne Rich looks to the early semimythical Amazon women for inspiration.[56] Others find their ideal in the prebiblical world of polytheism, where there was still room for tolerance of differences, and no distinction between the normative and the "other."[57] The vast proliferation of literature that has developed around the topic depicts an age and certain pagan cultures in which the division of power between the sexes and the relationship to women differed considerably from what subsequently emerged in the Bible, allowing for greater female participation in religious ritual. According to this picture, the battle against fertility cults and the institution of sharp distinctions between the pure and the impure that emerged with monotheism denigrated the importance of women's sexuality and reproductive powers. But this debasing was the least of the consequences. It also did away with a whole culture that held women's existence to be at the very center of what is necessary and sacred. Neopaganist restorativists maintain that this focus deserves to be resurrected in the modern religious consciousness.

Postmonotheistic spiritualism

Another version of the theological response to third-stage feminism, known as *spiritual,* or *postmonotheistic* feminism, abandons the restorativist move entirely. Christian feminists adopting this approach (such as Daphne Hampson or Mary Daly in later works)[58] believe that nothing in the past can sustain the feminist critique; what is required is a total break with tradition. Dressing up the stereotypical monotheistic images with a skirt will not do, but neither will a return to polytheism suffice. The theology promoted by such post-Christian feminists, while still theistic, tends to adopt an impersonal concept of God: a divine force, or a power that constitutes "another dimension of reality." Instead of the patriarchal Western dichotomy, whereby God's greatness is in contrast to our weaknesses, God is conceived as the fullness of our potentiality. Unlike the world, which is external to us, God is the foundation of our being, and what connects us to the greater whole, giving us a sense of and allowing us to become our true selves. Although this God does not stand over and above us as an object or heteronomous "other" within the realm of reciprocity, He does not simply reside within the self, submerged in our subjectivity. When we speak of God, we are referring to something real both in and beyond ourselves, a power interwoven within the world of which we are also a part, upon which we can draw for healing and spiritual strength. Such an understanding tends to a conception of the divine that is called *panentheistic:* all the world is part of God, but God is also infinitely more.

The authority for this postmonotheistic conception of the divine is grounded not on revelation or history, but rather on the felt experience of women themselves; a sense that there is more to reality than meets the eye, an added dimension available for all to discern. Women adopting this model of God speak of their immediate awareness and sense of profound connectedness to a spiritual presence on which they may draw, a presence beyond the self, of power, love, a drive for the good, and a greater purposiveness in the world. It is this presence, as well as the receptivity and openness to the whole that it affords, that they wish to identify with religious experience. Such awareness and receptivity do not *imply* God; awareness and receptivity are what God is.

If spiritual feminism, as neopaganism, is not a sensibility grounded on revelation, and thus generates few formal and specific prescriptions for ritual practice, this is not to say that it has no effect on daily life. Such a religion encourages certain ways of being in the world that allow us to maintain a sense of wonder, without mandating otherworldliness and loss of the sense of self. Its adherents assert the value of prayer, but as a way to interconnect mind and body, rather than as a dialogic stance. Particular virtues, and their attendant practices, are fostered because they cause our lives to take a particular shape, enabling greater openness to God, as well as attentiveness to others; facilitating compassion and concern rather than domination.

The spiritual feminist's belief is that virtues such as compassion and consideration conform to the way the world really is. They are grounded in the inherent structure of reality. Such ways of being exist in saintly and spiritual people of all denominations, and may be part of existing religions. However—as Hampson, a prominent exponent of this type of spirituality sees it—this feminist variety of religious praxis also includes a different ethos, one that seeks to affirm rather than deny and overcome a here and now that is already given; an ethos that is opposed to self-sacrifice, humility, and obedience. It leads to a sense of finding our place in the world and feeling at home in it, rather than looking out to an external God and a life beyond.[59]

Jewish appropriation of the theological track

At previous stages of the feminist critique, striking similarities could be found among the three great monotheistic traditions. It is mainly feminists raised on the Christian tradition, however, who have allowed themselves the liberty of criticizing the theological premises of their religion to the breaking point. One may surmise that Islamic feminists whose identities are bound up with Arab nationalisms generally feel less free to push their critique beyond procedural questions and practical application. Any more profound critique of Islam could be construed as a political statement of identification with the cultural imperialism of the West and its values. Christianity, by contrast, never defined the personal, communal, or ethnic identity of its adherents. This historic difference could be one reason why Christian feminists have felt less inhibited in critiquing substantive theological issues. The more intense interest of Christian feminists in theology could be explained on a theoretical level as well, by the fact that the very essence of Christianity is bound up with a greater emphasis upon dogma. In Christianity, it is allegiance to a specific set of beliefs, rather than to a very demanding way of life, that determines one's identity as a believer.

Most Jewish feminists opt for more muted responses to the theological critique of their tradition on both accounts. The sociocultural ramifications for a Jew who chooses to leave the religious fold are much greater than for a lapsed Christian. Jews—like Moslems—cannot divorce their spiritual experience from their social and cultural ties without incurring some form of identity crisis. Religious observance in the modern age has become for many a symbolic mode of communal identification, a sociological sign of one's "Jewishness." (For others, Zionism fills this role.) For some Jewish feminists, this constraint is further reinforced by the experience of the Holocaust.[60] Reluctance to dishonor the dead by defection may be accompanied by the suspicion that the outside world will never accept a Jew, even when she rejects her original religious affiliation. As for more ideological concerns, Judaism has always maintained a decidedly legalistic bent, viewing *halakhah,* or religious practice, as its main vehicle for worship and spiritual expression. Perhaps for this reason, Jewish theology has always managed to retain a considerable degree of latitude in the interpretation of doctrine, by according a primary role to *midrash* and biblical exegesis. All these factors help to explain why, even in non-Orthodox circles, theological dissent generally does not involve a complete break with the Jewish religious tradition.

Nonetheless, major calls to move beyond the confines of traditional monotheistic "God-talk" are not unknown among Jewish feminists. Some non-Orthodox feminists are attempting theological revision, but because they strive to rectify matters without overstepping the boundaries of tradition, they prefer to couple the theological track with a restorativism that maintains continuity with familiar forms of Jewish spirituality and worship.

Judith Plaskow's augmenting of male monotheism. In "The Right Question is Theological," a rebuttal of Cynthia Ozick's position, Judith Plaskow claims that Ozick's fixation on sociology and her reluctance to explore the "theological underpinnings" of women's status still leaves her situated firmly in the mainstream of Jewish feminism. This, Plaskow says, remains a civil rights movement rather than a movement for "women's liberation," focused on "getting women a piece of the Jewish pie." It has not wanted to bake a new one:[61]

If the Jewish women's movement addresses itself only to the fruits but not the bases of discrimination, it is apt to settle for too little in the way of change. It may find that the full participation of women in Jewish life—should it come—will only bring to light deeper contradictions in Jewish imagery and symbolism, And, most likely, far-reaching change will not come until these contradictions are examined and exorcised. It is time, therefore, to confront the full extent of our disablement as Jewish women in order that we may understand the full implications of our struggle.[62]

One aspect to confront is how the "Otherness" of women in tradition is given dramatic expression in its language about God. According to Plaskow, although Ozick recognizes the predominance of male imagery in Jewish tradition, she too lightly dismisses feminist misgivings as "quibbles about the incompetence of pronouns."[63] She fails to appreciate that the normative language about God serves only to reinforce the tendency to exclude women from participation in Jewish religious life and in the development of *halakhah*: "Male imagery both tells us about God's nature (it is, after all, the only way we know God) and justifies a human community which reserves power and authority to men."[64] Moreover, Plaskow charges, Ozick overlooks the possibility that this exclusion is reflected not only in the content of *halakhah* but even in its very form.

We must recognize, argues Plaskow, that true equality of women is not the same as integrating women into male institutions and systems. There is no guarantee that *halakhah* will remain the chief medium of expression and repair if the tradition comes to reflect women's voices as well as men's. "The implications of Jewish feminism, while they include halakhic restructuring, reach beyond *halakhah* to transform the bases of Jewish life." A new understanding of Torah must begin with acknowledgment of the profound injustice of Torah itself in discriminating between men and women. A new understanding of God must reflect and support an inclusive redefinition of Jewish humanity by incorporating feminine imagery in the language of ritual. And a new understanding of the community of Israel must include the voice of women who speak and name their experience for themselves.[65]

In expressing these sentiments, Plaskow has become one of the most prominent and cogent exponents of the more radical wave of Jewish feminism, which believes that only by renovation on the theological plane can full religious participation and creativity on the part of women be transformed into a social reality. Yet, despite the revolutionary nature of her project, Plaskow remains in the restorativist mode, rather than completely cutting ties with a past that in her opinion can only cause women pain. Her insistence on this, as that of other third-stage Jewish feminists, is based on their understanding of the role of the Jewish past in shaping Jewish identity and self-understanding.

In all the so-called historical religions, religious ritual has a history not only because it has its origins in the past, but also because it repeats, reproduces, and carries into the future, acts that have been repeated and reproduced again and again in the course of the religion. At the Passover seder, for example, participants are enjoined to regard the ritual as a personal and communal enactment of the Exodus from Egypt; on Shavuot, we renew the original covenant at Sinai, and on Sukkot, we live in temporary dwellings (*sukkot*) for a week and experience the utter dependency upon God that our ancestors knew in the desert. If the possibility of creating a present totally discontinuous with the past is questionable within any historical textual tradition, Plaskow regards it as doubly problematic in Judaism, as "memory is not simply a given but a religious obligation."[66] In challenging the traditional depiction of God, then, Plaskow concentrates mainly on replenishing and enhancing the understanding of the divine that emerges from the existing religious imagery and language of prayer. She has no intention of rejecting the monotheistic conception; rather, she wishes to strike a balance between the differing conceptions of self and world that arise from the male and female perspective. This balance is to be effected through the use of metaphors that, as feminist poet Marcia Falk has expressed it, portray the one God as "an embracing *unity* of a *multiplicity of images*." Or, in the words of one alternative prayer book, "Countless visions we have named You; Through all visions You are One."[67]

The debate over the form that reimaging the deity should take echoes the debates of radical feminism at large.[68] All agree that maintaining exclusively male God-talk would be repeating the mistakes of second-stage liberal feminism, along with its implicit assumption of male values as supreme. But should male and female qualities be merged in some more evenhanded androgynous manner? Or should female imaging take over completely? Many non-Orthodox Jewish feminists favor addressing prayer to the *Shekhinah* (representing the feminine aspect of the divine in Jewish mystic tradition) and using female pronouns. This preference is defended on various grounds. One is the belief that introducing female imagery leads us to more positive attitudes toward women's bodies and sexuality. Another is that the force for renewal in the everyday world is most dramatic at the birth of new life. Thus it is only natural to view God, the creative life force of the universe, immanent or all-present, in female terms. And while describing God in gender-neutral terms reflects a philosophical understanding that the divine force is surely abstract and ungendered,[69] to appreciate this transcendence of gender human beings may need feminine imagery as a counterbalance to the male images instilled by traditional liturgy. Rita Gross, among others, supports the use of gendered language, to preserve the sense of personal relationship with God that is not captured by abstract pronouns.[70]

Plaskow recommends an additional avenue of response to the critique of third-stage feminism: developing new ways to flesh out collective memory so as to include the experience of women. Here too, as with female God-language and imagery, Plaskow stops short of leaving the traditionalist medium altogether, relying on what she terms the "woman-spaces" created by the sex role divisions of traditional Judaism in the past. As she puts it:

Whether it was in the market or the ritual bath, or whether it was in the form-creating idle chatter of the women's side of the synagogue, women shared a common life that we deeply desire and yet lost when liberal Judaism gave us the precious right sometimes to act as men. What women did with this common life is now our task to discover."[71]

Plaskow is aware that "woman-spaces, like halakhic tinkering, can help preserve an unjust system by rendering it bearable and providing shared self-validation which does not threaten the status-quo." Her solution, however, is "to use those spaces in a way which is transforming, knowing that we have not invented them, that we have a heritage of power to draw on."[72] In the style of the sociological revisionists, this entails finding an interpretive framework for understanding the past broad enough to include data at odds with its selective memory. Capitalizing upon the ambiguity and sometimes cryptic nature of classical texts or their commentaries can accomplish this. It also entails, however, both the creation of new women's *midrash* based on our own contemporary experience, and enacting this experience through new ritual and liturgy that will reshape the Jewish memory. One such effort is a midrashic myth, "Applesource," which she created together with a few other women, retelling the Garden of Eden story in a manner that portrays the sisterhood of Lilith and Eve.[73] Concerned for Jewish continuity, Plaskow defends such filling in of the "woman-spaces" left between the lines of the biblical text as a fleshing out of its original message, even when it transforms rather than merely uncovers "what really happened" according to the traditional view. Such techniques, she insists, do not violate historical canons, but are rather an enactment of commitment to the fruitfulness and relevance of biblical texts and to the building of links between our stories and those of our foremothers.[74]

Orthodox appropriation of the third-stage methods. The response of Orthodox Jewish feminism to theological revisionism has been minimal and qualified. Nevertheless, there are some notable points of contact between feminists of a more traditional orientation and those who agitate for revision of the classical God-talk of monotheism. These points serve to blur the boundaries between sociological and theological modes of response.

First, as I have already indicated in chapter 2, there exists an ironic similarity between the radical defenders of female God-language and the conservative wave of ultra-Orthodox female apologists who seek to make peace with tradition as it stands by identifying God more closely with women's experience. The apologists, however, limit this identification to the exegetical level. They would actively object to actually replacing traditional male images of God or infusing the language of the liturgy with more gender-inclusive terms. The same may be said of Modern Orthodox feminists who have ventured beyond the first stages of the feminist critique and appreciate the crucial role that religious language and imagery play in developing and reflecting our self-images and social structures. They too evince far less interest in diverging from the language of the traditional prayer book and the sacred texts. Minor revisions of phrasing in order to acknowledge the presence of women, both single and married, within the congregation, to circumvent the blessing of "*shelo asani isha,*" or to include the names of the four biblical mothers alongside the forefathers in some of the prayers, are about as far as most would go. This lack of interest in revision beyond the anthropological level stems from ideological commitment to the *halakhah,* which stipulates the inviolability of standard prayer formulations fixed by the Rabbis. It is also dictated by the wish to avoid schisms, and by genuine attachment to the formulations themselves, which are both venerable and familiar. Thus, resistance to change may well be accompanied by recognition that such language is not ideally suited to feminine sensibilities or to the moral intuitions of the age.[75]

On another level, however, even ultra-Orthodox women share, to a limited extent, the growing interest in forming communities willing to engage creatively in ceremonies that commemorate life-cycle events and other significant occasions in the lives of women.[76] Admittedly the radical revisionists go further, including such typically feminine milestones as onset of menstruation or menopause, and marking crises unnoticed by the world of patriarchy: abuse, miscarriage, divorce. The ceremonies that have thus far penetrated more traditional circles fall into two categories: life-cycle celebrations that parallel male rituals (for example, ceremonies welcoming a baby girl in lieu of male circumcision rites or bat mitzvah celebrations of a girl's reaching the age of religious responsibility) and the revival of previously established customs (such as celebrations of the new month [Rosh Hodesh], regarded as a women's festival in ancient times). Among the ultra-Orthodox such celebrations tend to be woman-only affairs, while among the Modern Orthodox the life-cycle events usually take place in mixed company, and increasingly on synagogue premises. Whatever the setting, the very notion of publicly celebrating women's spiritual milestones is a notable development in Orthodoxy.

The feminist critique has had some influence upon the Orthodox mainstream even in the realm of Torah scholarship. This influence can be seen in a heightened concern for countering the androcentric slant in tradition by uncovering and highlighting the few existing texts in which women figure prominently. In the past few decades, a new genre of writing on "the image of woman" in the Bible, the Talmud, or in Judaism at large has been produced even by the most traditionalist circles. Apologists are contributing their share to a veritable flood of popular articles and more substantial studies seeking to redress the longtime absence of women's voices in the shaping of Jewish public life and letters. The thrust of this conservative literature, however, is that the rare exceptions to the general rule of female invisibility in the sources corroborate traditional conceptions of role stratification and confirm the halakhic status quo.[77] The underlying assumption is that one predefined eternal view of woman is being played out throughout the centuries. The more fanciful midrashic efforts of the radical restorativists are often regarded as in poor taste, if not as sacrilegious.

This genre functions largely as a vehicle for enlarging upon the conventional religious view, by idealizing biblical texts as the fulfillment of current egalitarian visions.[78] In contrast, some of the inventive biblical interpretations that are now emanating from more consciously feminist Orthodox quarters occasionally bear striking affinity to those produced by the radical feminists in their robust and independent vision of female spirituality.[79]

Orthodox feminists are also beginning to exploit other opportunities to designate women as religious personalities. One example of this is a growing interest in ceremonial commemoration of Miriam the prophetess at the Passover seder. Notice of Miriam's vital role in the release of the Israelites from bondage in Egypt is linked with mention of those women of today who still await similar release from bondage to husbands refusing divorce. A custom of inviting the foremothers as metaphysical guests (*ushpizin*) during the festival of Sukkot is also gaining popularity. Such practices straddle the border between bolstering feminine spirituality and self-worth and reshaping the sanctified memories of a patriarchal tradition.

Jenny Kien's Jewish neopaganism: Reinstating the divine goddess. Any mode of theological restorativism more radical than that represented by Plakow has held little attraction for most Jewish feminists, and especially not for the more traditionalist among them. Nevertheless, I would like to introduce one example of such an effort before evaluating the usefulness and viability of restorative third-stage Jewish feminism. I believe it will highlight in greater relief—through a type of reductio ad absurdum—some of the difficulties posed by theological restorativism in particular. This last response seeks to go beyond the normative framework of monotheistic tradition altogether by uncovering the goddesses of older polytheistic forms of Israelite religion.

Thus, Jenny Kien, an Australian-born professor of biology who teaches in Israel, attempts to find support for a "thealogy" (rather than theology) more congenial to women by revealing traces still buried in biblical texts of goddess worship throughout both Temple periods. In her book *Reinstating the Divine Woman In Judaism*[80] (which she published privately after despairing of getting any established publisher to disseminate her radical brand of Jewish feminism), Kien asserts that monotheism, like every other social change, had its roots in the social and political history of the Judahite and Israelite cultures. Basing her conclusions on extrabiblical textual evidence, as well as historical and archeological research, she contends that human culture was originally matricentric, citing various psychological, economic, political, and anthropological explanations for its eventual overtaking by patriarchy.[81] Her careful reading of the Bible reveals traces of the polemic between various religious groups in the transition from pre-Jewish goddess worship to the competition between Jahweh, Baal, and Asherah, followed by Jahweh polytheism until the eventual victory of the Jahweh-alone position and appropriate revision of the canon. Paralleling these struggles is the story of the gradual exclusion of women from active participation in cultic activities, as well as the development of a negative attitude to female sexuality through its exclusion from the divine.

On the strength of these claims, Kien argues that making Judaism a religion that deeply empowers women mandates the provision of a strong, sexual, fully female goddess. She believes that remaining strictly monotheistic, merely "feminizing" the male God with the addition of female symbols and imagery, is insufficient, while gender-neutral metaphors leave us with a one-sided theological abstraction. Even experiments with new female names for the divine, such as Merciful Mother (*Rachemah*) or Womb (*Rechem*) of the Universe, focusing upon the uterus as the source of life, do not dare far enough, skirting the issue of female sexuality per se.[82] What is required is an all-inclusive deity in which both the male and the female aspect are embedded, much as the boy and the girl child are carried in the mother's womb. Kien equates such goddess worship with a feminist approach to the world, in that it reinstates a divine presence "whose essence is its inclusiveness, with an imagery of acceptance of otherness, of many parallel truths and many causes and effects, an imagery in which justice is not based upon sin and retribution, but upon the consequences of losing connectedness."[83]

Kien admits that although the type of female deity she is proposing might formally be defined as monotheistic, it would soon, in everyday use, give rise to a pantheon of gods and goddesses that would most probably take us far beyond monotheistic confines. Nevertheless, she is not deterred by this possibility. Being Jewish is in her eyes something broader than accepting the monotheistic tradition. It represents a community experience of manifold traditions, rituals, and culture, all of which create a way of looking at things, and a more general approach to the world that to her mind is best expressed by a pluralistic polytheism allowing for affirmation of women's experience.

Kien's neopaganism leads her to favor an approach to biblical texts supporting this interest. She obviously rejects the conservative reading of the Torah as representing *the* one ideal, definitive Jewish view of woman. She also does not see much point in the quasi-apologetic effort to peel off later layers that have accrued to the text in order to reveal a latent egalitarianism, or in inventing new *midrashim* to flesh out a more affirmative feminine story from the text's empty spaces. Her preference is to adopt what she describes as a more backwards-going working with the text, taking the text at face value.[84] This approach mandates honoring what these themes and symbols in the text referred to at the time that they were written or edited, enabling the modern reader to identify political moves to desecrate traces of the goddess and to thereby subdue women.

Kien believes that the pernicious effect of classical religious texts can be transcended only once their "simple meaning" is confronted honestly in this way. Her recommended mode of study benefits from the academic research of scholars in the past twenty years who, sympathetic to critical feminist interests, search the Bible for evidence indicating censorship of lingering antipatriarchal motifs that oppose the dominant voice of the victors.[85] On the strength of their assumption that the Bible is not homogeneous, but rather a composite work, such scholars attempt to find traces of protest and struggle on the part of polytheistic countertraditions. Kien, however, wishes to go further than these attempts. Her reading of Adam's naming of Eve as the Mother of All Living Things reveals a polemic masterpiece of political propaganda that conveyed to readers in biblical times the demoting by Jahweh of the great goddess Asherah. Previously the bearer of Adam and creator of the universe, Asherah is transformed into a human woman, herself created by and out of a male.[86]

Kien recognizes that her view of Judaism diverges radically from the traditional Jewish self-understanding. She quite frankly acknowledges that her main interest in solving the feminist dilemma via this rather convoluted restorativist response, relating goddess worship to precisely those traces of precedent with which the biblical text is at war, stems from the wish to maintain continuity with her Jewish roots and communal identity. It is this wish, rather than any compelling theological features of Judaism, that causes her to seek validation for her ideas from a mainstream Jewish text instead of associating herself with more general neopaganism or the modern feminist spirituality movement. In addition, her awareness of the difficulties in contriving new imagery, at a level deep enough to move us toward connectedness with it, brings her to pragmatic appreciation of the importance of relying on existing traditions rather than simply inventing new ideas.[87] It is doubtful, however, whether the tactics she employs are anywhere near equal to the task.

CHAPTER 7

Evaluating Revisionism

Third-stage revisionism carries obvious appeal in its promise to make a clean break with the problems at the heart of the feminist critique of religion. It appears more honest and thoroughgoing—after admitting the vulnerability of the religious tradition to external influences or limited androcentric perspectives—to tackle the feminist critique on a more deep-seated attitudinal level, rather than taking the path of apologetics or merely tinkering with the halakhic system. Unencumbered by ill-suited baggage, be it sociological or theological, the faith community is left free to rebuild its belief system in a manner better attuned to feminine interests and experience.

Moreover, when coupled with some form of restorativism, the revisionist project allows the third-stage feminist to give religious credence to her self-perception as a woman, without engaging in a head-on confrontation with her tradition and disowning her roots completely. Fortified by claims of valid precedent in the tradition, she is able to challenge patriarchy on its own grounds. If male domination has not always prevailed as the necessary or only possible order, she may now suggest that it is not a faithful reflection of the true ideals of Judaism or of an inevitable cosmic reality. Contradictory precedents in legal and religious traditions provide an important source of authority for divergence from current norms. Such precedents make room for the claim that perhaps the feminist notion of justice is the natural moral state of society. On this basis, present injustices in the tradition may even be regarded as a deviation from the true faith.

Nevertheless, I find the promise of third-stage feminism overstated or problematic on several accounts: historical, pragmatic, and theological.

Questions of Historical Accuracy: Are Monotheism and Women's Oppression Necessarily Linked?

The distortions of false nostalgia. One difficulty in a revisionism that relies on the authenticating powers of precedent lies in its anachronistic tendency to whitewash the past. Initially, the willingness of the revisionist to own up to shortcomings in her tradition creates an impression of intellectual honesty. Yet in the zeal to discover sociological or theological precedent for change, revisionism (no less than mainstream meta-halakhic formulations or conservative apologetics) is often not above unself-consciously projecting onto historical and textual evidence from the past whatever interpretation best serves the interests of the contemporary agenda. Rigorous historical research may indeed show how firmly the texts of tradition and their application are anchored in the particularities of their own time and place. But when such analyses are pressed into the mill of restorativist interests, they become grist for the construction of overromanticized pictures of bygone eras.

This complaint applies especially to sociological revisionists who apply the "golden thread" argument in order to pin their restorativist hopes on dominant motifs of the far-distant biblical period. Depatriarchalizing projects after the fashion of Trible do not seem capable of covering all the ground necessary in reappropriating the Bible for feminist purposes. While such readings may deflect something of the unconscious male bias with respect to a select list of biblical narratives—such as the story of Adam and Eve, and the Book of Ruth—many other narratives are still left wanting. (Indeed, as Mary Daly has quipped in this connection, a depatriarchalized Bible would leave us with no more than a book of pamphlet size).[1] On the other hand, reinterpretating the textual and historical evidence in the manner of Antonelli—implying that the Torah given at Sinai originally conveyed a blueprint for society that tallies with our progressive egalitarian notions and present-day sensibilities—ignores the basically hierarchical view that dominates biblical visions of justice. Moreover, neither Trible nor Antonelli have attempted tackling the androcentric imaging of God and attendant views of His relationship to His creation; nor would it be easy for them to extend their interpretive skills to these. Salvaging the Torah's morality by highlighting a general inclination to gender blindness is equally unsatisfactory. Despite the biblical statement that "male and female created He them," women's role is mainly biological even in the Bible. Women's status is established by social criteria rather than by considerations of holiness, and women appear in biblical law as a subdivision of humanity, rather than as members of the main class.[2]

While theological revisionists may show greater freedom from dogmatic constraints of loyalty to the biblical text as it stands, they too fall prey to tendentiousness. Such feminists appear no less naive or guilty of false nostalgia than the "sociologists" when they hark back to matriarchal religion in search of a more equitable social order. Are certain structures of religious belief in and of themselves really more emancipatory or enslaving than others? Is there so obviously a simple and clear-cut causal relationship between the character and gender of the gods imagined by a particular society and the power held by the corresponding sex on the anthropological level?[3]

Were polytheistic societies indeed less hierarchical and did they have a better record in their treatment of women? Recent studies of religion adopting greater levels of methodological sophistication in their analyses suggest that it is much too facile to assess the character of a religion and the social relations of its adherents merely on the basis of its imagery for the divine.[4] Anthropological and historical studies indicate that the notion of patriarchy was widespread in ancient times and embraced almost all the great civilizations of that world, even those that had nothing to do with Jewish monotheism. According to Frymer-Kensky, "A comparison of biblical laws with those of Assyria readily shows that the Bible did not rival Assyria in the extent to which it subordinated women.[5] Although both Kien and Plaskow imply that the demand of female goddesses for child sacrifice is merely a polemic allegation,[6] this claim too is open to debate.[7]

Inappropriate standards of assessment. Viewing monotheism—as many radical feminists are wont to do—solely as the creation or projection of male concerns, seems excessively reductionist. Monotheism then, they claim, continues as a ploy, to preserve men's present privileged status. Yet a good case can be made for the idea that patriarchal religion, in many contexts, has addressed various anthropological needs that serve men and women alike.[8]

To this day, popular folktales are fond of depicting women voluntarily choosing to subscribe to what has been termed "mythical male dominance," playing a game of deference in order to compensate their menfolk for the ways in which the balance of power works in women's favor.[9] Although such humor does not cater to feminist tastes, one should not dismiss the possibility that real or mythical male dominance may indeed have originated in a genuine anthropological need to render less threatening a natural asymmetry of power created by women's ability to give birth.[10] If that is the case, leaving men some room to maneuver and feel a sense of worth may have been a joint concern that Jewish monotheism addressed. Moreover, although Jewish tradition continued throughout its history to give religious legitimacy to male dominance in its social structures, this dominance was not unrelated to women's concerns. The home as the woman's sphere of activity was often an important outlet of female power despite her restrictions in the public sphere, and answered to a variety of uniquely feminine needs. Would an egalitarian distribution of power in accordance with contemporary feminist ideals inevitably have contributed to women's spiritual flourishing or made them happier?

In the same vein, the proverbial "red tent" or the equivalents to which menstruating women are banished in traditional society[11] (a practice—contrary to popular misconceptions—not limited to patriarchal regimes) need not be dismissed categorically as a tool of male dominance. It may have provided a much-needed venue for female empowerment as well as the convenience of privacy in an age lacking the hygienic amenities of our day.[12]

Anthropologist Mary Douglas suggests that the appropriation of biological anomalies by religious regulation and ritual also serves a more subtle cultural function of imposing order on an otherwise chaotic reality in a manner that may be meaningful to all human beings, irrespective of gender.[13]

Are these more positive readings of ancient religious practices simply the product of a false consciousness? Who does the deciding? Portraying women in patriarchy either as unwilling prisoners of oppression or as dupes of misplaced perceptions created by a system whose attitudes are completely shaped by male values is problematic in its monolithic understanding of women's possible responses. The very assessment of women's lot in terms of power may be the imposition of male standards uncongenial to women's experience or scale of values in certain cultural settings. Only when we supplement history with the undocumented and nonliterate story of women, can we understand the true balance of power, even in male terms.[14] The final test of these explanations, however, must not be how they measure up to any preconceived standard, but rather the extent to which they work for those directly concerned and produce results that are deemed worthy or convincing.

The mitigating influence of extraneous factors. Another reason why it is not easy to stipulate straightforward linkage between monotheism and women's oppression is that the factors determining how a particular religious view gets translated in practice are never bound exclusively to the realm of theology. Even in a traditional society, religion as it is lived is much more nuanced and subtle than its doctrine might indicate. In addition to influential primary religious symbols, physical and emotional needs and broader cultural, geographical, economic, and political considerations come into play. In many instances people are not in a hurry to align their practice with the formal requirements of their religion, or with what one may have expected to be the natural effect of its religious symbolism.

The striking diversity that has emerged within and among the various streams of historic Judaism, despite their common heritage of religious imagery, should surely make Jewish feminists think twice about the critical influence of androcentric imagery. Greater attention to the details of Jewish life over the ages reveals that, imagery notwithstanding, Jewish women participated in a history rich with complexity. The disparity between the image of women in biblical versus talmudic times, or between the Ashkenazic and Sephardic communities of the Middle Ages is immense, indicating that the varying degrees to which the patriarchal idea dominated the lives of our foremothers had far more to do with the state of the general cultural surroundings than with whether male or female language figured in their prayers. Differing contexts must also be taken into account. The same may be said for the contemporary status of women in Judaism; despite retention of male imagery, it too cannot be summed up by the laws of segregation in the synagogue (*mehitzah*), obsessive preoccupation with obligations of modesty, and denigrating aphorisms of the sages. Moreover, although our social structures may not be free of the impact of theology, the opposite is equally true. When the cultural climate calls for adjustments, basically androcentric images and practices are sometimes transformed and turned on their head by layers of more nuanced conceptions and interpretations of transcendence that accrue—at times even within the confines of severe constraints.

Feminizing influences upon the monotheistic agenda. Many *aggadot* of the Rabbis are strikingly compatible with feminist thought in their mode of thinking and in the values they embody. God may be the king and judge, but He also suffers with His children and follows them into exile.[15] When Rabbi Eliezer is outvoted by his opponents in the Sanhedrin despite a voice from heaven supporting him, God Himself concedes that orderly procedures of legal adjudication carry more weight than heavenly messages. Yet when the court goes on to victimize R. Eliezer by excommunicating him, God's anger is aroused, and Rabbi Gamliel, as leader of the majority, eventually loses his life.[16] What concerns the aggadic mode of thinking in general are human relationships, feelings, and the meaning of life as it is lived, rather than the law and formal abstractions.

In like manner, perhaps part of the attraction of Jewish mysticism in today's world is its emphasis on spirituality and its congeniality to the feminist agenda in other ways as well. Indeed, this double appeal is corroborated by traces of a genuine historical connection between feminist calls for a return of the divine goddess and the appropriation of more immanent notions of God, promoted by movements as mainstream to Judaism as the Kabbalah and Hassidism (Erich Neumann, a disciple of Carl Jung's, was influenced by these movements and contemporary feminists in turn were influenced by Neumann).[17]

Kabbalah translates the female sense of God's immanence into a rich vocabulary of metaphors for God.[18] It seeks to give expression not simply to God's presence in ordinary events and situations, but more specifically to the discovery of God's presence moving in and among women. It not only uses female metaphors for the *Shekhinah* aspect of God, but also images of God birthing, nursing, and nurturing the world after protecting its initial emanations in the womb of *Binah,* the higher Mother. In Kabbalah, God is not a being outside us, over and against us, who manipulates and controls, and raises some people over others. God is the source and wellspring of life in its infinite diversity and is present in all its aspects. God is present not just as father and protector but as the force that empowers us to act creatively ourselves. God is inside and outside us; transcendent, but only in the way that community transcends the individual within it. The pinnacle of the Godhead—*Ein-Sof,* the Infinite One—embraces the inexhaustible particularities of all communities and is named fully by none. The feminist preference in ritual for circles that empower all present and imply rejection of hierarchical leadership is also echoed in kabbalistic symbolism, which equates the feminine aspect of God with a self-contained circle, as opposed to the masculine as a progressing line.

We have already seen in our discussion of conservative apologetics that a vision of women as superior appears in several kabbalistic and Hassidic depictions of the Messianic age.[19] The introduction of a more gender-inclusive vision of Messianic times is another strategy for broadening the scope and formative influence of symbols designating a supreme male deity. On a more profound level, Rabbi A. I. Kook's preference for the abolition of binary dualisms and the promise of their eventual transformation into various stages of a harmonious continuum is spelled out in many far-reaching applications reminiscent of radical feminist theology. Take, for example, his preference for a panentheistic picture of the relationship between the world and God, with the two as part of one continuum, rather than a theistic one, that entails a clearly demarcated hierarchy with God above and His creatures down below and on an utterly different plane.[20] R. Kook's preference for describing creation as a process of emanation, rather than as ex nihilo, and the reasons he gives for this[21]—that there is no point at which God is not, so that we are connected to Him even before our potential for existence is realized—are also congenial to the feminine sensibility, as is his definition of holiness as optimal inclusiveness rather than a state of separation.[22] Even a critique of monotheism as a type of idolatry is clearly expressed in his writings. The following passage, a case in point, contrasts "the majestic idea of Israel" to the usual understanding of monotheism:

We do not speak of nor do we even contemplate the Source of all Sources, but from the very fact that we do not deny him, everything lives and exists forever. This is Israel's majestic idea, eternal, even if in the end this also is revealed only through the *Shechina*. What of it! Nothingness and I (*Ain* and *Ani*) are composed of the same letters. This is not monotheism which negates practical talents, friendship, and beauty. Monotheism is a fabrication of gentiles, an imprecise translation, a sort of self-contradictory comprehensible infinity, and therefore can lead to nothing. This is not the source of the name of the God of Israel, the infinite, incomprehensible root of all existence, because He is the existence (the preserver) of the world, who can be comprehended and spoken of only through the nuances of colors, through (his) many deeds and abundant peace, his profusion of love and courage. (Only) Israel, who proclaims "this is my God and I will adorn him," can say this, not the barren wilderness of Islamic monotheism, nor Buddhism's negation (of earthly life); only the highest existence, which brings joy to all and gives life to everything, revealed through the subjective revelation of all hearts who seek and comprehend him.[23]

The features reminiscent of feminine ways of thinking in this passage are striking. This is evident not only in R. Kook's portrayal of the divine[24] and insistence that the exclusive reliance upon one image is a type of idolatry. The parallels also appear in his emphasis upon the *Shekhinah* aspect of the divine, and in his describing God as the source of vitality, revealed in the subjective experience of his followers and in their enthusiastic affirmation of the concrete here and now.

The particular concept of God that R. Kook promotes is that of a metaphysical entity requiring the quality of potentiality and its resultant dynamic urge toward betterment and growth as supplement to His static perfection.[25] R. Kook regards traditional monotheism as merely a stepping-stone, serving as a vestibule or "reception hall" to the second more pantheistic or panentheistic vision.[26] A number of Christian feminist theologians have been drawn to a similar image of God in what has come to be known as *process theology*.[27] Unlike the God of Western theism, process theology denies the immutability and omnipotence of God. All of reality is interrelated. The God of process theology allows "Himself" to be affected and changed by the activity of human beings, for each individual introduces novel arrangements into the world that become contained within God. At the same time, God is said to respond to the world, taking up the particular circumstances that pertain and bringing new possibilities into being. God changes human beings, inasmuch as we construct each actual moment from the possibilities God presents.

Although variations on the monotheistic model can serve feminist purposes, the expression feminists would desire on the anthropological level is not inevitable. R. Kook's theology is a case in point. However congenial it might seem to feminine sensibilities, his more practical notions regarding women can be characterized (as already noted) as benign paternalism at best.[28] All this attests further to the folly of assuming predictable social consequences on the strength of hard-line theological stereotypes. Arguably, the lesson to be learned from history is that simply reinstating the goddess within Judaism even in a manner tempered by the needs of our time will not lead willy-nilly to a form of worship geared to enhance the power of women and their sense of self-worth. Nor does remaining with the old symbolism necessarily perpetuate the opposite. The possibility of a male God who enjoins Abraham, "Whatever Sarah tells you, do as she says" (Genesis 21:12), does not end with the Bible.

Pragmatic Considerations: Can and Should Contemporary Judaism Revise Classic God Imagery?

The irrelevance of theoretical argument to the living religious reality. Even if we were to grant revisionists who take the theological track some form of linkage between feminine imagery for the divine and women's well-being, those who insist upon reinstating goddess terminology tend to overlook the fact that we are different persons today. Over and above debates regarding the historical accuracy of theological revisionists' accounts of matriarchal religion, I find it far-fetched to argue that the way men and women formulated their understanding of the goddess in an ancient Near Eastern culture can serve as a relevant model for the present age.

To be fair, Kien herself does not envisage that uncovering and reviving the goddess of old in the Torah will ever bring a return to the ancient forms of worshiping her. "We must re-interpret her in light of the millennia that have passed, and within the context of our current social, political and religious cultures."[29] In the interest of promoting revision of primary religious symbols, however, while still maintaining their Jewish character, both she and Plaskow are led to engage in theological and historical arguments asserting an obvious and simple connection between goddess imagery and present-day Judaism. These arguments involve them in basic questions of definition. At what point does a theology cease to be Jewish? The two authors answer differently, and Plaskow dissociates her own views from some of those that Kien defends. Nonetheless, the very similar theological and historical contentions that they enlist betray their shared disregard for the weight and significance of the living religious reality that they seek to refute.

In theological terms, both Plaskow and Kien suggest that the prophetic invective of the Hebrew Bible against such worship may not portray it accurately.[30] Plaskow, in this connection, criticizes Ozick's "hysterical and historically false" jump from goddess worship to charges of human sacrifice and idolatry.[31] She attempts to sort out the issues that lie behind the "pagan" label so as to determine "when, if ever, they are legitimate and when they reflect either religious prejudice or continuing attachment to patriarchal aspects of Judaism that might better be transformed."[32] In battling against the instant revulsion traditional Jews feel regarding female imaging of God, she invokes logic: "Rationally, it seems contradictory to argue that the Jewish God transcends sexuality, that anthropomorphism is not to be taken literally, and at the same time insist that new metaphors slander and sully monotheism."[33]

Kien too strives to overcome the influence of Deuteronomic diatribes, which she believes have prejudiced many people against pagan imagery because they are convinced that the figures are worshiped as deities in themselves. This unfair portrayal of polytheistic religions equates the religious use of physical symbols in paganism with its most primitive and uneducated understanding. In the eyes of the educated pagan, such images are really nonverbal metaphors, forming a complex symbolic grammar on which to meditate and achieve other-than-everyday states of mind. Such a form of worship is surely reminiscent of some of the complex rituals traditional Judaism has woven around the Torah, treating it as a holy object so as to change our attitude toward it in study and open our minds to its words in a special way.[34] In a vein similar to that of Plaskow, Kien tries to combat the instinctive negative reaction of traditional Jews to the ancient anthropomorphic symbols of paganism. Why, she asks, do Jews kiss a mezuzah or Torah scroll and explain that it is not the symbol itself that is worshiped but rather the divinely inspired words within, yet recoil from figures that serve to focus sacred energy and help us reach closer to the divine? And why does goddess terminology or any name for divinity implying a clearly female (i.e., sexual) body, rather than the abstract concept of mothering, immediately provoke fear of idolatry among the same Jews who are prepared to appropriate female names from Kabbalah or other abstract female attributes?

On the historical level, both Plaskow and Kien point out that the struggle between exclusive Yahweh worship and Canaanite modes of worship continued for a good span of Israelite history. Plaskow nonetheless draws the line at polytheism, implying that a single deity is a more defining characteristic of Judaism than the precise nature of the symbols and rituals we develop for thinking about the One God. In contrast, Kien contends that because Jewish monotheism developed over time and involved a struggle, it cannot be regarded as the exclusive definitive element of Judaism and sharply distinguished from its original Canaanite roots.[35]

Following this debate down to its bottom line, one is hard put even on the theological plane to distinguish between Kien's ignoring the biblical injunction against polytheism and Plaskow's overriding of its predominantly male imagery. But aside from quibbling over the relative legitimacy of their positions in terms of the authenticity of their definitions of Judaism, the main problem I find with all such arguments is that they are conducted on a hypothetical level—that is to say, from the outsider's point of view. This perspective ignores the living reality of de facto Judaism as it has been absorbed and practiced by the community of believers for centuries. The knee-jerk reaction of most Jews would surely still be to identify with Ozick's incredulity over the "preposterous" suggestion that "millennia after the cleansing purity of Abraham's vision of the One Creator," we return to "a resurrection of every ancient idolatry the Jewish idea came into the world to drive out." Is it only by infiltrating female imagery and deity figures into Jewish thought that we may enhance the self-esteem of women and mend the injustice of their status in tradition? Says Ozick, "The answer stuns with its crudity."[36]

It is true that any harking back to ancient traditions must contend with the fact that since the time of Abraham, Isaac, and Jacob, the notion of the Jewish God has undergone a thing or two. *Of course* the interpretive overlays were imposed upon a struggle that was formulated in terms that may no longer be ours. *Of course* the likelihood is that had we begun in this era we would choose to proceed differently. But we cannot—nor should we wish to—leapfrog over two thousand years of rabbinic tradition in order to revise (according to Plaskow) or even rip out in one fell swoop (according to Kien) the foundations of the entire grand halakhic, philosophical, and theological edifice built in its wake.

In this connection it is illuminating to bring the testimony of Gilla Rosen, a contemporary Modern Orthodox educator who relates her experience in the early 1970s when, as a college freshman, she was approached by a fellow student eager to "convert" her to feminism. The conversation began with her being asked how she could possibly relate to a totally male God.

I stared at the poor girl in astonishment. Her question intrigued me. If Judaism had a male God, I hadn't noticed. . . . I had been brought up on the God of Maimonides—starkly incorporeal and abstract, omnipresent yet invisible, almost colorless, devoid of anthropmorphic characteristics.

If there was a fault in my education, it was that God was left too abstract for a child—unimaginable, inscrutable, unreachable—approachable only through the set prayers of the Siddur. If the language used to describe God sounded masculine in English translation—in Hebrew it lacked that connotation for me.

Later that day, I sat in class musing about that strange non-meeting of minds . . . and eventually it dawned upon me that my perception of God was truly different from the expectations of my questioner. I already knew intuitively that truth lay hidden within a kaleidoscopic multiplicity of metaphors. That if God was indeed my father, my shepherd, my king, my beloved, my judge and my craftsman (to name but a few employed in the Bible), then certainly "He" was both all of these and not exactly any of them. One cannot pray on Rosh Hashanah—even as a child—without sensing this.[37]

What is to be learned from such testimonies is that whether the prophetic caricature of Canaanite polytheism and goddess worship as literal belief in sticks and stones (and morally corrupt practice) conforms to the biblical reality or is a mythical construct may be interesting for historians. But surely it is not what will determine the Jewishness and acceptability of new ways of conceiving of God. Once the abstract but exclusive and predominantly male God has been established as Jewish canon and absorbed by its adherents as the basis of their Jewish identity, the enlisting of historical or rational arguments in order to bypass these parameters appears irrelevant. The same may be said of the preservation of derivative theological concepts and symbols, such as trembling before the voice of the mighty God, or acquiescing to the sacrifice of Isaac, which have come to signify for us a transcendent and awesome dimension of reality even though at face value they hardly reflect the life experience and sensibilities of the modern Jew.

This argument applies equally to anthropological repercussions on the religious life. We may, for example, reduce to a cultural construct (à la Foucault) the obsession—so pathological to modern eyes—of rabbinic sources with female seductiveness, and say that this construct was set up in order to serve male power interests. But does this justify bypassing a whole world of Jewish gender identity internalized in its wake? If ethnologists attribute the source of laws governing menstruant women to primitive man's fear of the destructive powers in women's bodily secretions, is this sufficient cause for eradicating the aura of holiness that has been woven around the concept of family purity over the course of time?[38] Such examples are no different in principle from the case of several of our sacred festivals. Distinctly religious interpretations have lent deep meaning to what are possibly simply remnants of agricultural practices or even of pagan rituals common to many tribal cultures of the ancient East.

Particularly for those who wish to adopt a form of spirituality continuous with the past, it seems beside the point to dredge up a far-distant precedent from the archives of history that ignores all subsequent sensibilities and interpretations that have accrued to it and been adopted by the community of believers. Ultimately, once a tradition becomes established, it is never again possible to retreat to some neutral territory that ignores what previously prevailed in order to build a new and antiseptic future. Any future developments must negotiate with what already exists.

The intrinsic value of hierarchic theological conceptions. The conservative regard for what has already been established is not motivated by pragmatics alone. In addition to practical considerations of feasibility, the theology and imagery of any religion, after all is said and done, must be viewed primarily in terms of its main function: capturing the nature of the divine and enhancing the spiritual capacity of human beings for experiencing it. Questions of male or female pronouns aside, monotheism and the concept of a transcendent God do shape the stance we adopt toward the world and the way we relate to spirituality. All of this may have intrinsic value irrespective of gender and sexual politics. The vision of God as outside ourselves may be crucial to the experience of prayer as a dialogic activity.[39] The notion of divine providence may be as necessary to the development of human morality and social responsibility as policing is to the preservation of law and order. And the notion of a God who stands over and above creation may be valuable in imaging a God who is more than the projection of our subjective desires.

Listening to much of the non-Jewish contemporary feminist discussion of goddess thealogy, one gets the impression that such preferences stem from a more general theological position of nonrealism. By this I mean a position that views the entire purpose of religion not as reflecting a real metaphysical entity with any objective claims, but rather as facilitating a lifestyle that is spiritually satisfying and contributes to human flourishing. In such a system, talk of the goddess does not refer to an actual divinity who fits the description "female," but may function more as a glorified metaphor for the sacred power of the human self.[40] It is a real question whether religious belief in general and Judaism in particular can afford the forgoing of *any* claims to metaphysics.[41]

In sum, religious models and norms born of a monotheistic worldview cannot all can be judged one-sidedly in terms of "the woman question" alone. There are certain aspects of religiosity and the human condition that men and women share, and in which they have a common interest, despite the danger of adverse anthropological repercussions from a feminist point of view. Nor can such models and norms be evaluated merely in terms of their original significance. The irrational emotions, collective memories, customs, rituals, mystic, and even magical meanings that have accrued over the generations all interweave to form the invisible thicket that constitutes our sense of who we are.[42] Because of these additional strands and the complex ties and reciprocal relations that have developed among them over the course of time (without our always being conscious of their existence, let alone their significance), theological selectivity is an impossible affair. Submitting our traditional God imagery to radical gender transformation can have profoundly distorting effects, of which we cannot begin to be aware, upon our core identity as Jews.

This is not to claim that there is no room whatsoever for modification of the models and norms that a religion adopts. But the ability of any proposed change to be absorbed successfully by the religious mainstream depends much upon the extent to which it relates to the entire range of its historical development. Revamping Judaism by superimposing an additional transplant upon its basically androcentric symbolism, while totally ignoring (as Kien) or significantly discounting (as Plaskow) an entire body of law, lore, and literature that has developed in its wake—including various accommodations, compromises, and trade-offs for women—has little chance of resonating with the central body of its loyal practitioners. Insistence upon the "given" nature not only of the Bible itself, but also of its accumulated tradition, as material that is not to be challenged or doubted, is built into the very fabric of Jewish tradition.

Going even further, I think it would be fair to say that the ultimate message of Judaism, over and above the notion of monotheism, is the centrality of *halakhah* to the religious way of life. Both before and after Judaism was established, other forms of monotheism existed.[43] Even the concept of a one-time revelation never to be repeated, which comes to teach that human spirituality mandates continuity with what went on before, is a veneration of traditionalism common to the three great monotheistic religions alike. Addressing this revelation to a collective, however, in the form of concrete commands, conveys a uniquely Jewish notion that spirituality is best expressed and experienced via immersion in the real world and within community.

Admittedly there has been some debate over the generations as to whether observance of the law should be the regarded as "the essence of Judaism." Questioning the centrality of law to the religious life was not restricted to the schism between Christianity and Pharisaic Judaism. It was also reflected in tensions evidenced within various streams of rationalism and mysticism and in the conflict between Hassidim and their opponents, the Mitnaggedim, as well as between other forms of pietistic inwardness and halakhic behaviorism. Among the Modern Orthodox as well, differences of opinion continue as to the degree to which *halakhah* should be viewed as the exclusive and uniquely distinctive characteristic of Judaism.[44] In this connection, it may be instructive to summarize the last two centuries of Jewish life as a two-hundred-year search for an alternative to the halakhic rigor of traditional Judaism.[45] Aside from assimilation and secular Zionism, alternatives range from viewing Judaism as an expression of political liberalism, whereby all of Jewish identity is subordinated to the pursuit of social justice (*tikkun olam*) and a return to prophetic ethics suitably shorn of their traditional metaphysical claims, to a New Age type of spirituality more reminiscent of Eastern religions. Nevertheless, I think it is still fair to say that historic attempts at preserving Judaism without reference to *halakhah* as an essential bridge to the divine never remained Jewish for long.[46] What can be surely be said with an even greater measure of certainty is that in the eyes of a traditional Jew, for whom a reading of Torah bereft of the rich mediation of the Oral Law is inconceivable, the suggestions of Plaskow and Kien would not appear plausible on any grand scale.

Viewed in this light, the agenda of third-stage feminism need not be male God-bashing. Rather, as the "sociologists" suggest, the question may still be what to do today about those deep-seated hierarchical aspects of Judaism affecting contemporary women adversely on the halakhic level. The limitations of positivism, restorativism, and the seeking of precedents indicate that a different model for addressing this agenda must be developed. This conclusion, however, is premature, pending confrontation with another set of assumptions implied by third-stage feminism that are far more problematic theologically. Any revisionism, be it sociological or theological, that seeks to improve upon biblical tradition poses a serious threat to the notion of divine revelation.

The Ultimate Theological Question: Is the Torah from Heaven?

Faulting biblical justice. The critique of all third-stage revisionists harks back to the Bible itself in one form or another, implying that not all or even most of what is written there supports current notions of justice. We have seen that "multiple thread" revisionists quite frankly seek to improve on the dominant biblical model. But even a "golden thread" or "principle of charity" methodology that relies on selective reading of the Torah or on appeal to the talmudic period (and sometimes only to its dissonant voices at that) is problematic. Viewing Oral Law as a necessary corrective implicitly casts aspersions on God's original message. Assuming that absolute justice means equality, and then acknowledging that the Bible is patriarchal and does not treat all humans as equals, is tantamount to saying that the Bible contains a fundamental moral flaw.

A case in point is Cynthia Ozick's assertion that we must be clear-eyed about the case of women and admit that the Torah has failed to provide us with a timeless law, allowing itself instead to reflect the norms of the world in its time. Past rabbinic efforts to ameliorate women's condition do not, in her opinion, suffice to establish justice, but only the voluntary and unreliable

ceding of a privilege. Though explicators of *halakhah* explain biblical inequality in terms of complementarity, when the norm is male and female is a
deviation (as in rabbinic literature) then the norm will always be understood
to be superior. Justice in this case can be achieved "only through restoring to
the Torah the cleansing precept of justice itself." As we noted in the last
chapter,[47] Ozick calls for no less than an eleventh commandment: "Thou
shalt not lessen the humanity of women."

The taking of such liberties with what is presumably a divine text is religiously problematic. Faulty rabbinic interpretations, while uncomfortable,
may be excused by invoking human limitations. But such excuses do not
work when a message is said to be divine. What authority does Ozick offer
for pitting her twentieth-century notions of justice against the Bible's? If she
admits that her a priori perception of equality does not derive from or tally
with biblical teaching, she may be indicating that God is not her only or
even her final arbiter of morality. It seems, however, that she still attempts to
understand Torah as a divine text providing us with absolute moral values
that are meant to transcend nature and society. If the principle of equality
for women is meant to be included among these, as she maintains, we need
an explanation that she does not offer us for the Torah's lapse in this one
case. Why should a divine text that speaks in the name of absolute justice be
inconsistent in its application? Attributing contradictory messages to the
Bible is surely problematic theologically for a religion based on the belief in
divine revelation. It requires theological justification.

Orthodox feminist Judith Antonelli does indeed address this problem:

> If the Torah were written by men (or even three men and one woman), an apparently
> sexist Torah passage could simply be dismissed as anachronistic and only the mean-
> ingful passages retained. One who believes in divine revelation, however, cannot dis-
> miss some parts of the Torah while embracing others. It is one Torah and one God.
> The fabric cannot be torn apart into separate threads.

Antonelli's solution to this "existential dilemma"[48] is to build, as did Berkovits, upon Maimonides' notion of the Torah as a pedagogic work. In the
attempt to explain the biblical acceptance of animal sacrifice, the medieval
commentator suggests that the long-term goal of the Torah is to wean humanity gradually to higher moral standards; in order to be truly effective,
however, God had to take into account the moral state of the surrounding
culture at the time of revelation. In other words, the Torah deliberately
failed to apply its ideal of justice to all biblical law, for pedagogic reasons.

Antonelli and Berkovits apply this reasoning to biblical attitudes toward
women. But this solution involves a legal non sequitur. Acknowledging that
the original formulation of a law is influenced by surrounding circumstances
does not necessarily mean that the law may be revoked when those circumstances no longer pertain. A formalist position, especially regarding biblical norms, would hold that the law is the law no matter what the original

reasons for its formulation. There is every indication that even Maimonides—who purportedly viewed the Torah as an educational document embodying more spiritual values—did not view his understanding of biblical acceptance of animal sacrifice as a basis for future revoking of sacrificial laws. Another problem with Antonelli's position: If we allow for the possibility that some parts of the Torah merely reflect passing social norms, on what authority do we distinguish between what is temporary and the influence of sociology and what is permanent and divine? We have no guarantee that such distinctions themselves are clean of subjective bias.[49]

Faulting biblical theology. These reservations are by no means the end of the story. As Judith Plaskow is quick to note, Ozick is not oblivious to a deeper level of difficulty although she does not address it in her sociological response to the moral priorities of the Bible. Indeed, she postpones its very mention to the end of her paper,[50] evidence of her reluctance to explore it. However, as Plaskow defines this level, in the wake of Ozick's own formulation, it concerns the possibility of a more inherent link between injustice and the nature of biblical theology. Hence, Plaskow asks:

what if the Otherness of women is not simply a matter of Jewish incorporation of surrounding social attitudes but is in part created and sustained by Torah itself? What if the subordination of women in Judaism is rooted in theology, in the very foundation of the Jewish tradition?[51]

Audacious, but I believe that even such questions fail to probe the full depth of the theological challenge posed by the feminist critique. As Plaskow would have it, the most damaging aspect of an all-pervasive male bias in the Torah is the influence upon attitudes to women on the anthropological level: if the Torah places males at the center and images God as male, it also leads to a set of cultural attitudes and structures particularly suited to patriarchal social forms. The all-powerful Creator God, who rules over the universe and commands humanity like a king of kings (even if He be regarded also as a kindly father figure) is incontrovertibly male, not so much in sex as in role. And this role then strengthens, reciprocally, the notion of patriarchy as a sort of imitatio Dei, whereby man's relationship to the beings under him is as God's relationship to him: one of separation and dominion.

We have already noted that Orthodox feminists generally do not enter this level of critique. Indeed, they studiously avoid it; not necessarily because they identify more fully with the attitudes implied by the sanctified formulas of tradition, but because of the claim of these formulas to divine origin. The Torah may indeed have been phrased in the terms of a patriarchal and pagan society, but we as mere flesh and blood may not change at will a tradition based upon a divine document. Lurking in the background, however, of the critique of biblical morality and theology is a more radical conclusion, usually unarticulated, that nevertheless exerts its corrosive influence on the very foundations of traditional Jewish belief. What third-stage feminism ultimately implies is that this document that all traditional Jews consider divine and which has served as the authoritative basis of the Jewish way of life for millenia cannot possibly be attributed to God at all.

How is this so?

Undermining the plausibility of divine authorship. As we have seen, third-stage feminism problematizes the assumption that the Torah begins with a "pure" and uniquely Jewish view that is not inimical to women's interests, only requiring adjustments here and there in order to accommodate new societal concerns and realities. Yet unless we are prepared to accept the notion that God Himself is unjust, such suggestions already begin to call into question the divine character of the Torah. In its commitment to a fixed hierarchy of gender, the biblical social order is seen to reflect a set of assumptions traceable to palpably "ungodly" forces in history. Such assumptions are not pure or distinctly Jewish at all. They also do not reveal the type of even-handedness that women would expect the deity to display in protecting their interests and concerns, alongside those of men.

Over and above considerations of divine justice or an androcentric theology, however, what third-stage feminism of the theological variety teaches us is that the divine word bears a more *pervasive* male bias that is so implicit and subtle that the innocent reader usually remains unaware of its existence. The problem is not merely the profoundly normative character of maleness in the Torah and in Jewish tradition per se, or the inequality that this implies. Neither is it a question of male pronouns and images of the divine and whether it is necessary, desirable, or even permissible for monotheists to initiate talk about God as a She rather than a He, or to depict the nature of God in more woman-friendly terms. Rather, even the very need for an explanation of how the world came into existence can be said to reflect a male brand of curiosity. That this explanation relies upon analogy with someone making something outside of themselves and by command, that the world is portrayed as an ordered realm of demarcated beings; that our spiritual and physical well-beings are said to depend upon our performing a detailed series of acts that are mandated for us—*all* these reflect a specifically male way of thinking. It corroborates feminist assertions we saw earlier: that gender bias has an impact upon knowledge in general (see chapter 1) and upon the development of the monotheistic idea in particular (see chapter 6).

The importance of this observation is not academic. For each of the four assumptions above we might imagine a different assumption, yielding an alternative image not only of God, but also of ourselves, of our relationship to God, of our relationship to one another, and of what it means to be close to God. The very awareness of a masculine bias suggests a contrasting set of attitudes, feminine in nature, that could have given us quite a different picture of creation. Feminist retellings adopting the literary forms of *midrash* are born precisely of the need that some women feel to imagine this.

If the Torah had been written from a woman's perspective, argue the feminists, different concepts of the divine—more pantheistic or panentheistic in nature—would have been favored. Perhaps, instead of viewing the act of creation as God making something out of nothing, the Torah would have opened with the analogy of God giving birth to the world, as we find in other religions of the time. This imagery would have been a poetic celebration of a sense of our abiding intimacy with God in a world that at times seems hostile and unintelligible. Perhaps this narrative would have stressed the interrelated texture of the self at the expense of an atomized, fragmented conception, or the immanent nature of God as opposed to His transcendence, or a sense of the cooperative element in the relationship between God and His creatures. Rather than the primacy of law and obedience to authority, such a rendition would emphasize the importance of religious feeling and the presence of God in the immediate experiences of motherhood and the domestic routine of everyday life; in the biological sensibilities particular to women; and in women's view of themselves as serving God through concrete acts of charity and kindness toward others. Third-stage feminists contend that such emphases would more strikingly convey the emotionality, personal nature, and intimacy of women's piety. (Whether this religious orientation stems from a distinctly feminine perspective that is innate to all women or is culturally shaped by patriarchal society is an interesting question but really irrelevant to the feminist critique at this point.

Quite apart, then, from questions of justice or of the penetration of outside influences upon the Torah, discovery of the extent to which the biblical mind-set and its specific picture of reality is derived from the male point of view calls its divine character into question on more general grounds: if the Torah is from God, it should be above *any* human conditionality. But if the Torah's portrayal of the world and God so clearly reflects a quintessentially male point of view, how are we to view the source of such a Torah? What sort of God would ignore the voices, insights, and experiences of half the human race? Because the perspective of the Torah is limited, can we really credit it with being divine? Is it really describing God in words that God has revealed to us or might these words be merely the projection of our own wishes or social systems onto the cosmos—in a religious language that is socially shaped and culture-bound, and therefore not binding upon us? Perhaps our Torah is really only a male Torah, parading under the cloak of universality?

These questions bear extremely upsetting implications for prevailing Orthodox concepts of revelation and the divine nature of the Torah. The feminist reading of the Torah, which begins in suspicion of its male bias and continues by attempting to redress injustice with the addition of a female perspective, often ends up refusing to understand the text as divine revelation. This denial may be inevitable when the text seems simply to establish and express in a multitude of ways the one-sided particularities of a male perspective. On this view, however, the ultimate problem raised by third-stage revisionism is whether a document that so subtly and thoroughly represents partiality of *any* sort can truly be regarded as divine. Feminist revisionists who highlight those aspects of divine revelation that seem to betray a thoroughgoing male bias must eventually move the focus of their critique beyond the nature of God and our religious imagery to the notion of divine revelation itself.

Undermining the authority of halakhah. As I see it, these implications that discovery of the profoundly male bias in Torah bear for the very possibility of verbal revelation are the ultimate problem raised by the feminist critique. The disturbing nature of this threat is intensified when we realize that all halakhic legislation and its attendant rabbinic commentary is based on the premise that every word of this Torah stems directly from God. Although Judaism is best described as a religion of practice and not of dogma, observance of *halakhah* does of necessity entail certain basic theological assumptions; otherwise such observance is rendered meaningless or at least loses most of its binding force. One of the most central understandings is that this Torah upon which *halakhah* is grounded is indeed from Heaven. A growing number of self-described traditional Jews find difficulty in accepting the premise of Torah from Heaven although it is a tenet of Orthodoxy, and they revere the Orthodox body of legislation and commentary nonetheless. Yet it is this connection between the authority of *halakhah* and its claim to divine origins that defined the character of Jewish spirituality for generations.

Many third-stage feminists are untroubled by such observations. Some are totally indifferent to the constitutive role that the halakhic medium has played in the self-image of Jews and in the definition of Judaism. Others would dismiss the halakhic medium altogether as symptomatic of an oppressive male mode of religious expression. Plaskow, however, is not oblivious to the diminished authority of traditional sources that third-stage feminism implies. Concerned about preserving some semblance of continuity as the sanctified collective memory of Jewish tradition is reshaped by feminist insights, she registers awareness that these insights diminish the authority of traditional sources. As she admits:

In seeking to restore the history of Jewish women, the Jewish feminist historian is not "simply" trying to revolutionize the writing of history but is also implicitly or explicitly acting as theologian, claiming to amplify Torah, and thus questioning the finality of the Torah we have.[52]

In spelling this problem out, however briefly, she is one of the few Jewish feminists who articulates the importance of confronting the view of Torah that feminist revision entails.[53] Her response, however, seems to be giving up on the traditionalist game from the start, making peace with a watering down of biblical rights to metaphysical claims. The necessity of tempering biblical authority with the lessons of human experience may indeed imply flaws in the message. But if the more practical implication of a diluted notion of revelation is that it undermines the authority of *halakhah* as a system predicated on biblical fiat, Plaskow is willing to pay this price.

As fellow third-stage feminist Rachel Adler has observed, "Plaskow is profoundly ambivalent about *halakhah*."[54] On the one hand, Plaskow does acknowledge an integral relationship between Torah and *halakhah,* and that "law certainly constitutes an important part of Jewish teaching, if not its center."[55] Moreover, in *Standing Again at Sinai* she rejects the more sweeping antinomian charges of non-Jewish feminists, who regard law per se as a product of male ways of thinking. She recognizes norm-defining as a human need.[56] She also, however, identifies with the radical critique of *halakhah* that regards it as an unsuitable tool for remedying women's status in tradition because of its most fundamental assumption of woman as Other. She therefore asserts that any reform of *halakhah* designed to restore justice to women "would entail a recognition of women as women" that goes beyond "a system that renders women's status invisible."[57]

Elsewhere, Plaskow questions the suitability of halakhic form, irrespective of its content, as a suitable medium for expressing women's Jewishness,[58] and doubts whether the rational abstractions of law can adequately accommodate more fluid, spontaneous spirituality or be responsive to the concreteness of individual moments.[59] Her final conclusion is that any feminist choice to work with *halakhah* "entails rejecting the argument that *halakhah* cannot be altered because it represents the will of God."[60] Feminism and recognition of the human origins of *halakhah* are logically intertwined. Hence Plaskow entertains the vision of a feminist future in which varying models of relationship or nonrelationship to *halakhah* and understandings of the roles that it should play in Jewish life exist side by side.[61]

Rachel Adler, in expressing her feminist vision, adopts a more affirmative attitude to the halakhic medium. Her writing does not shy away from the multidisciplinary techniques with which the revisionists retrieve the voices of protest from traditional sources. She also shares the willingness of her more radical third-stage sisters to develop and create new theological imagery and ritual practices. Nevertheless, the special interest of her writings for the traditionalist lies in the fact that she is far more concerned than feminists such as Plaskow in expressing her vision of Judaism in a halakhic mode. Adler understands that those who most feel the claim of *halakhah* upon their lives are the least likely to abandon their Jewish lifestyle and identity.[62] Appreciating the difficulty of "extricat[ing] thought from praxis in a living Judaism"[63] leads her to search for methods of constructing a viable framework for halakhic living, without remaining caught up in the straitjacket of positivism or the vulnerability of judges to judicial bias. In such a framework Adler seeks not only ground rules for overcoming the view of *halakhah* as "a closed system of obsolete and unjust rules," but also "a way for communities of Jews to generate and embody their Jewish moral visions,"[64] without seeking support for these in any more grandiose metaphysical claims. Looking at both the strengths of her proposals and their shortcomings may shed light on what Orthodox feminists need to realize in their own moral visions.

CHAPTER 8

Halakhic Proactivism

The approaches we have seen thus far in our exploration of feminism's challenges to the halakhic system are fairly polarized. Either *hala-khah* is a system that is consistent with its own internal standards or it is controlled by passing, outside influences. This polarized view extends to the nature of the Torah as well: either it is divinely revealed or it is a humanly authored document reflecting male interests and biases. In the realm of *halakhah*, Modern Orthodoxy has attempted to mitigate the rigidity of this polarization somewhat by introducing the notion of fixed and contingent elements. While the fixed elements are indeed untouched and untouchable, the contingent ones are open to change. Third-stage feminism critiques this distinction and finds it wanting. It reveals that no portion of the Torah or of *halakhah* is immune to social conditioning, and even the apologetic attempt to create a distinction is itself the product of contingent and subjective cultural demands.

Acknowledging the vulnerability of *halakhah* and even the Torah to the influence of androcentric bias leads feminists to disillusion with positivist approaches. The shortcoming of such approaches lies in their assumption of what may be termed "naive objectivism": the belief that truth "corresponds" to some neutrally defined, universal, irreducible, and self-evident reality that already exists, quite apart from our subjective formulations, and that observers can, in perceiving it, overcome the mediation of their own bias or point of view. Adler's search for a new halakhic model induces her to seek a method of interpretation that does not posit so sharp a distinction between a fixed, objective meaning of the text and a subjective understanding of it, but rather acknowledges a more fluid mode of interaction between them.

Adler is not alone in this project. The growing influence of historicism and critical awareness in the traditional study of Jewish legal sources, and the ensuing "loss of innocence," have provoked the interest of a growing number of halakhic theoreticians to explore the potential for less objectivist theories of law. Generally these theorists are not *poskim* but academically

trained rabbis who are affected by the impact of historical research conducted in the past few decades by several halakhically observant historians
and talmudic scholars—among them Yaakov Katz, Yisrael Ta-Shma, and
Yitzhak Gilat. These new exponents of halakhic theory also strive to take
the "external" point of view of the outside observer into account and incorporate the insights of this perspective in understanding the true impetus for
the decisions of the internal players—the "officials," or judges, within the
system. Increasingly skeptical of the positivist notion of a fixed, eternal element of the *halakhah* embedded in the standards and precedents established
in the Torah, these new philosophers of *halakhah* look to some of the more
recent formulations of Anglo-American legal philosophy for a viable theory
of jurisprudence.

Post-positivist Trends in Legal Theory

Post-postivist legal theory is still in its infancy. It is only beginning to face the
need for articulating a vision of law more constructive than the critical
thinking of the external observer, while still taking the radically biased nature of human perspectives and their fluctuating foundations into account.
All such attempts acknowledge the futility of implying that legal procedures
are so malleable that they can be construed to support any position. All realize that saying that the law can be interpreted to mean anything is tantamount to declaring that nothing at all can be called illegal. Their flight from
nihilism or anarchy relies upon the recognition that, while it is certainly important to question our traditions continually because of their contingent
nature, escaping them altogether would leave us nowhere. The differences
between their various formulations rest on the precise models they offer for
maintaining the adequacy of our traditions despite these traditions' limitations and biases. The degree to which such models can provide solid interpretive tools for maintaining our socially situated and contingent traditions
and practices without slipping back into the mode of naive objectivism that
they purport to reject is the critical measure of their success.

Dworkin's serial novel model. One effort that initially looks promising is the
model of jurisprudence developed by Ronald Dworkin. Dworkin regards
legal systems as a multilayered hierarchy of concrete rules, abstract principles, and even more broadly based policies that usually work in tandem and
are sometimes weighed against each other in the complicated effort to
achieve legally actionable decisions.[1] Still regarded as very much part of the
mainstream school of Anglo-American positivism, he has nevertheless
argued that laws need to be determined with reference to society's political
and moral conceptions, even though these conceptions cannot themselves be
tested against some standard of objective morality.[2]

In Dworkin's more recent work, he describes law as a text that must be reconstituted, and he invokes the image of a mythical judge, Hercules, who is able to perform this difficult task. Much like an author charged with the task of writing a new chapter for a serial novel, Hercules must make his text as plausible and coherent as possible when extending the legal tradition and applying his understanding of what is internal to it. This charge entails the assumption that the law is or can be understood to be coherent, and that there is an identifiable theory or rationale unifying the recorded decisions in a particular area of law. Such an assumption does not allow Hercules license to do whatever he wants; there is a level beyond which the interpreter no longer remains an interpreter, but is actually writing a new text. As long as he does not cross that line, however, he is justified in "hard cases" of doubt to exercise the principle of charity[3] in his interpretation (much as Ozick has done in her understanding of the biblical attitude to women),[4] in order to present the law in the best possible light. Even if case law is split on a given question, Hercules will make the "right" decision based upon his commitment to integrity, equality, and due process.

Dworkin's description of the interpreter seems to be especially suited to the reading of religious texts; and indeed, his comparison of the judge to the author of a serial novel has already been referred to favorably by several Orthodox meta-halakhists.[5] A religious believer is certainly committed to the principle of charity, opting for the most favorable interpretation of the holy sources. Out of a sense of intimacy with God, such readers are most likely to identify God's concepts of justice with their most deeply internalized moral intuitions.

Moreover, a model that posits continuity as a criterion for distinguishing between legitimate and illegitimate interpretation holds additional appeal for theoreticians of law in general. This attraction reflects a significant difference between legal hermeneutics and other forms of interpretation, in terms of their methods of justification on the rhetorical level, if not in practice. Although literary and legal interpretations are equally determined by the traditions of their respective interpretive communities, a new literary interpretation is justified when addressing a contradiction or ambiguity in the old. For this reason, the subject of analysis is always the primary text. In law, on the other hand, judges examine precedents not in search of weakness, but to make connections to the case at hand. Therefore, in legal interpretation the primary text grows with each interpretation to include not only the original text, but also the accumulated tradition that has adhered to it.[6] This growth again holds especially true for the Jewish legal tradition, rendering the criterion of continuity especially important.

What Dworkin's critics are quick to note, however, is that while the model of a developing text pays lip service to the need for both an external and internal perspective on the legal system, it still fosters a certain bias for the status quo. Dworkin's model lacks a neutral vantage point from which to determine when an external view is legitimately incorporated, because it is merely adding a "chapter" to the same "novel," and when it must be delegitimized because it is really writing a different story. Determining whether a judge is interpreting or changing the law already involves a prior decision as to what the legal history is. Reliance upon precedent is as much an interpretation of the legal tradition as is showing that a precedent is irrelevant to a case or simply mistaken. Leaving such decisions exclusively in the hands of the Herculean judge essentially means wholesale privileging of the opinions of the regnant legal establishment. As David Kairys, a radical critic of legal positivism, has put it, "The dominant system of values has been declared value-free; it then follows that all others suffer from bias and can be thoughtlessly dismissed."[7] In effect, Dworkin's position may be regarded as combining the worst features of positivism and legal realism, in that the biased interpretation of judges in problematic cases can run unbridled, masked under the cover of universally accepted textual constraints.

An illustration of these weaknesses can be seen in an article written several years ago by Rabbi Jonathan Sacks, chief rabbi of England, which refers approvingly to Dworkin's vision of law.[8] In this article on creativity and innovation in *halakhah,* Sacks applies Dworkin's model of "hard cases" to halakhic deliberation. Not surprisingly, issues dealing with women figure prominently as test cases. But wholesale identification with the baseline attitudes held by the ruling establishment renders Sacks incapable of dealing with feminist claims that the very core of *halakhah* is gendered. He is also left with no room for dealing with the important sociological finding that in other matters as well the opinions of the halakhic authorities tend to correlate with their inescapably situated political and ideological orientations. And his lack of an objective means for distinguishing between text and interpretation leaves him with uncritical wholesale acceptance of existing Orthodox ideology and its definition of core text.

A telling example is Sacks's rejection of the Conservative position regarding women's entry to the rabbinate.[9] Alongside objections of a more technical nature, Sacks invokes a meta-halakhic argument that this decision constitutes a break with the halakhic past.[10] But the question of coherence and continuity with the past or change and innovation is itself a matter of interpretation. No matter how Herculean the judge, such an enterprise can never be conducted from some neutral and bias-free vantage point. The attempt to contrast the U.S. Conservative movement's view that Jewish law evolves "even in its ultimate conceptions of value and purpose" with an Orthodox position that allows for development "only in its detailed actualization"[11] emerges as artificial and strained.

In placing the full burden of interpretation on the judge, Dworkin's position does not provide a satisfactory jurisprudential model for feminists. Despite the awareness he displays (as do all secular positivists) of law as the social construction of legal principles and despite his willingness to blur the sharp distinction between text and interpretation, he still believes in the overall ability of texts to delimit interpretation uniformly. In so doing, he does not take sufficient account of the continuing role of bias and other contingent factors in the interpretive process. Feminists do derive inspiration, however, from other critics of legal positivism who understand the meaning of law in a more open-ended manner.

Cover's model of law as a bridge. A school of legal theory in the United States that is especially attractive to Jewish and non-Jewish feminists[12] is that which has come to be known as the school of Critical Legal Studies. The approach suggested by the late Robert Cover, a chief exponent of this school, is relatively free of fixed constraints, even when expressed in formal terms. It is also more inclusive in its understanding of the interpretive process. As such, feminists regard it either as a source of hope for deliverance from despair over law's stultification[13] or as a first step that feminism develops and improves upon.[14] Cover's ideas figure prominently in Rachel Adler's feminist project of developing a *halakhic* system that is both "proactive" and inclusive of women.

Cover draws expressly on the Jewish legal tradition as inspiration for a model of law that can successfully address some of the current dilemmas that American law faces in maintaining a coherent legal system while allowing for pluralism in its interpretation and practice. In so doing, he represents a current vogue among contemporary American scholars of literary and legal theory: pointing to certain parallels between postmodernist theory and the classic rabbinic mode of midrashic exegesis. Such parallels come to challenge the commonly held view of *halakhah* as a predetermined system overwhelmingly constrained by hierarchical rankings of authority and precedent.[15]

One feature common to *midrash* and postmodernism that these circles emphasize is the interpreter's role in the formation of meaning. If postmodernism speaks of the futility of absolute predefined truths that exist independent of subjective perception, rabbinic tradition also stipulates that "the Torah is not in Heaven"[16] and recognizes the importance of human interaction with the text in establishing the ultimate meaning of Torah. If in postmodernism this understanding leads to the notion of multiple truths, rabbinic thought appears to foster a spirit of pluralism as well. This spirit is evident in the talmudic declaration that "there are seventy faces to Torah"[17] and in the story of the heavenly voice that mediated the conflicting legal opinions of the Schools of Hillel and Shammai by proclaiming that both "these and these are the words of the living God."[18] The Rabbis acknowledged the human factor that led to indeterminacy when interpreting the received tradition, and they understood God as attaching religious value to human participation in the process of deliberation and the overcoming of ambiguities. Even when allowing for the possibility of divine intervention in the determination of law, rabbinic tradition does not dismiss the validity or worthiness of alternative approaches to the norm. This breadth of understanding on their part allowed disagreement (*mahloket*) to be recorded as an essential part of the canon.[19]

Critics of this trend warn against getting carried away with analogies. Some scholars have expressed serious reservations about drawing parallels in the realm of literary theory.[20] Others question the inspiration that some legal theoreticians claim to have found in the Jewish model, and they reject the attempt to apply its multifaceted notion of truth to a secular system of law.[21]

Undoubtedly there is a significant difference, beyond semantics, between the claim that the received word of God contains infinite possibilities of interpretation and the postmodernist rejection of metaphysics and the notion of universal truth altogether. For the Rabbis, the grounding of various views in a common metaphysical source indicated that a point exists at which they are all ultimately reconcilable. In the words of the Talmud, conflicting opinions are all valid because "all of them are given from one shepherd."[22] The postmodernist attitude, by contrast, tends to deflate the pretensions of any point of view's claims to truth. As I have indicated, the postmodernists would regard all choices as random selections from arbitrary collections of isolated and unconnected viewpoints, whose relative worth can be understood or assessed only from within their own partial terms.

Moreover, as noted talmudic scholar Professor David Weiss-Halivni has observed, the fluid approach of the Rabbis pertained only to the text of Torah.[23] Even here there is more interpretive flexibility evident in *midrash aggadah* than in *midrash halakhah;* diversity is much more accepted as there is not the same imperative for uniformity in nonlegal matters.[24] At any rate, we have no indication that the Rabbis would have been prepared to apply their view of the significance of reader participation to any text other than the biblical one. When this fluid approach to truth is limited to Torah, it fosters in the religious believer an attitude of respect toward every point of view, as the bearer of significant meaning on a theoretical level, yet still attaches great importance to which opinion is to be applied in practice, signifying the precise method of interaction between God's truth and a finite temporal reality.

Nevertheless, what does appear common to both postmodernism and the rabbinic mode of midrashi exegesis is an initial impression of joyous anarchy. Ostensibly, there are no constraints and one can interpret however one likes. No doubt the Rabbis would have denied this lack of constraint in their methods of procedure, at least with regard to their methods of legal exegesis, but as Weiss-Halivni states, "de facto, the rabbis did give the reader-interpreter great leeway in shaping the meaning of a text."[25] Such leeway in effect dissolves distinctions between the function of interpretation as determining original authorial intent and its role in extending the meaning of texts.

Returning to Cover, some of the salient features that he finds in the Jewish model—beyond its celebration of multiple opinions and its rejection of fixed and objective notions of "truth"—are its relative independence of authoritative institutional structures, and the transformative power that this dependence on voluntary commitment gives the community of its practitioners in defining the meaning of law. Because of the contrast that Cover's view presents to the positivist portrayals of *halakhah* favored by modern Orthodoxy, it is worth examining it in some detail.

The conception that Cover puts forward (most notably in his masterly essay "Nomos and Narrative")[26] is that no legal system is reducible to a static body of laws that we must master and adapt. A legal system is rather the reflection of a universe that we inhabit. In addition to legal precepts and principles, this universe—or *nomos* (a term taken from the Greek for "that which is customary and accepted" in practice)[27]—consists of the norms and values embedded in the narratives that every community weaves around the legal tradition to which it is committed. Narratives are not the mere telling of stories, but any act that lends meaning to law, by providing it with a context and envisioning the possible and plausible states of affairs to which it may apply. Without this linkage to narrative, legal meaning does not exist.

Cover cites in this connection the biblical tradition that an oldest son is entitled to succeed his father as head of the family and receive a double portion of the family inheritance.[28] The thrust of a rich set of biblical narratives showing the younger son as preferred is subversive, contesting the simple rule of succession and problematizing in various ways the notion of inheritance by divine destiny. The function of subsequent legal interpretation is to provide a concrete link between the codified ruling and the implications of the narrative that accompanies it. Hence law is not to be conceived as a static entity, but rather as a bridge between the present norms and values of the community and the as yet unrealized moral visions toward which it reaches.

Cover suggests that the bridge that law creates is, ideally, maintained by the coexistence in dynamic equilibrium of two distinct elements of legal development. The first (which in terms of Jewish tradition corresponds to the function of the prophet) is described by Cover as the *paideic* or world-creating mode and refers to that element which generates new narratives and visions of legal meaning. The term comes from the Greek word for a teacher or guide, because this mode sees law as pedagogic, leading to something that is internalized personally. Because society is never monolithic, however, this mode leads to variegated interpretations. The second element (which in terms of Jewish tradition corresponds to the function of the rabbinic sage) is described as the *imperial* or world-maintaining mode. Its function is to counteract the instability created by the diversity of interpretation that invariably develops within a social context. Ideally, this function is accomplished not only by enforcing universal institutional norms, but also by adapting some mechanisms of tolerance for pluralism: creating legal fictions, unearthing little-known precedents and minority opinions, publicizing technical loopholes, or maintaining silence. Such policies allow divergent and minority views some freedom and autonomy and enable diverse interpretations to coexist harmoniously. Thus, for example, ruling authorities may choose not to exercise their full powers against conscientious objectors to military enlistment or will find grounds for government funding of sectarian religious schools, despite an acknowledged principle of separation between church and state.

One well-acknowledged avenue for staying in tune with the ideals and particular worldview that the community distills from its legal codes and traditions is via the ongoing decisions of its judges, as Dworkin would prescribe.[29] Applying the law in individual cases affords them the opportunity to improve and articulate more exactly the self-understanding of the community as implied in its narratives. Because "every legal instruction demands being related to a narrative," every new application of the law represents the efforts of the judges "to connect with the moral identity of the community."[30] But although lawmaking is often understood as a monopoly of the imperial bodies of the community, the example Cover derives from the Jewish legal tradition is that of a system in which law is defined not by reference to the authority and power of the state, but rather by the commitment of a legal community to voluntarily accepted legal obligations.

The Jewish example shows the imperial and paideic elements of any legal system interacting constantly through complicated processes of mutual influence and negotiation. In addition to the official lawmakers and their mainstream followers, other members of the legal community are also engaged in making their own selections from the patterns of received tradition that fit or make sense in their lives. If a law does not speak authentically to their experience, it may be ignored or transformed through the new normative significance (or narrative) attached to it by their section of the community. To the extent that subsections of the law-abiding community are willing to act upon their variant visions even in the face of state opposition, these divergent narratives also have the potential to remake legal meaning.

Cover brings several striking examples from the annals of American legal history to illustrate the power of commitment to variant narrative in redeeming law. One of these is drawn from the American antislavery movement of the nineteenth century. When the escaped slave Frederick Douglass and other abolitionists insisted that the U.S. Constitution did not permit slavery, despite professional consensus to the contrary, the vision they embraced of an American legal system guaranteeing freedom eventually led to the transformation of the legal landscape.[31]

In another example of a competing normative vision, the U.S. Supreme Court held that the Internal Revenue Service had rightfully exercised their statutory authority in denying tax-exempt status to a Christian university that discriminated on the basis of race.[32] The Court based its decision on a public policy requirement specific to the Internal Revenue Code, rather than on the constitutional dimensions of the policy of discouraging racial discrimination in education. The Mennonite Church, although it did not share the racist premises of the litigant, submitted a brief objecting to the ruling. It charged that the Court had failed to recognize that the university authorities were asserting a competing claim of value; they appealed to the American commitment to separation of church and state, as established in the First Amendment to the Constitution. In basing its rejection of the university's appeal on jurisdictional doctrine and hiding behind this lower authority, the Court in effect abandoned the protection of religious freedom—that of the Mennonites and other religious minorities alike—to the whim of public policy. Its duty, claimed the Mennonites, was to commit itself to an interpretation of the Constitution that clearly affirmed the unconstitutionality of publicly subsidized racism.

Cover understands this as the assertion of a normative community. The Mennonites were not merely protesting a court decision. They were also creating legal meaning by asserting their commitment to U.S. law, in the context of a history in which their opposition to regnant law demanded a real and high price.[33] Because they represent a cohesive community dedicated to a set of moral ideals and defined by a particular narrative, their vision of the First Amendment has as much claim to the word "law" as the opinion of the Supreme Court.

The fact that legal meaning is created by the manner in which precepts and narratives are interwoven in a web of interpretive commitments is equally evidenced in less dramatic instances. People may choose, for example, to drive faster than the speed limit on quiet country roads in defiance of state law or they may choose to yield to its dictates. The state may choose to impose sanctions upon such defiance or to ignore it. In each of these cases, legal narratives and commitments are being tested and established. The decisions as to when to stand resolute and when to give way make a difference in the life and the law of the community and are as much a part of the law as any of their other normative texts.

What Cover comes to teach us is that the willingness of a community to adopt a particular narrative and to live by it is the ultimate source of its authority, and its final justification. The meaning of the law that is established by such acts of commitment "counts" as a legitimate interpretation not because something in the text makes it so, nor because the community's authoritative bodies hegemonically declared it so. Public acceptance is "proof" of the truth of the interpretations the community adopts simply because such acceptance is what enables an underlying narrative to hold us in the grip of its perspective in a way that gives substance and body to all the other justifications that are then applied. The nomic reality to which this narrative leads fulfills the role of an interpretation in practice—a role that is possible only in a social context.

Cover's understanding of the meaning of law allows him to extend the role of legal interpretation beyond the purely conservative function of preserving stability and continuity with the present system. His appreciation of the influence on legal meaning of narrative and commitment enables him to view jurisprudence as dynamic, providing the mechanism for transforming narratives into new nomic realities and implementing their redemptive visions. It also enables him to transfer the criteria for the determination of legal meaning from the realm of the legal establishment to the realm of the community of practitioners at large.

Rachel Adler's Feminist Application of Cover to *Halakhah*

The understanding of *halakhah* that Rachel Adler proposes is a notable appropriation of Cover's thought. She seeks a method of jurisprudence that does not merely address the need for coherence within an existing system, but can also strike out for something new: an "engendered" Judaism that men and women "recreate and renew together as equals," breaking the monopoly on "rules, categories, and the transmission of authority" of Jewish law as we know it. [34] Drawing a distinction between "classical" and "liberal" *halakhah*, she dismisses the relevance of the former in today's world.[35] She also charges the latter, however, with evading critical questions of authority and structure in its attempts to reconcile *halakhah* and modernity.

Applying Cover's ideas of law as bridge to the halakhic framework, Adler rejects the model of legal positivism, which would reduce *halakhah* to formal rules or principles embedded in the texts, and the model of legal realism, which would relegate the determination of law completely to the discretionary power of judges. What ultimately generates law, she argues, is the ability of its community of adherents to envision the possibilities implicit in their canonized texts and traditions, and the willingness to live some of them out in practice. Law is maintained or remade not by orthodoxies but by commitments of communities either to obey the law as it stands or to resist and reject it in order to live out alternative legal visions.[36] Her book culminates in such a vision: a Jewish wedding ceremony and *ketubah* (contract) that retain traditional metaphors of covenant but rely on partnership law rather than property law to provide the legal underpinnings.

In other areas, too, Adler suggests that the corrective to the stultification and androcentric orientation of present-day *halakhah* lies in the hands of those who refuse to make peace with its drawbacks. In order to institute change, the halakhic narrative itself must be reinterpreted more inclusively by its practitioners, encompassing the perspective of women as well as the perspective of all other groups that have thus far not been taken into account. Such a project is not merely a matter of applying another bandage to the wounds of the existing system. It involves, rather, using the tools of a variety of disciplines to engage traditional texts and create a broader framework, a more general universe of legal meanings that will include some of the secular values that have been assumed in modern times: equal respect, inclusivity, diversity, and pluralism.[37]

Adler is not prepared to give up on the halakhic mode altogether, because (unlike Plaskow) she believes that no form of Judaism can exist without it. She places no limits, however, on how the halakhic *nomos* and narrative can be convincingly engaged. What she seems to believe is that so long as there is a corresponding narrative, no matter what its nature, then any reading of the sources is possible and available in the effort to adjust the nomic reality we now inhabit to the one toward which we strive.

Evaluating Adler in Light of the Halakhic System's Constraints

Adler's understanding of law as determined by collective cultural understanding has appeal. Any legal system that is not enforced by a totalitarian regime depends on popular acceptance. Such is especially true of the Jewish legal system, which is precisely why Cover uses it as a model. *Halakhah*, even as conceived of in Maimonides' codes of law, includes recognition of the role of the lay community both in establishing customs (*minhagim*) which may eventually become law and in determining law in cases of doubt. Communal acceptance also constitutes a decisive factor in invalidating edicts that the community of ordinary practitioners is not capable of living up to (*gezerah she-ein hatzibbur yakhol laamod ba*).[38] With the authority of the institutional bodies of the *halakhah* at an all-time low in our day, the influence of popular grassroots initiative has increased, reinforcing the understanding that communal will is a powerful force in halakhic deliberation.

Understanding communal commitment to a particular narrative as the primary factor determining the legitimacy of any legal interpretation has additional appeal for feminists who have been persuaded by the critique of meta-halakhic positivism. Rejecting the notion of a predetermined stable truth embedded in the law, they prefer simply to describe how the *halakhah* works in practice, removing the issue of halakhic legitimacy from debatable ideological premises. The beliefs and principles that purport to justify halakhic decisions may now be understood as inseparable from the way of life that lends them their meaning and significance, rather than as external "objective" criteria that must be fulfilled.

For these reasons, I believe that Adler's plan for concentrating upon community as a primary source of halakhic development has promise. But when the community is presented—as it is by Adler—as the sole arbiter in the establishment of legal meaning, I find the suggestion still requires considerable fine-tuning.

In order to effect changes that the existing halakhic system could assimilate, it is not enough for would-be reformers simply to invoke a new redemptive vision via an alternative reading of canonized texts, and then hope it will be accepted if they live it out in practice. Adler's rejection of positivism and its assumption of law's determinate meaning fails to take into account that complete interpretive freedom is never available. For one thing, there are certain inherent constraints that are built into any legal system as such. Even if the definition of law is liable to some gradual shifting, it does still embody provisional standards and methods of procedure that are integral to its interpretive tradition. Cover's image of law as a bridge applies not only to where the law is going, but also to where it is coming from; Adler's contrasting emphasis ("we need to look not just at where [the laws] were, but at where they are pointing")[39] disregards the fact that these standards and rules do control—at least to some immediate extent—the nature of the bridge that is to be formed. Any new suggestion will be measured against them. Furthermore, if a new narrative is to have any effect on the larger community of the halakhically committed, it must be capable of engaging with the sensibilities and interpretive traditions of the chief players within the system. The moderating influence of these factors is especially powerful in the case of legal systems, such as the *halakhah*, that also bear religious claims.

The spirit in which I raise these caveats is, like Cover's theory itself, not normative but pragmatic. Nevertheless, I am aware that the moment I begin to speak of constraints internal to the halakhic system, or of the need for continuity with its accumulated interpretive tradition and existing community of practitioners, I immediately lay myself bare to the accusations that were leveled against Dworkin: defining such constraints and continuities in terms of an interpretive bias that supports my position.

Undoubtedly, my halakhic community differs from Rachel Adler's. This difference is reflected in our choice of texts, the relative weight we give them, the exegetical tools we adopt in reading them, and how they fit in the overall arguments that we construct. I do believe, however, that our use of the term *halakhah*—if it is to have any sense at all—must entail some overlap; that is, taking into account prevailing notions of the concept. Adler, claiming the term "because it is the authentic Jewish language for articulating the system of obligations that constitute the content of the covenant," nonetheless writes off the possibility of covenant with those whose definitions are more traditional than hers.

Any interpretation must contend with certain existing frames of reference in order to qualify as relevant and worthy of consideration in the eyes of the traditionalist. Irrespective of more specific and substantive considerations of content, three elements are indispensable: appeal to the consensus of experts, solidarity with the larger community in which the transformative narrative is to be played out, and acknowledgment of the law's claims to transcendence.

Appeal to the consensus of the experts. To the extent that anarchy is "understood to mean the absence of rulers, not the absence of law," Cover has defined his position as "close to a classical anarchist one."[40] The *nomos* he describes "requires no state."[41] Indeed, much of his attraction to the Jewish model of law lies in its lack of control by authoritative bodies capable of stifling competing interpretations. Yet despite the anarchic propensities of Cover himself and of halakhic reformers who would often prefer to overlook the inconvenience of authority, a functioning legal system cannot completely do away with the judgment of its experts or the appeal to their guidance regarding custom and practice.

As I noted early in chapter 3, a combination of political and historical factors has indeed brought about a situation whereby most halakhically observant Jews live from day to day without recourse to any official halakhic body. Some would even regard this, in the spirit of Cover, as a welcome development. Precisely because the *halakhah* is ultimately a matter between God and the individual, it is fitting that most decisions be left to personal discretion. Nonetheless, even for Jews influenced by modernity and its emphasis upon personal autonomy, and despite the lack of opportunity to appeal to a centralized institutional body in our day, there still remain some compelling considerations for working hand in hand with institutional representation of the law.

Irrespective of our opinion on any given question of law, in order for a ruling to be legally viable it must be formulated in accordance with accepted procedural rules and conventions of the legal tradition.[42] Certain issues require a very broad consensus if any new interpretation is to be effective: most notably those in the area of criminal law or those that require formal litigation, such as inheritance and property disputes or breaking contracts. Some issues of personal status, such as conversion to Judaism, require agreement across the board if the rule of law is not to collapse altogether. This feature of the law is not merely a necessary evil of societal politics. It is precisely the existence of such rules and conventions that enable legal deliberation and provide the basis for the internal consistency critical to rule of law.

In this connection, there is a difference between merely ascertaining what has already been determined as existing halakhic practice and more active decision-making; that is, applying and adjusting the existing law to changing conditions. When resolving an issue involves no more than a basic inquiry, formal ratification by a recognized authority is usually unnecessary. When, however, the situation is more complicated, even the learned layman will feel the need to turn to a recognized rabbinical decisor who can investigate the original sources, alongside the interpretations of the early and late expositors, and then decide what the law should be. Aside from his greater proficiency, such a scholar has a global view of the system, enabling him to make sure that his decision will cohere holistically and "fit" according to *some* conception of the law. The component of piety (*yirat shamayim*) that has been traditionally regarded as a necessary attribute of the halakhic decisor lends an added dimension of religious weight and earnestness to halakhic deliberation that distinguishes it from ordinary legal discussion. This added weight is another reason that those who seek to observe the law in a religious context often prefer to turn to an authority figure in order to ensure that their final decisions are free from illegitimate forms of self-interest.

There are, to be sure, hazards in privileging the opinions and lawmaking powers of a ruling body of experts, in exposing the interpretation of the law to their class biases. Simply denigrating the intransigence of the halakhic establishment, however (as some feminists are wont to do), or writing it off altogether (as Adler seems to) negates the possibility of willingness within the system to engage with the dissidents. Something important is going on when the experts struggle mightily to discover internally legitimate solutions in light of the recognized rules, principles, and policies of the law as they appear to them. The self-perception of the experts cannot be dismissed as completely illusory—a type of Marxist "false consciousness" with no basis to speak of. It is precisely the appeal of halakhic authorities to a unique method of legal reasoning and its genuinely felt constraints that is critical for the translation of new claims into objectified legal meaning. And if the role of the official religious establishment is neutralized by the pressures of community, who indeed will be the instrument of new policy and translate the changes that have been effected into the formal language of law? Such considerations make it undesirable and sometimes even impossible to forgo all appeal to due process of law (no matter how decentralized *halakhah* is in our day), to its institutional methods of procedure, and to formal approval by its acknowledged representatives in the formulation of legal meaning.

Appeal to the larger community of the halakhically committed. As Cover himself has noted: "If law reflects a tension between what is and what might be, law can be maintained only as long as the two are close enough to reveal a line of human endeavor that brings them into temporary or partial reconciliation."[43] In citing the example of escaped slave Frederick Douglass to illustrate the power of commitment to the regnant legal system in determining law's meaning, Cover contrasts him to William Lloyd Garrison and other radical Garrisonian abolitionists. The Garrisonians refused to accept the U.S. Constitution, which they (like the reactionaries) read as countenancing slavery. Cover argues that it was precisely in their eschewing of the state and its law that they forfeited the possibility of changing its meaning. In a similar

vein, Cover demonstrates that what gave the Mennonites' argument its force
was their commitment, based on their understanding of scripture, to obey
the secular law of the government under which they lived. Adler is not the
only formerly Orthodox feminist to opt in the end for a more "Garrisonian"
mode; as a disciple of Cover, however, she should appreciate the consequences of this move, in terms of affecting "classical" *halakhah*.

Various streams or denominations, each with its own authoritative bodies, are part of Jewish communal life today. As the modern history of denominational strife in Jewish life has borne out, sometimes communal unity
demands a very high price, and the wish to remain part of the halakhic community often forces would-be reformers to settle for compromises with fellow religionists committed to halakhic interpretation as it stands. Indeed,
the inability to transcend factionalism has proven the greatest stumbling
block in solving the problem of *agunot* in our day. Even though the traditional community may seem oblivious to their plight, many women will still
prefer to refrain from remarrying, even attaching religious virtue to the sacrifice, in order to avoid exposing themselves to charges of an invalid divorce
procedure and thereby condemning any future children of theirs born of a
new alliance to bastard (*mamzer*) status. So long as the authoritative bodies
of the more traditional segments of the community refuse to recognize divorces on the basis of legal solutions suggested by those whose halakhic
commitment they question, or whose arguments appear flimsy on other
grounds, other women will be pressed to pay a very tangible price in order
to remain part of the overall community. Yet the conservative elements show
no signs of relenting in their steadfast commitment to their own interpretations. Their passion and fervor is fueled by the conviction that they are performing God's will. While the commitment of such elements preserves their
status as chief players in the system, the women who are most dedicated to
keeping the law ironically suffer the most.

Adler suggests that if traditionalists and reformers cannot reach agreement and occupy the same track, they might run on parallel tracks, coexist-
ing without concurring. Her contention is that if traditionalists would only
recognize precedents within *halakhah* that relegate some status questions
and ceremonies to areas outside their halakhic jurisdiction, it would be possible to bring about a detente between Orthodox and non-Orthodox worldviews.[44] This contention is absolutely correct. But if the traditional establishment is not prepared to see things her way, is there any use in preaching
only to the converted? Although Jewish feminists may profess to cherish the
same religious values and sacred texts as the rest of the halakhic community,
there is no guarantee that the dominant community being challenged—and
its institutional bodies—will exhibit any degree of tolerance for the alternative visions implicit in new interpretations. They may decide, instead, to reject those who choose to act upon such visions, regarding them as outsiders
to the established tradition.

Appeal to a dimension of transcendence. In addition to the appeal to halakhic expertise, its traditional methods of procedure, and to the halakhic
understanding of the larger community in which the transformative narrative is to be played out, any new vision must be framed in terms of the
broader interpretive tradition to which it relates, conforming to its acknowledged premises and tenets. While a new interpretation may sometimes challenge one or more of the existing "rules of the game," if it goes overboard
and undermines too many such principles, or even one that is too firmly
rooted in the interpretive tradition, it most likely will not be accepted as
convincing. In tendering a proposal, its promoters may suddenly find themselves outside the system because their suggestion is regarded as mistaken or
deviant and therefore irrelevant.

There is no denying the illuminating insights of feminists such as Adler
who demonstrate that "historical understandings of gender affect all Jewish
texts and contexts"[45] and that "halakhic categories and methods as they
stand cannot remedy gender injustices."[46] But while Adler's narrative relates
in richly imaginative ways to the sacred texts, the terminology and hermeneutic tools that she employs, the range of texts she calls upon (as well as
those she omits), and the redemptive vision that her narrative embodies represent a radical transformation of the existing interpretive tradition. As
such, her narrative does not prescribe a way of relating and negotiating with
this established tradition, whose proponents revere the same core texts that
she does. Her project's most glaring flaw is its lack of appeal to transcendence as a source of legitimacy for its new interpretation.

As we have seen, Orthodox Judaism—including even its modernist elements—continues to cling to a naive historicism that holds that what the sacred text reports indeed occurred in precisely that way. Adler responds by
declaring that the premises of modern historiography "are incompatible
with the belief that *halakhah* was divinely revealed in a single event and reflects an eternal and immutable divine will."[47] She discounts the usual ideological bases for the authority of *halakhah*: traditional notions affirming
Torah as the revealed word of God, the historical experience of the people of
Israel as continuing revelation, or the self-justifying assent to an ultimate
internal principle, or *Grundnorm*. Yet she offers no alternative paradigm
that may serve as grounds for justification in its stead, other than the ability
of our interpretations to fit the world we now inhabit. The most that she demands of any theology is that it "allow the texts of the tradition and the
lived experiences of religious communities to keep revealing themselves to
one another so that the sacred meanings of both can be renewed." "In the
course of this process," she adds, "God becomes present in our midst."[48] But
why would anyone be drawn to wrestle with and draw sacred meanings
from a text that does not uphold the metaphysical grounding upon which
this activity is usually based?

It would seem obvious that Torah can function as the source of a living religion based on passion and commitment only to the degree that it makes some compelling appeal to truth and a connection with the divine. If Adler's response to the male bias of the Torah is simply to conclude that the Torah itself (and not only its rabbinic applications) is fallible, time-bound, and socially conditioned, then what claim, beyond folklore and cultural loyalties, can this text possibly have upon us today? In today's global world, it is not enough simply to respond: "Because it is ours." Such parochial loyalties are not compelling enough to sustain a living faith. As Judaic scholar Martin Jaffee has phrased it: "Jewish practice without grounding in the divine has no more compelling a claim to the religious attention of Jews than the Code of Hammurabi."[49] A halakhic narrative that completely dispenses with transcendence (mythic or otherwise) and leaves all its interpretation's claims to authority up to contemporary communal life and its interpretive ingenuity will inevitably lose its fervor and passion—and the reason for its existence. Community (unlike God) does not demand total devotion. A reconstructed legal narrative that is unaccompanied by an equally thoughtful reconstruction of its connection to the divine is, ultimately, a hermeneutic failure. It may engender a new *nomos,* but that new *nomos* will not be *halakhah.*

It would therefore appear that if the feminist critique in its Jewish mold threatens to relativize and make conditional the whole corpus of traditional *halakhah,* halakhically committed Jews stand in desperate need of a contemporary understanding of revelation that will accommodate the following two requisites: (1) ability to acknowledge with a maximum of intellectual integrity the degree to which the Torah is formulated in a time- and culture-bound social mold; and (2) the ability to assert that this same Torah is nevertheless the voice of God speaking to us, with every word of that voice equally holy and indispensable, even finding theological meaning in the fact that our sacred and revered texts have been bound to androcentric premises.

Does this mean that women who recognize the necessity of appeal to the halakhic establishment, its existing interpretive tradition, and the halakhic community most committed to its current practice must despair and give up their redemptive vision? No. As we shall see, Orthodox women living out an egalitarian reality are precisely the ones most capable of building upon Adler's model. In order to provide them with the proper tools for doing so, however, we would do well to examine more closely the theoretical background behind the Coverian-Adler approach. Identifying its philosophical underpinnings will help us locate interpretive insights that could prove useful in overcoming its deficiencies.

•PART IV•

Beyond the Third Stage: Expanding the Palace of Torah

The options thus far for resolving the conflict between feminism and Jewish tradition have been limited to conserving women's status as it stands, seeking room for improvement within its fixed constraints, or revamping it through some more radical form of sociological or theological revisionism or unbridled halakhic innovation. I contend that the rapprochement between feminism and tradition must take a different tack, conflating the distinction between original traditional assumptions and the need to respond to changing circumstances. This approach, which builds upon a feminist propensity for dissolving binary opposites by blurring distinctions between them, resonates with some current aspects of postmodernist thinking. More significant, it comports with some strikingly fluid notions of the divine word that are rooted in Jewish tradition but tend to get bypassed in times of ideological stress.

In delineating this method of conflating text and its interpretation, I begin with the practical level, demonstrating how diversity and change can be accommodated even within an authoritarian religious framework when accompanied by strong commitment to a vibrant halakhic community and its existing interpretive tradition. Relying upon some of the hermeneutic insights of Hans Gadamer and Stanley Fish, I argue that it is precisely Orthodox women experiencing the highest degree of tension between their current secular reality and their more immediate universe of religious discourse who are the ideal agents for this model of change. While the methods of negotiation I recommend cannot entirely eliminate uncertainty or stress, I believe that they are capable of keeping these at a minimum, opening up promising avenues of innovation by expanding upon the guidelines of well-established constraints.

In the chapter that follows, I attempt to establish theological justification for this more dynamic model. I begin with a survey of various non-Orthodox and Orthodox responses to the challenge that modernity poses to the notion of a divine Torah. These responses are found either in terms of their ability to sustain Jewish belief and practice or in terms of their philosophical finesse and intellectual honesty. Such criticism leads to my call for a reformulation of the meaning of religious language and truth claims, as essential to a more adequate understanding of the notion of divine communication. Here I introduce an approach to the divine message that I term "cumulative revelation." Rejecting the view of Torah as a fixed and rigidly stable message that is passed on intact from generation to generation, I prefer instead to extrapolate an alternative vision from insights to be found in the thought of Rabbi A. I. Kook and other traditionalists. These thinkers discover the ultimate meaning of Torah word in the inevitable dialectic between the original revelation at Sinai and the progressive unfolding of history and human understanding. Building upon some of their more creative extensions of the meaning of God's message, this approach rejects the notion of revelation as a static legacy hermetically sealed against the influence of external forces and impervious to the developing moral intuitions of the faith community. Instead, it regards these factors as heaven-sent tools for revealing God's will.

Possible difficulties posed by the approach of accumulating revelation have already been anticipated in one form or another by Christian theologians concerned with issues of divine justice and their repercussions upon human initiative and responsibility. They are also foreshadowed by some Orthodox Jews who are reluctant to bind their religious interpretations to more grandiose metaphysical claims. In conclusion, I address myself briefly to these concerns.

CHAPTER 9

Halakhah Contextualized

Nonfoundationalism and the Role of Interpretive Traditions

Nonfoundationalism: The Theoretical Background

Rachel Adler does not dwell overmuch upon the deeper philosophical underpinnings and ramifications of her interpretive method. Nonetheless, in order to appreciate the precise nature of her contribution and attempt to address its difficulties, we would do well to note its affinity with an element of postmodernist theory known as *nonfoundationalism*.

Nonfoundationalism is a contemporary epistemological position. It stems from various sources; as a general approach to knowledge claims in different fields, however, it may be characterized as, on the one hand, the view that there is indeed no firm "foundation" that serves as the basis for our knowledge. In other words, there are no "raw chunks of reality" to which our notions of truth correspond. In this sense, nonfoundationalists, no less than postmodernists in general, reject naively objectivist conceptions of truth.[1] On the other hand, in some contexts appropriation of this term is meant to indicate a deliberate distancing on the part of its proponents from an unduly postmodernist focus on the diversity of knowledge and the self-indulgent subjectivism that it is said to generate, leading to the notion that "anything goes." The reaction of most self-professed nonfoundationalists to the bogey of postmodernist relativism is to insist that their rejection of fixed notions of truth is not to be equated with nihilism and anarchy. Refusing to shed philosophical responsibility, members of this camp usually see themselves as continuing to employ—no less than their modernist protagonists—firm criteria for interpretation and decision-making.[2]

To use the imagery suggested by a contemporary American philosopher, Ernest Sosa,[3] nonfoundationalists consider it far more appropriate to understand knowledge as a "raft" that we construct or repair from bits and pieces taken from our surroundings, than as a "pyramid" built on solid foundations. The raft image evokes a picture of truth as a network of interlocking claims that are held together or justified by reciprocal relations, rather than by their grounding in ultimate, indubitable, or self-certifying propositions.

Instead of viewing the project of truth-seeking as the attempt to capture something predefined in the physical or metaphysical world, we now understand it as a dialectic process of negotiation between the perceiver and the "object" of his/her perception. The search for truth becomes the search for "the widest possible inter-subjective agreement"[4] with regard to a dynamic floating body of knowledge, rather than the reaching down to some firm and stable foundation. This process takes place "conversationally"[5] from *within* a ground that the truth-seeker shares with a wider community, rather than in the form of an individual search conducted on some neutral territory in the beyond.

As opposed to judging particular truth claims in terms of theoretical, philosophical, or theological beliefs purporting to be neutral, most non-foundationalists prefer to justify these claims simply in terms of their coherence with other beliefs and opinions drawn from the traditions of the wider community. The nonfoundationalist insistence upon clear criteria becomes perfectly understandable once we realize that the insight that we are never neutral in our perception does not merely modify the earlier objectivist model of "interpretation as discovery." It is not that the nonfoundationalist still admits the presence of the raw object "out there," yet now acknowledges that our only access to it is through the biased lenses of our subjective perspectives. Such an understanding would leave us no other option than to admit and accept that our fate is rooted in our subjectivity. Instead, the nonfoundationalist adopts a more nuanced understanding of the relationship between the observer and the object of his observation, blurring the distinction between them.

Philosophers influenced by Ludwig Wittgenstein have understood this search for coherence as a give-and-take between various opinions and perspectives that continues until some "picture" is arrived at from *within* these, one that connects the various details that we observe or facilitates coordinated rather than disjointed action. As Hilary Putnam, a contemporary American philosopher of mind and language has put it, "The important thing . . . is to find a picture that enables us to make sense of the phenomena from within our world and our practice, rather than to seek a God's-eye View."[6] The powerful "grip" of this picture on our sensibilities is what makes us consider it inescapably true for us. Its messages then become self-evident and require no further justification.

Nonfoundationalism and the "conversational" method of arriving at intersubjective agreement is particularly congenial to a dominant stream of feminist epistemology. As I have shown in my discussion of feminist epistemology in chapter 1, dissolving dichotomies by blurring the distinctions between binary opposites is particularly popular with third-stage feminists who seek to remove polarities not only in the realm of gender but also in the conceptualization of reality at large. Many such feminists also identify with the school of thought known as *standpoint theory,* which posits that all knowledge is situated and attempts to overcome this liability by incorporating as many views as possible in the formulation of truth.[7] Feminism's contribution here is evident in the effect that it has had in developing the art of conciliation as a method of conflict resolving in legal dispute. Conciliation is also gaining popularity in the methodologies of other disciplines,[8] seeking liminal areas of overlap that eliminate the need for either-or choices between sharply defined options that are mutually exclusive.

The chief criticism that has been leveled against the influence of nonfoundationalism upon jurisprudence is that it does not provide sufficiently precise tools for the determination of law.[9] If the establishment of a particular interpretation as correct is determined only with reference to society's current cultural, political, and moral conceptions, the measure of the interpretation's legitimacy must ultimately remain retroactive; that is, dependent upon the degree of its acceptance by the interpretive community. This retrospective may be useful for literary interpretation. Religious beliefs too might be capable of waiting for the retroactive decree of history. In the realm of legal procedure, however, the internal players of the system cannot do without concrete tools for determining a valid interpretation in any given situation *before* its universal acceptance. They must be provided with sufficient basis on which to proceed when there are precedents to support both sides of an argument. They also require more practical instructions as to how any new interpretation may be engaged with the existing system, as well as clear guidelines for incorporating more proactive legal measures. Without these, the nonfoundationalist approach remains an insufficient basis for conducting legal activity.

This charge, which has already been leveled against Cover, appears to be doubly true with regard to Adler. In adopting a nonfoundationalist vision of law, she does not seem to harbor any constraints as to the form her suggested feminist redemptive vision may take beyond her own moral convictions, and perhaps those of a particular stratum of Jewish society. She appreciates full well that "an engendered Judaism needs the materials of the tradition to make credible theology."[10] Given her lack of commitment to what she terms "classical *halakhah*," however, the usefulness of this understanding for its practical transformation is limited. Eschewing the precedents of the past in favor of social engineering does not yet preclude the necessity of wild, unprincipled "leaps in the dark." Reliance upon shifting norms and values does not yet prescribe any a priori workable formula for deciding when to ignore the precedents of classical *halakhah* and endorse a new social vision and when to reject it. And in religious terms, such reliance certainly does not provide the mythic vocabulary that might support incorporation of such aims as "mutual respect, diversity, pluralism" into our halakhic lives—values that are avowedly secular.[11]

In sum, more substance is required to fill in the gaps that Adler leaves between real and ideal. Her attempt to affect authentic halakhic change is stymied by the lack of a method that could enable her external criticism to be assimilated in terms of the *halakhah*'s own internal language, standards, and procedures.

Hermeneutics and the Dilemma of Relativism

A first step in confronting this task is to take a closer look at more fluid and subjectivist approaches that have been absorbed in the realm of hermeneutics (the theory of interpretation). Because the process of legal deliberation itself is essentially an interpretive one, there is a natural affinity between hermeneutics and law. In fact, implicit to any legal argument is a more comprehensive hermeneutic approach.[12] Delving into hermeneutics does not completely absolve us of the necessity of painstakingly identifying the contingent principles of law that are appropriate for us in our present situation. Nonetheless, it should provide some guidelines for minimizing the Sisyphean nature of this task. At the very least, it might yield a game plan less amorphous than that provided by Adler for women interested in halakhic deliberation.

In turning to the contribution of hermeneutics as a solution for halakhic praxis, we are actually reversing the contemporary trend represented by Cover: instead of drawing on Jewish tradition in order to address contemporary problems in literary and legal theory, we look at what such theory contributes to resolving current questions in the Jewish context. This "back-to-front" method of approach might appear questionable at the outset. After all, despite its openness to contingent factors, rabbinic method has been around for much longer than nonfoundationalism. The justification for this appeal to contemporary thought is the discrepancy between our conscious evaluation of rabbinic process, and the relatively unreflective practice of the Rabbis themselves. In the wake of greater awareness of the role of the interpreter in creating meaning, fresh insights have emerged. Our modern loss of innocence—the loss of belief in the detachment of rabbinic method from subjective bias and external influences—lead us to them.

Hans Gadamer's and Stanley Fish's contribution. The attempt to address the loss of firm foundations without lapsing into relativism or anarchic nihilism has benefited from the contribution of various hermeneutic approaches, beyond Wittgenstein's influence, that have been developed in the past few decades. Particularly illuminating are the implications of approaches developed by Hans Gadamer[13] and by Stanley Fish, both leading proponents of hermeneutic theory in the second half of the twentieth century.[14] They share the nonfoundationalist understanding that the interpretation of "texts" (which are defined broadly to include not only literary productions but all cultural products given to inquiry, whether or not transmitted in written form) involves more than merely employing the proper tools and hence discovering a predefined meaning with a clearly independent existence. Seeing and describing are no longer taken to be entirely passive or neutral activities. In profound yet often undetected ways, our perceptions are shaped by our previous conceptions, biases, and interests, so that the simple act of observing already involves a significant amount of processing, on the basis of the hopes, fears, expectations, and "intellectual baggage" that we bring with us to the text.

Gadamer maintains that every interpretive effort is also an act of translating the author's original intent into the terms of the inner world and prior subjective biases of the reader. The belief that it is possible to reconstruct the text in an objective manner free of biases is perhaps the most subjective bias of them all. Claiming that one interpretation is better than another because it is more faithful to the general intent of the original is futile not because there never was such a general intent, but because its very definition involves an interpretive act. Because we can never be neutral at any stage, there is no sense in speaking of a virgin meaning embedded in the text, simply waiting to be revealed.

Gadamer's first contribution to the loss of belief in interpretive neutrality is his refusal to define this lack of objectivity as a problem. The subjective involvement of the interpreter and the interpreter's initial biases is in fact what enables the act of interpretation to take place; the more laden these prejudices are, the fuller the interpretation. We are reminded of the work of the anthropologists: bringing a rich tradition of inquiry—based on the empirical examination of the cultures of other societies and the interpretation of what they have in common with the society under investigation—could enable a better understanding of the lives of the natives than the natives have of themselves.

Gadamer's second contribution to this "conversational" model of truth-seeking is to draw our attention to the social construction of the space within which the dialectical process of interpretation takes place. The initial hypothesis of the observer, which stems from subjective intuitions, must afterward be subjected to the test of the evidence supplied by the object or text to be interpreted. This dialectic process of negotiation forward and backward, between the observer and the object of interpretation, always takes place within the unique cultural climate in which the individual observer is rooted. The very way in which the observer approaches the object of his perception is always contextual and situated. The beliefs and practices to which he appeals are never merely his own, but are always shaped by the norms, traditions, and conventions of his surrounding society.

What emerges from Gadamer's insights is that admitting to the role of subjectivity in interpretation does not mean that the reader is free to interpret the text however he likes. Rather, he *already finds himself in* the beliefs and opinions that enable discovery of a text's meaning as something that derives necessarily from the general sociopolitical context in which he and the words take part. Because it is impossible to separate the broader cultural baggage the individual reader brings to reading the text and his own understanding, he is never entirely free to "impose" meaning upon the text in a manner that ignores the burden of his interpretive tradition. This limitation derives necessarily from the general sociopolitical context in which he and the words take part. Interpreters *always* "see" from within their context because no other way of seeing exists. This explains why certain interpretations in certain periods and circumstances appear perfectly plausible, yet are utterly implausible in another setting. Thus the hermeneutic process, according to Gadamer, is neither objective nor subjective. It is rather the combined product of the reader, the tradition of established conventions that he brings with him to the text, and the power of the text to delimit and guide his interpretive quest.

While Gadamer defines the interpretive moment as the "merging of horizons" between text or author intent and the reader, Fish represents a more extreme view. He removes the entire focus of the interpretive process from the internal world of the author to that of the reader. Not only is there no "objective" meaning to texts, but even the texts themselves, according to Fish, do not exist as such, independent of the reader's interpretation. In principle, no formal and predefined ground rules limit our manner of identifying the original text itself. One observer may see in the chicken-scratch stone etchings of an archaeological finding the scribbling of primitives. Another may view them as exciting hieroglyphics. The criteria that delimit the nature and structure of any text, as well as its meaning, are no more than the sum total of conventions adopted by the "interpretive community" within which both the text and its interpreters function.

However, even on Fish's more fluid understanding of the interpretive act, the claim that not only the *meaning* of texts but even *the texts themselves* do not have a stable, identifiable existence apart from their observers does not lead to utter relativism. Such a conclusion would be justified only if interpreters could be perceived as acting entirely alone, arbitrarily deciding whatever they pleased. But Fish, no less than Gadamer, does not see this as possible. The validity of a new interpretation is always determined by its acceptance as good or correct. This acceptance depends on the interpreter's success in persuading the interpretive community of the justice of his reading. His methods of persuasion are also part and parcel of the working principles and operative methods that characterize the interpretive community and guarantee its continuity despite change.

In sum, the joint contribution of Gadamer and Fish to hermeneutics and thus to postmodernist notions of interpretation is: (a) acknowledging the role of the reader's preliminary biases in determining the meaning of texts, while understanding that there is no absolute or objective yardstick to evaluate such biases; (b) recognizing both the role of society in constructing such biases and the critical restraining force of the interpretive tradition of the community in their implementation; and (c) denying that this modified view of the truth-seeking process, which is based on sociopolitical rather than naively objectivist justifications, diminishes in any way the commitment to honest and disinterested inquiry. Rejection of the strict dichotomy between reader and text (or subjective bias and objective truth) does not entail denial of criteria for preferring one interpretation to another. What it does change is our understanding of how dependent they are upon context.

The Solution of Orthodox Jewish Women: Innovation within Constraints

What do the insights of Gadamer and Fish add to Adler's description? Do they contribute anything further to the development of proper tools for legal practice? There is no denying that their descriptions still remain the phenomenological accounts of external observers, without spelling out for us what our own contingent values and standards at any set moment should be. And as philosophers, they still speak *about* interpretive theory without entering *into* the practice of interpretation and articulating the precise rationale or theory that should drive us in ensuring that we choose the best reading possible. Their teachings do not absolve us of the responsibility to tackle the more substantive questions that face us when making legal decisions. We still are left with the difficult task of defining the precise biases of the interpretive tradition to which we are committed. We also must pinpoint the considerations that are to guide us in determining when formal rules and precedents are to prevail at all costs and when they may be contextualized or overridden by more overarching and abstract principles. Nevertheless, the teachings of Gadamer and Fish do underscore the qualifying role of interpretive traditions, the demands of their distinct methods of procedure, and the degree to which acceptability in the eyes of a reference group in question delimits the range of possible interpretations.

This appreciation for the constraining influences of interpretive traditions sits well with the classic ideal of the Torah student who, although not a passive recipient, both molds and is molded by the divine word and its multilayered interpretive tradition.[15] It also comports with the weightier attitude of respect for all opinions that is fostered by the rabbinic notion of the divine word's all-inclusiveness, as opposed to the random and free-wheeling choices of postmodernism. It is the Torah that must absorb the world rather than the world the Torah, and it is the skill of its adherents in doing so, in a manner that is coherent in their eyes with its existing network of beliefs and practices, that constitutes its vitality. Tradition must function as the ever-present lens through which *halakhah* views the contingencies of contemporary experiences *as they arise* rather than seeing them as an object of inquiry whose religiously significant or literal meaning is located in some fixed and objective standard either within or outside itself.[16]

Bearing in mind these qualifications, as well as Cover's own assertion of the need to engage the primary interpretive community addressed, I believe that the vision of law that Adler relies upon can indeed provide the greatest encouragement for precisely the group of people who experience the highest degree of tension with the current halakhic stalemate: Orthodox women living in an egalitarian reality in their secular lives. Gadamer and Fish cannot define for such women the precise parameters of the community from which they do not want to be cut off. What can be concluded from their insights, however, is that those in the best position to negotiate the encounter between Judaism and modernity are those who are most intensely affected by the conflict of loyalties that it has engendered. Deeply immersed in the rabbinic tradition and maintaining a high degree of allegiance to its standards and practices, Orthodox women with feminist sensibilities are the very personification of the qualifications required for Adler's project. Precisely because they are the ones who have been forced to the greatest extent to develop concrete ways of reconciling these loyalties *within* the tradition, the potential for engendering classical halakhic development lies largely in their hands. Able to approach *halakhah* critically without rejecting it and to manipulate a viable position for themselves within it without abandoning its internal vocabulary, they are the ideal formulators of new legal meaning.

The meshing of rival values that such women are managing as a result of this conflict turns them into a fascinating example of legal dynamics in general. Bound by their common sense of exclusion from major portions of the tradition, and by a growing sense of confidence and conviction in the halakhic impropriety of this situation, they are forming a sisterhood of women that represents a uniquely powerful agent of change. This power stems from their ability, despite their involvement in a new narrative, to maintain a way of life that can still be contained within the present interpretive tradition of the *halakhah* and can answer to the three constraints enumerated in the previous chapter: appeal to the consensus of experts; commitment to the halakhic community in which the transformative narrative is to be played out; and commitment to this narrative's claims to a dimension of transcendence.

Enhancing rabbinic power within the existing halakhic reality. The very formation of a critical mass of women who—because of their intensified commitment to Jewish learning and tradition—are interested in seeking out the opinion of the experts provides halakhic authorities with a wide and stable constituency. The expansion of such a constituency reinforces the relevance of halakhic authority, even while it mandates taking the women and their problems into account. Willing to turn to halakhic authorities for guidance, the devoutly religious women who tread the fine line between tradition and modernity may constitute precisely the factor that enables such authorities to widen the scope of their decision-making.

I do not belittle here the influence of peripheral groups and their protest upon the "heartland." Sometimes those who place themselves outside the system forge new paths that, once trodden, modify the concepts of even the more conservative elements as to the range of the possible. When I was a child, for example, ritual celebration of the birth of a daughter or of her becoming *bat mitzvah* was unknown in the Orthodox community. The innovations of non-Orthodox denominations and New Age Judaism paved the way for the widespread acceptance of these rituals in Orthodox circles today. But when the thrust of dissent is directed at the establishment prior to the internalization of change by a community committed to establishment rule, then more often than not institutional defense mechanisms bar what might conceivably be permitted.

Another powerful tool of this newly formed sisterhood of the halakhically committed is its potential for educating women from its ranks, providing them with the skills necessary for entering the world of halakhic dialogue and engaging it on its own terms. As *halakhah*-abiding women enter this discourse, their persistence in raising the "woman question," articulating their dissatisfaction with the status quo and suggesting innovative arguments and methodologies, will inevitably spur the advent of practical solutions that address their newly recognized spiritual needs.

There is, however, a third, much more profound manner in which Orthodox women are already bridging the gap between their present unredeemed reality and the ideal that they envision. This method conforms more closely than the previous two strategies to the lawmaking image promoted by Adler and Cover.

Transforming narrative and affecting halakhic reality. When Orthodox women speak to the existing establishment from within a specified set of common interests and concerns, they would like to assume that the halakhic establishment will hear their words. They profess a common language due to a manifest level of formal agreement regarding the authority of individual rules and values and the procedures for applying them. Employing this level of discourse, women attempt to "demonstrate" or "prove" that certain strategies of interpretation are acceptable and halakhic solutions possible. A more lasting bridge is created, however, when communication is based not merely on a common language in this limited sense, but rather upon a joint way of thinking stemming from a more intimately shared participation in a new narrative. In such a situation the novel interpretations called for are accepted simply because they appear so obvious, natural, and correct that further argument and persuasion are superfluous.

For example, despite the fact that according to established *halakhah,* a woman does not inherit the estate of her late husband, rabbinic courts allow for this possibility as a matter of course.[17] And generations of *poskim* have disregarded Maimonides' instruction that a husband should prevent his wife from leaving her home more than once or twice a month.[18] In our day, the late Nehama Leibowitz, a universally acclaimed Orthodox pedagogue and biblical scholar, received unprecedented invitations to teach classes at a Modern Orthodox men's yeshiva in Israel and at various convocations of Orthodox rabbis visiting Israel from abroad. Leibowitz on many occasions reiterated her belief in the primacy of women's roles as wives and mothers. She also accorded rabbis great respect, usually addressing them in the third person. Yet she clearly regarded as stuff and nonsense the notion that she, as a woman, should not be devoting herself to serious Torah study or should not be teaching men out of considerations of modesty. The fact that she perceived herself in this way and acted upon it within the halakhic community as a matter of course facilitated the halakhic acceptability of her self-perception.

Men interacting with women living out an alternative narrative are forced to experience the same sense of dissonance that the women themselves feel when they encounter equality of opportunity and status in the everyday secular sphere and discrimination in the synagogue and other communal religious institutions. It is this anomaly that creates the environment for the "correctness" of a different reading of the legal sources. On this level of influence, the power of Orthodox women is not in constituting an external force that influences the religious establishment or the community at large simply by appealing to its authoritative bodies or engaging them on their terms. Rather, it lies in the fact that such women situate the interpretation of *halakhah* in a particular context by living out their new vision while still remaining part of the community. In this way they play an instrumental role in determining how interpretation will go.

Are God's words to Eve "And he shall rule over you" (Gen. 3:16), a normative prescription for all time or an escapable curse? Much depends on the social context in which they are read. But surely in this day and age this verse will not be regarded (as it has been at times) as a recipe for marital bliss, but rather as an evil to be overcome—much as God's words to Adam, "By the sweat of your brow shall you get bread" (Gen. 3:18), are not understood as countermanding the use of technology to overcome the constraints of nature. The new reading is not perceived as a dishonest "twist" in order to accommodate newfangled desires, but rather as the inevitable meaning of Torah. And the more prevalent a new reading becomes, the more "obvious" the legal meaning it implies, as more and more people relate their practice to that particular interpretation.

An example of the difference between the two levels of persuasion can be gleaned from the article by Rabbi Sacks referred to in the previous chapter. Writing of his search for a halakhic formula that would allow him to express the same joy over the birth of his daughter as over the birth of a son, he expresses his satisfaction at finding a valid solution.[19] Yet a few pages later he rejects twentieth-century views of what is sexist or undemocratic on the grounds that this "modern consciousness, deeply affronted that there might be significant role differences given by birth" is "radically subversive of tradition of all kinds."[20] Rabbi Sacks has not yet faced the fact that his very wish to give ritual expression to his joy upon the birth of a daughter is quite likely a product of that same modern consciousness, as most likely will be his wish that she receive a rich grounding in Torah, and his sense of discomfort if she trains to be a lawyer or rabbinic pleader but remains unable to sign a testimony of witness. (Interestingly enough, several male Orthodox feminists confess to having been "converted to the cause" by thoughts of their daughters' limitations under the *halakhah*, rather than those of their wives.)

To the extent that halakhic response to the feminist dilemma suffices with formal adjustments here and there of the sort Rabbi Sacks offers, while continuing to dismiss women's new visions as an import foreign to the "inner" viewpoint of tradition, women's lives under *halakhah* will still reflect the old reality. To the extent, however, that the very presence of halakhically observant women who feel a dissonance between their understanding of Torah and the regnant interpretation compels the men in their community—their rabbis and teachers, husbands, fathers, brothers, and sons—to share their more pervasive sense of anomaly, women's lives under the *halakhah* will change.

What Orthodox women who tread the border between the existing halakhic reality and that envisioned by their new narrative are essentially declaring is this: "It is true that we Modern Orthodox women are part of Western liberal civilization. It is true that we are affected by the current modern consciousness and deeply affronted by the contention that certain hierarchical relations and role differences are predetermined by birth. But it is as misplaced to accuse us for this reason of importing into Judaism outside values that have no basis in tradition, as it would be to accuse the Torah of Moses of importing patriarchy into tradition. Where these values started is irrelevant. What is relevant is that they have affected and become an inextricable part of our everyday lives, and they are part of the everyday lives of the halakhic authorities themselves.[21] And as the old conceptions become more and more inconceivable as the basis for substantive halakhic decisions beyond the level of rhetoric, we are confident that new ways will be found to accommodate our emerging narrative into the meaning of Torah, incorporating the feminist vision of a different future."

Pessimists may disparage the influence of this type of statement as negligible in that it has not thus far produced substantial change in *halakhah*. Apologists of a conservative bent will also choose to diminish its significance, by casting the women's declarations as the propaganda of pleaders for a cause still requiring establishment approval. But this belittlement would be a misreading of the situation.[22] Women who play out their tension with modernity within the community of the halakhically committed, setting up an alternative narrative without severing their connections with current understandings, do not function only as advocates for change. More significant, they are engaged in creating the conditions for that change, by exposing new possibilities of meaning in the existing corpus of Jewish tradition and acting upon them within the community most resistant to such developments. Orthodox women are promoting prenuptial agreements, establishing women's Torah study halls (*batei midrash*) and prayer groups, devising new rituals marking uniquely feminine concerns, developing programs for the training of women leaders, and otherwise acting upon a deeply felt sense of themselves as equal participants in the tradition. In doing so, these women are, in effect, saying: "We do not need to change the law. We may transform its meaning by simply weaving it into a different narrative."

Accepting the interpretive tradition's framing of the range of the possible. The decision of Orthodox women not to cross the line—not to declare their commitment to feminism as the overriding one when it conflicts with the formal demands of existing *halakhah*—is made possible by devising ingenuous ways of realizing their new redemptive vision within the limitations of clearly defined constraints. In choosing to maneuver within the bounds of the permissible, they appear to be opting for one of two familiar models of halakhic change. These models can be extrapolated from the halakhic tradition, even without recourse to the debatable meta-halakhic theories of Modern Orthodoxy.

The first model involves those changes that are imposed on the community of believers from without, because of forces beyond their control. Such changes, even when they involve a blatant transgression of previous norms and not merely a subtle deviation from their spirit, are tolerated by the halakhic system so long as they can be regarded as a temporary measure (a *horaat shaah*), to be revoked the moment external factors make this possible. Even when the change is no longer resisted, the hope lingers that someday circumstances will allow a reinstatement of halakhic practice as originally conceived. Some ultra-Orthodox Jewish men must still make their peace, at least on the rhetorical level, with allowing "their women" to vote in Israeli elections, for example, or even with affording them greater opportunities for acquiring Torah literacy. Rabbi Avraham Wolf, the principal of one ultra-Orthodox women's seminary in Bnei Brak, is known to have informed his students: "We are giving you an education so that your granddaughters will no longer have the need for one." The thrust of his message is the hope that women's education will return to the home, conducted through the example of their mother's domestic practices.

Most Orthodox women, however, do not view the changes in their lives as a necessary evil. They would more readily identify these with the second model of halakhic change: divergence from past practice or attitude by individual believers who are motivated by internal religious considerations. A prime example of this divergence is when women nowadays take on the obligation of hearing the blowing of *shofar* on the High Holidays despite the fact that they are formally exempt. The same may be said in our day for women who take on optional *mitzvot,* such as setting aside regular hours for the study of Torah, wearing *tzitzit,* donning *tefillin,* or counting the *omer* period from Passover to Shavuot. These deviations are justified as voluntary acceptance of greater stringency than the usual norms dictate, a stringency that is not necessarily incumbent on the community of halakhically observant women at large. Such divergence from accepted norms falls—in accordance with most understandings at least[23]—under the category of similar efforts to move beyond the letter of the law (*lifnim meshurat hadin*). The women's self-imposed limitations (for example, avoiding prayers formally requiring a male quorum when participating in a women-only prayer group) make it particularly difficult for their wider community categorically to delegitimize the new narrative and its concomitant *nomos.* The limitations also make it difficult to ignore the need for overcoming the anomalies within the current halakhic reality that are created as these innovations become more widespread.

Symptomatic of these difficulties is (as we have seen in chapter 5) the tendency of halakhic authorities to be reduced, for want of better grounding, to ad hominem attacks upon the motivation of the women concerned. An illuminating contrast is seen in the objection to women's prayer groups versus the condoning of married women's use of wigs in fulfillment of the halakhic requirement to cover their hair in the interests of modesty (a practice described earlier). Impugning the women's motivation is an inaccurate way of framing the issue at stake. Do women driven by a concern that their outward appearance conform with contemporary Western standards of fashion, rendering themselves virtually indistinguishable from their nonmarried sisters, display a higher level of religious motivation than women seeking more spiritually meaningful forms of religious worship? After the fact, some halakhists have rationalized that wigs are preferable to hats and scarves because they can be relied upon more thoroughly to do the job of leaving no strand of hair uncovered.[24] Despite the attempt to put a legal face on it, however, what those who object to prayer groups and similar developments are really saying is: "Although we cannot find formal fault with the new practice, we do not sympathize with the narrative of the women concerned and do not respect the redemptive vision that drives them. Their narrative does not lead to an image of women and the religious life that we can share."

Rationalizations aside, the degree of slack between the interpretive community with which we align and the one to its right from which we do not wish to be cut off is what finally determines the range of possibilities in any halakhic decision. The "imperial" elements of the halakhic community would like to have us believe that the keys to this range remain exclusively in their hands. The truth is, however, no matter how much the halakhic establishment seeks to privilege its authority, in reality the lived experience of the community of the committed cannot be ignored, and the final outcome is always some form of dialectic and negotiation between the two.

Choosing to limit our issues only to those that may conceivably be tolerated within the current Orthodox framework makes the statement that although feminism is an important value, it is not the exclusive yardstick by which everything else in our lives is measured. Occasionally this value is offset by other values equally dear. We recognize that we may be called upon to prioritize values and sacrifice some of our feminist aspirations and deeply held convictions in the interests of halakhic conformity and of acceptance by a community embodying a hierarchy of values that differs from our own. In this hierarchy women's interests are not always paramount. Nevertheless, it is this choice of commitment that renders the battles we *do* find necessary to wage relevant and influential, in a manner that no outsider stance can match.

Some feminists will regard the moral, social, or ideological price of life in a traditional community as not worth paying. Jewish feminists, as well as other halakhic observers experiencing the tension with modernity, harbor a natural yearning to erect grand theoretical edifices comprehensive enough to solve every problem in a way that is spiritually and intellectually satisfying on all levels. As Adler has expressed this: "The obligation to be truthful and the yearning to be whole . . . to be faithful to the covenant requires that we infuse the whole of our existence with our religious commitments."[25] My hunch, however, is that the real work of halakhic building in feminist issues will be accomplished by those small groups of traditionally inclined women who, in the course of the next few decades, unravel their halakhic lives into a multiplicity of fine component threads and then weave these together with equally fine threads drawn from other of their life experiences. This experimentation will take the form of various trade-offs, negotiations, and unexpected instances of compliance and compromise—thus promoting the sort of variety-in-unity that is characteristic of true halakhic stability.

The Fallacy of the Bloodless Battle

Having said all this, we should not harbor illusions. The commitment of Orthodox women to the tradition provides them with unique tools that are particularly suited to the task of engaging external criticism with the *halakhah*'s own internal language and procedural methods. The tradition provides a more viable model for religious continuity than such responses as conservative apologetics, halakhic positivism (or liberal feminism), or any more thoroughgoing form of revisionism (or radical feminism). Nevertheless, the practical effectiveness of the path taken by women who choose to accommodate their redemptive vision within an unredeemed halakhic reality will not eliminate all tension. Though the protagonists are determined to wear kid gloves, their battles cannot always remain bloodless, nor can the exercise of halakhic caution guarantee total circumventing of those "unruly moments" that, according to Cover, are the most likely finally to impel resolution of legislative impasse.[26] Such disruptive moments can occur in the lives of even the most halakhically committed women when solidarity with the feminist narrative appears to demand stronger measures than simply maneuvering within the confines of those well-acknowledged lacunae or ambiguities mercifully left by current halakhic rulings.

Typically, these moments occur in what appear to be a quite narrowly circumscribed range of "hard cases." In these cases, the halakhic community is strongly committed to an existing nomic reality, despite the fact that its own declared standards and methods of procedure clearly do not support this reality and in fact could be construed as equally supportive of the feminist vision. It is here that a protracted process of give-and-take may develop, and this process does involve uncertainty and risk. In such cases, there is no clearly delineated interpretive tradition that can ensure the best decision is always reached, even when working within the established constraints.

Shapiro versus Henkin: Women's aliyot to the Torah as a test case. The delicateness of these decisions and the negotiations involved can be illustrated by close analysis of a halakhic exchange that developed in reaction to Mendel Shapiro's study defending women's right to be called up to the Torah, described in chapter 5.[27] Shapiro met with difficulty when he first tried to publish the fruit of his research in the mainstream publications of Modern Orthodoxy in the United States. It was dismissed either as unsuitable or as requiring certain changes. Eventually, however, he did manage to get his article unmodified into the electronic journal of *Edah,* an American Orthodox organization that has undertaken to address women's issues and other challenges of modernity creatively.

A conservative response was soon forthcoming; it expresses reservations about a reading of the Talmud that contextualizes the concept of *kevod hatzibbur.*[28] In the eyes of respondent Abe Katz, who does not profess to be a rabbi or a Talmud scholar, a much simpler and more convincing reading of the original ruling is that women can in principle have *aliyot* but in practice may *never* do so because of *kevod hatzibbur.* On this reading, *kevod hatzibbur* is an overriding principle bearing an "objective" definition that cannot be changed at the whim of the community. What is at stake is indeed the "objectivity of *halakhah*" and deviation from the simple meaning (*peshat*) of the sources.

Another response, of greater interest to the nonfoundationalist, was that of Rabbi Yehuda Henkin, like Shapiro, an American-born Jerusalemite. Henkin has established himself in some circles as a halakhic authority and has displayed a refreshing responsiveness to women's interests, despite his taking great care not to violate established halakhic procedure. His halakhic writings previous to the response to Shapiro already exhibit a sophisticated understanding of legal procedure. Not unlike the Modern Orthodox meta-halakhic positivists of chapters 4 and 5, he speaks in the name of a "pure ha-lakhic argument" that can be distilled from the sources alone and distinguished from "ideological positions."[29] Nevertheless, he also acknowledges that, de facto, halakhic interpretation sometimes involves long-term "negotiation" based upon a complicated conglomeration of factors, the relative merits of which may never be determined conclusively.[30] In this process of give-and-take, the degree of conformity with what the *posek* sees as the original intent of any given source is an important factor, but not the only, nor the most conclusive one in establishing the correctness of an interpretation. He sees three components to a halakhic decision: "The first is the optimal, or 'pure' Halakha determined from the sources alone. The second is the *metzi'ut,* 'reality,' the situation on the ground. To bridge any gap between the two comes the third element, *hora'ah,* literally 'ruling.'"[31]

Applying these insights to the issue of women's *aliyot,* R. Henkin accepts Shapiro's essential argument, with a few reservations. His final comment,[32] however, is the most instructive for our purposes:

Where does all this leave us? Regardless of the arguments that can be proffered . . . women's *aliyot* remain outside the consensus, and a congregation that institutes them is not Orthodox in name and will not long remain Orthodox in practice. In my judgment, this is an accurate statement now and for the foreseeable future, and I see no point in arguing about it. This leaves us with the possible exception. I have already written . . . that if done without fanfare, an occasional *aliyah* by a woman in a private minyan of men held on Shabbat in a home and not in a synagogue sanctuary or hall can perhaps be countenanced or at least overlooked.

What are we to learn from this reaction?

Henkin's observation that women's *aliyot* remain outside the consensus of Orthodoxy, despite their permissibility according to current principles of halakhic procedure, might be understood in Coverian terms as noting that they do not conform with current narrative regarding women's place in ritual. The bone that Henkin throws to Shapiro is that halakhic authorities might be prepared to condone this practice, or to look the other way, if women keep a very low profile and do not blow *aliyot* up into a revolutionary ideological statement. Shapiro responds, however, that this move still does not satisfy him on several accounts. I shall look at both the theoretical and practical considerations in the course of my discussion,[33] but it is the latter that are germane here.

Shapiro insists that if women's *aliyot* are formally permissible, they must be allowed. As he demands: "If my halakhic analysis is tenable—and Rav Henkin seems to agree that it is—by what moral justification may women be denied a halakhic privilege if they exercise it in self-selected [mixed-gender] groups without directly impinging on others' sensibilities? Why should the fact that women's *aliyot* are outside of the Orthodox consensus be a complete explanation of why they may not be instituted?"[34] What remains particularly puzzling or "opaque" in Shapiro's eyes is the significance of R. Henkin's seeming reluctance to phrase his objection to synagogue *aliyot* categorically. Is the formulation that women's *aliyot* remain "outside the consensus . . . now and for the foreseeable future" intentionally equivocal, leaving the way open for more private spread of the phenomenon (and thereby encouraging the possibility of its eventual incorporation into regular synagogue life)? There is support for Shapiro's suspicion: R. Henkin is well aware that such were the origins of other untraditional practices, such as women reciting *kaddish* or reading the *megillah* for themselves on Purim.[35] Does Henkin think we might stand elsewhere "tomorrow"? asks Shapiro. Or must we simply understand his judgment as an out-and-out condemnation of the untraditional practice?

R. Henkin's words may well be an example of the favorable exercise of "imperial discretion" (in Cover's terms), whereby judges strive to maintain halakhic stability by enabling a more inclusive vision of the law that is capable of accommodating minority interests. Henkin's acceptance of the innovation before the larger community of the halakhically committed is prepared to accept it could backfire and his authority be undermined. If this indeed is all that his cautious phrasing implies, he is simply acting in accordance with a well-known constraint upon halakhic authorities not to devalue *halakhah* (creating halakhic *ziluta*) by issuing a ruling that will not be respected. Nonetheless, this constraint itself may also imply a wish to protect a conception of the legal decisor's role that accords completely with Cover's ideal (providing the interpretive solution best equipped to articulate the current self-understanding of the community, while not closing the opportunity for new narratives to weave their way in gradually).[36] This accord is accomplished by Henkin's attempt to pave the way covertly, if necessary, for gradual mainstream acceptance of a hitherto untraditional practice, taking into account shared traditions and aspirations and employing an ad hoc mixture of logic, history, common sense, sociology, precedent, and personal prejudice.

Applying this understanding to the issue at hand, would-be innovators find the practical conclusion clear. If several individuals share Shapiro's interpretation of the sources and are willing to act upon it privately, and if this practice becomes intelligible to the wider halakhic community, quite possibly the practice will eventually be accepted, at the very least, as a tolerable variation of the mainstream view. Such a vision of halakhic development conforms completely with the optimistic belief of R. Kook that if the urge for a particular halakhic innovation becomes widespread, no doubt the additional necessary factors for its acceptance (a genuinely conceived interpretation and institutional approval) will be forthcoming.[37] This comes alongside his warning against wholesale adoption of the innovation before the rest of the community is ready for it. Until that time, nothing is to stop individuals from privately assuming such standards for themselves, though imposing them on the public at large could only cause harm.

The truth is, however, that although this vision of halakhic change minimizes disparity between reality and the desired ideal, it does not dissolve it completely. Even so judiciously phrased a response as that of Rabbi Henkin does not bridge the gap between the limited dispensation for occasional private readings and the desire for more public adoption of a practice admitted to be permissible on commonly accepted formal grounds.

As noted, a handful of congregations have made the unauthorized leap over the uncharted territory demarcating Orthodox exception from non-Orthodox rule, by transferring the innovative practice from home to synagogue. On what basis do individuals and communities decide? As Shapiro points out to Henkin, if they believe that the practice that accords with the divine will is by definition that which becomes accepted as normative by communal consensus, and a new consensus begins to solidify, then it may be legitimate to act upon it. Are there no *inherent* methods of assessing the nature of the divine will? he asks.

At this juncture, we would do well to reiterate the point made by Gadamer and Fish, as well as other nonfoundationalists: The absence of stable boundaries and the indeterminacy of meaning that results should not be confused with absence of valid criteria altogether. Neither should this indeterminacy be equated with the type of hermeneutic nihilism that asserts that anything can be taken to mean whatever we want it to, so long as we want it badly enough (akin to Blu Greenberg's "when there is a rabbinic will, there is a halakhic way"). The lack of absolute limits, in principle, to halakhic interpretation does not mean that *any* interpretation can be developed with equal honesty. It does mean, however, that any consensually agreed-upon limitations restricting halakhic decision-making are themselves the products of interpretation; as such their content and import are always (at least hypothetically) open to reevaluation and reconsideration.

Perhaps some or all of these limitations will reveal themselves as permanent features of Judaism, but then again, perhaps not. Only God knows how His Torah will be understood in the future. Recognizing that we cannot dismiss any potential development as utterly impossible in principle does not dictate relating to our present understanding of the Torah as tentative or conditional, or being any the less committed to the authority of *halakhah* as we understand it. All that this recognition implies is that any development is logically possible, though not equally plausible, and this open-endedness may occasion choice and even tension between the "paideic" and "imperial" forces in the community.

When faced with such circumstances, each woman is left to choose the extent to which she is prepared to serve as martyr for her redemptive vision and to endure the opposition emanating from the dominant halakhic mainstream. It is at this point that a woman must face the limits of theory and of judicial authority and even of the "grip" of the picture created by the traditional way of life to which she is committed. Other factors of considerable weight muddy the issues, among them: the spiritual cost of disrupting time-honored patterns of devotion and communal worship or of distancing oneself from the familiarity and solidity of an established Jewish identity and its halo of sacred associations. While some practices may not be strictly mandated by the letter of the law, they have become so entrenched in the traditional way of life and integral to communal self-perception that diverging from them appears tantamount to transgressing the law itself. By association, such practices may appear inextricably bound to a tried-and-true form of spirituality that even an Orthodox feminist may still be reluctant to forgo.[38]

After balancing all these considerations, all that the Orthodox feminist is left with is an educated guess as to the best option in light of background factors and pragmatic considerations. In the last resort, there is no a priori workable formula for deciding when to ignore precedents and endorse a new vision even when this vision appears capable of being assimilated by the tradition's own standards. In the absence of such a formula, the final measure of her decision will be not the degree to which it is grounded in halakhic niceties but its results. The nature and intensity of religious commitment among those who are drawn to this option, the degree of their continued immersion in the tradition, the amount of spiritual good that the deviance does or does not seem to accomplish—these will be the factors ultimately determining her choice.

In an ideal world, this self-determination might not be the way to establish a legal reality. It is not what we would choose if we were starting with a clean slate. When dealing with a rich and complex tradition constituted of the meeting between so many variegated communities, over so long a period of time, however, it may be precisely the recourse to local decision-making, in the form of ad hoc solutions and piecemeal victories won case by case—and even recourse to the silences of halakhic authorities who look the other way—that is most effective in building long-term solutions. At any rate, it seems to hold greater promise on purely pragmatic grounds than sweeping and bombastic ideological declarations that fail to make connections with the present nomic reality of the halakhically committed. As the noted twentieth-century German architect Ludwig Mies van der Rohe declared, in describing his minimalist style and worldview, "Sometimes less is more."

These reflections bring us to the third and most critical requirement for effecting halakhic change in a manner that can be viewed as authentic from an internal perspective: commitment to the interpretive tradition's divine authority. Demonstrating how a feminist critique of women is not antithetical to the notion of a divine Torah is the focus of the following chapter.

CHAPTER 10

The Word of God Contextualized

Successive Hearings and the
Decree of History

One of my sons once remarked to me that most of his women acquaintances were much more sophisticated religiously than his male friends. The reason was obvious to him: a Jewish girl raised in the Orthodox tradition realizes from the outset that she must adopt a more complicated relationship to the classic sources, because so much of the picture of women in the sources simply does not correspond to what she knows herself to be. Like Molière's Monsieur Jourdain, who suddenly discovers that he has been speaking prose all his life, Orthodox women are constantly appropriating a nuanced approach to Torah. I do not claim that all such women are active theologians with a common position regarding the validity of "external" influences upon the religious life, or even that they are consciously involved in developing one. To the extent, however, that they are capable in practice of relating to tradition and its dissonance with their contemporary experience *in a manner consonant with its mythic vocabulary,* they have much to teach us. Fortified by a more sophisticated understanding of the relationship between inner and outer dimensions of the divine word, Orthodox women may be able to offer a unique theological contribution, in reconciling a feminist self-image with the notion of a divine Torah.

Precedents to the Feminist Critique of Revelation

Before embarking on any attempt to articulate such an understanding, I should first note that the challenge that feminism poses to the divinity of God's word—highlighting its vulnerability to the distortions of limited human perspectives—is not really unique to feminism at all. In demonstrating the extent to which the worldview of revelation has been filtered through male spectacles, feminism is, in a sense, merely reviving with a vengeance the old threat of historicism that was raised in the nineteenth century by the *Haskalah* (the Jewish Enlightenment movement), by Reform Judaism, and by the school of *Wissenschaft des Judentums* (the historical-philological study of Jewish sources). The writings of the Rabbis tacitly acknowledge human imprints on sacred texts and even the subjectivity of Moses and his generation in absorbing the divine message of Torah. Over the generations Jews have exhibited awareness of the time- and culture-bound nature of biblical statements in many areas. The nature, scope, and intensity of their questions, however, have changed over time.

In medieval times it was the challenge of rationalism as represented by Aristotelian physics and metaphysics that highlighted what appeared to be imperfections in the divine message. Theological and philosophical problems abounded: Can we say that God is angry and jealous, has a strong arm, or speaks or reacts in time? Can the fixedness of the laws of nature allow for the possibility of miracles? These difficulties were resolved by the classic solution of Maimonides: "The gates of interpretation are never sealed."[1] In other words, whenever the literal meaning of the Torah can be incontrovertibly refuted, this is clear indication that the text was meant to be understood allegorically, with deeper meanings to be extracted by the more philosophically inclined. The form of the Torah was indeed affected by human fallibility; rather than indicating human authorship, however, this condescension to human nature reflects the didactic wisdom of the divine Author, and His ability to accommodate the message of the Torah to all levels of intelligence and sophistication.[2]

In the early modern period, the critique moved on to the natural sciences: Does the earth have four corners? Was the world created in six days? Is it really only five thousand years old? As these disciplines developed, the questions became far more advanced and exacting. The bearing of paleontology on the age of the earth, Darwinism on the origins of the species, and archaeological discoveries on biblical accounts of history, to name but a few examples, raised difficulties that were compounded by broader critiques of biblical morality. The biblical acceptance of genocide, capital punishment, and slavery, among other social institutions we today regard as morally inferior, make the outlook of the text appear dated, bound by the conceptions of a civilization long extinct. As the gap between contemporary understandings of reality and the plain sense of religious truths became wider, even the elasticity afforded by allegorical readings was often not enough to extend their credibility as divine messages untouched by the limitations of human perception.

Another major factor contributing to modern difficulties in viewing the Bible as a divine text was the development of Wellhausen's documentary hypothesis. Julius Wellhausen understood the Torah as a composite work, consisting of four separate documents that can be identified on the basis of various stylistic, linguistic, and other differences (beginning with the use of different names for God). He concluded that these documents were compiled over time and finally made canonic long after Moses' death. His hypothesis appears to remove the text even further from God's hands: not

only because it contests the historical accuracy of the traditional account of
the Torah's literary genesis, but also because the notion that biblical ideas
underwent historical development appears to contradict flatly the tradition
that God dictated to Moses every word of the Torah.

The development of the study of ancient civilization and comparative religion has made it even more difficult to employ the medieval allegorist's distinction between form and content as a tool for salvaging the divinity of the
text. Explanations that focus on God's sublime purpose in phrasing His
message in allegoric terms—presenting textual anomalies as trappings specially contrived by a benign Teacher so as to render eternal truths more intelligible or palatable to temporal beings and finite minds—lose their persuasiveness when such difficulties are more elegantly explained by reference
to their historical setting. Furthermore, as modern literary theory has taught
us that in all cultures the form in which ideas are expressed is closely related
to their content, allegory itself is now understood to be a culture-specific
phenomenon, with various contemporary factors determining when and
where it is to be used. For this reason too, most readers now find it more
plausible to chalk up difficulties with what appears to be the plain meaning
of various biblical passages to the direct input that imperfect human beings
had in formulating the text.

What makes the feminist analysis unique is that the ultimate question it
raises does not concern any *particular* difficulty in the contents of the Torah
(be it moral, scientific, or theological). Nor does it concern the accuracy of
the historical account of its literary genesis. Highlighting an all-pervasive
male bias in the Torah seems to display a more general skepticism regarding
divine revelation that is much more profound. What it drives us to ask is,
Can any *verbal* message claiming revelatory status really be divine? Because
language itself is shaped by the cultural context in which it is formulated,
and because it must of necessity be bound to a particular standpoint, is a divine and eternally valid message at all possible? Can a verbal message
transcend its cultural framework? With these questions, the clash between
Orthodoxy and historicism is transformed from a dispute over the facts of
the matter to a debate over issues of general bias and the ubiquitous traces of
cultural relativism. And it is here that the insufficiency of traditional pana-
ceas comes into bold relief. Allegorical interpretations of problematic passages in the Torah will not solve anything in this case. The male bias cannot
be limited to specific terms or passages; it is all over the text.

There are, to be sure, other instances of cultural bias that might be regarded as equally pervasive. One example is the blatantly pagan mind-set
that emerges from the Torah. It is not only Moses and the Israelites who appear as polytheistic idolaters when they cry out in praise: "Who is like you,
O Lord, among the gods? (Exod. 15:11). The Torah itself, when speaking
of God often employs highly anthropomorphic imagery, despite injunctions
against graven images and such warnings as: "No one shall see me and

live" (Exod. 33:20). Moreover, the Torah depicts a God who is not always wise, omnipotent, and just—forcing those adopting its imagery once again into confrontation with the issue of biblical limitations and traces of dated human conceptions upon what purports to be a timeless text. Chapters and chapters devoted to the ritual details of animal sacrifice are much more readily explained by the beliefs of human authors than as God's deliberate compromise with the weaknesses of human nature and the everlasting danger of idolatry.

The theological dilemma as highlighted by feminism is more acute simply because of the direct influence it has on everyday life. The undesirable effects of continued reference to God's mighty arm can be satisfactorily muted by allegory, even if it does leave some garbled anthropomorphic image in the mind of the believer who is not philosophically inclined. Whether or not this image is the residual influence of pagan thinking does not matter, so long as there are no more discernibly harmful results. By the same token, slavery or animal sacrifices may be ignored because they are not options for the moment. Yet if language wields a subtle negative influence on human behavior, as feminist thinkers charge, the visions in the book of Hosea—of a God who relates to the disobedient people of Israel as does an abusive husband to his whoring wife—have contemporary ramifications.[3] For an increasing number of Jewish women (and men), the aspersions that the overwhelmingly patriarchal nature of the Torah seem to cast on its own divinity are more troubling because the conception of a fixed hierarchical relationship between the sexes is still capable of affecting today's women adversely.

Non-Orthodox Responses to the Question of Divine Revelation

Mordecai Kaplan's Reconstructionism. Outside the camp of Orthodox Judaism, one response to the dilemma can be found in the naturalist theology of Mordecai Kaplan.[4] Kaplan rejects religious claims to metaphysics and transcendence altogether, viewing revelation rather as the human "discovery" of how to live religiously. To say that religion is a creation of human beings does not imply that it is a fiction; religion flows naturally and intuitively from an innate religious impulse. Nonetheless, acknowledging this "discovery" ascribes to humans an infinitely more creative and decisive role in shaping the content of revelation. That content merely expresses the function of God as a process or power *within* the natural order.

Kaplan's view of revelation ultimately shifts the authority of Torah radically, from God to the human community. The text of Torah is sacred only because it has emerged out of the collective life of the Jewish community. Jewish belief and practice change as the community changes. Each generation of Jews formulates afresh its search for a meaningful existence in accordance with its own insights and limitations. As Neil Gillman, professor of theology, explains: "It is this theoretical framework that gives Kaplan the right to 'reconstruct' Judaism for our day. Hence the movement inspired by Kaplan's teachings is called Reconstructionism."[5]

The school of dialectical theology. There have been several attempts to develop a more nuanced understanding of revelation that does not reject biblical claims to metaphysics altogether.[6] All of them appear to be variations of the view developed by Martin Buber that has come to be known as "dialectical theology." It is represented in the theological writings of Franz Rosenzweig, Abraham Joshua Heschel, Louis Jacobs, and others.[7] This more complex approach to the biblical text understands everything said about God as a human effort to convey or recapture certain religious moments. Although such moments represent genuine meetings with the divine, they were inevitably experienced in a particular linguistic and cultural context that structured the nature of the experience and its interpretation. It is also the nature of such moments that no written or oral report can successfully convey them in terms entirely free of the influence of historical context.

Thus dialectical theology sees in the Torah an account of the experiencing of the divine that is, on the one hand, incomplete. On the other hand, the very fact that the text that emerges has succeeded in arousing others and providing them with a sense of meaning demonstrates that it indeed reflects an authentic experience. Hence the Torah should be viewed as the attempt of a concrete historical community to remember and realize in its life the encounter at Sinai with a God who turns to a particular people and determines its destiny. The significance of this true meeting is wrapped up in its limited language. What is left for us is to extract the eternal illuminations that the Torah communicates to us from those trappings that are the fruit of passing human experience.

Although the memory of standing at Sinai when the Torah was revealed is at the core of Judith Plaskow's feminist theology, she does not devote much attention in her writing to the concept of revelation. From the little she does say, however, it would appear that she herself leans toward dialectical theology and the selectivity between the human and the divine that it allows, rather than denying any supernatural element in history, after the fashion of Reconstructionist Judaism.[8] While denying the plausibility of God communicating to human beings via a verbal message transmitted in a text free of human fallibility and bias, Plaskow does not forgo the possibility of "moments of intense religious experience." She regards the Torah, however, as only a partial record of such experiences: in principle these moments "cannot be pinned down and reproduced; they can only be suggested and pointed to so that readers or listeners may from time to time catch for themselves the deeper reality vibrating behind the text."[9] Moreover, Plaskow recognizes that such experiences are shaped even in their original reception by their cultural contexts; therefore they cannot be free of human constructions.[10]

A dialectical account of revelation does indeed appear more satisfactory than traditionalist formulations in its ability to contend with the critical findings of feminist literary and historic analysis comprehensively, without rejecting biblical claims to a supernatural source. Dialectical theology avoids the impossible exercise of distinguishing sharply between the form of Torah and its content, as we saw Judith Antonelli and Eliezer Berkovits attempt to do. In the words of Louis Jacobs, who describes himself as a "liberal super-naturalist," the assertion that there is both a human and a divine element in the Torah does not mean to say "that one can go through the Pentateuch or the Psalms or the Mishnah or the Talmud with a pencil ticking the passages which appeal to us as divine and those which do not as human."[11] It is rather, he suggests, that "God is behind the whole process." Nonetheless, because Jacobs holds that the Torah, after all is said and done, was produced by humans, and "is eternity expressing itself in time," it still contains "higher and lower, error as well as truth, the ignoble as well as the noble."[12]

Dialectical theology does not, however, satisfy the traditional requirement that the *entire* Torah be viewed as the word of God and its authority be considered as binding in all of its detail. Indeed, according to the *Mishnah,* those who suggest that Moses said even one sentence of the Torah on his own rather than receiving it from God are precisely those who have "denigrated the word of God" in denying the principle of "Torah from Heaven" (*Torah min hashamayim*).[13] Perhaps this is the reason that dialectical theology has not held much appeal for mainstream Orthodoxy.

Orthodox Responses to Biblical Criticism

To the extent that Orthodox Judaism has turned its attention at all beyond lower criticism—investigating issues of textual accuracy—to questions of content, it has thus far not moved much past medieval-style treatment of isolated texts.[14] The traditionalist still seeks to weather storms raised by apparent difficulties in the surface meaning of a passage through recourse to modernist counterarguments that address the difficulties as localized factual issues of science and religion. (By "modernist" and "modernism," I refer to a worldview based on the assumption of rigid and stable notions of truth. Such a view supports the belief that tradition speaks in the name of a neutral rationality that serves as its justification).[15] Questionable features of biblical morality are solved in a similar ad hoc manner; the existence of a biblical worldview with more pervasive biases of a dated or parochial nature is not considered.

As we have seen, Berkovits and Antonelli belong to this camp. They are willing to take into account the role of historical factors in shaping the divine message. They acknowledge the impact of the surrounding culture on certain biblical formulations with regard to women that now seem morally questionable. This recognition, however, does not address the more subtle and pervasive male bias highlighted by third-stage feminists, nor the broader issues raised by feminist readings of the text—such as the image of a distant transcendent God who exists apart from His creation and the authority-based relationship established between the two. Moreover, the approach of Berkovits and Antonelli ignores evidence that the differences between "Torah-authentic" and "Torah-tolerated" norms are the product of a natural historical process in which human beings took part.

Two other notable attempts have been made to relate to contemporary findings of biblical criticism regarding the literary genesis of the Torah and the difficulties these findings pose to the traditional account of a one-time revelation at Sinai. Although the bottom-line conclusions (like those of Berkovits and Antonelli) continue to uphold the notion of an original revelation dictated by God to Moses in a manner transcending historical process and human input, these efforts have met with much resistance in the Orthodox community. In many quarters they are regarded as extremely controversial, if not entirely beyond the pale.

Rabbi Breuer's sanctification of biblical criticism. The first of these attempts is that of Rabbi Mordecai Breuer, an Orthodox Torah scholar whose method has had considerable influence in modern yeshiva circles in Israel— in contrast to the intellectual bastions of Modern Orthodoxy in the United States, where (to the extent that his approach is recognized at all) it has been greeted with much graver reservations and even suspicion.[16] Breuer begins by acknowledging the problematics highlighted by Wellhausen's documentary hypothesis, and the nature and extent of contradictions it exposes in the biblical text. As he puts it, "the power of these inferences, based on solid argument and internally consistent premises, will not be denied by intellectually honest persons."[17] Though he accepts the evidence to which this school of biblical scholars points, he nonetheless dissents from their explanations and offers others in their stead.

Like Berkovits and Antonelli, Breuer sees the purpose of contradictory literary strata in the Torah as educational. But rather than limiting his explanation to God's need to wean humanity gradually from the inferior moral standards of a primitive society, Breuer understands the complex composition of the Torah revealed by the extensive findings of the documentary hypothesis as constituting an elaborate divine code. This code speaks to different generations of Jews in different voices. A multitude of meanings often moves beyond the plain sense of specific portions of the text. Only through this complex structure can the many complementary aspects of creation be conveyed. The Creator, who is beyond time and space, and not subject to the laws of historical development, presents these conflicting perspectives simultaneously. The secular scholar, who approaches the biblical text as the natural product of human culture, sees each perspective as a disparate document; woven together, the strands reflect for him the differing subjective perspectives of various human authors. The religious believer, by contrast, will dwell upon the conflicts and differing nuances in the text in order to discover the manifold divine secrets buried in its original design. And indeed, Breuer has built an impressive interpretive edifice by careful attention to all the discrepancies revealed by the methods of higher biblical criticism, while avoiding their heretical conclusions.

Breuer's belief in the divinity of the Torah is predicated on belief in the unique receptivity of Moses, who was able to absorb and transmit the primordial Torah that served as the blueprint of creation without the distortion of human mediation. Because the prophecy of Moses transcended his particular time and surroundings and conveyed the words of the living God using a content and style totally independent of his personality, there is no disparity in the Torah between God's authorial intent and the final written product. Breuer allows for the possibility that God addressed some sections of the Torah to a primary audience consisting of the generation of Israelites in the desert, but he is convinced that there is also a second level of authorial intent that comprises the Torah's deeper meaning, even though it may not have been penetrated by this primary audience.

Breuer insists that this linkage between the sanctified status of the Torah and the uniqueness of Moses' reliability as scribe was central to how the doctrine of divine revelation was understood throughout the generations. His insistence stems from a belief that the divinity of the Torah logically depends upon its having been transmitted in a manner that transcends historical process and the subjectivity of its receipient.

As various scholars have pointed out, this claim is overstated.[18] Aside from the theological non-sequitur involved (does the divinity of the Torah logically depend upon its literary genesis and manner of transmission?) Breuer's position is simply not born out by the facts, ignoring evidence that the Rabbis themselves did not regard the Torah written by Moses as emerging in a documentary void. Despite strong doctrinal emphasis upon the uniqueness of the Mosaic revelation, a few rabbinic sources register awareness that the Torah incorporated divine messages and written texts predating the life of Moses.[19] Moreover, several other rabbinic sources and medieval commentaries allow for the possibility of later interpolations to the Torah extending far beyond the time of Moses.[20]

In addition to inaccurate portrayal of traditional doctrine regarding revelation, Breuer's approach involves several methodological difficulties.[21] One of these is his excessive commitment to the findings of Wellhausen, despite revisions that have been made by Wellhausen's followers and more modern scholars in the field. Breuer's tenacity in building his entire exegetical edifice upon these findings ignores the fact that they are not the proven facts of an exact science. What constitutes a contradiction is very much a function of the reader's prior assumptions, and these necessarily undergo development and change in the course of time.[22] The same can be said of deciding how to interpret the significance of a contradiction. Hence, the conclusions that are built upon Wellhausen's findings must also be altered accordingly. Moreover, if planting contradictions via bogus shifts in style and content is indeed God's method for conveying His message to human beings, it is difficult to understand why such an important exegetical principle was so well hidden that we had to wait for Breuer to reveal it.[23]

Prof. Weiss-Halivni's maculated Torah. A second traditionalist approach to apparent flaws in the biblical text is that of the noted talmudic scholar, Professor David Weiss-Halivni.[24] Halivni strays further than Breuer from current Orthodox understandings of revelation; he is ready to attribute textual flaws to a historical process. He does not explicitly state to what extent the corruption he refers to extends beyond the minor textual inconsistencies that even the most traditional Torah scholar would not deny, and how far such corruption tallies with the more radical findings of "higher criticism" and source theory. Halivni finds evidence for his assumption of "maculation"—evidence of tampering with the text or scribal error—in biblical and talmudic references that link negligence of halakhic observance in the first Temple period with failure to preserve the original scriptural revelation properly. On the basis of these references, he concludes that the biblical text we now have dates from the time of Ezra the Scribe.

According to Halivni, Ezra initiated a process of "rehabilitating" sections of the Torah that had suffered corruption, in order to align their import with the original version of revelation. This rehabilitation was usually accomplished not by revising blemished texts (Ezra did not feel he possessed sufficient authority to do this), but rather by initiating a method for reinstating the original meaning through authoritative midrashic interpretation. There are various instances in which the *halakhah* reflects a later rabbinic understanding of what the biblical text once said; the paradigmatic example is the displacing of the simple meaning of "an eye for an eye" with the notion of monetary compensation. From this Halivni learns a humbling but religiously valuable lesson: no divine message entrusted to human hands can remain perfect for long. Nevertheless, we ought to relate (as Ezra did) to this flawed remnant of God's word with the same awe and respect that the original would command.[25]

If the greatest threat to traditional Judaism in Breuer's eyes is any doubt regarding the perfection of the biblical text as it stands, Halivni appears more concerned with ensuring the authenticity of the Oral Law and its interpretive agenda. Evidently he believes that defending the legitimacy of halakhic practice as established in rabbinic Judaism is a preferable method of guaranteeing the alignment of our present Torah with the divine will.

Halivni's assumptions about Ezra's halakhic exegesis are not without difficulties of their own,[26] difficulties that may be born of an apologetic impulse in defense of *midrash halakhah*. The original revelation no longer bears the weight of faithfully transmitting the divine will; this responsibility is now transferred to the Oral Law and we can be reassured that in leading the halakhic life we are following the divine will. In divorcing the issue of biblical textual accuracy from its divinity, Halivni frees himself of the dogmatic constraint to deny any evidence of changes and reversals in the original text over the course of time. He also avoids the rather anthropomorphic view of God laboriously composing conflicting messages, one in the form of an explicit norm addressed to a primary but temporary audience, and another more implicit, waiting to be discovered—the problematic image evoked not only by Breuer's approach, but even by the more muted distinction between Torah-authentic and Torah-tolerated norms of Berkovits and Antonelli. The ultimate shortcoming of Halivni's solution, however, is that he too does not address the heart of the problem raised by radical feminism, which calls into question the very possibility of verbal revelation.

I believe that this issue points to a new theological dimension that should rivet the attention of every traditional Jew who sees any measure of justice in the reluctance of women in our day to continue to submit to patriarchy as the ideal societal mold. The challenge when rethinking the past is how to alter traditions without compromising their authority. In forcing this issue, and pressing for a more adequate solution than that provided by the positivist/restorativist mode, the feminist critique creates one of those decisive historical moments when faith can be lost—or strengthened through its refinement. As R. Kook would have it: "in general, this is an important rule in the struggle of ideas: we should not immediately refute any idea which comes to contradict anything in the Torah, but rather we should expand the palace of Torah above it, and through this exaltation the ideas are revealed."[27] Indeed, what we now face is a rare opportunity for expanding the palace of Torah.

Dissolving the Problem:
Recasting the Meaning of Religious Language

All the approaches to the divinity of Torah that we have seen thus far view traditional formulations of revelation as simple statements of fact. If literal meanings are problematic, we must reject the formulations, qualify them, or bring logical argument and empiric evidence in order to resolve the difficulties they raise. I suggest that this is the wrong way to proceed: it entails a misconception of what traditional descriptions mean to the believer in the context of religious life. When an Orthodox Jew says, "I believe in Torah from Heaven," her primary concern is not to discuss facts or establish history, but to make a statement on an entirely different plane. It reflects her wish to establish a much stronger claim that will regulate her entire life. It is a statement that may bring her to take risks or make sacrifices that she would never dream of for the sake of opinions that she knows to be far better grounded from a scientific point of view. Her belief in the divine origins of Torah serves as the primary basis for a way of life and worldview to which she is inextricably bound in a multitude of ways by personal conviction, passion, and practical considerations.

Does this understanding of the function of religious statements mean that she regards the divine origin of Torah as less true than scientific beliefs? No. But because the two statements are of a different nature, the evidence for each is different. What we normally think of as evidence in a scientific context is quite irrelevant for substantiating a religious belief.

Thus, for example, even if we were able to locate the original Mount Sinai, find fragments of the first tablets broken by Moses, and read a parchment diary by an Israelite who witnessed and documented the event of revelation firsthand, none of this would change what the believer means by saying that the Torah is divine. The purpose of this assertion is to affirm the ultimate meaning and value of a way of life and worldview. Because of its different aim, the scientific basis for this assertion might be exceedingly flimsy evidence or nonexistent. The considerations brought to bear in determining the validity of such religious statements is taken from *within* the religious framework itself. Validity must be formulated in terms of the context from which a statement derives its meaning.

In pursuing this track I am following a recent trend in the philosophy of religion, one that has developed as a result of the increasing breakdown of belief in the literal meaning of religious language. In the past few decades, theological thinking has turned away from the by-now-overworked modernist attempts to try to defend religion's portrayal of reality on an empiric level. Instead theology is now typified by an altogether new focus upon the significance of religious language. Much of this trend has been influenced by the thought of the Austrian-born philosopher Ludwig Wittgenstein, whose work combines in a unique way ideas derived from both the Continental European and the British analytic traditions.[28] His insights regarding language and its uses—and the implications of these insights for questions of metaphysics, evidence, and belief—have had great impact. A significant number of philosophers and theologians have applied his views to their religious understandings. Something like the Wittgensteinian attitude to religious belief can also be discerned in the writings of a few contemporary Jewish thinkers, such as David Hartman, Eliezer Goldman, and Yeshayahu Leibowitz.[29] A similar attitude is rooted more profoundly in some modern formulations of older mystic traditions of Judaism.[30]

What Wittgenstein taught is that language does not serve the same purpose in all contexts; there are many kinds of things that can be said. To illustrate the diversity of discourse, Wittgenstein introduces the concepts of "language games" and "forms of life." The different functions or substructures of language comprise different "language games," each doing a particular job, conveying certain meanings to those who participate in its particular discourse. If the waitress in a coffee shop asks what I'd like to order and I reply demurely, "I am waiting for the Messiah," she would be quite justified in keeping an anxious eye on me. If I utter the same statement in the context of synagogue prayer, however, it is not only appropriate, but even expected. Someone who says "Great performance!" is participating in the language game of praising. Someone who says "I see two red chairs" is participating in the language game of describing. Each "language game" is part of a "form of life"; that is, a whole complex of natural and cultural presuppositions that constitute a worldview and enable its expression in practice. By saying "Good morning," we are not necessarily describing the weather, but we are certainly participating in the language game known as "greeting." This last example illustrates that human life is complicated; we often participate in many language games at one and the same time. It is only when we get different types of discourse mixed up with one another that we are led to blunders and confusion. This intermixing, to my mind, is what plagues certain spokesmen of Modern Orthodox thinking in their strident attempts to stipulate what may or may not be legitimately believed.[31]

Religious language is a long-established form of discourse that does a particular set of jobs, imparting its own particular "form of life" to those who participate in its "language game." The participants employing religious discourse are engaging a system of symbols that legitimate their most basic patterns of thought, feeling, and behavior. This "form of life" is not merely a set of practices. It also reflects a "picture" of reality that shapes and produces profound sentiments, attitudes, and awarenesses.

Emphasizing the distinctiveness of religious discourse does not imply that this discourse is totally unrelated to other "language games" and unaffected by them. On the contrary, Wittgenstein's insights have led to a growing recognition that the religious language game, like others of a similar nature, is long established and a much more complex form of discourse than most. A religious language game performs many and various linguistic functions that are closely related and internally dependent on each other. For example, when a religious Jew is asked, "How are you?" and answers, "Barukh Hashem" (Blessed be God), she is engaged in an act of praising the Lord; she may also, however, employ this formula noncommittally or even when things are not going well at all. By pairing "Barukh Hashem" with "My teenagers are driving me crazy," or even with "I've just been diagnosed with cancer," she is expressing her faith in God's management of the world, whatever her troubles. And as she returns the question and receives the same preface to the answer, she is also participating in a ritual of mutual empathy. When religion operates as the ultimate value against which all else is measured, it serves as the prism through which many other experiences of the world will be filtered. This absorption process may modify the specific meaning attached to a religious formula, but it will not serve as the basis for upholding or dislodging it.

If we return with this view of the multifaceted functions of language to the belief in divine revelation, we see that the difficulties raised by the feminist critique may alter how this belief is to be understood in the religious "language game." Its validity, however, will rise or fall on other grounds that have more to do with the "form of life" that it supports, and the grip that its particular "picture" has on the loyalties and convictions of the believer.

Witnessing informal debates of a theological nature, I have observed that almost invariably, there comes a point when, after the obvious logical, scientific, or philosophical arguments have been exhausted, one of the parties will exclaim, "But how can you possibly posit belief X (for example, that the Torah was not all given to Moses or that God allowed injustice to women)? Don't you realize that if you do, this necessarily leads to 'form of life' Y (the death of *halakhah,* or atheism)?" Generally, this slip into a different mode of argument is made unconsciously, without realizing that it is tantamount to an admission that religious doctrines are generally shaped by our prior interest in a particular form of life, rather than the other way around. My point here is not to repeat the banality that intellectual argument is never totally clean of personal bias. Nor is it to deny the validity or justice of that bias. It is instead to suggest that the main purpose of religious doctrine is indeed to grant meaning to the "form of life" through which we live by attributing to it divine purpose.

Religious believers generally assume this attitude to the function of religious doctrine unreflectively. They simply allow the concrete experience of their everyday lives to be constituted and shaped by the truth claims of their religious traditions. Most believers employ these claims quite naturally as the grammar to be used when speaking about their ultimate values, without dwelling overmuch on their doctrinal content. Belief in divine revelation for traditional Jews simply means loyalty to the Torah and the way of life that it propagates, without needing to delve into greater detail and explore what this doctrine implies. Intuitively, they will have mastered the skill of stating their belief in a manner that does not overstep the context and regulative purpose for which the statement was meant: to impress upon us the ultimate authority of the halakhic way of life. Employing religious beliefs in this manner will have negotiated such believers into a spiritual orientation and practical kind of "knowing" that seems natural and satisfying without their experiencing a need for further proof beyond the form of life that ratifies this knowing.

This is not to say that *any* understanding of doctrine will serve the purpose. Although religious belief is not proven or falsified on rational grounds, inability to reconcile a religious truth claim with reason or with other religious beliefs (such as God's justice, or His transcendence) may well be an obstacle to its acceptance (unless irrationality itself is part of the religious "picture"). As Rabbi A. I. Kook has observed: "Belief to which reason cannot acquiesce gives rise to anger and cruelty, because the most sublime aspect of humanity—which is reason—is, as a result, impoverished."[32] Therefore, when doctrines that are part and parcel of the religious form of life appear untenable, the believer must subject them to a more deliberate and conscious process of interpretation that will remove such complaints. Conveying reasonable import is not their main function. Nonetheless, a strong sense that they are *un*reasonable may well render the doctrines ineffective in accomplishing the regulative function for which they *are* meant: to compose the "picture" that stands behind the religious form of life. What is more, the interpretive adjustment must be conducted in terms consistent with the rules of the religious "language game" itself.

Can this be done with regard to the belief in divine revelation? I believe so.

The Cumulativist Solution: Three Assumptions

Jewish tradition provides precedents for a view of divine revelation that can assimilate feminist exposure of a pervasive male bias in Scripture, without resorting to untenable conceptions of God and His methods of communication. In brief, this is accomplished by reappropriating three additional assumptions that already exist in tradition. These assumptions enable belief that the Torah is divinely revealed, without denying human involvement (hence male interest and biases). Instead of purporting to distinguish a fixed, objective meaning on the part of God versus subjective human understanding, they provide a more subtle definition of the relationship between divine intent and human interpretation.

The first assumption I draw upon is that revelation is a cumulative process: a dynamic unfolding of the original Torah transmitted at Sinai that reveals in time its ultimate significance. This deviation from the common picture of an absolute and one-time affair at Sinai favors a more fluid view of Torah as a series of ongoing "hearings" of the voice at Sinai throughout Jewish history. The idea that this voice is always there waiting to be heard is well anchored in the sources. Rabbi Isaiah Horowitz (known by the Hebrew acronym of his magnum opus, *Shnei Luhot Habrit,* as "the Shlah") notes the use of the *present tense* in the Mishnaic saying: "Every day a voice goes out from Mount Horeb and announces . . ."[33] This voice, he says, is the same one that was heard at Sinai. "We find that God gave the Torah and He continues to give the Torah at every moment," continues the Shlah. "The flowing fountain does not cease, and what He gives is on the strength of what He gave."[34]

The second assumption, implicit in the Shlah's statement, is that God's voice does not express itself through the reverberation of vocal chords (not

His, nor those of a "created voice" as some commentators suggested in order to avoid the problem of anthropomorphic visions of God).[35] His word is heard rather through the rabbinical interpretation of the texts, which may or may not be accompanied by an evolution in human understanding, and through the mouthpiece of history. If that same voice from Sinai reverberates throughout the world every day, and even in our day, it must be a spiritual voice. Our "hearing" may sometimes take the form of quasi-prophetic inspiration (*ruah hakodesh*); at other times necessary adjustments to the constraints of the era and the ideas that they bring forth may also constitute "hearing." History, and particularly what happens to the Jewish people—the ideas and forms they accept as well as the process of determining those they reject—is essentially another form of ongoing revelation, a surrogate prophecy.

The third assumption is that although successive hearings of God's Torah sometimes *appear* to contradict His original message, that message is never replaced. As I shall explain, it always remains as the primary cultural-linguistic filter through which these new deviations are heard and understood.

Some believers of a theistic bent will prefer to understand ongoing revelations in a more personified manner as manifestations of a continuing divine providence. Those of a more mystic propensity will view them more abstractly, as a gradual exposure of the metaphysical divine essence on its earthly level. Either way, I am contending that unfreezing our concept of revelation—moving away from the simplistic metaphor of God dictating the entire Torah to Moses—does not require a nontraditional theological framework. Revisionist history or creative rereadings that ignore the halakhic tradition are not the only sources or the best ones for expansion of Torah and the meaning of revelation. The conception of a Written Torah whose full meaning is only revealed incrementally, via the prism of history, exists within mainstream Jewish tradition. In an essay entitled "Continuous Revelation—Three Directions," Hebrew University professor of Jewish thought Shalom Rosenberg points to three versions of this conception in the sources: Torah as the wellspring from which all subsequent interpretations are drawn; "acceptance by the nation," which relies on accord between the will of the Jewish people and the divine will; and halakhic authority as the true medium for expressing the divine will.[36] The approach I would like to develop, which I call "accumulating revelation," combines elements that appear in each.

One could say, then, that I too am proposing a theological restorativism of sorts, in the sense of seeking to reclaim motifs that already exist in the tradition but have been neglected, forgotten, or abandoned for various reasons. My restorativism, however, is directed not to Jewish notions of social justice or to our ways of imaging God, but rather to the nature of Torah as a divine text—something even more profound and fundamental in terms of the Jewish way of life. Irrespective of whether the place certain motifs occupied in the past was of major or minor importance, restorativism in the usual sense hopes that in resurrecting these elements we bring the authority of the past as justification for their replication in the present. In applying the notion of cumulative revelation to the concept of restorativism itself, however, I would like to assert something more nuanced than this: that with respect to the past we are never capable of repeating it intact. Neither can we totally release ourselves from its hold upon us in order to invent something entirely new. We are forever investing new meanings in the ideas that have become part and parcel of our own identity, in a manner that conjoins the two. This same notion applies to our understanding of Torah.

As noted in chapter 8, rabbinic tradition has always maintained a sense of the "meaning" of Torah that is looser and richer than a strictly literal historical understanding. The creative potential this implies is fortified by the notion that the nature of the Hebrew language is inexhaustible. Such breadth allowed for great interpretive fluidity, as evidenced in the classical notion that Torah can be explained in different ways, according to its plain (*peshat*), applied (*derash*), implied (*remez*), and esoteric (*sod*) meanings. Despite the special status of the talmudic Rabbis, the legitimacy of innovation was not limited to the talmudic period. In the realm of *halakhah* there exists a whole literature of commentary, known as "novellae" (*hiddushim*), in which scholars from the Middle Ages until the present day, present their original interpretations of canonized texts.[37] In this genre, originality and creativity are not just acceptable; they are encouraged. This creativity is not viewed as threatening to tradition, or as changing the Torah, but simply as elaborating upon its original meaning. The same may be said for the rich legacy that Jewish tradition has produced over time in the nonlegal realm of Jewish thought and philosophy, often turning the original import of basic Jewish concepts on their head.

The idea of accumulating revelation may be regarded as a natural outgrowth of this traditional understanding of the nature of rabbinic interpretation and its relationship to the Written Torah. What it adds is merely the conviction that if these free-flung interpretations of the Torah have evolved in a certain way, there is likely something of significance to be derived from this particular evolvement. As Michael Berger has already expressed it:

Judaism, like several other theistic traditions, does not restrict the level of divine involvement in human affairs strictly to the realm of prophecy. There is also the cardinal belief in God's supervision of the world's events, at both the collective and the individual levels. . . . In a similar vein, it could be argued that the revelation of the Torah, whether at Sinai or throughout the forty years of wandering in the desert, was not a one-time event, but rather that God has continued to supervise the history of the development of halakha ever since.[38]

Belief in God's involvement in the development of the Oral Law does not necessarily entail the claim that all rabbinic authorities were endowed with heavenly gifts of prophecy or divine inspiration. It does, however, involve faith in some attunement between the character of the original prophetic message and its subsequent human exposition. It also expresses a theological affirmation of the background conditions leading to the interpretive status quo. It allows for the possibility that although certain interpretations may for the moment appear limited or even flawed due to the shortcomings of human understanding, in the end they are capable of achieving God's ultimate purpose. It confirms the function of religious belief itself as an affirmation of life, and of our determination to view reality and the flow of events as something other than meaningless chaos.

Although such an approach is particularly suited to Jewish theology because of the rabbinic concept of the Oral Law, it has found expression in the thought of some Christian feminists as well. It is especially congenial to Catholics, who also tend to think in terms of an evolving tradition. Because of this similarity, they too can easily accept the idea that the will of a transcendent God is revealed not only in His original revelation, singular though it may be, but also in the interpretive adaptations to canonized tradition. These adaptations have been either generated by the continuing insights of inspired teachers or compelled by the developments of history. This approach, while still affirming the past as normative—making binding claims upon us—allows for development, based on the belief that there is a divine purpose in history that unfolds stage by stage.

As in Judaism, such a Christian cumulativism favors a more theistic theology that sees God as outside of history, yet actively involved in it—as revealed in certain *kairoi* (a Greek term referring to special junctures, unlike normal linear time, that God brings about by creating situations that are particularly pregnant or opportune). When people are inspired to take advantage of these situations and take action, God's will is revealed.[39] An alternative source for the conflating of God and history, in a manner more reminiscent of the Jewish mystic tradition, is provided by Christian process theology (described in chapter 7). That system of thought also conceives of the relationship among God, human beings, and nature progressing together into a future that integrates past realities with new permutations. Ideal possibilities of ever-increasing complexity can thus be realized.

Traditional precedents for cumulative revelation

In Judaism, the blurring of boundaries between the divine word and the human interpreter finds particular emphasis in those streams of thought that could be described as more "feminine" by nature. Support exists for one or another of the components of a more dynamic understanding of revelation in various *aggadot*, in kabbalistic literature, and in the writings of many of the Hassidic masters. It may be that it is precisely the predilection of these expressions of traditional Judaism for less binary modes of thinking that also leads them to support a more fluid view of Torah, one that does not pose God and His word as utterly distinct and separate from the flow of history and human subjectivity. Although the idea of an accumulating revelation does not appear elsewhere in exactly the form I present here, it combines various strands that exist separately in order to construct a more extensive and cohesive theology. My appeal to these varying strands is not based on any conception of their combined common *authority*. It comes simply to illustrate the extent to which tradition itself already provides valuable tools and precedents for expanding the meaning of Torah.

In brief, the fluid notion of Torah suggested by these softer conceptions presents the Sinai revelation of God's word as the initiator of a series of revelations in the form of inspired interpretations throughout the ages. The ideal meaning of the Sinaitic revelation is eked out only with these accumulated interpretations. The various strata are then absorbed as an integral part of the primary text, expanding upon and sometimes even transforming its original meaning, while forever remaining rooted in its precise language and frames of reference. All of this together forms one integral unity that represents the true intent of Torah. Through this unified prism we look out onto the world, and we understand it too as an extension of the text.

Aggadic differentiation: The primordial and the Written Torah. It is in midrashic literature, for example, that we already find a distinction between the "primordial Torah" (*Torah kedumah*) and the "Written Torah" which was received by Moses. We may term the latter the *human* Torah; that is, the Torah of Moses. The primordial Torah is, so to speak, the reflection of God in His essence, the secret world of His infinite wisdom, untouched by the finite dimensions of human understanding. The sages refer to this infinite aspect of Torah when they establish that "God looked into the Torah and created the world."[40] This primordial Torah retains a spiritual existence beyond this world even after creation.[41] The Written Torah of Moses embodies that supernal Torah; of necessity, however, it does so in a more limited and time-bound context, for God's infinite thought can never be exhausted or contained by finite human minds. In this vein, the Kabbalah's central text, the *Zohar,* subsequently establishes that the supernal Torah, when descending into the world, must clothe itself in coarser "garments" in order to make itself intelligible to creatures of flesh and blood. That is to say, the worldly Torah in a sense hides the Torah Above and its revealing is only made possible by a measure of concealment.[42]

Some *midrashim,* furthermore, could be understood as teaching that it is in the nature of religious experience that no oral or written record can emerge entirely free from the subjectivity of the person receiving the divine message. Several *midrashim* speak of the voice of God as being transmitted and modulated to each person of Israel "according to his strength" (*lefi koho*). Even Moses, despite biblical emphasis upon the directness of God's speech to him (especially encapsulated in the "dictation" metaphor), hears "according to his strength."[43] In broader contemporary terms, these midrashic accounts of variegated reception of prophecy could also be understood as reflecting the psychological, sociological, cultural, and other conditions and limitations of the generation to which the Torah was given.

The relationship between the primordial Torah and the human Torah, as manifested at Sinai, is depicted in a remarkable *midrash:*

> The Torah that God gave to Moses was given to him as white fire engraved upon by black fire. It is fire mixed with fire, cut from fire, and given from fire.[44]

Mystic tradition builds upon this enigmatic but profoundly suggestive imagery, indicating that the limitations of Moses' Written Torah also rest on the fact that it is not final and complete. The vision of the white fire, representing nothing less than God's transcendent mind, was engraved upon by black fire; what Moses caught sight of was only a reflection or shadow of that awesome, infinite, uncontainable, and inchoate form which fire represents.

This vision, however, was only the beginning of revelation, initiating a process that would bring the Torah progressively closer to human understanding.[45] In the language of the *midrash,* the white fire was made to differentiate itself into elements. Instead of being a pure, transcendent unity, it began to have recognizable parts: "black fire mixed with white." As the vision continued, this simple duality became more complex. The black fire formed itself into the twenty-two letters that form the Hebrew alphabet. According to *Sefer Yetzirah,* one of the earliest writings of the Jewish mystic tradition, these letters joined into various combinations that eventually emerged as the various names of God. Through these names all the phenomena of the universe were created.[46] As these letters metamorphosed into longer and longer configurations, they eventually formed themselves into one long holy mystical name of God that can be read in various ways, indicating the untold potential contained within.

Kabbalistic views of successive unfolding in history. This dynamic conception of Torah was later developed by medieval halakhists, who further embellished the idea of successive unfolding of the supernal Torah. This development, which is based on a conflating of the Written and the Oral Law, is represented powerfully by the thirteenth-century Tosafists of Ashkenaz. They regarded the difference between revelation and interpretation as a matter of degree, but not a difference in kind. The meaning of Torah, as they saw it, is eked out in the interpretive enterprise of the scholars, but "the spirit of God hovers over the *bet midrash* (study hall)."[47] In other words, divine providence exerts some influence on the direction of scholarly discussions so that the authenticity of halakhic decisions is ensured. Centuries later, in his inimitable fashion, Rabbi A. I. Kook reformulated the idea of continued prophetic influence upon the development of the Oral Law by appeal to the difference between the Babylonian and the Jerusalem Talmuds. The lengthiness of the former, he explains, is because this protocol of rabbinic discussion originated in the Diaspora, where the spirit of prophecy did not have full reign. Therefore the rabbis took longer to arrive at conclusions, while their Palestinian colleagues were able to grasp the issues in half the time![48]

Nachmanides, the classical medieval commentator better known as the Ramban, continues the mystic tradition in asserting that Moses was given two ways of interpreting the final great name of God:

It would appear that in the Torah written with letters of black fire upon a background of white fire, the writing was contiguous, without being broken up into words. This made it possible to be read either according to the division into divine names or according to our normal reading, which makes explicit the Torah and the commandments. Both interpretations were given to our teacher Moses: the division of words that express the commandments was given to him in written form, and the rendition that consists of the divine names was transmitted to him orally.[49]

This assertion serves to fortify the traditional belief of the sages that everything knowable by the human mind can be found in the Torah.[50] The developing nature of such knowledge is revealed in the changing nature of its trappings.[51]

A more elaborate version of this notion is manifest in what has come to be known as *Torat hashemitot,* a theory appearing in *Sefer Hatemunah,* a hallowed mystic work of the thirteenth century. In this view, time is divided into seven cosmic eras (*shemitot*), each of which reflects one of the seven lower manifestations (*sefirot*) of the Infinite One (*Ein-Sof*). In each of these eras, the original Torah is read differently. Its letters combine in new configurations; some disappear or are reinstated. Thus, the text takes on various forms, displaying just those meanings that reflect the particular characteristics of its era. In each, the Torah represents only one stage of a process that continues through all seven eras, it still retains its divine nature. According to *Sefer Hatemunah,* the cosmic era prior to the Sinaitic Torah was an era of *hessed* (the creative principle of all-encompassing expansiveness and undivided unity). In this era, the Torah did not read as commandments and prohibitions.[52] But our current cosmic era is the era of *din* (the principle of strict judgment and limitations), in which the evil urge exists as an independent reality. Therefore, our Torah now appears in the form of obligations and restrictions. In the next era we are destined to have a Torah of *rahamim* (compassion), which combines *din with hessed.*[53] On the kabbalistic understanding, what renders differing hearings of God's word in different stages of history as divine is the conviction that they reflect varying aspects of the Divine Being. Such metaphysical structures repeat themselves all the way down to the Torah and then to our worldly natural and cultural realities. Thus we may understand that even the hierarchical and patriarchal aspects, in the world, in the Torah, and in God, mirror one another.

The role of human receptivity and history in revelation. The dynamic understanding of the Torah as a reflection of God's metaphysical unfolding gains
an added dimension when it merges with another idea: that the "hearings"
of the Torah even on the biblical level are not one-directional, from above to
below. One source for this idea is a *midrash* that depicts the angels protesting to God, "How is it that you give the Torah to Moses? Are you not afraid
that he may add to it on his own?" Although God answers, "Heaven forfend
that Moses do such a thing!" He immediately continues, "But if he does, he
is trusted throughout my household" (Num. 12:7).[54] Even if Moses were to
say something on his own, divine approval is given in advance, for he is
known to be a trustworthy mouthpiece for exactly what God intends to express. Human participation in the giving of Moses' Torah is also clearly
brought home in the text itself. According to the Book of Numbers (9:1–8),
it is only after Moses turns to God that he receives divine assent to the institution of a second Passover for those who could not bring the Paschal sacrifice because of their ritual impurity.[55]

Sometimes it is not Moses who is the initiator, but other biblical figures.
For example, the princes of the tribes of Israel decide on their own accord
what sacrifices should be brought to the dedication of the Sanctuary; only
subsequently does Moses serve as the medium for God's decision as to
which to accept (Num. 7:1–9).[56] Similarly, demand by the daughters of Tzelofhad to inherit their father's lot (Num. 27:1–7) is only subsequently con-
firmed by God through Moses.[57]

As for later rabbinic interpretations, another *midrash* has two of the
sages arguing over the meaning of a biblical passage, without reaching
agreement. When one of them subsequently meets Elijah the Prophet (who
is known to solve all riddles) and asks him what God was saying at the time
of their dispute, the answer given is that God Himself simply repeated the
words of the Rabbis, learning Torah—as it were—from their mouths.[58]

In subsequent generations, this idea was expanded to mean that God
sometimes takes into account the contemporary predilections of the Jewish
people when revealing His will. Thus, for example, it is suggested that only
when the Israelites insisted upon having a king did God develop His Torah
in accordance with this idea.[59] If we are not all prophets, we are at least de-
scendants of prophets, and even the intuitive wishes of the people are in accordance with the divine will and have an influence on the way it flows, revealing itself in each generation.

Another significant contribution to the idea of a fluid revelation is the
teaching that sometimes God's will is revealed in processes that seem to be
working against His originally declared intentions. An echo of this understanding can be found in Rabbi Yosef Eliyahu Henkin's suggestion that we
see an act of providence in the impossibility of renewing the institutions of
semikhah (ordination from the last in a chain of teachers stretching back to
Moses) and the Sanhedrin (the court of the sages). It comes to prevent the

reinstating of corporal punishment, thus heralding messianic times.[60] This motif appears in different form in the suggestion by R. Kook that we must make peace with our inability, in the absence of stipulated preconditions, to observe the *mitzvot* of chastising the sinner in our day[61] or completely eradicating the seed of Amalek.[62] In another remarkable passage, R. Kook states that the outbreak of certain transgressions of the Torah (presumably by the secularist pioneer settlers of the land of Israel in his day) should be regarded as a phenomenon that "saddens the heart in terms of external manifestations, but gladdens it in terms of its internal significance"; sometimes even such outbreaks are a sign of God's will.[63]

This idea is taken one step further in R. Kook's writings when he locates expression of God's dynamically changing will beyond those factors that facilitate or obstruct our practical ability to observe certain *mitzvot*. The divine will can also be discerned in those factors that encourage or discourage our ability to entertain certain ideas on the spiritual or ideological plane. This notion appears with respect to the development of our moral intuitions in R. Kook's correspondence with a disciple who was troubled by the Torah's compliance with slavery. In his reply, R. Kook first contends that some races are naturally predisposed to subordination (a view that has caused considerable embarrassment to some of his more liberal admirers); he then notes that slavery can exhibit many forms and exists even today in our capitalist society. Because certain elements of society are inherently prone to being underdogs, the attempts of the Torah to mitigate the injustices of slavery still apply.

Having done with these apologetic efforts, R. Kook then implies that the Torah laws pertaining to slavery were also meant as an educational device, in order to wean humanity away from the institution of slavery altogether. When his correspondent apparently then assails him with a response to the effect of "Aha! So you too believe in an evolving Torah!" R. Kook vociferously objects. He insists upon a distinction between reformers who see the development of Torah as arbitrary and his own concept. By positing a supernal Torah and successive unfolding of that Torah as progressive revelations of a preexistent ideal, R. Kook concludes that if certain unprecedented ideas or norms become absorbed within tradition, it is a fair indication of the workings of divine providence. Such providence is attuned not only to our physical needs, but also to our gradually maturing spiritual sensibilities.[64]

If the community of believers and its authoritative bodies manage to find what they believe to be genuine support for their emerging worldviews in a new reading of the existing Torah, one can rest assured that such interpretive virtuosity is a true reflection of the divine will. The ultimate test of the validity of a new interpretation is its final acceptance by the interpretive community. For the believer, if any particular idea or social form, no matter what its source, takes hold and informs the life of Jews committed to Torah, this is a sign that it stems from God and was meant to be.

And if a question arises about some law of the Torah, which ethical notions indicate should be understood in a different way, then truly, if the Great Court decides that this law pertains only to conditions which no longer exist, a source in the Torah will certainly be found for it. The conjunction of events [that prompted the new interpretation], with [the reinstatement of] the power of the courts and the interpretation of Torah is not a coincidence. They are rather signs of the light of the Torah and the truth of the Torah's Oral Law, for we are obligated to accept [the rulings] of the judge that will be in those days [a reference to Jeremiah 2:3].[65]

Such a process is not what R. Kook terms "a deleterious type of 'evolution,'" but rather a new "hearing" of God's voice emerging from Sinai even in our day.

It is not only in the providential juxtaposition of events, judicial institutions, and their ability to accommodate new currents in their interpretation of Torah, however, that we see God's will. Even the rejection of certain scientific, theological, or moral convictions traditionally associated with religious belief may be interpreted as a sign, as may the birth of new ideas that appear to stray from belief, heralding a new unfolding of that primordial Torah that is revealed by divine providence.

The crux of the matter is that there is a special significance attached to the timing and effect of every idea. Nothing is haphazard. . . . When you understand this, you will know that there is sublime value in what is revealed and in what is hidden.[66]

R. Kook's religious reversal of historical reductionism. In viewing history as a medium of revelation, R. Kook provides traditionalists with an important avenue of rapprochement with feminist insights.[67] Irrespective of the substance of the feminist critique, there is something about its very methods that initially appears totally antithetical to a religion based on the notion of divine revelation. Believers generally recoil from historical, sociological, anthropological, or psychological explanations of key customs and tenets. In their eyes, the strength of Jewish beliefs and mores lies in the immediacy of their connection with the divine, and any suggestion of the influence of historical circumstances or comparison with surrounding cultures of the times is anathema. In feminist discussion, on the other hand, metaphysical or even scientific lines of argument typically brought by philosophers or theologians in the name of pure truth are rejected as irrelevant, owing to the decisive influence of subjective and contingent considerations upon such arguments. Thus it would seem as if there is hardly any common basis in the respective ground rules that would allow for dialogue between traditional religious belief and the feminist critique of religion.

Yet what R. Kook manages to do with his view of revelation through history is to turn the reductionist conclusions of historicism and the external observer on their heads. He dismisses the consternation of some of his religious contemporaries when confronted by superficial similarities between the Torah and Assyrian civilization.

Regarding the comparison of deeds [between pre-Sinaitic Israelites and their pagan surroundings] it is already a commonplace at least from the time of Maimonides (and indeed even before him in the words of the Rabbis) that prophecy adjusts itself to the nature of man, inasmuch as man's nature and inclination must necessarily be elevated by divine guidance.[68]

It is as if R. Kook is saying: "Of course revelation is influenced by history and the evolution of ideas (even when such ideas or their parallels are to be found in non-Jewish sources), but history and the evolution of ideas themselves are also the tools of revelation!" As opposed to Maimonides (and the track taken by Berkovits and Antonelli in his wake), R. Kook's acknowledgment of the influence of historical circumstances upon Judaism takes into account not only the need to struggle against negative aspects of the culture at large, but also the absorption and refinement of whatever positive elements it has to offer. On his understanding, revolutionary developments in the world of ideas are the most significant tools of all; they are a clear sign that humanity has outgrown more primitive forms of spirituality and is ready for a new, more sublime level.[69]

The foundational status of patriarchy

At this point it is important to note that according to R. Kook and all the more traditional understandings of revelation, expansion of the Torah does not involve devaluing or supplanting the previous norms of tradition. On a formal level these remain as authoritative as when they first appeared in the canonic texts. Even when the faith community absorbs new understandings, such understandings never displace the original heritage. Subsequent revelations may transform a former "hearing" by building upon it, but they cannot skip over it entirely. The sanctified formulations of the canonic texts of tradition are immutable foundations, defining the absolute, rock-bottom parameters of Jewish belief and practice.

It is this feature that distinguishes the approach of an accumulating revelation offered here from several of the less traditional understandings of revelation previously described. On the surface, the theory of "continuous" or "progressive" revelation offered by Louis Jacobs is very similar. In Judith Plaskow's writings, she too describes an evolving Torah, drawing on the mystic distinction between the "primordial Torah" and the "Written Torah."[70] Unlike the more traditional sources, however, both Jacobs and Plaskow then proceed to demonstrate the imperfect nature of the Written Torah by casting it as a partial record of that attempt by mortals to capture their encounters with the divine. The Written Torah is thus relativized, after the fashion of dialectical theology, by making it out to be the word of humans, *rather* than the word of God. It is the Torah *of* God only in the sense of being a Torah *about* God, and in response *to* God.

I have no interest in artificially blowing up ideological differences between different denominations in Judaism. Nevertheless, I believe that theologically this point is crucial. What is unique about the cumulativist notion in tradition is that it allows for the possibility that the Torah can be all human and all divine, at one and the same time, because even the trappings of Torah are a reflection of the divine.

Thus, according to the kabbalistic conception of evolving eras, the shift from *din* to *rahamim* that involves a merging with *hessed* is not an abrupt change, discontinuous with the past, but is gradual and incorporates *din* within it. To be sure, *Torat hashemitot* teaches that in the era of *rahamim* legal and hierarchical forms will no longer dominate the Torah. The Torah letters will recombine, and missing letters will appear. But it is significant that the kabbalistic idea perceives a gradual development from an era that was almost exclusively *din* to a synthesis between *din* and *hessed*. In this synthesis, the principle of categorization and division of *din* is to open out in a new way to the antihierarchical principle of *hessed*, combining the best of tradition with the best of the feminist critique. In contrast, the feminist critique at its most radical calls for *replacement* of the old order with the new.

Similarly, R. Kook's preference for viewing the relationship between God and the world as a continuum rather than according to the usual theistic picture,[71] includes his insistence that humanity must experience the first model, understanding God as transcendent, before it can begin to approach the more harmonious view.[72] He conceives of the shift as an evolving process that unfolds as our spiritual understanding matures. We ourselves are the products of a long history of emerging values, a history begun and massively shaped by holy texts, by our ancestors' way of life, by their teachings and their example. We humbly recognize that we stand to our past not as superior moral beings looking back upon morally depraved forebears, but as dwarfs who can see more than the giant simply because they stand on his shoulders.

But if the evolution of events and ideas is to be viewed as a cumulative manifestation of God's divine providence, then the very fact that the Jewish community of believers accepted the canonized foundational Torah when they did is an expression of God's will. So too may the subsequent interpretations of that foundational Judaism, the ideas and social norms that the community of committed Jews accept or reject, be viewed as an expression of that will. It is only natural that I, as a cumulativist, attach religious importance not only to the circumstances precipitating interpretations of the primary revelation of Sinai, but also to the fact that it was the Sinaitic revelation that came first and that was accorded foundational value.

Rabbi Tzadok Hacohen, a leading late-nineteenth-century Hassidic thinker, intimates that it is not chance that this revelation took place in a culture that was dominated by paganism. The Talmud informs us (in Tractate *Yoma* 69b) that prophecy ceased after the destruction of the First Temple and (in Tractate *Sanhedrin* 102b) that paganism ended at the same time. R. Tzadok hints at the connection. Every great shortcoming, he teaches, contains the potential for a commensurate good. Paganism, with all its errors and evils, still allowed people to experience the overwhelming immediacy of divine presence. From this we may conclude that it was precisely the raw, childlike passion of primitive perceptions, uninhibited by moral and theological sophistication, that facilitated direct and uncomplicated communion with God.[73]

In a similar vein, I as a cumulativist would strive to put a religious face even on the fact that Israel reached its understanding of God and its own destiny at a time that patriarchy was being consolidated throughout the ancient Near East. Cumulative revelation can find meaning in the knowledge that this theological model helped to institute, support, and reinforce the historical development of male hegemony rather than dispute it. That Jewish tradition has preserved just those memories that express the history of men and their androcentric interests as the basic constitutive vocabulary of tradition, from which all further interpretations will necessarily evolve, must have some divine logic. Phrasing the canonical literature in the masculine may be a necessary "scaffolding" for certain features of patriarchal society valuable to the religious life. It may serve as protection from other dislocations, confusions, and excesses that we are liable to face if the core illumination of the feminist undertaking is embraced without reservation.

What could possibly be the value of being tied down to obsolete formulations of a patriarchal society? For a cumulativist feminist, the answers will change with the times, but a number of factors can be brought to bear. In addition to the anthropological and theological benefits of patriarchy cited in chapter 7, maintenance of sexual boundaries and gender distinctions works to ensure preservation of the traditional family unit. Despite protestations of radical feminists to the contrary, no better vehicle has yet been found for the transmission of values from one generation to the next and the promotion of human welfare.[74] Another undeniable benefit of role-differentiation between the sexes is the general attractiveness that people find in cultural differences. Moreover, as feminist philosopher Janet Radcliffe Richards has observed, in emphasizing specific talents and character traits in each gender, "it is not just *difference* which is attractive, but also its rooting in tradition."[75] And, after all is said and done, the fact that, hypothetically, things could have been otherwise is not sufficient reason for reversing the course of history once the existing order has already been established. "Even though the wishes and expectations men and women have of each other may be culturally induced and not an inevitable part of their natures, that is not the slightest reason for ignoring them. A liberator must allow people *as they actually are* to make their own choices, because their culturally determined preferences are still theirs."[76] (This does not, of course, obviate the need to eradicate whatever evils do become evident in the patriarchal model during the course of time.)

The revelatory status of feminism

Feminists may look askance at considering patriarchy a manifestation of divine providence or a gradual unfolding of the divine being. By the same token, however, we may also consider the emergence of feminism as a new revelation of the divine will; we may see a newly evolving appreciation of the importance, integrity, and value of female spirituality in our time as a rare religious privilege. The cumulative understanding of revelation allows us to view the phenomenon of feminism itself—even if it appears to stem from sources outside of Judaism—as a gift from God. In this sense, assimilating feminism into Judaism is no different than the imbibing of Aristotelianism by Maimonidean rationalism or the absorption of certain ideas from Gnosticism and the Neoplatonic tradition by the Kabbalah, among other examples. What we are now beginning to know is being bestowed upon us. We are the beneficiaries of what has gone before us, as we grope toward a new light reaching out to us from God. Listening to feminist claims with sympathy and understanding need not be thought of as a deep violation of Jewish tradition. Instead, it should be regarded as a spiritual undertaking of the first order (an *avodat kodesh,* or holy task).

If feminism is indeed thrust upon us today in a manner that cannot be avoided or ignored, this constraint is not a problem but an agenda to be addressed and incorporated positively into Jewish religious life. A cumulativist view of revelation permits us to entertain the thought that some feminist understandings reflect more refined moral sensibilities that ought to accrue to the original religious model and even alter its meaning. At the same time, such accretions do not violate in any way the formal status of that model as an immutable element of our foundational canon. For men, regarding feminism as the manifestation of higher moral sensibilities, instead of as a necessary evil or as pandering to the spirit of the times, may mean voluntarily ceding the privileges of hierarchy for the sake of greater equality and justice. For women, it represents the taking on of greater active participation and responsibility in the religious life, instead of merely enjoying vicarious merit through the accomplishments of the menfolk. Patriarchy, in this scheme, is not an eternally fixed and ideal social form, but rather something necessary for its time, which can now be recognized as a stepping-stone, the residual traces of which continue to function as a necessary prism for the achievement of greater moral sensibilities.

In sum, the importance of a cumulativist understanding of God's revelation, as communicated in a gradual manner via natural historical process, is twofold. First, it allows for the very possibility of divine communication, despite the inevitability of cultural bias. It also provides a way of accommodating feminist claims to hearing a new message free of that bias, without undermining the authority of the original. In seeing the initial core divine message as scaffolding to build upon, the understanding of revelation as accumulating embodies one of the most important contributions that historic religion can offer to the feminist enterprise.

Valuing the past is a central feature of the religious sensibility. It comes to teach us that there is a powerful spirituality in uniting with that which went before. Tradition is the special way our parents and grandparents spoke and sang to God. And while a good measure of nostalgia is no doubt present whenever an old tune is sung, it is not only nostalgia that makes us sing. Maintaining the practices of the past allows us not only to unite with our immediate community, but also with all our coreligionists all over the world. It connects us to those no longer with us—and even to those as yet unborn: according to *midrash* (Shmot Rabbah 28), they also participated in the revelation at Sinai. It adds the weight of precedent and continuity to the authority and legitimacy of our current endeavors. It allows us to incorporate valuable sources of inspiration from the past in fleshing out the empty spaces of our here and now. It affords us a bond with something larger than ourselves, and establishes our contemporary way of doing things as the realization of an ancient dream, rather than merely a passing whim. It expresses the insight that no human being can create ex nihilo, and that there is no neutral territory we can escape to in developing our present and our future. Abandoning tradition is tantamount to abandoning language itself.

At its deepest level, the feminist critique would most likely take this hymn to the past as evidence of my profound assumption of male categories of thought. Indeed, feminist theologian Daphne Hampson regards seeking meaning in continuity with a past history, beyond the here and now, as a narrowly male way of experiencing the spiritual dimension of reality. In her eyes, theologies of revelation or of history do not place human beings at the center of the stage. In a theology of revelation, truth is not found within; it must be revealed precisely because it is other than the self. And in a theology of history, "the problem is not that the self has to base itself on that which is other than itself, but rather that there is little concentration on the individual self at all." As opposed to feminism's fundamental concern for the individual, and the transformation of individual lives, "the person knows salvation only as he or she is caught up in a greater whole which will be redeemed, and that scarcely in that person's lifetime!"[77]

I disagree. It is precisely traditionalist religion and a cumulativist merging with history that is consonant with the uniquely feminine view of self as enmeshed in a web of relationships. Through tradition women may approach life in a manner that sees the greater significance of the passing moment not because they seek to transcend it, but because they see in it the reflection of other moments, and do not view the present as something discontinuous and atomized all on its own. Especially when traditionalism is linked with the concepts of process theology, it is precisely the emphasis on the inter-connectedness of all reality that resonates to female sensibilities, potentially avoiding the dualism that has plagued so many conceptions of monotheism and its concomitant tendency to dichotomized thinking. Such traditional-ism teaches that there is no basis for drawing strict boundaries between dif-fering moral conceptions and separating them from the past in which they are grounded.

CHAPTER 11

Some Theological Remarks for the More Philosophically Inclined

Having already acknowledged that views very much like accumulating revelation have emerged in the discussions of Christian feminist theologians, I would like to consider and comment upon some of the more universal objections that have been raised in that context. These objections touch upon several interlocking questions: the totality of God's justice; the image of God that this entails; the extent to which this image leaves room for human initiative and avoids the pitfalls of complacency; how to relate to the interim of time before the determination of God's will and judge behavior that conforms with options that are eventually dismissed. Other objections derive from ideas more integral to Jewish tradition. They stem from the wish to limit divine revelation to a one-time affair in the Sinai desert.

Philosophical reflection is not to everyone's taste. For many believers the persuasiveness of religious models is not dependent on logical argument, but rather on the light that such models shed in practice over the spiritual landscape of our lives. Nevertheless, the power of religious models is also dependent upon our ability to translate their images into terms that are logically consistent with each other and with the rest of human experience.

Divine Justice and Human Responsibility

The larger universal questions begin with the theodicy problem: If God is in full control of history, then this implies that God saw nothing wrong with how things used to be. When an erstwhile norm is blatantly unjust, the claim that an improved future makes up for the deficiencies of the past will not do. If God were truly involved in the direction of human history, surely He could have interfered sooner.

One response to this problem is a theology that effects a greater equation between God and history. God need not be thought of as transcending history or acting as an agent in history, but rather as a sacred force that is present within history, inspiring a vision of liberation that progresses from age to age. Daphne Hampson identifies this tendency in the writings of Christian feminist liberation theologian Rosemary Ruether, who proclaims:

Feminist theology must fundamentally reject . . . the concept of spirit and transcendence as rootless, antinatural, originating in an "other world" beyond the cosmos, ever repudiating and fleeing from nature, body, and the visible world. Feminist theology needs to affirm the God of Exodus, of liberation and new being, but as rooted in the foundations of being rather than as its antithesis.[1]

Ruether presents a vision of liberation that progresses from age to age. "God liberates us from this false and alienated world . . . as a constant breakthrough that points us to new possibilities that are, at the same time, the regrounding of ourselves in the primordial matrix, the original harmony."[2]

Hampson, as a critic of liberation or process theology, regards vindicating God in this manner as too high a price to pay: to conflate God with history may solve the problem of God's justice, but not without creating other problems of its own. She argues that process theology leads to what is, in the eyes of the theist, a very watered-down notion of God. In a Marxist-Hegelian approach, theism seems to be forfeited entirely and all reality is collapsed into history. God is reduced to being simply a "transcendent life principle,"[3] which is nothing other than a human conception. Hampson, questioning whether Ruether's thought is a theology, as opposed to simply a political agenda for the liberation of people, remarks that Ruether never speaks of God, but rather of people's concept of God, which may spur them on in their striving for justice.[4]

Another difficulty created by identifying God too closely with historical process, Hampson claims, is the crippling effect this has on moral initiative: encouraging a type of passivity detrimental to the assumption of human responsibility. "The God of process theology, though a kindly father, is still very much in charge. Indeed, there is something about process thought which is profoundly paternalistic."[5] Such an approach leaves us floundering, especially when augmented with the Hegelian notion of historical dialectics, which assumes that even what appears to be regression is really just part of a dialectic move forward. It does not allow for the possibility that the evolution of history may not correspond to our notions of progress.

The same point is made by Rachel Adler. She warns that when taken to its extreme, sacralization of history begets a "conventionalism" that makes moral initiative superfluous because "whatever is, is right." As she formulates it:

Attributing change to the invisible hand of history relieves us of responsibility for consciously and reflectively shaping the future. We could simply wait for history to drag us in its wake. Conventionalism is a perversion of the doctrine of revelation through history, but it suggests a cautionary lesson: God may speak through history, but what God is saying may be less than obvious.[6]

Christian process theologians—correctly, in my opinion—reject this assessment of their position. Far from prescribing passivity, they argue, process theology emphasizes change as the foundation of reality and stresses the importance of the creative activity of human beings in bringing change about.[7] The existence of a divine force in history does not determine the course of our destiny; on the contrary, it preserves our sense of autonomy and responsibility vis-à-vis the world. As Mary Ellen Ross, a feminist moral philosopher sympathetic to process theology, has noted: "Such a scheme removes theological obstacles to human agency and creativity."[8]

At least in the Jewish context, I believe the process theologians have a case. Traditional theistic conceptions of divinity are no less liable to produce an attitude of moral passivity than mystical conceptions, given the stress that the former place on God's ultimate power over humanity and nature. Indeed, R. Kook regards a strictly theistic model as inferior precisely because of the crippling effects that it can have on human initiative, tending to diminish a person's confidence in her or his own creative ability and value.[9] In Lurianic Kabbalah in general, it is the notion of the substantive connection between God and the world and their interdependence that emphasizes the responsibility of human beings for the cosmic state of affairs. Because the kabbalistic scheme of reality stipulates the interconnectedness of all being, God differs from human beings primarily in the sense that God contains all possibilities in addition to all actualities. But God in no sense dominates or controls human beings, depriving them of their sense of agency. Rather, the relationship between God and human beings is one of mutual need and completion.[10]

As for the allegation of a watered-down conception of God, one of the characteristic features of Jewish mysticism is the recognition that no *one* model is adequate to the description of God. Personalistic attributes figure alongside portrayals of God as an impersonal force, typically in such abstract terms as light, holiness, will, wisdom, bounty, and the like. Images of immanence are mingled with images that are more transcendent.

Admittedly, the notion of God as process deflects the theodicy problem on the level of ultimate truth. When God is not conceived of as a being or force that exists outside of the world, there is no room for asking why there is evil or so much of it in the world. Instead we ask, What is the nature of evil? What is its power and function? How are we to overcome the suffering it brings? But Jewish mysticism does not belittle the human need for answers from our limited perspective. Even the impersonal God is by no means absolved of the responsibility of meeting the human demand for justice, as we perceive it.

Most suited to the notion of an accumulating revelation for resolving the problem of evil, if a more personal concept of God is assumed, is the argument of moral contextualism; that is, adopting a concept of justice that, in defining what morality entails, takes into account prevailing notions of the times.[11] A view of divine revelation as an ongoing, accumulating process, even when allowing for the role of future interpretation, does require the believer to justify the meaning of the text as it was understood in the past as valid at least *for that time*. Its meaning can be universal only to the extent that striving for perfection is universal and human flourishing is an overarching ethical ideal. The theological requirement to uphold the justice of biblical morality, however, leads to rejecting the translation of the universal ideal into a priori considerations or formal logical principles that are forever true *regardless of context*. Instead, the cumulativist will say that patriarchy may not be a societal ideal today, but such was not always the case.

I am well aware that this view of morality is unpalatable to many feminists today. Current feminist thinking tends to adopt an ethical absolutism that denounces patriarchy as wrong for all time, irrespective of the surrounding circumstances. Claiming the existence of moral universals in a timeless forever, such a position mandates the adoption of a single true moral code that is and always was binding upon all societies. Assuming that the principle of human equality is one of these universals, this feminist view would deny justification for real differences in evaluating the morality of different cultures at different times and places in their treatment of women. I believe, however, that moral contextualism is a view that *can* be defended on philosophical as well as dogmatic religious grounds. Moral ideals and standards are not totally arbitrary and do not develop in a contextual void. Their value and significance are derived not only from our personal wants and desires, but also from the understandings and needs of the larger social group in which this behavior is played out.

In consonance with this way of thinking, I believe that the feminist reading of history as a long-standing power struggle between the sexes is (like the class struggle of Marxist ideology) an exaggerated and overstated mythical construct with flimsy basis in historical fact. Instead of alleging a male conspiracy, it is more accurate to say that given certain economic, sociological, and other factors in society, the patriarchal model for centuries served the interests of society in general. By the same token, the institution of slavery also prevailed as long as it did because it reflected the vestiges of an economy that was not viable without the existence of a serving class. In both instances, the sense of dissatisfaction and injustice became widespread only when circumstances so changed as to make the disadvantages blatantly clear to the oppressed group. As other socioeconomic structures became feasible, they could afford to rebel and even hope to convince the oppressors of the justice of their claims.

The contemporary American philosopher, Michael Walzer, has made a similar point: "Justice is relative to social meanings. . . . A given society is just if its substantive life is lived in a certain way—that is, in a way that is faithful to the shared understanding of the members."[12]

Walzer is saying that any notion of justice is embedded within a given culture. Even the community's sense of right and wrong behavior always has a larger frame of reference. Because the community's political and moral conceptions cannot be tested against some objective moral standard, their legitimacy too is largely contextual, and usually developed on strong anthropological grounds. Hence, it makes no sense to speak of patriarchy as wrong for all human beings, as if the injustice of patriarchy was part of the furniture of the universe.

The idea of accumulating revelation does not entirely eliminate the urge to condemn certain rulings even in light of the standards that prevailed at the time that they were made. A cumulativist might entertain the belief that an array of positive moralities, recent as well as past, have so much in common despite their differences that a single minimalist set of principles will eventually come to be accepted by all. In the name of that belief in human progress, a cumulativist might even reject certain aspects of biblical morality as absolutely unjust from *our* point of view and therefore conclude that from *our* point of view they should be uniformly relinquished. But this concession does not preclude the argument that within the context of biblical times, gender stratification of the sexes was an equitable social arrangement. Morality does not demand the high degree of homogeneity that some versions of feminism seem to imply.

Divine Ambiguity and Human Culpability

Another question raised by notions of accumulating revelation and moral contextualism is the question of human culpability. Imaging divine providence over history in terms of a personal God orchestrating the affairs of the world from above in response to changing requirements does not guarantee us clear-cut messages. How do we know when God is speaking to us, and how are we to be sure of what He is saying? How are we to decide when we are meant to comply with the established course of history and when we are meant to diverge and follow the call to a new course that has been revealed? How are we to distinguish between this call from those negative moments in history that are simply a test of faith and should be battled rather than embraced? This problem is merely intensified by any more extensive identification of God with history, after the fashion of liberation or process theology. As Hampson writes, equating God's will with the revelations of history makes it difficult "to adduce abstract principles which should have a life of their own, quite apart from whether they have been exemplified within history, which may be used to judge history."[13]

Such questions apply even to the original revelatory experience at Sinai. Talmudic *aggadah* speaks of God imposing Mount Sinai like a barrel over the heads of the Israelites. What nonfoundationalist approaches help us to appreciate is that no truth has the power simply to bang us over the head and compel us to understand it as such. Even the original revelation could be acknowledged as God's word only when filtered through the prism of past cultural symbols and traditions. Acceptance of the biblical rendition of that experience as the authoritative and definitive foundation of Jewish belief and practice to which all else must answer is no less an interpretive act than are subsequent rabbinic understandings of the biblical text. Because experience is always a matter of interpretation, each experience or meeting with a text is constrained by the interpretive tools brought to the material.

On this view, the basis for accepting (in our eyes) a palpably androcentric Bible as a true hearing of the divine word, rather than as a decidedly human projection of male interests, has nothing to do with its literary or historical genesis. The fact that the Jewish people accepted this text as the divine word and that we continue to maintain a form of life that is grounded on this belief is what renders it as such. Even such insights, however, do not eliminate risk entirely or spare us the quandaries of uncertainty.

This quandary is especially evident in certain Hassidic writings that struggle with the destabilizing possibility that God's true will does not always conform with His apparent instruction. Thus, R. Mordecai Yosef Leiner understands that the real trial of Abraham in the story of the binding of Isaac lay in the ambiguity of God's command to Abraham to "raise" his son as an offering. This phrasing left it unclear as to whether Abraham was meant actually to kill Isaac (as against God's explicit instruction against killing and His promise that Abraham's lineage would be continued by Isaac) or was merely to perform the symbolic act of placing him on the altar.[14] According to these writings, one cannot go too far wrong when playing it safe and conforming to the clear guidelines of the past. But sometimes the mark of the saint (or *tzaddik*) lies precisely in the ability to take on the risks of epistemological ambiguity and break with the accepted norm on the strength of the certainty of a new vision. Even a *tzaddik*, however, faces the danger of slipping into self-deception, rationalizing his personal desires on religious grounds by identifying his will with that of God. The main guarantee offered in Hassidic thought for ensuring genuine recognition of God's will lies in cleansing the heart of personal biases and negating all egotistic interest.

On a practical plane we have seen that although the risk of wrong decisions can never be eliminated entirely, it can be considerably minimized by conforming to the constraints of the interpretive tradition within which such decisions are made. The principles and standards of the interpretive tradition in which we are grounded enable us to relate to this text as sacred and prevent us from interpreting it in a totally instrumentalist manner so as to comply with our own self-serving interests.

On a theological level, however, some need for clarification still remains. If we admit that normative standards are sometimes established only over a considerable span of several generations (if ever), how are we then to understand that time period before a consensus has solidified? And how are we to judge those who placed their bets on a decision that is ultimately rejected? Applying these points to the issue of women's *aliyot,* Mendel Shapiro challenges Yehuda Henkin's qualified response which indicates that, despite their formal legitimacy, they are not to be adopted as the norm because they do not conform with present Orthodox practice.

To this I would respond that only within a foundationalist view of truth does it make sense to question the status of those who act during the time before consensus is solidified. Foundationalism assumes an objectivity based on self-contained standards, beyond the perimeters of discussion, and a divine will that is empirically verifiable. Even in this context, however, such a question can be dismissed as the illegitimate by-product of oversimplified religious literalism. In asking how to appraise the merit of those whose behavior eventually proves deviant, Shapiro and others appear to be questioning divine bookkeeping policies too closely. The image of God judging may be metaphysically true, but the exact considerations that He brings to bear are beyond our ken. We may *think* we know what factors enter into God's considerations, but we should never be so presumptuous as to believe that we can fathom them all. This submission ties in with the notion of moral contextualism: understanding that the relative worth of human activity can never be divorced from the general fabric of beliefs, attitudes, hopes, and fears to which it relates. Something of this notion is faintly captured in the religious cliché that only God can truly understand our motives and judge human behavior.

Moreover, as Maimonides, Immanuel Kant, and other philosophers have already taught us, time itself is a category indigenous to human thought but not to the divine reality. This being so, we must recognize that trying to align our decisions with God's assessments in terms of precise dates and times is an inappropriate extension of human conceptions to the mysteries of divine agency. This insight sits well with rabbinic pronouncements such as "These and these are the words of the living God, but *halakhah* is according to the decisions of the school of Hillel" (referring to debates between the halakhic schools of the two great Rabbis, Hillel and Shammai). Such pronouncements serve to qualify further the significance of halakhic determinacy beyond a certain realm, on the basis of similar recognition of an inherent gap between the nature of finite human truth and infinite divine truth.

In a nonfoundationalist context the inadequacy of a divine bookkeeper model is predicated on an understanding that is more radical and far-reaching. The very image of God's judging and deciding must be viewed within the context of the religious language game. As such, its function is constructive rather than descriptive, shaping our attitudes to reality rather than providing us with precise metaphysical information. Hence, the attempt to assess the halakhic status of practices conducted before their normativity is determined is entirely misplaced.

As explained in chapter 10, failure to distinguish between different types of discourse—as highlighted by Wittgenstein—leads to errors and confusion. A believer who understands the grammatical rules governing theological discourse develops a skill for applying the assertions of the doctrinal tradition to the ever-changing circumstances of life, culture, and history. As Katherine Tanner, a representative of Christian nonfoundationalist religion, has suggested:

Making a decision about proper action or belief seems less a matter of application of explicit precept and more a matter of tact and good timing—knowing what affirmation or action to add to a situation so that its various elements form some sort of agreeable balance or harmony. . . . Using that sort of sense or feel for the game . . . one figures out, for example, that talk of God's love is better than talk of God's wrath when conversing with others about their infirmity. Or, that it is better to draw initially on a religious repertory of lament rather than songs of praise for God when confronted with grave injustice and its perpetrators—on the one and then the other, in a proper order and timed well to meet the situation specific responses of one's adversaries in ways that highlight the unacceptability of injustice in God's eyes."[15]

Applying Tanner's insights to Shapiro's dilemma, the notion of God judging at a particular point in time is a way of granting ultimate meaning to human behavior. It induces us to attach great responsibility to our moral decisions. Extending this notion, however, in a manner that engenders the existential anxiety induced by temporary halakhic indeterminacy is to misunderstand the grammar of the religious language game. Its function is not to make empiric statements, but rather to facilitate the construction and expression of a religious mind-set. To press the implications of the judgment model beyond its limits is as inappropriate to religious discourse as would be the attempt of the religious supplicant to shout his prayers more loudly so that God might "hear" them better.

My refusal—as a Wittgensteinian who understands the rules of the religious language game—to take the type of theological questions raised by Shapiro seriously may frustrate the literal-minded who want to know how many celestial "brownie points" accrue to a given action before they decide to carry it out. Nonetheless, I find it unnecessary to conclude (as Shapiro seems to) from the lack of precise and unequivocal criteria for assessing the acceptability of halakhic innovations in any given situation *before* they become commonly accepted, that "halakhic change is by its nature a mean-spirited, opportunistic affair."[16] What this reluctance should teach us instead is the folly of using the same criteria that we apply to the ordinary statements of our everyday world when relating to religious metaphors. This teaching holds true even when taking the risk of opting for behavior that may eventually prove wrong in practical halakhic terms.

Interpretive versus Historic Cumulativism

A different type of objection to cumulativism comes from another quarter:[17] Jewish traditionalists who are not enthusiastic about embracing a doctrine of accumulating revelations or "hearings" via the conduit of history. Preferring alternative theologies that do not submit history to such grandiose claims, they choose to rely on a rival tradition that is represented by Maimonides, who was interested in establishing a clear line of demarcation between texts representing revelation and the rabbinic interpretation of such texts.

As we have seen, the Tosafists and their followers through the ages (including R. Kook) seem to have been driven by the wish to convey their sense of rabbinic alignment with the divine will. They therefore speak of rabbinic interpretations as divinely inspired. In contrast, what seems to be at stake for Maimonides (and those who preferred to follow his tradition) is the need to protect the supremacy and inviolability of Mosaic law from the upheaval of further claims to prophetic inspiration. It was this interest that led Maimonides, in opposition to many predecessors in the Gaonic period,[18] to sharply distinguish between the role of the prophet who *reveals* God's word and the sage who *interprets* it. The role of prophecy and its appeal to charismatic authority is severely circumscribed. Hence, prophetic powers play no role in the development of the Oral Law.[19] This restriction appeals to some contemporary theologians who wish to emphasize the role of human autonomy in the interpretive process.[20]

Such theologians would argue that because the potential for new interpretations is so well accepted in the traditional Jewish concept of Torah, one need not bind the resolution of current halakhic dilemmas to cumulativist claims of God's continuous revelation in history. Given that rabbinic tradition already recognizes the manifold interpretive possibilities of the revelation at Sinai, even a view that posits the finality of the Sinaitic revelation need not pose any obstacle in principle to the predicament of women today. On the contrary, it is precisely the belief in the completeness and perfection of that revelation that should serve as the founding principle of its continued relevance. This relevance is ensured by the work of the scholars of every generation, who can and do uncover more of its original meaning without the benefit of any divine intervention. What they uncover is regarded as always having "been there"; new ideas are neither invented nor continuously revealed but discovered.

Such a view does not, of course, guarantee that future interpretation will take any particular direction. The absence of predefined limits to the Mosaic Torah and the resulting indeterminacy of its meaning should not be confused with skepticism about the possibility of meaning at all. It also should not be identified with a type of hermeneutic nihilism, asserting that anything can be taken to mean whatever we want so long as we want it enough. There are certain accepted interpretive procedures, so that not every direction can be developed with equal honesty. Nevertheless, given Judaism's powerful commitment to the belief in a righteous God whose Torah is just, it is both valid and appropriate that moral concerns play an important part in creating the need for new interpretation and in its formulation. If one adds this factor to the flexibility afforded by the notion of many levels of meaning in Torah, one might claim that any resolution to the feminist predicament (and to other instances of conflict between modernity and tradition) can be accommodated even within a Sinaitic framework, without resort to the concept of accumulating revelation.

If feminist morality is more than a passing fad, it is likely that the interpretive tradition will discover that some of the values expressed by the feminists are indeed those of the Torah and should be pursued accordingly. The fluidity of meaning that allows for this does not require that we understand that the Sinaitic revelation was incomplete. Other feminist values may be considered as opposing the values of the Torah and as such be rejected. Still other matters may remain in the realm of the permissible but not obligatory. Such a solution could be no less effective than claims to divine intervention in history in avoiding the theological pitfall of faulting the existing biblical text. Sufficient to this task should be an underlying assumption that the multiple meanings inherent in a divine message become apparent only through a protracted process of rabbinic interpretation.

In sum, even those who are reluctant to link the process of rabbinic interpretation to metaphysical claims of revelation can still maintain intellectual honesty regarding the various texts of the canon. Even when these appear to be reflections of particular (patriarchal) historical contexts, they need not sacrifice hope for a future accommodation of the Torah with feminist values. What is more, they need not resort to a contextual view of morality in order to resolve the question of God's justice. It might suffice them to explain the discrepancies between current practice and ancient religious sensibilities by pointing to the inability of ordinary human beings to absorb an ideal message already revealed to Moses in full. Alternatively, they may interpret such discrepancies in terms of the adaptation of perfect fixed principles to the vicissitudes of imperfect and changing situations.[21]

These differing (though not mutually exclusive) interests lead to differing nuances and emphases in the mythic vocabulary of each approach. Cumulativists who prefer the notion of divine influence upon the course of interpretation would speak of a primordial Torah as the infinite divine message that history is out to reconstruct, by constantly stretching the meaning of the primary but time-bound revelation at Sinai. The never-ending opportunities provided by history for fleshing out the Sinaitic revelation are designed gradually to increase the compatibility of that Written Torah with the original preverbal Torah that served as God's blueprint for the world. Those who prefer to regard the Sinaitic Torah as a one-time, complete, and perfect revelation in and of itself will shy away from rhetoric that accords further interpretations any revelatory status. According to them, the function of hermeneutics is to discover what is already buried there in potentia, rather than to stretch it to mean anything new.

I can imagine that some readers will query the importance of all this theological nitpicking. Indeed, it would be well to keep the stakes of this argument in perspective. When all is said and done, it is not a debate over the "facts of the matter." Rather, the argument revolves around which theological approach can best express and maintain faith and loyalty to a Judaism and *halakhah* that grants us some intimation of the Ultimate Being, the object of all religious belief. Nevertheless, I believe that, despite the fact that both positions outlined here confirm the dynamic possibilities of Torah, they do entail different sensibilities.

I personally find the doctrine of revelation through history more appealing theologically, for a variety of reasons. Viewing the Sinaitic Torah as merely the earthly reflection of a metaphysical Torah, which must be supplemented by history, avoids imposing the burden of infinite interpretive possibilities upon the former text alone. Any verbal message as such must be contextualized; its very commitment to language renders it time- and culture-bound. Therefore, I find it more convincing to load the potential for limitless interpretations exclusively upon a primordial, preverbal Torah. The primacy of the Torah of Sinai is still maintained in the understanding that it is precisely that revelation, together with the additional interpretations accruing to it over time, that provides us with the formula for reconstructing the earlier Torah to which all history leads.

The notion of an accumulating revelation also affords a view of God and the way He interacts with the world that I find more plausible. Relegating the notion of an infinite Torah to a metaphysical realm, beyond creation, avoids the necessity for grotesque anthropomorphism or other elements of the fantastic, allowing us to understand the transmission of God's word in a naturalistic manner (just as every miracle, once it occurs in the natural world, is subject to explanation by natural law). It even allows for the liberty of conceiving of the Torah of Moses in terms of a revelation that occurred over a period of time, via a process that is totally consonant with the findings of biblical criticism and archaeological discoveries (to the extent that these are scientifically verifiable and convincing). At the same time, we can still accept that process as God-given.

A final point is that belief in accumulating revelation grants religious significance to the events of history and the development of the human spirit. It also allows us to recognize that even when interpreting Torah "from the inside," the impact of outside forces on our definition of that view is never far behind. The ultimate decision as to what the Sinaitic Torah means is arrived at by a dialectic between inside and outside forces, with both subsumed under the larger interpretive goal: to achieve a holistic understanding of the divine will.

Although I prefer the doctrine of revelation through history for all these reasons, in the context of this discussion I am much more interested in simply spelling out the value of the challenge to our current raw and undeveloped state of theological thinking. My interest is no less in stimulating others to address this challenge than in promoting any specific suggestion of my own. Undoubtedly, feminism has become such a volatile issue within Judaism precisely because it highlights the fact that the current modernist defense of revelation appropriated by Orthodoxy is inadequate. It is incapable of dealing with a critique that bears the potential for particularly unsettling disruptions to the continuity of religious life as it has been known for the past two thousand years. This Orthodox approach has outlived its adequacy and needs to be replaced. Blanket appeals to the "mystery" of revelation will not suffice in addressing the philosophical difficulties of a simplistic view. Whatever theology is developed, it can only be effective in its confrontation with the modern world, and in its revalidation of the primacy of the halakhic rubric for approaching contemporary problems, if it both faces the feminist critique squarely and incorporates some of its genuine insights into halakhic reality.

•PART V•

Epilogue

Prophecy—as the sages have taught us (BT Baba Batra 12b)—has ever since the destruction of the Temple been given only to fools and children. Moreover, although ideas shape the course of events, they are also shaped by them. I therefore do not believe that, as a teacher and philosophical observer, I have any privileged vantage point from which to predict the future of feminism and its relationship with Judaism. Nevertheless, one can safely say that we are now living in the midst of a major process of societal change. Some features of this process can be resisted; others have already effected a considerable erosion of traditional gender roles. To the extent that such phenomena become more widespread, changes in the balance of power and increased participation of women in the more public aspects of religious life and leadership will inevitably lead to more substantive modifications of male-oriented definitions of spirituality and the religious life.

In this final chapter, I suggest that the innovative message of feminism converges at least in part with some more general tendencies gestating within Modern Orthodoxy, particularly in Israel. These include affirmation of openness to the manifold lessons of human experience, a growing democratization of religious authority, and response to the demand for greater individuality, spontaneity, and personalization in forms of religious worship.

I conclude with the contention that these destabilizing tendencies, when forced into healthy tension with the constraints of a rich and established spiritual legacy and tempered by humility and respect for the wisdom of the ages, have an important contribution to make to Judaism and to human civilization at large. In the eyes of the external observer, Jewish feminism in this sense may provide a unique model of cultural continuity, demonstrating how the benefits of a rich and long-standing tradition can be transformed without undermining its authority. For the believer it represents something deeper: "expanding the palace of Torah."

CHAPTER 12

Visions for the Future

Practical Developments

The converging of various forces of modern life has sparked revolutionary changes in the status of women. These developments not only diverge significantly from the thrust of Jewish tradition for the past two thousand years, but also go far beyond what most feminists of the past have ever imagined. The technological advances that have increased women's life expectancies and encouraged them to pursue careers outside the home and to achieve full economic independence; the discoveries of medical research that enable complete separation between sex and the powers of reproduction; the emphasis of Western society upon the values of self-fulfillment, individual autonomy and freedom of choice; and the pervasive influence of the mass media, which allows these ideas to surround us constantly—all seem to be cooperating in a conspiracy geared toward the establishment of new gender definitions and family patterns. Even the most insular of Jewish communities cannot remain untouched.

At the same time, we cannot discount the possibility that it is precisely the revolutionary quality of these very forces that will provide the catalyst for an extreme backlash from anti-Western fundamentalist circles. The background of events accompanying the writing of this book include the overtaking of Afghanistan by the Taliban and their drastic curtailing of women's basic liberties. A fundamentalist trend can already be discerned in important pockets of previously Westernized Orthodox Jewry that now seem intent upon tightening halakhic strictures on social mingling between the sexes and upon intensifying the ideology of role stratification. Even when not brought up this way themselves, many parents are moved by the conviction that such stringency provides necessary protection in today's world against the pernicious influences of modernity and that it promotes the dedication and long-term commitments central to the religious life. Demographic trends and the success of extensive outreach activities generated by such circles indicate that this variety of Orthodoxy will continue to flourish and exert a powerful influence upon the future of Judaism. Although even these strongholds of tradition cannot help being affected by the sociological implications of the broader economic and technological forces surrounding them, the process is far more muted and slower paced, thanks to sustained efforts to maintain cultural insularity.

Outside these circles, however, it is reasonable to expect a steady intensification of the current trend toward greater inclusion of women in the more public and authoritative centers of Jewish religious activity. There is no doubt that the sheer energy generated by the increased participation of women will considerably change the face of the more modernized segment of Orthodoxy on many fronts. On the practical level, some of these changes are already evident and will only gain strength in the coming years.

Allowing women their own voice

One clear effect of feminism's influence is its imbuing Orthodox women—even those who do not consciously identify with feminist ideology—with the confidence to find their own voice. A few of the yeshiva-like institutions for higher-level learning that have opened up for women in North America and in Israel are beginning to show signs of serving a similar function to that of the women's consciousness-raising groups in the 1960s and 1970s. At that time, it was the very convening of women as women to discuss issues related to home and family, on their own, without a male presence, that encouraged development of their own perspective on their situation. In like manner, the concentration of women now opening the books for themselves and gradually gaining the ability to confront their image as a unique social class, a "people unto themselves" in the sources, without having the texts mediated by male authority figures, affords them opportunity to express specifically feminine concerns and develop their own responses.

To be sure, even after having tasted of the "forbidden fruit," not all the women who are part of the new wave of learning are dissatisfied with their present situation. A goodly number of the Modern Orthodox participants in the learning revolution are still happy with their lot and find in it a complete world of spiritual satisfaction. Many of them vigorously object to any attempt to connect their study of Torah with new social and cultural tendencies that smack of feminism. Torah study, they will say, need not spill over into any more revolutionary changes in the status quo. This attitude especially typifies the centers of women's learning in Israel, where synagogue ritual is not the focus of religious life, so that women's lack of participation in public worship appears less of an issue.

Over the years, however, the situation has changed somewhat. The general globalization of Jewish life and intensified connections between the Diaspora and Israel has seen a gradual melding of interests and mutual influence between two distinct varieties of Orthodox feminism centered in the United States and in Israel. Only a few years ago, the circle of more militant North American women could be dismissed as peripheral to the halakhic heartland, while the more moderate Israeli women appeared to be quite satisfied with their status quo so long as their opportunities for learning were ensured. Now, the activists' anger is being somewhat dissipated into a greater zeal for learning, whereas the patience of some of the women involved in learning is thinning as they attempt to translate their knowledge into acceptable avenues of expression.

In the United States, many long-time Orthodox feminists now find their spiritual home in Drisha, a women's institution in New York dedicated to advancement of women's greater proficiency in the Oral Law, and they are instrumental in promoting women's study groups around the country. Israel, on the other hand, has seen the establishment of Kolech, an activist Orthodox women's forum that goes beyond the advancement of women's learning and includes more political objectives among its declared goals. It enjoys the unqualified support of many women involved in the learning revolution.

This impression of converging interests is corroborated by the comparison of two sociological studies of the women's learning movement. The first study, carried out by Lauren Granite,[1] examined the religious influence of higher-level study of Torah among women based on fieldwork conducted in Israel in the 1980s. The conclusion she reached was that the more women entered into the activity of Torah learning, the more they were at peace with Jewish tradition as it stands. The reasons for this finding are not clear. It may be that the thrill and excitement of the first generation of women students finally to be granted access to male realms of knowledge allowed them to identify with the internal rules of the halakhic discipline. It may also be that at the initial stage all of the learning was mediated by males, for lack of sufficiently proficient women teachers. It would be only natural for these men to structure the material in a manner that was congenial to the existing social structure. Without any deliberate intentions of censorship, they would tend to deemphasize material that would be spiritually devastating to the sensibilities of the new wave of female religious enthusiasts.

However, as women have begun to gain the skills that enable them to approach the sources independently, the tone has become less conciliatory. A more clear-eyed appraisal of difficulties is beginning to emerge. It is probably for this reason that it is only in the more recent study of Israeli anthropologist Tamar El-Or that the potentially revolutionary flavor of the women's learning revolution has been articulated.[2] El-Or spent a year observing various women's learning centers in Israel, focusing in particular on the women's *midrashah* of Bar-Ilan University. She concluded that the new phenomenon of women's learning has already begun creating deep inroads that may serve to change the face of Orthodoxy within a short period of time. In addition to introducing shifts in the traditional balance of power

between the sexes that has been the norm in religious society for generations, women's learning may also introduce alternatives to the exclusive
hold that male ways of thinking have had on determining the contents and
cultural values of the religious tradition.[3]

As feminist research gradually uncovers the extent to which a predominantly male perspective has been instrumental in shaping the development
of *halakhah,* women are gaining the courage to look at its background narrative more critically and voice aloud their hitherto unspoken skepticism regarding its objectivity. In the face of men presuming to define who women
are and what they should be feeling about themselves, the Jewish feminist
movement has empowered women to turn the tables round: it is now they
who are (perhaps gratuitously) both telling men what *men's* essential nature
is and passing judgment on *their* motives.

A striking example of this newfound "audacity" on the part of Orthodox
women (and a glimpse of their potential as a collective) was seen at the first
international conference of Kolech in the summer of 1999. On this occasion
each of the hundreds of Torah-observant women attending found a detailed
scientific questionnaire in her conference packet. The purpose of this questionnaire, composed by rabbinic pleader Rachel Levmore, was to check the
current validity of the talmudic statement that women prefer to be married
to any man rather than to live alone.[4] As a halakhic assumption upon which
rabbinic courts operate to this day, this statement serves as justification for
their pressuring women to remain locked in undesired and sometimes physi-
cally abusive marriages. Although Levmore's initiative was conducted in the
form of an academic survey, and the questions were carefully worded so as
not to affect the answers—pro or con—the very impetus for conducting
such a survey implies the understanding that invalidation of the original assumption could ultimately affect halakhic rulings in our day. By challenging
paternalistic rabbinic observations (which may have held true under certain
socioeconomic circumstances, but do not apply universally today) and even
subjecting these to empiric examination, women are voicing their refusal to
allow male judgments about their nature to play a determining role in halakhic deliberations.

Women and the halakhic establishment:
Encroaching upon a male preserve

Despite their allegiance to tradition, a corollary of the above development is
a growing realization on the part of some Orthodox women and their male
sympathizers that even the most benign male attempts to bring change into
the *halakhah* are incapable of going far enough in meeting the feminist critique. This incapacity will continue to be the case as long as male halakhic
authorities unself-consciously continue the traditional practice of looking
out on women, thus perpetuating the exclusion of women's perspectives

from the interpretive powers of Judaism. Women, learned women, must be centrally included in the actual process of halakhic deliberation. And if there are not enough learned women around, then the community of traditional Judaism must cultivate and encourage their emergence. Without this step halakhic development is destined to forfeit important nuances of feminist experience, leading to continued discrimination and moral failure. Moreover, in a world in which women are being propelled into positions demanding a high level of secular education, it is incongruous to bar them from similar employment of their training in Torah. The contemporary halakhic world cannot afford to dispense with the potential contribution of women's unique insights and methods of approach, if it hopes to retain its credibility and authority in the long run.

As we have noted in previous discussion, the move to intensify women's knowledge of Torah was not originally motivated by any political agenda of rebellion against the exclusivity of male rabbinic authority, but rather by a genuinely conceived need both to intensify women's attachment to the Jewish tradition and upgrade women's Jewish literacy to the level of their general knowledge. Nonetheless, irrespective of the original catalyst or purposes, there is no denying that the phenomenon of women's learning has become a time bomb, in providing women potential access to positions of leadership and authority that were traditionally held only by men.

No longer are women restricting the application of their talents to what have traditionally been regarded as "women's tasks," such as attending to the material and aesthetic arrangements at synagogue functions, or personal acts of charity and good works. Their new roles consist in part of administrative activities, such as serving on synagogue boards in North America or being elected to membership of religious councils in Israel. They also include a few inroads into the traditionally male role of pulpit rabbi (as in the official appointment of female "rabbinic interns" at two avant-garde Orthodox synagogues in New York and in the unofficial function of a handful of learned women who serve in pastoral and educational capacities in privately organized synagogue communities in Israel). More significant, however, women's newfound proficiency in learning has found an outlet in their assumption of teaching positions in top-level areas of learning previously relegated only to men. Female instructors are teaching Talmud in women's *yeshivot* and in private study circles or *batei midrash*.

Symptomatic of this new phenomenon and its problematic aspects for Orthodoxy was a Torah-learning marathon organized for and by women that took place in Jerusalem in May 1999. Although the organizers of this mammoth event strove to avoid any hint of revolutionary political overtones, their decision to grant all presenters the title of *Rabbanit* (the feminine for rabbi), despite the fact that most of them were not married to rabbis,[5] inadvertently highlighted the untraditional communal implications of the women's learning revolution. While their particular choice of title was hardly relevant, the very need to improvise one was significant, testifying to the growth of an unprecedented phenomenon: a cadre of women that is gradually taking upon itself roles that in the past were the exclusive preserve of men, as natural outlets for employing the intensified Torah scholarship they have acquired for themselves. This development cannot but be accompanied by gradual erosion of exclusive male privilege in the most influential realm of halakhic deliberation.

Literacy is the great democratic equalizer, blotting out class differences as it grants access to power and privilege. Especially in a society that accords the highest value to learning as a religious activity, every student of Torah is in principle on his or her way to becoming a fully active participant in the interpretive process.[6] Therefore the ultimate key to women's entry into the male-dominated realm of halakhic interpretation lies in their intensive participation in study of the Oral Law. To the extent that women scholars transfer their learning activity to this traditionally male province, gaining proficiency in the employment of its tools, rules of procedure, and terminology, they pave the way for the eventual entry of women into positions of halakhic authority as well. Although the prospect of women's active participation in the halakhic process evokes deep visceral opposition in some sections of the Orthodox community, their exclusion is actually more a sociological aftereffect of their traditional role in Jewish society than a strictly halakhic issue. Israel's Sephardic chief rabbi has declared that "women may be great talmudists (*gedolei hador*) and they may serve as arbiters of the law (*morei horaah*) and as teachers of Torah and practical *halakhah,* because the authority for these positions flows from the individual's talents."[7]

It is crucial that feminist sympathizers do not make light of the work ahead and harbor inflated delusions about present achievements. Considering their present level of achievement, Jewish women have several generations to go before training first-rank *poskim* and preparing the ground for their acceptance. But first steps toward women's penetration into this field can already be discerned in the publication of the first compendium of Jewish legal writings written exclusively by women,[8] and a few isolated cases of women publishing studies on halakhic topics in journals that have always been regarded as a male preserve. A growing partnership has also begun between rabbis and women professionals (psychologists, social workers, and the like) in devising practical solutions to halakhic problems in areas such as adoption.

Intensification of the rapidly growing disparity between the traditional view of women and their newly emerging status is also reflected in the recently established courses for the training of women pleaders (*toanot rabbaniyot*), who function as advocates for women seeking divorce in the Israeli rabbinic courts. Wives of recalcitrant husbands feel much easier discussing the intimate details of their marriages with a woman and having her represent their case; nonetheless, this institution used to be the exclusive preserve of yeshiva-trained men, or secularly trained women lawyers unfamiliar with the details of rabbinic law. In the last decade, a few of the women's seminaries for higher education, after a struggle with the Chief Rabbinate, were finally granted permission to train their students to qualify for entry into this profession. In the few years that female graduates have been working in the courts, they have managed to achieve the acceptance and cooperation of the exclusively male establishment of judges who preside over divorce cases, despite some wariness of the competition that female pleaders present to their male colleagues.

Another milestone has been the initiation of an innovative program to train women counselors in the laws of family purity. The wish to save women the embarrassment of turning to male rabbis with intimate personal details and even samples of their genital secretions, in order to determine their menstrual status and whether or not they may engage in sexual relations with their husbands, has contributed to growing approval of this program in Modern Orthodox circles.

Given the link between literacy and authority, it is not surprising that certain traditionalists today make a great effort to prevent women from entering the field of Oral Law. When obstructing proves difficult, they strive at the very least to introduce new distinctions, approving women's study for practical purposes (leading either to greater appreciation of the law or to intensification of religious commitment) for women but endorsing in-depth study "for its own sake" only for men. Such innovations as women learning Talmud may thereby be assimilated by the existing traditional hierarchy. The traditionalists also create a mystique around the dedication required of any student of *halakhah* who would qualify as a rabbinic decisor, their implication being that no woman with normal motherly instincts would wish to take on such a burden.

Female compliance with this attempt to prevent rocking of the boat is evidenced in the caution taken by the initiators of training for the family purity counselors, insisting that their graduates be called "advisers" and not "*poskot*" (female halakhic decisors).[9] It is doubtful, however, that even diplomacy and a rhetoric of distinction can continue to disguise the revolutionary thrust of such innovations for long. Barring a flagging of interest on the part of the women themselves, no degree of effort expended upon making fine distinctions (between learning for general purposes of spiritual enrichment or for practical knowledge of *halakhah,* versus learning for the sake of more informed influence upon halakhic decision-making) will be able to keep the lid on agitation for greater participation by women in the halakhic process. Just as the Hafetz Hayim's original dispensation allowing women to learn simple religious texts of Torah[10] opened up the gates— from study of the commentaries on the Pentateuch, to study of the *Mishnah* and Talmud on stenciled sheets, and then to learning Talmud from the talmudic text itself (*lefi haseder*)—so too with the "slippery slope" of women assuming active roles in various new areas of religious leadership, including increased participation in the most influential areas of halakhic deliberation.

Substantive Developments

The sociological ramifications of women taking on positions of religious authority are not insignificant, even in cases that are clearly condoned by *halakhah*. Such developments will serve to erode further the role stratification that has marked Jewish society for centuries. The implications of women's gradual entry into the realm of halakhic deliberation, however, may prove to be far more profound than this, influencing its substance as well.

Direct exposure to the sources has brought women to examine with a more critical eye male definitions of women's nature and interests that stand in the background of certain halakhic decisions. In times gone by, women were never regarded as a class; it was always assumed that their interests would be sufficiently represented by their male counterparts. It is this assumption that has been modified by a heightened awareness of the limitations in today's world of a unilaterally male perspective in *halakhah*. Of particular interest is that a few women from ultra-Orthodox circles who have undertaken training as rabbinic pleaders are also undergoing such exposure, and confronting difficult sources in the halakhic tradition to which they are not ordinarily exposed, sources that strongly undermine the "separate but equal" argument. The training and work alongside Modern Orthodox feminists raises their consciousness as well, with respect to one of the most problematic areas of tension between halakhic tradition and the constraints of modern life.

Exposure to the male bias in Jewish tradition, and the courage to articulate that such bias exists, does not in itself entail a negation of respect for rabbinic authority (*kevod hakhamim*). Nevertheless, women are increasingly aware that even when leading and reputable *poskim* try hard to be objective and disinterested in rendering the word of God as they see it, there is significance in the *halakhah*'s having been molded primarily by men, and this significance needs to be explored. The process of halakhic decision-making today, almost by definition, leaves no scope for independent accounts of women's practical experience and expertise. No matter how benign to women, the considerations that are taken into account by male *poskim* must of necessity remain on some level typically male.

Greater focus on questions of female concern

I do not suggest that any given *halakhah* would necessarily be decided differently by a woman. But it is probable that an active female presence in halakhic discussion will, at the very least, encourage special focus on issues of concern to women, and encourage greater attention to the variety of halakhic precedent and possibilities. To draw a parallel, no one expected women who took up senior positions in the medical establishment to suggest different medical strategies for known diseases. Yet, as more female oncologists and gynecologists entered senior positions, they developed new alternatives to radical mastectomies and instituted changes in the facilities of hospital delivery rooms. An example of a similar connection between women's involvement in the halakhic process and the effects this can have on the face of *halakhah* is evident in the current public campaign against wife abuse in the Orthodox community,[11] and in a growing willingness to respond to testimony of sexual harassment or worse on the part of male authority figures and educators of young women. In the past, such issues were rarely discussed in public. Another example is the new sensitivity to women's presence in the synagogue, which is creating new directions in synagogue architecture, rather than assuming that the women's section must always take the form of a balcony, or a smaller and more crowded area behind that of the men.

Even on this level changes are likely to be more extensive in *halakhah* than in any other discipline, such as medicine or psychology, given the length of time that direct representation of women's perspectives has been excluded from halakhic discussion. The potential influence of women's involvement in halakhic deliberation, however, does not end here.

Changes in criteria of assessment

In addition to bringing new women's issues to the fore, women's involvement in the halakhic process is bound to impact more subtly on the nature of considerations brought to bear on any particular issue. A number of factors come into play here.

Refusal to resolve public policy issues at the cost of women's interests. The more women learn, the more they are able to discern whether decisions are based on arguments generally regarded as strictly halakhic or whether they are governed by more social considerations that may be weighty but are not absolutely compelling in legal terms, even by contemporary authoritative consensus. Greater proficiency in the independent study of the sources allows women not only to appreciate the absolute limits of the *halakhah,* but also the extent to which it is possible to extend limits whenever societal and moral pressures threaten to render halakhic observance impractical or irrelevant.

Equipped with their heightened critical awareness and recognition of the role that nonjuridical considerations play in the application of halakhic principles, women participating in halakhic deliberation will inevitably come to challenge the regnant scale of values governing public policy issues that affect their concerns. Firsthand familiarity with the sources promotes the understanding that although stringency is sometimes a matter of religious zeal, at other times it reflects either a fear of the unknown or ignorance of the wealth of halakhic considerations and avenues for flexibility. To the extent that women who have gained such familiarity participate in halakhic discussion, they will serve as a natural restraint upon any tendency of the halakhic establishment to fight conservative battles for communal identity on the back of women's interests.

Thus, for example, women protest when, for the sake of maintaining halakhic stability and avoiding change per se, authorities dismiss recognized precedents for releasing women from the grip of recalcitrant husbands. The objections that *halakhah*-abiding women are now raising to what they see as the sacrifice of their interests and sensibilities on the shrine of "halakhic integrity"(especially in questions of marriage and divorce) are fired by a moral pathos that refuses to be marginalized as irrelevant to religious practice. In the implicit compliance of the rabbinical courts with financial extortion by the husband in many divorce proceedings, or their binding a woman against her will to a violent or philandering husband in the name of "domestic peace" (*shlom bayit*), women see a travesty of justice and an admission of moral turbidity on the part of the rabbinical establishment.

On another level, Orthodox women are also questioning the validity of decisions by male rabbinic authorities that forbid them from voluntarily assuming certain halakhic practices simply out of the wish to delineate artificial differences between Orthodoxy and other denominations. One halakhic move that might open up new possibilities in terms of women's more active participation in ritual has been suggested by Orthodox Rabbi Yoel Bin-Nun of Israel. Bin-Nun begins with the assumption that in principle women's halakhic obligation to perform *mitzvot* is equal to that of men. In accordance with the reasoning of Abudraham and Maimonides and, more directly, the teachings of his immediate spiritual mentor, Rabbi Z. Y. Kook, he concludes that women's exemption from time-bound obligations in the past was due simply to their dependent status, whereby their time was not under their control. Basing his conclusion on the fact that a goodly number of contemporary women no longer regard themselves as subject to the authority of their fathers or husbands, Bin-Nun maintains that they constitute a totally distinct halakhic category of *bnot horin* (independent women), to whom the traditional concept of "woman" simply does not apply[12] (in most instances).[13]

Relying further upon a classical halakhic authority of the seventeenth century, Rabbi Abraham Gombiner (known as the Magen Avraham), who declares that a woman voluntarily taking on the performance of a *mitzvah* may transform its status to that of a compulsory obligation,[14] Bin-Nun concludes that if a group of modern *bnot horin* consistently take on the obligation of prayer, this practice allows them to form a proper *minyan* (prayer quorum) for themselves and recite all the blessings that generally require a male quorum (*devarim shebikdushah*). This ruling could obviously be extended to other time-bound *mitzvot*.[15]

A more radical target of feminist protest is the assertion that a male-only *minyan* is "not to be indicted for oppressiveness" for it is merely "a technical construct true to its own categories."[16] Women's ineligibility for inclusion has been cited as one example among many of halakhic recognition of men and women's different roles and obligations within Judaism.[17] Beyond the denial of any halakhic basis for counting women as part of a quorum, charging that it "would make a *hukha utelula* [mockery] of traditional forms by appearing to concede to the feminist charge of oppressive discrimination of inequality" does not wash well with some Orthodox women. Although the "technical construct" argument is perfectly sound, it is not inconceivable that, in due time, even the most traditional of halakhists will be forced to take note of changing circumstances and communal readiness for innovation.[18]

Inventive legal solutions have been found for resolving problematic aspects of other *halakhot* that assume a now-obsolete social, political, or economic reality. A much-cited example of such a corrective is the *heter iskah,* which was developed in order to sidestep the biblical prohibition against usury by recasting the transaction as a profit-sharing partnership. This legal stratagem provided a bridge between, on the one hand, a halakhic system based upon the assumptions of a small-time barter economy and, on the other, a money-based society that relied upon the provision of credit.[19]

Sometimes, even when reliance upon previous codified sources is invoked in support of the new solution, the reasoning involved is so flimsy that its subordination to popular custom or unprecedented social need is absolutely transparent.[20] Consideration of changed circumstances has been invoked (as we have seen in chapter 3) as the basis for obligating today's women to recline at the *seder* table and for the far more influential dispensation to extend their Torah literacy. Modern Orthodox women might similarly invoke a societal application of the *nishtanu hatevaim* (nature has changed) argument to assert that women of today are different from those of earlier generations and may be regarded as part of the *edah.*[21] Indeed, Bin-Nun's assertion that today's *bnot horin* differ from women as traditionally defined by *halakhah* could also be used to that effect. Yet it is worth noting that Bin-Nun explicitly dissociates himself from any application of his theory to mixed-sex prayer groups.

As Bin-Nun sees it, the need for constraint stems from considerations of modesty, which he believes should be applied more stringently in the synagogue than in ordinary life. Bin-Nun regards this constraint—rather than more theoretical issues of theology and historicism—as the great divide between the Orthodox and Conservative movements in today's world. Although he regrets the factionalism that it creates, such constraint constitutes sufficient basis in his eyes for opposing even a less radical response to the wish for egalitarian inclusion of women in mixed-sex settings (as already adopted by the Israeli congregation Shira Hadasha and a few Orthodox communities on American college campuses): waiting for the presence of ten women, in addition to the required quorum of ten men, before commencing with services.

In a rapidly shifting reality, where women are already delivering Torah homilies and assuming other more active roles in public ritual, this application of the modesty principle may not last long. As another Orthodox rabbi in Israel recently suggested, with rare candor and insight, much of the difference between Orthodox and Conservative Judaism has less to do with matters of substance and more to do with matters of rhetoric and pace.[22] By the same token, whether or not more egalitarian forms of worship will become widespread in Orthodox communities has less to do with legal definitions, technicalities, and formal constraints than with the significance that women's issues have assumed as "symbolic absolutes" that establish a clear sense of sexual or communal identity. This role as symbol does not necessarily diminish the importance of such considerations; it *does*, however, demand that they be recognized for what they are.

Despite the predilections of liberal second-stage feminists, it may be that most Orthodox women will still prefer to remain with their relative freedom from the male-defined forms of religious worship and their compulsory rotes. Some women may still appreciate the need for token bottom-line demarcations between Orthodoxy and non-Orthodox denominations, even when these consist of anarchic vestiges of female exclusion from the public sphere. They may also seriously weigh the cost of dislodging a principle so deeply entrenched in their interpretive tradition against the ostensible benefits of incorporating moral sensibilities of their secular reality into their religious lives. The likelihood, however, is that the introduction of women's perspectives upon the weight of such considerations will have some impact upon the practical outcome of future halakhic rulings.

Questioning the male-centered orientation of halakhic assumptions. Reflecting a more profound change in criteria, women's entry into halakhic discourse is already raising previously unthinkable questions about more basic halakhic assumptions that seem to reflect an exclusively male point of view. Following upon the learning revolution and the issue of women's active participation in prayer, the new frontier appears to be rulings affecting sexual relations. Because of their intimate nature, such matters have traditionally been hidden by a veil of secrecy and certainly not discussed in public. Yet the combination of a more open attitude to sex in modern society and the new found voice of women has changed this situation; matters that were previously taboo are now aired even in mixed company.[23] Despite the fact that such openness violates a treasured atmosphere of delicacy and sanctity in which Jewish attitudes to sex have often been ensconced, it does afford women an unprecedented opportunity to take a fresh look at how *their* interests and perspectives figure in the overall balance of halakhic considerations.

To take one example, women are now beginning to question the fact that the traditional laws of modesty are always framed in terms of the temptation women pose to men.[24] In the eyes of a feminist, the assumption that it is only men who are sexually aroused and incapable of controlling their desires inappropriately places the halakhic onus on women. Must the solution lie in unilateral curtailing of women's freedom, rather than charging males with more responsibility for the exercise of self-control?

Likewise, the assumptions of the stringent laws of family purity are queried. Biblical law requires women to separate from their husbands only while menstruating and to undertake ritual immersion in the *mikveh* on the evening of the eighth day. However, obligations of ritual purity affecting flow of blood outside of the menstrual period (*zivah*) have been superimposed by rabbinical decree on the laws of *niddah* (which affect sexual relations alone). This imposition is despite the fact that ever since the destruction of the Second Temple, both men and women are regarded ritually defiled to the highest degree (*temeiei metim*) without any means of purification from such defilement.

The practical upshot of this conflation is, first, that a woman must count an extra seven "clean" days beyond the days of actual bleeding before she may engage in any form of physical contact with her husband. While occasional precedents for leniency exist, taking into account men's sexual needs[25] or the need to enhance women's ability to conceive,[26] there is no corresponding consideration of women's psychological needs for physical expressions of affection that do not necessarily entail full sexual relations. This denial is particularly problematic in the modern reality; the conception of marital relations has become highly romanticized and personalized and women's expectations of intimacy with their husbands extend far beyond the minimal satisfaction of sexual desires.[27] Sensitivity to women's sexual desires is not lacking in the Talmud and medieval sources. However, exhortations to husbands regarding such matters are typically phrased in terms of *men's* perceptions of women's requirements. Women now question whether their own perceptions might not also be heeded and taken into account.

Over and above this practical outcome of conflation between the laws of *niddah* and definitions of ritual impurity, however, is the fact that the language of defilement has been unnecessarily retained as something that applies to women only. This factor has contributed to the perpetuation of negative attitudes regarding women's bodies; to regarding them as inherently more impure than those of men. Such attitudes spill over subtly into women's own self-perceptions. They also affect folk practice and ritual in inappropriate ways, as reflected in the widespread notion that women may not touch a Torah scroll when menstruant, even though Torah scrolls by halakhic definition do not contract impurity.[28]

A third issue is the relegation of authority in determining whether or not excretions issuing from a woman's body are menstrual. Women engaging in the study of sources question the advisability of men serving as experts on questions that are more readily answered from the immediacy of women's personal experience and knowledge of their own bodies. As noted above, the wish to spare women the embarrassment of turning to men with unsavory blood samples is being answered by the growing popularity of women halakhic advisers who have been trained specifically for this purpose. This improvement notwithstanding, the very notion that women must submit themselves to this method of outside surveillance is questionable. In a day and age when standard kits have been developed by medical labs even for home pregnancy exams, why should similar procedures not be developed for determining women's menstrual status? The mystique surrounding the degree of expertise such questions require raises the suspicion that here is merely another device for keeping women in their place.

Orthodox feminists are now also beginning to explore those areas of *halakhah* that address fertility and reproduction, probing the basic assumptions that are brought into play and highlighting the fact that these reflect male objectives and considerations, without the direct input of women's sensibilities. That a wife's role in reproduction is legally defined in terms of enabling her husband to fulfill his obligation to be fruitful and multiply bears certain deep-seated cultural implications. What influence have traditional conceptions of gender and women's identity had on rulings about birth control, abortion, artificial insemination, in vitro fertilization, and surrogate motherhood? Does male bias in halakhic decision-making, for example, create differences in halakhic attitudes toward artificial insemination (usually resorted to when the problem is male infertility) as opposed to attitudes regarding in vitro fertilization or surrogate motherhood (where the problem is usually the infertility of the woman)? What is the effect of such bias upon rulings on birth control that limit women's opportunities to develop an identity independent of home and family? How will potentially upsetting answers to such previously ignored questions be integrated with the regard for family, for giving and caring, for the moral affirmation of life and the optimistic trust in the future that have always been the pride and backbone of Jewish tradition?

Even in cases not directly relating to sex and gender, the likelihood is that women entering halakhic discussion will have their own unique input regarding the implications of any given issue. Bringing different considerations to bear may lead to different judgments. Even when acknowledging regnant considerations, women may well work with different criteria for assessing their relative weight, based on a different hierarchy of values. To the extent that there is a typically feminine way of looking at the overall balance, these different criteria too could lead at times to modified conclusions.

Openness to influence of the academic disciplines. Women's relative freedom from existing traditions of learning allows them to think in ways unencumbered by past conventions. The lack of conditioning into traditional ways of reading text, which may leave them unconvinced by male interpretations, is the "price"—as Orthodox feminist Rivka Lubitch has put it[29]— that men must now pay for two thousand years of female exclusion from halakhic discourse. The criticism leveled by rabbis that women's autodidactic Torah study is not authentic because it does not continue the chain of learning that originated in Sinai[30] cannot count for much when women were never part of that chain. Unlike their male counterparts, the women interested in advanced talmudic study today are generally those who have also been exposed to academia, which allows them more naturally to incorporate scientific methods into their understanding of Torah. This influence can already be noted in the type of biblical exegesis (*divrei Torah*) they produce[31] which is easily distinguished by its more polished style and unabashed use of the tools of textual and historical analysis. Of particular importance is their growing exposure to the expanding influence of gender studies on various disciplines.[32] To the extent that women develop proficiency in the Oral Law, their academic training is also likely to have its effect on their procedural methods of determining *halakhah*.

Diminished emphasis on denominational politics. Another influence of women's greater participation in halakhic process may be a diminished emphasis on delineating sharp denominational boundaries. Such tendencies can already be noted in the willingness of Orthodox feminists to convene and dialogue with their Conservative and Reform sisters, to the extent that they share common interests—a striking deviation from usual Orthodox politics.[33] I believe that this dialogue has less to do with the supposedly liberal leanings of Orthodox feminists than with a general disinclination among women for playing the institutional games men seem to require to establish their identities.

Diminished emphasis on legal formalism as the exclusive determinant of halakhah *and the religious life.* Despite the fact that women's initial exposure to texts is largely mediated by male teachers, and the entire tradition is dominated by male ways of thought, I find it reasonable to assume that women will never assimilate the masculine love of formalism to an equal degree. No matter how great her intellectual conditioning, a woman would be hard put to come up with the idea of epitomizing the religious significance of the Passover *seder* experience with the legal imperative of swallowing a measure of *matzah* equivalent to the mass of a giant olive (*shiur kezayit*) within three minutes flat.[34]

On a more profound level, one may expect that women's participation in the halakhic process will reflect the influence of a more general devaluation in Orthodoxy of the formalistic halakhic mentality. As we have seen, some feminists regard the very notion of a religion that is law-governed, dependent upon our performing a detailed series of mandated acts, as expressive of a typically male way of thinking. Rather than placing formal obedience to rules at the top of their list of moral and spiritual priorities, women might emphasize the importance of religious feeling and a sense of the presence of God. By the same token, some exponents of feminist theory have argued that women tend to develop a value system that is more pragmatic than formal, less concerned with the law itself than with how the law affects daily life.[35]

This essentialist view can be contested and has been. All human beings have an interest in maintaining law and order; one cannot claim that antilegalist sentiments are exclusively a female preserve. Many Orthodox Jews today, regardless of gender, sense a dry legalism dominating contemporary halakhic discussion,[36] a lack of spirituality and emotion in the synagogue, a widespread insensitivity to broader issues of "making the world a better place" (tikkun olam), and an almost all-pervasive communal divisiveness. Moreover, one can of course find other examples in Jewish history of a spiritual and moral revival rooted in a male world that superseded legal formalism (as in the critique of some aspects of the dominant rabbinic ideology engendered by the Hassidic and musar movements). Nowadays, however, this corrective is being revived in an analogously powerful manner by the heightened influence of women's sensibilities. One example is the new emphasis on more personalized, creative, and meaningful forms of ritual and prayer, initiated in the Orthodox world almost exclusively by women.

To the extent that women enter the arena of halakhic discourse, their appreciation for less formalistic considerations will no doubt extend to the nature of halakhah itself. There is no denying that halakhah is basically a formalistic legal system, in the sense that it is grounded in particularistic and concrete norms, rather than in abstract principles. Its discussion of routine cases is rule-oriented; legal questions are decided on the basis of casuistic reasoning and close analysis of the language of the codified texts. The uniqueness of Jewish law, however, traditionally manifested itself in the leeway that poskim found to veer from these constraints and respond to the tension between standard rules and larger principles that potentially exists in every law. In pre-modern times, the readiness in principle of poskim to show such flexibility exhibited itself not only in "hard cases" where the language of the law was ambiguous, but whenever justice or other implicit goals of the law warranted deviation from the rule.[37] The supremacy of law, or the integrity of the legal system itself, was not the ultimate goal. Indeed, some observers have viewed in this very flexibility of halakhah evidence of its essentially "feminine" nature, even when it does not concern itself with explicitly feminist concerns.[38] Thus the entry of women into contemporary halakhic discourse may eventually serve the function of restoring to the halakhah some of the flexibility that once characterized its method, in placing moral and spiritual considerations over and above political ones, or even above the adherence to formal rules.

Communal Developments

Shifting the burden of authority and decision-making to the community

Nearly all of the recent changes in women's halakhic status have been propelled by their initiative. In the case of women's learning, most rabbis eventually came around to appreciating the positive potential in women's religious literacy, so that today they prefer to vie in taking the credit for promoting this cause.[39] The practical effect is that the network of Beth Jacob seminaries, stemming as we saw earlier, from Sarah Schenirer's 1918 initiative, now works hand in hand with the once-reluctant religious establishment and serves as a powerhouse for the forces of religious conservativism.

In the absence of a comparably empathic response from today's rabbinic establishment, however, the likelihood is that as a critical mass of Orthodox women Torah scholars develops, the more revolutionary effects of their advances in learning will encounter greater resistance. To the extent that the halakhic establishment persists in ignoring the burgeoning political force of Jewish women's self-awareness as a collective and their unique spiritual and practical needs, preferring instead to work exclusively with the conservative segments of Jewish society, it is in danger of losing much of its clout and practical relevance. When leading *poskim* cannot arrive at solutions to women's issues that alleviate the human suffering and the sense of spiritual diminishment and moral outrage such issues engender, the women involved are apt to dwell on the ineffectiveness of the existing halakhic establishment, its lack of religious viability, and the inadequacy of its tools. The result is a sense of futility in seeking authoritative halakhic response.

That women themselves, propelled by a combination of desperation and newfound confidence, are launching grassroots initiatives in search of solutions for various halakhic problems could be perceived as a threat to the formal authority of the rabbis. Such initiatives encourage the development of an alternative to the conventional institutional model for halakhic decision-making, which consists of devising independent solutions to halakhic problems without the need for sanctioning by any official religious establishment or any authoritative halakhic response.

Such tensions between communal will or special interest groups and rabbinic authority are not unprecedented in Jewish tradition.[40] As we have already noted, even beyond talmudic accounts of women's voluntary acceptance of *mitzvot* or added stringencies, the annals of subsequent responsa literature testify to occasional individual or collective pressure on the part of women—and the headaches their expressions of independence have presented for halakhic authorities.[41] In our day, however, this trend is doubly powerful, joining forces with a growing phenomenon in Israel, as well as in a few Diaspora communities, of many members of the observant community being well versed in *halakhah*. Such communities have dispensed with the appointment of official rabbis, as the same legal resources that serve the rabbi are equally accessible to the educated layperson. Bypassing the role of rabbis as final decisors in all communal matters leaves them with the function of technical advisers at best.

One could view such developments as a welcome revival of the old Jewish ideal of the aristocracy of learning. A communion of learning between men and women could serve to foster leadership that is based on genuine excellence in Torah scholarship and piety, rather than on official appointments (although the assumption here—that scholars whose authority stems from rabbinic learning and not from official titles would be less subject to political pressures—may be no more than a utopian dream). The trend toward halakhic privatization, however, is not without problems, the dearth of halakhic leaders within the Modern Orthodox community who command the required authority, and the lack of inclination in modern life to turn to authority figures altogether notwithstanding. As I noted in my critique of the Coverian model of lawmaking in chapter 8, important considerations for some form of appeal to rabbinic authority still remain. In the case of women, these considerations might prove doubly important. Women still have much to gain from the sympathy and cooperation of leading rabbinic scholars who are willing to help them reach true standards of excellence in learning and facilitate their entry and acceptance within the halakhic establishment. But what will remain of traditional rabbinic authority when it is threatened by the growing self-awareness, literacy, power, and activism of women independently articulating their own sense of themselves, establishing their own religious realities, and exerting their influence on more general forms of Jewish spirituality?

The wish to avoid such schisms[42] is one of the reasons that Orthodox feminism, despite the remarkable effects of the learning revolution in uniting the ranks of women and creating a new level of sisterhood, still houses within it two contradictory trends. On the one hand, there is an all-around acknowledgment of disparity between women's de jure status in *halakhah* and their de facto situation in everyday secular life. A sense of the injustice of this disparity, however, is vocalized far more often by the generation of the founding mothers of the movement, who still prefer to dwell upon the unresolved problems of the *agunah;* the lack of equal opportunities for women to assume active roles in public synagogue worship; the restrictive laws of modesty; the harmful influence of existing halakhic terminology, which encourages abusive attitudes toward women in the family and in the religious courts; and so forth.

On the other hand, while the younger generation of women enjoy the fruits of the educational revolution and the transformation it has wrought on their spiritual demands, many of them show great reluctance to engage in militant, angry identification with feminist causes. Feminism, if it represents the right to equal opportunities in learning and the development of strong religious role models for women, is something they will almost all defend to the hilt. Some will also display enthusiasm for women's *megillah* readings, and innovative ritual practices that build upon women's life experiences and spiritual predilections (for example, welcoming rituals for newborn girls, bat mitzvah ceremonies, Rosh Hodesh celebrations, and creative ways of understanding Torah). A few may occasionally participate in separate women's prayer groups. However, if any of this leads to more radical talk of changing traditional arrangements in the synagogue or liturgy, or to speaking about the *halakhah* and rabbinic authority in funereal terms, there is a lack of interest, and even antagonism.[43]

The reasons for this lack of interest are various. One is that tradition-bashing is a lonely and soul-destroying activity, estranging one from one's roots and natural social context. It is not very comfortable to stand at a distance and constantly view one's tradition through the lens of an outsider. A second reason is that many of the benefits of tradition, and even some of its essentialist assumptions regarding the nature of women's spirituality, have been genuinely internalized by these women. Halakhic definitions of modesty are for many not just an excuse for keeping women from the centers of power, or denying them their rights to ownership of public space. They breed virtues that are truly cherished, and their own aesthetic and spiritual benefits may not endure in quite the same way if forced to undergo a radical feminist transformation. The image of woman that feminism appears to encourage is, by comparison, quite simply *unattractive* in the eyes of such young women, especially when accompanied by the bitterness and stridence that are a natural hazard of all reformers.

A third factor lies in the spiritual temper implied by respect for authority in general. Some women would, admittedly, reject as antirationalist dogma the demand that they acquiesce to a given ruling merely because someone with a formal title—whether male or female—so decrees. Others subscribe to a view of the ideal religious personality as one who disciplines herself uncritically to obey heteronomous decrees.[44] Such women may be alienated by alternative concepts of spirituality. Whatever the merits of a feminist religious understanding, how it can be reconciled with traditional religious notions of submission to God's authority (*kabbalat ol malkhut shamayim*) and the concept of a transcendent God is a serious question. I hope that the idea of accumulating revelation will be of assistance here, but striking the delicate balance between the two values is no simple matter.

Intertwined with these substantive considerations is a fourth motive that is more tactical. Many Orthodox women intuit what every experienced legislator accepts as a given: in order for legal initiative to succeed, one must not only be right; one must also be clever. In this connection, the head of one of the leading women's seminaries in Jerusalem, which fosters a relatively conservative and low-key profile in terms of feminist militancy, prides herself on having initiated some of the most important breakthroughs in paving the way for women's active participation in the halakhic process. She has no doubt that this has been accomplished simply by virtue of her rhetoric; she refuses to speak of the *halakhah* as a wounded system in need of repair. The vision for women implicit in her initiatives may be revolutionary. Because it is not presented as revolutionary, however, but rather suggested in a spirit of cooperation and compliance with the halakhic establishment, her proposals pass with much less opposition than had they assumed a more strident face. In this position diplomacy and sincerity of attitude are mingled. Her overall faith in the system and her optimistic belief that peace shall prevail redeem the revolutionary implications of her moves, absolving them of any possibly objectionable rankle.

The maintenance of such a nonconfrontational facade is sometimes derided as Pollyannaish self-delusion. Opponents feel that this mode of response provides a dangerous smoke screen, masking the more difficult problems and lulling women into a state of denial or passive acquiescence. Throwing bones to women by allowing them to appear in court as representatives of women chained to recalcitrant husbands does not resolve the deeper issues of women's status in Jewish marriage law, they will say. Neither does it change the fact that under current circumstances the judges will always be male. Giving two hundred women space for their own *bet midrash* does not overcome the absurdity of their having to scrounge around for a *minyan* of ten men and stand segregated behind a *mehitza* in their own study hall before being able to recite prayers of penitence (*Selihot*) in the days preceding the High Holidays.[45] Relaxing some of the rigidities of the hierarchy does not yet remove the glass ceiling and its anomalies.

These tensions within Orthodox feminism are merely a more rarefied and nuanced expression of the larger debate between radical and moderate revisionism in the feminist movement at large. As time passes and the ranks become more solidified, it will be easier to predict which way the wind blows. Although it is unlikely that there will ever be total consensus in these matters, the general thrust—whether quicker- or slower-paced—is undoubtedly toward the breaking down of gender-based barriers and the establishment of pockets of Orthodoxy committed to total equality in fact if not in name. As the movement grows, the hope of its well-wishers is that a greater overlap between the two trends will emerge that will serve to their mutual advantage. The initial satisfaction of the younger women with learning, and their new sense of themselves as spiritual beings whose prayer and study is important, will lead them to positions of responsibility in other realms of community leadership and halakhic guidance. Once this happens, they will be thrust, whether they like it or not, into confrontation with the more practical problems of discrimination in worship and law.

With the development of a cadre of learned and halakhically responsible women from these ranks, and the effect they will have on the breakdown of old rabbinic attitudes, the mistrust between rabbis and their female constituents should gradually erode. This mutual respect could engender a new generation capable of working in greater harmony with institutional bodies of authority. As always, however, the decisive push will come from below, in consonance with the general current trend of Modern Orthodoxy toward more modest perceptions of the rabbinic decisor's role vis-à-vis community.

Israel as the future powerhouse of Orthodox feminism

Despite the Western origins of Orthodox feminism, its most exciting developments will now most probably arise in what was previously regarded as its slower-moving, more traditionalist Israeli base. This paradox has to do with a number of significant differences between Jewish life in Israel and in the Diaspora. The first is that, as opposed to Modern Orthodoxy in the Diaspora, its counterpart in Israel is more clearly demarcated from ultra-Orthodox circles and therefore less affected by its opinions. Moreover, official Orthodoxy in Israel is characterized by a weak rabbinate facing a more halakhically literate laity that has greater confidence in its ability to make independent judgments. The second difference is that in Israel religious life revolves less along organizational lines, so that the most influential terms of reference still remain the classic sources and other more substantive considerations, rather than practical politics and the need to react to rival denominations. The fact that in Israel those involved in feminist issues are more steeped in Jewish learning also makes for more profound treatment of these issues.

A third difference is that Jews in the Diaspora tend to respond to any conflict between their religious and secular lives by constructing an artificial "bubble" of holiness in which they continue to abide by the norms of tradition, cordoned off, as it were, by a myriad of practices designed to create barriers between themselves and their secular surroundings. Though difficult on a cognitive level, such bifurcation is still workable where the main business of modernity and the secular values it generates can be left to the gentiles. Thus Orthodox Jews in the Diaspora as a minority culture may flirt with modernity to whatever limited extent they wish, without assuming real responsibility for its nature or direction. Israeli Orthodox Jews, in contrast, cannot so easily afford the luxury of distancing themselves from their surroundings. Living in a predominantly Jewish state does not lend itself to maintaining dissonance between one's halakhic reality and the public space of everyday life. To take but one example, the development of the arts and a culture of leisure and recreation demands halakhically problematic materials and practices. "Exceptions for the religious"—such as special choir, dance, and theater programs performed only for and by women—may be workable on ghetto terms but do not fully resolve issues of modesty or antinomian outbursts of ideological heresy. Developing more nuanced standards for "clean" art, literature, and films in order to avoid the clash with halakhic strictures may likewise enable greater artistic freedom of expression on an individual basis.

When such issues apply on a national scale, however, they become much
more urgent and demand more substantial response. Thus, life for religiously committed Jews living in Israel becomes an ideological hotbed. The
grappling with such issues is richer and more intense.

Broader Ramifications

There is no doubt that on an ideological level, the feminist critique of the ostensibly patriarchal orientation of tradition poses formidable questions.
With respect to some of the modifications of practical norms that the critique dictates, it seems as if Orthodoxy has no choice but to accept them—
at the very least to regard such change as a necessary evil imposed by forces
beyond its control. Such is the case, for example, when the ultra-Orthodox
ideal of men's exclusive dedication to Torah study is dependent upon
women's participation in the workforce, or when the continued existence of
the religious political parties in Israel is inconceivable without religious
women being able to cast their votes alongside the men.

There is still the option of building a higher wall between the halakhic reality and the outside world to avoid other modifications and allow the old
norms to continue to prevail. This option remains with regard to the preservation of male privilege in rhetoric, ritual, and Jewish law, to the extent that
these areas are not subject to the direct influence and control of the secular
world. The thrust of this book, however, has been to suggest that even for
the religiously committed there is yet a third possibility. This possibility lies
in the recognition that Jewish tradition can accommodate the newfound reluctance of both women and men to maintain patriarchy as the ideal societal
model and can even view such accommodation as genuinely "expanding the
palace of Torah." This does not mean that any particular societal model is to
be adopted by all Jews in all situations at all times. It *does* allow for a more
pluralistic view of the variety of models that can be absorbed by canonic
texts bearing an initially patriarchal slant. On this view, the "picture" and
"form of life" that these texts generate within the interpretive community
most committed to their study and practice ultimately determine which
models take hold.

To the extent that this accommodation takes hold, the significance of the
confrontation between feminism and Orthodoxy reaches far beyond its
practical effect on Jewish life. A solution to the challenge of feminism that
accommodates newly emerging moral intuitions amid the globalization of
human society, in terms consonant with the necessarily limited founding
principles of Jewish tradition, stands to teach us something much more profound about the nature of religion, law, and humanity in general. In submitting itself to the filter of a historic religion that firmly binds its adherents to
the authority of foundational texts while still exhibiting great interpretive

latitude, this brand of feminism may emerge as the provider of a singularly valuable paradigm for human existence. By making it possible to transform the meaning of traditional texts, its cumulativist premise comes to convey that only when we have a past from which to draw and a future toward which to strive can there be a meaningful present. Despite ideological protestations to the contrary, I believe that Orthodox Judaism's growing accommodation of feminism's redemptive vision is providing dramatic confirmation of this premise before our very eyes.

Notes

Preface (pp. ix–xxii)

1. Janet Radcliffe Richards, *The Sceptical Feminist* (Middlesex, England: Penguin Books, 1982), p. 323.
2. Blu Greenberg, *On Women and Judaism: A View from Tradition* (Philadelphia: Jewish Publication Society, 1981; reprint, 1996).
3. "Can the Demand for Change in the Status of Women Be Halakhically Legitimated?" *Judaism* 42:4 (fall 1993), pp. 478–492.
4. This talk was the kernel of a fuller article, subsequently coauthored by myself and Yehuda Gellman. See "The Implications of Feminism for Orthodox Jewish Theology" (in Hebrew), in *Rav-Tarbutiyut Bemedina Democratit Veyehudit*, edited by Menachem Mautner, Avi Sagi, and Ronen Shamir (Tel Aviv: Ramot Publishing–University of Tel Aviv, 1998), pp. 443–465. It also provided some of the material included in chapters 7 and 10 of this book.
5. Tamar Ross, "Modern Orthodoxy and the Challenge of Feminism," in *Jews and Gender: The Challenge to Hierarchy*, edited by Jonathan Frankel (New York: Oxford University Press, 2000), pp. 3–39.
6. Yeshayahu Leibowitz, *Emunah, Historia Vearakhim* (Jerusalem: Akademon, 1982), pp. 71–75.
The article appears in English translation as "The Status of Women: Halakhah and Meta-Halakhah," in Yeshayahu Leibowitz, *Judaism, Human Values, and the Jewish State*, edited and translated by Eliezer Goldman et al. (Cambridge, Mass.: Harvard University Press, 1995), pp. 128–132.
7. Ibid., p. 128.
8. Such as that of Joel B. Wolowelsky, *Women, Jewish Law, and Modernity: New Opportunities in a Post-Feminist Age* (New York: Ktav, 1997), whose analysis of the halakhic issues is conducted in a laudably evenhanded manner, while suggesting (p. x) that "it is now time to move past this fear of feminism."
9. This talk was subsequently expanded into an article. See "Can We Still Speak to God the Father?" (in Hebrew), in *Ayin Tovah: Du-Siah Vepulmus Betarbut Yisrael*, edited by Nahem Ilan (Tel Aviv: Hakibbutz Hameuchad/Neemanei Torah ve-Avoda, 1999), pp. 264–278.
10. Rabbi A. I. Kook, *Orot Haemunah* (Brooklyn, N.Y.: Langsam, 1985), p. 25. For further discussion of R. Kook's understanding of the function of religious truth statements, see Tamar Ross, "The Cognitive Value of Religious Truth Statements: Rabbi A. I. Kook and Postmodernism," in *Hazon Nahum: Studies in Jewish Law, Thought, and History Presented to Dr. Norman Lamm on the Occasion of His*

Seventieth Birthday, edited by Yaakov Elman and Jeffrey S. Gurock (New York: Yeshiva University Press, 1997), pp. 479–528.

11. Ludwig Wittgenstein, *Culture and Value,* translated by Peter Winch (Oxford: Basil Blackwell, 1980), p. 76.

12. Ibid., p. 73.

1. Feminism and the Halakhic Tradition (pp. 3–24)

1. For a clear, comprehensive and updated survey of the many varieties of feminism, see Rosemarie Putnam Tong, *Feminist Thought: A More Comprehensive Introduction* (Boulder, Colo.: Westview, 1998). See also Judith Lorber, *Gender Inequality: Feminist Theories and Politics* (Los Angeles: Roxbury Publishing, 1998) for additional source material illustrating the various trends.

2. Mary Wollstonecraft, *A Vindication of the Rights of Women,* edited by Carol H. Poston (New York: Norton, 1975), preface.

3. John Stuart Mill, "The Subjection of Women," in *Collected Works of J. S. Mill* (Toronto: University of Toronto Press; London: Routledge and Kegan Paul, 1984), 21:261–340.

4. Betty Friedan, *The Feminist Mystique* (New York: Dell, 1974; first published in 1963).

5. Simone de Beauvoir, *The Second Sex,* translated and edited by H. M. Parshley (New York: Knopf, 1953).

6. Ibid., p. 267.

7. Sigmund Freud, "The Passing of the Oedipus Complex," in *Sexuality and the Psychology of Love* (New York: Collier Books, 1968), p. 181.

8. See Judith Lorber, *Paradoxes of Gender* (New Haven: Yale University Press, 1994), pp. 13–36.

9. Nancy Chodorow, *The Reproduction of Mothering: Psychoanalysis and the Sociology of Gender* (Berkeley and Los Angeles: University of California Press, 1978).

10. For bibliographical guidance on Marxist feminism, see Lorber, *Gender Inequality,* p. 44; Tong, *Feminist Thought,* pp. 329–333.

11. See, for example, Deborah Rhode: "The Ideology and Biology of Gender Difference," *Southern Journal of Philosophy* 34 (1996, supplement), pp. 73–98.

12. Jane Flax, "Postmodernism and Gender Relations in Feminist Theory," in *Signs: Journal of Women in Culture and Society* 12 (1987), pp. 626–627, 641–643, quoted in Lorber, *Gender Inequality,* pp. 175, 177–178.

13. Critics have pointed to the fact that anti-essentialism, taken to its postmodernist extreme, leads to a paradox: The very ability to speak of feminism depends in an important way upon just the sense of group identity, interest, and shared experience that it seeks to challenge. The tendency of most recent feminist thinking, therefore, is to try and find ways of acknowledging the existence of sex-linked qualities without perpetuating their constraints. This acknowledgment is accomplished by viewing gender differences as elements on a continuum rather than diametrically opposed and also by focusing less on the contingent nature of such differences and more on methods of overcoming the inequality that they create.

14. Wollstonecraft, *A Vindication of the Rights of Women,* p. 29.

15. Lorber, *Paradoxes of Gender,* p. 33.

16. Margaret Mead, *Male and Female: A Study of the Sexes in a Changing World* (New York: Morrow, 1949), pp. 159–160.

17. Kate Millet, *Sexual Politics* (Garden City, N.Y.: Doubleday, 1970).

18. For many illustrations of this thesis, see Jean Baker Miller, *Toward a New Psychology of Women* (Boston: Beacon, 1986).

19. Chodorow, *The Reproduction of Mothering.*

20. See Genevieve Lloyd's critique of Descartes in *Women, Knowledge, and Reality: Explorations in Feminist Philosophy,* edited by Ann Garry and Marilyn Pearsall (Boston: Unwin Hyman, 1989), pp. 149–165, and Allison Jagger's similar critique of artificial distinctions between reason and emotion in the same volume, pp. 166–190.

21. For a discussion of this example and its more general implications, see Hilary Korenblith, "Distrusting Reason," *Midwest Studies in Philosophy* 23 (1999), pp. 181–196.

22. Ibid.

23. Vrinda Dalmiya and Linda Alcoff, "Are Old Wives Tales Justified?" in *Feminist Epistemologies,* edited by Linda Alcoff and Elizabeth Potter (New York: Routledge, 1993), pp. 217–244.

24. Ibid., p. 223.

25. See Lynn Hankinson Nelson, "Who Knows? What Can They Know? And When?" in Garry and Pearsall, eds., *Women, Knowledge, and Reality,* pp. 286–297; Sandra Harding, "Rethinking Standpoint Epistemology: What is Strong Objectivity?" in *Feminism and Science,* edited by Evelyn Fox Keller and Helen E. Longino (Oxford: Oxford University Press, 1996), pp. 235–248; Louise M. Antony, "Quine as Feminist: The Radical Import of Naturalized Epistemology," in *A Mind of One's Own,* edited by Louise M. Antony and Charlotte Witt (Boulder, Colo.: Westview, 1993), pp. 185–225.

26. Dalmiya and Alcoff, "Are 'Old Wives' Tales Justified?" p. 223.

27. For reference to the superior understanding of subordinated groups, see Jean Baker Miller, *Toward a New Psychology of Women* (Boston: Beacon, 1976; 2d ed. 1986), pp. 10–11.

28. See, for example, Jean Grimshaw, *Feminist Philosophers: Women's Perspectives on Philosophical Traditions* (Boulder, Colo.: Wheatsheaf Books, 1986), pp. 29–49; Nel Noddings, *Caring: A Feminine Approach to Ethics and Moral Education* (Berkeley and Los Angeles: University of California Press, 1984).

29. Carol Gilligan, *In a Different Voice* (Cambridge: Harvard University Press, 1982).

30. One of the most prominent pioneers in this field has been Mary Daly, beginning with her first major work: *Beyond God the Father: Toward a Philosophy of Women's Liberation* (Boston: Beacon, 1985). A more recent exponent of the feminist critique of monotheistic religions is Daphne Hampson; see her *Theology and Feminism* (Oxford: Basil Blackwell, 1990) and *After Christianity* (London: SCM Press, 1996). For a general survey of the impact of gender awareness on the study of religion, see Nancy Frankenberry, "Philosophy of Religion in Different Voices," in *Philosophy in a Feminist Voice: Critiques and Reconstructions,* edited by Janet Kourany (Princeton: Princeton University Press, 1998), pp. 50–65; Rita Gross, *Feminism and Religion* (Boston: Beacon, 1996).

31. The halakhic background provided in this section draws heavily upon formulations appearing in the introduction and first chapter of Michael Berger's *Rabbinic Authority* (New York: Oxford University Press, 1998). See also Adin Steinsaltz, *The Essential Talmud* (London: Weidenfeld and Nicolson, 1976).

32. The expression is found in the Babylonian Talmud (hereafter abbreviated BT) *Eruvin* 21b. Cf. *Menahot* 29b.

33. Berger, *Rabbinic Authority,* p. 5.

34. Ibid. As Berger notes, however, some scholars have suggested that awareness of the distinction between biblical law and its interpretation did not obtain

throughout the entire rabbinic period but evolved only in its later phases. For references, see *Rabbinic Authority*, p. 159 n.15.

35. *Hazal,* an acronym for *hakhameinu zikhronam livrakha* (our sages of blessed memory) not only refers to these Rabbis of the Mishnaic and talmudic period, but also to the halahkic and aggadic literature of the period in general. As Berger notes, in some traditional circles use of the term "immediately instills awe and reverence in the reader or listener." See *Rabbinic Authority*, p. 9.

36. For a balanced and judicious summary of some of the major aspects of women's status under Jewish law, informed by a professed feminist interest and historicist view, see Rachel Biale, *Women and Jewish Law: An Exploration of Women's Issues in Halakhic Sources* (New York: Schocken, 1984). For a more practical guide for contemporary Orthodox women, see Elyakim Ellinson, *Haisha Vehamitzvot* (Jerusalem: World Zionist Organization, 1984).

37. See relevant discussion of this in chapter 6 below.

38. See, for example, Leviticus 27:1–8, where the Torah appears to place a different "price tag" on men and women, although the basis for this is not clear at all.

39. See, for example, *Tosefta* on *Berakhot* 6:22 in the standard editions of BT *Berakhot* or 6:18 in the Lieberman edition. For a literary analysis supporting the contention of Mishnaic linkage between degree of obligation to Mitzvot and legal status, see Noam J. Zohar, "Women, Men and Religious Status: Deciphering a Chapter in Mishnah," *Approaches to Ancient Judaism,* edited by Herbert Basser and Simha Fishbane,vol.5 (Atlanta: Scholar's Press, 1993), chapter 2.

40. From the wording of the *Tosefta* on *Berakhot* (ibid.), it might seem that according to the Torah women were not obligated to observe *any mitzvot*. However, two rabbinic scholars, the fourteenth-century Menahem Ben-Solomon Meiri (Hameiri) and the twelfth-century Eliezer Ben-Yoel Halevi of Bonn (Ravia), understand the *Tosefta* as saying that women are not obliged to perform *all* of the *mitzvot,* and this seems to be the amended reading of the sages, as evidenced in the Palestinian Talmud (see Saul Lieberman's *Tosefta Ki-Fshutah*). As against this, see Rashba on BT *Kiddushin* 34a, suggesting that the initial halakhic assumption is that women are not obliged to the commandments, as "all of the Torah was written in the male gender." For further instances of halakhic discussions that reiterate women's status as outsider in a male-built society, see Eliezer Berkovits, *Jewish Women in Time and Torah* (Hoboken, N.J.: Ktav, 1990), pp. 4–7. The first example Berkovits cites is a discussion concerning the question whether women's obligation to say grace after meals (which includes thanking God for the covenant He has sealed in our flesh and the Torah He has taught us) is biblical (*mideoraita*) or rabbinical (*miderabbanan*). While the discussion on this matter in BT *Berakhot* 20b reaches no conclusion, the Tosafists of the thirteenth century suggest that women's biblical exemption stems from the fact that women are neither circumcised nor obligated to study Torah, thus implying that they really were not participants in the covenant (not circumcised) nor recipients of the Torah. In subsequent discussion, however, it emerges that a man who is obligated only rabbinically (e.g., if he ate less than the prescribed measure of food) may nevertheless recite grace for a man who is biblically obliged, in accordance with the principle that "all Israel are responsible for each other." A woman, however, cannot do this since, according to the Rosh, the principle of collective responsibility for *mitzva,* performance does not refer to women (see Rosh on BT *Berakhot* 20b).

41. Mishnah *Kiddushin* 1:7.

42. Many Orthodox Jews fulfill this obligation nowadays by going "beyond the call of duty" and wearing a fringed four-cornered garment (*tallit katan*) as a regular part of daily dress. It is also fulfilled by the custom of donning a four-cornered prayer shawl (*tallit*) during the morning prayers.

43. For an interesting survey of the history of this principle's application and its reflection of the move to greater inclusiveness of women in halakhic obligation, see Uri Ehrlich, "'They Too Were Witness to That Miracle': The Evolution of an Egalitarian Argument in the World of *Halakhah*" (in Hebrew), in *Ayin Tovah: Du-Siah Vepulmus Betarbut Yisrael*, edited by Nahem Ilan (Tel Aviv: Hakibbutz Hameuchad/Neemanei Torah veAvoda, 1999), pp. 142–160. See also Chana and Shmuel Safrai's article of the same title (in Hebrew), *Sefer Yeshurum*, edited by Michael Shashar (Jerusalem: Shashar/Yeshurum, 1999), pp. 197–213.

44. See, for example, BT *Hagigah* 2a.

45. Mishhah *Kiddushin* 1:7. The positive time-bound *mitzvot* from which women are exempt include many (but not all) holiday-related *mitzvot* (such as *shofar, sukkah,* and *lulav*), as well as many (but not all) *mitzvot* that need to be fulfilled during certain parts of the day or week (such as reciting the *Shema, tzitzit,* and *tefillin*).

46. Time-bound *mitzvot* from which women are not exempt include the obligation to eat *matzah* on Passover (Deut. 16:3), rejoice on holidays, and participate in the mass assembly for reading the Torah (*hakhel*) every seventh year (Deut. 31:12). Positive *mitzvot* from which women are exempt that are not time-bound include the study of Torah, procreation (*periyah ureviyah*), and the symbolic redeeming of firstborn sons from service to the priesthood (*pidyon haben*).

47. Mishnah *Horayot* 3:7.

48. Mishnah *Horayot* 3:7, with amplifications and qualifications in later rabbinic sources. Women's rights override those of men in the obligation to ransom captives, because of the threat of rape. But here too, if a man faces this threat as well (in a homosexual context), his right to be ransomed precedes, on the assumption that he will be less used to this type of sexual contact (*Shulhan Arukh, Yoreh Deah* 252:8).

49. The Rema on the *Shulhan Arukh, Yoreh Deah* 252:8, and commentary of the Taz, *simman katan* 6.

50. See chapter 2 below, note 21, p. 261. The objection to women learning was generally limited to muted disapproval (see *Shulhan Arukh, Yoreh Deah* 246:6), in light of Maimonides' position (*MT, Hilkhot Talmud Torah* 1:13): Women are not to be taught because most of them are not attuned to study. If they take up study on their own initiative, however, they do merit reward, though less than that of the male who is commanded to engage in this activity. Maimonides also distinguishes in this context between the Oral and Written Torah, regarding the prohibition against teaching women the former as most severe.

51. See Eliyahu Bakshi-Doron, *Binyan Av* (Jerusalem: 1982), responsum 65 (p. 287). See also *Sefer Hahinukh*, no. 158; *Birkhei Yosef, Hoshen Mishpat* 7:12; *Enziklopedyah Talmudit*, vol. 8 (p. 494, "*hora'ah*"), and the sources brought there in note 109.

52. Very rarely, women's opinions are quoted approvingly, but generally because as wives or daughters of well-renowned male scholars they had privileged inside knowledge. See, for example, BT *Ketubot* 85a, where Rava relies upon the daughter of Rav Hisda (who was his wife) in discounting a particular woman's oath in the absence of the required testimony of two male witnesses to this effect. This applies even to so independent a spirit as Beruria, the wife of R. Meir (see *Tosefta Kelim Baba Meziya* 1:3).

53. Deuteronomy 17:14 and the commentary of the Sifrei.

54. *MT, Hilkhot Melakhim* 1:4.

55. *Shulhan Arukh, Hoshen Mishpat* 7:4.

56. BT *Shevuot* 30a; *Baba Kama* 15a; *MT, Hilkhot Edut* 9:2. Occasional exceptions are made under special circumstances; see Moshe Meiselman, *Jewish Woman*

in Jewish Law (New York: Ktav/Yeshiva University Press, 1978), pp. 75–78, and Berkovits, *Jewish Women in Time and Torah,* pp. 47–48.

57. The term *"kevod hatzibbur,"* which literally means "the honor of the community," has been understood as a reference to sexual distraction, but is more usually taken to mean that the community is disgraced by the implication that no suitable male could be found of the task.

58. For a description of ultra-Orthodoxy, see chapter 3, pp. 58–59 below.

59. Although Meir's assumption of the position of prime minister was accepted by the religious Zionist parties, her 1946 appointment as head of the political department of the Jewish Agency aroused comment in *Hatzofeh,* the organ of the Orthodox National Religious Party (August 28). Acknowledging that Meir was, without question, "understanding, industrious, ethical, a distinguished woman," the article protested that she was "all that notwithstanding—a woman . . . There are boundaries and borders, and each sex needs to know its limits." (Quoted and translated by David Ellenson and Elissa Ben-Naim, in "Women and the Study of Torah," *Nashim* 4 [Fall 2001], p. 137, n.1.)

60. Various explanations for this are offered in the Talmud; for example, that men are the initiators in sexual relations (BT *Yevamot* 65b), that women's natural desire for children renders this specific commandment unnecessary for them (see the stories cited in BT *Ketubot* 62a–b), or that the exemption from this obligation affords women the option of birth control in life-threatening situations (BT *Yevamot* 12b). See also R. Meir of Dvinsk, *Meshekh Hokhma* on Genesis 9:7, who suggests that women are exempt from the mitzvah of procreation because the Torah whose "ways are pleasant" would not obligate them to undertake the risks of pregnancy and childbirth.

61. BT *Kiddushin* 29a; Tosafot Yeshanim on *Yomah* 82a; Tosafot *Nazir* 28b; *Magen Avraham, Orah Hayim* 616, *simman katan* 2; and *Mishnah Berurah* 616, *simman katan* 5.

62. BT *Sotah* 23b.

63. *MT, Hilkhot Ishut* 3:11, based on Deut. 22:16.

64. BT *Kiddushin* 41a.

65. Tosafot *Kiddushin* 41:1; *Shulhan Arukh, Even Haezer* 37:8 (In recent years a number of husbands of women seeking divorce have exploited this relaxation in an unscrupulous manner. See "New Leverage in Divorce for Orthodox Fathers," *New York Times,* Saturday, May 27, 1995, pp. 21–22.)

66. BT *Nazir* 24b; *Gittin* 77a.

67. See Yisrael Yuval, "Marital Finanacial Arrangements in Medieval Ashkenaz" (in Hebrew), in *Dat Vekalkalah: Yahasei Gomlin,* edited by Menahem Ben-Sasson (Jerusalem, 1995), pp. 191–207; Judith Hauptman, *Rereading the Rabbis: A Woman's Voice* (Boulder: Westview, 1998), pp. 183–184.

68. BT *Baba Kama* 87a.

69. *MT, Horayot* 3.

70. *Shulhan Arukh, Yoreh Deah* 248:4.

71. BT *Kiddushin* 6a.

72. *Mishnah Ketubot* 4:5; *Ketubot* 48a–b.

73. BT *Kiddushin* 30b.

74. Maimonides, *MT, Hilkhot Ishut* 15:20.

75. *MT, Hilkhot Ishut* 15:19. For discussion of how the demand upon a husband not to cast fear over his wife can be reconciled with the instruction that she fear him and be subordinate to all his needs, see: Berkovits, *Jewish Women in Time and Torah,* p. 56; Shoshana Pantel Zolty, *And All Your Children Shall Be Learned": Women and the Study of Torah in Jewish Law and History* (Northvale, N.J.: Jason Aronson, 1997), pp. 31–32, n.54.

76. *MT, Hilkhot Ishut* 12:2, based on Exodus 21:1. Nahmanides' alternative interpretation of this verse (in his commentary on Exod. 21:9), restricts the husband's biblical obligations only to the sexual realm, attributing the other two obligations to later rabbinic law. Even in the sexual realm, the obligations of husband are circumscribed by rabbinically established standards, whereas the women's obligation has been understood as availability at all times that are halakhically permissible, provided she is in good health. See responsa of the Hatam Sofer, l 7:25; *Iggerot Moshe, Orah Hayim* 4:75; Ran, BT *Nedarim,* end of chapter 2.

77. *MT, Hilkhot Ishut* 12:2.

78. As Eliezer Berkovits points out, "whether the ketubah is biblically prescribed or is one of the later *takkanot hakhamin* (rabbinical rulings) remains an unresolved issue in the Talmud and the major commentaries." For sources, see his *Jewish Women in Time and Torah,* pp. 8–9. See also Deborah Greniman, "The Origin of the Ketubah," *Nashim* 4 (fall 2001), pp. 84–119; Hanital Ofan, "The Ketubah: Origin and Meaning of a Legal Obligation" (in Hebrew), *Masekhet* 1 (Jerusalem: Matan, 2002), pp. 103–129.

79. BT *Ketubot* 59b. *MT, Hilkhot Ishut* 21:3.

80. BT Ketubot 61a–b; *MT, Hilkhot Ishut* 21:7.

81. Rashi on BT *Ketubot* 61a.

82. *MT, Hilkhot Ishut* 21:10. One may find cold comfort in the Ravad's gloss: "I have never heard of whipping being practiced, but rather the woman's needs and food should be diminished until she succumbs." *Halakhah* allows for the use of physical force against sinning males as well, but only the rabbinic court (*bet din*) may employ force. While there is also room to interpret Maimonides' ruling as intending that punishment be administered by the court rather than personally by the husband, some *poskim* do not stipulate this. The reason for the difference is that the wife is legally the responsibility of her husband and therefore directly subjugated to him. For further discussion and a list of relevant responsa, see Mikhal Wolf, "Taming of the Rebellious Wife" (in Hebrew), *Meimad* 11 (March–April 1998); Rachel Lebel's response, *Meimad* 12 (May–June 1998); and Wolf's rebuttal, *Meimad* 13 (July–August 1998). See also Avraham Grossman's discussion of this issue in *Hassidot Umordot: Nashim Yehudiyot beEiropa Biyemei Habeinayim* (Jerusalem: Mercaz Shazar, 2001), pp. 373–396.

83. Although a woman may not divorce her husband herself, she may—in certain cases—turn to the rabbinic court to influence or compel her husband to divorce her.

84. *Shulhan Arukh, Even Haezer* 119:6. The non-reciprocal right of the husband to divorce his wife by writing her a *get* is grounded ultimately on Deuteronomy 24:1–3.

85. See Rabbi Eliezer Waldenberg's detailed survey: idem, *Tzitz Eliezer* (Jerusalem, 1998), 19:44.

86. For some contemporary literary and legal perspectives on the plight of the *agunah,* see *Women in Chains: A Sourcebook on the Agunah,* edited by Jack Nusan Porter (Northvale, N.J./London: Jason Aronson, 1995).

87. See the studies cited below in chapter 2, note 70, p. 265. These support Meiselman's claim to this effect in *Jewish Woman in Jewish Law* (New York: Ktav/Yeshiva University Press, 1978), pp. 16–18.

88. Rachel Adler, "The Jew Who Wasn't There," *Davka* (summer 1972), pp. 7–11, reprinted in *On Being a Jewish Feminist: A Reader,* edited by Susannah Heschel (New York: Schocken, 1983), pp. 12–18; Paula Hyman, "The Other Half," *Conservative Judaism* 26 (summer 1972), pp. 14–21, reprinted in *The Jewish Woman: New Perspectives,* edited by Elizabeth Koltun (New York: Schocken, 1976), p. 105; Judith Plaskow, *Standing Again At Sinai* (San Francisco: Harper, 1990). An article by Plaskow under the same title appeared in *Tikkun* 1:2 (November 1986), pp. 28–35.

89. Plaskow, *Standing Again at Sinai,* pp. 25–27; Adler, "I've Had Nothing Yet So I Can't Take More," *Moment* 8:8 (September 1983), p. 22f.

90. The biological assumption of biblical times was that for up to three days following intercourse women may emit viable semen from their bodies and thus remain ritually impure. On this understanding, corroborated by the talmudic reading of this passage (see Mishnah *Shabbat,* chapter 9, and subsequent discussion in BT *Shabbat* 96a–97b), Moses enjoining the man not to approach women three days before the event of revelation was precisely to protect *women's* purity so that they would be able to participate in that moment.

91. Plaskow, *Standing Again at Sinai,* p. 26; Adler, "I've Had Nothing Yet," p. 23.

92. Adler, ibid. It is worth noting that several midrashic statements do come to explicitly deny women's exclusion. See Rashi's citation of the *Mekhilta* on Exodus 19:3 and BT *Shabbat* 87a; *Shmot Rabba* 28:1, 2; *Tanhuma* at end of *Metzora.* For a traditionalist apologetic based on these sources, see Dina Hacohen, "Women at the Giving of the Torah and in its Daily Acceptance" (in Hebrew), *Gevilin* 4 (Tammuz, 1991), pp. 69–80. Even on the midrashic phrasing, however, women are regarded as a separate class, rather than as part of the norm—the general thrust of which would not be regarded by the contemporary feminist as particularly complimentary (see *Shmot Rabba*). As against this, a later midrashic work (*Pirkei deRabbi Eliezer* [Higger edition] chapter 40) most likely stemming from eighth-century Palestine, attributes the singling out of the women before the men in Exodus 19:15 because it is the women's opinion that determines the path of the men.

93. BT *Shabbat* 62a.

94. BT *Berakhot* 57b.

95. As aptly put by Rachel Adler. See "I've Had Nothing Yet," pp. 22–23.

96. Saul Berman, "The Status of Women in Halakhic Judaism," *Tradition* (fall 1973), p. 8; reprinted in Kiltun, ed., *The Jewish Woman.*

97. BT *Berakhot* 17a. The understanding of the fifteenth-century commentator Isaac Arama is exceptional: his biblical commentary to Genesis 3:20 (*Akedat Yitzhak,* chapter 9) teaches that the patriarch Isaac, when rebuking his wife Rebecca for her anguish over her barrenness, asserted that bearing children is not the only purpose of a woman's life and she shared with men the purpose of devotional piety and wisdom.

98. Berkovits, *Jewish Women in Time and Torah,* p. 3.

99. See in BT *Baba Batra* 109b. For further examples, see Rachel Elior, "'Present But Absent,' 'Still Life,' and 'A Pretty Maiden Who Has No Eyes': On the Presence and Absence of Women in the Hebrew Language, in Jewish Culture, and in Israeli Life" in *Streams into the Sea: Studies in Jewish Culture and its Context,* edited by Rachel Livneh-Freudenthal and Elchanan Reiner (Tel Aviv: Alma College, 2001), especially pp. 196–197.

100. BT *Pesachim* 65a; *Sanhedrin* 100b. The latter source laments that the father of a daughter can't ever sleep at night: when she's small, for fear that she'll be seduced; during her adolescence, for fear that she'll be promiscuous; when she grows up, lest she not get married; when she marries, lest she not have children; and when she's aged, for fear that she'll engage in witchcraft.

101. BT *Niddah* 57b; see also *Shabbat* 152a.

102. See, for example, BT *Sanhedrin* 22b.

103. BT *Shabbat* 33:2.

104. JT *Pesahim* chapter 4, *halakhah* 4, in connection with *bedikat hametz; Shakh Yoreh Deah* 127, *simman katan* 30, in connection with *nikur ahoraim.*

105. BT *Berakhot* 48b.

106. BT *Kiddushin* 78b and see Rashi there.

107. For further discussion of this trend and sources, see Avraham Grossman, *Hassidot Umordot*, pp. 26–54.

108. BT *Yevamot* 62b.

109. Ibid.

110. BT *Menakhot* 22a.

111. See BT *Megillah* 14b and BT *Niddah* 45b.

112. *Bamidbar Rabbah* 3:4; BT *Sotah* 11, which states that it was due to the piety of the Israelite women in Egypt that the Jewish people merited the Exodus from Egypt.

113. Compare, for example, BT *Avodah Zarah* 39a, which portrays women molded entirely by the interests of their husbands and having no mind of their own, and *Genesis Rabbah* 17:7, which declares the same regarding men.

114. For a contrast between the mimetic traditions of old and certain current tendencies of Orthodoxy, see Haym Soloveitchik, "Rupture and Reconstruction: The Transformation of Contemporary Orthodoxy," *Tradition* 28, no. 4 (1994), pp. 64–130.

115. See Jacob Katz, "Orthodoxy in Historical Perspective," in *Studies in Contemporary Jewry,* edited by Peter Y. Medding (Bloomington: Indiana University Press, 1986), 2: 3–6; Moshe S. Samet, "The Beginnings of Orthodoxy," *Modern Judaism* 8 (1988), pp. 249–269 (a different version in Hebrew appeared in 1970).

116. George Santayana, *The Life of Reason,* vol. 3, *Reason in Religious Belief* (New York: Scribner's, 1905–6), p. 198.

2. Sources of Discontent and the Conservative Response
(pp. 25–45)

1. BT *Eruvin* 53b.

2. BT *Avot* 5:1.

3. See Rabbi Yehuda Henkin, *Equality Lost: Essays in Torah Commentary, Halacha, and Jewish Thought* (Jerusalem: Urim, 1999), pp. 83–84. The enigmatic image of Beruria, which serves as a role model for many contemporary Jewish women who aspire to religious excellence, has been the focus of much feminist scholarship. Although she is extolled in various talmudic sources for both her piety and her erudition, the value of these are thrown into question by a less flattering account of her life's end in the thirteenth-century commentary of Rashi (on BT *Avodah Zarah* 18b). According to this tragic rendition, R. Meir responded to her derision about the sages calling women light-headed by declaring that she was destined in the future to corroborate this judgment. At R. Meir's bidding, his disciple tested Beruria's faithfulness by persistently trying to seduce her. After she finally succumbed, she committed suicide in mortification. The tale is problematic on several accounts, giving rise to many discussions regarding its authenticity. For a fairly complete survey of this discussion and its ramifications, see Brenda Bacon in *Kolech* (Religious Women's Forum) 38 (3 Marheshvan, 2001) on the weekly portion of Noah (in Hebrew) and in *Nashim: Journal of Jewish Women's Studies and Gender Issues* 5 (fall 5673/2002), pp. 231–240. One scholarly opinion, naturally appealing to feminists, is that this legendary ending to Beruria's life is a later addition devised in order to emphasize the bitter consequences of women's learning. On the other hand, it should be noted that Rashi himself was known to have learned daughters who actively participated in disseminating their father's halakhic opinions.

4. BT *Berakhot* 51b; BT *Niddah* 20b.

5. A brief analysis of this anecdote appears in Judith S. Antonelli, *In the Image of God: A Feminist Commentary on the Torah* (Northvale, N.J.: Jason Aronson, 1997), pp. xxix–xxx. For a more suggestive discussion of some of the deeper implications of this story and another Yalta narrative (BT *Nedarim* 20b), see Rachel Adler, *Engendering Judaism: An Inclusive Theology and Ethics* (Philadelphia: Jewish Publication Society, 1998), pp. 53–58.

6. Avraham Grossman, *Hassidot Umordot: Nashim Yehudiyot beEiropa Biyemei Habeinayim* (Jerusalem: Mercaz Shazar, 2001).

7. Ibid., pp. 214–215.

8. Ibid., pp. 214–216.

9. Ibid., pp. 331–334.

10. Ibid., pp. 338, 506.

11. In halakhic terms, however, the husband retains his dominance in many non-Orthodox ceremonies by speaking first, for once he "acquires" his wife through his gift of a ring, her subsequent declarations of commitment or gifts to him have no legal significance.

12. Blu Greenberg, *On Women and Judaism: A View from Tradition* (Philadelphia: Jewish Publication Society, 1981; reprint 1996).

13. See Eliezer Berkovits, *Jewish Women in Time and Torah* (Hoboken, N.J.: Ktav, 1990); Saul Berman, "The Status of Women in Halakhic Judaism," *Tradition* (fall 1973), pp. 5–28.

14. For more on this topic, see Shlomo Riskin, *Women and Jewish Divorce: The Rebellious Wife, The Agunah and the Right of Women to Initiate Divorce in Jewish Law: A Halakhic Solution* (Hoboken, N.J.: Ktav, 1989); Berkovits, *Jewish Women,* pp. 100–127.

15. See Rachel Adler, "The Jew Who Wasn't There: Halakhah and the Jewish Woman," *Davka* (summer 1972), pp. 7–16, reprinted in *On Being A Jewish Feminist: A Reader,* edited by Susannah Heschel (New York: Schocken, 1983), p. 15. This was written when Adler identified herself as Orthodox.

16. The exclusion of women from a *minyan* is argued on a number of grounds. See Aryeh Frimer, "Women and Minyan," *Tradition* 23:4 (summer 1988), pp. 54–77; see also an earlier abbreviated version of this paper, "The Status of Woman in *Halakhah*: Women and Minyan" (in Hebrew), *Or Hamizrah,* 34:1–2 (Tishrei 5746 [1985]), pp. 69–86.

17. See reference to Berkovits's discussion of this question in chapter 1 above, note 40.

18. See chapter 1 above, note 57, p. 256.

19. For some discussions of this phenomenon and the issues involved, see Berkovits, *Jewish Women in Time and Torah,* pp. 70–74; Berman, "The Status of Women in Halakhic Judaism"; David Feldman, "Women's Role and Jewish Law," *Conservative Judaism* 26:4 (summer 1972), pp. 29–39; Aviva Cayam, "Fringe Benefits: Women and Tzitzit", *Jewish Legal Writings by Women,* edited by Micah D. Halpern and Chana Safrai (Jerusalem: Urim, 1998), pp. 119–143; Aliza Berger, "Wrapped Attention: May Women Wear Tefillin," ibid., 75–119.

20. It is perhaps for this reason that compliance with the obligation of married women to cover their hair has gained popularity among Orthodox newlyweds in recent years, after several generations of relative neglect, even by women who are not especially meticulous about other demands of the halakhic dress code. The need for distinguishing marks of religious identity also explains the prevailing emphasis in Orthodox circles against women wearing pants—even under skirts, and even when obviously designed for women, so that such apparel cannot be construed as violating conditions of modesty or the ban on women wearing men's clothing. For demonstra-

tion of the possible influence of this sociological function upon contemporary hala-khic rulings, see R. Ovadya Yosef, *Yabia Omer 6, Yoreh Deah* (1976), *simman* 14, in which he develops at length the argument that women's pants do not fall under the category of men's garb, yet in what appears to be a legal non sequitur nevertheless ends up strongly recommending that women be restricted to skirts.

21. The desirability of teaching a woman Torah is debated in the Talmud. Ben Azzai regards this as a father's obligation, whereas R. Eliezer likens it to teaching her lewdness (see BT *Sotah* 21b). According to Rashi, R. Eliezer implies that she will use her knowledge of Torah unscrupulously. Although the issue was never settled defini-tively, the dominant view for many centuries was that of R. Eliezer. For a brief sketch of some of the relevant halakhic sources, see Rachel Biale, *Women and Jewish Law,* pp. 29–41. For a survey of the gradual growth of more permissive attitudes toward women's Torah study, see Shoshana Pantel Zolty, *"And All Your Children Shall Be Learned": Women and the Study of Torah in Jewish Law and History* (Northvale, N. J.: Jason Aronson, 1997), pp. 55–95.

22. For additional details regarding the founding of the Beth Jacob network and its subsequent development, see Zolty, *"And All Your Children,"* pp. 263–300; Naomi G. Cohen, "Women and the Study of Talmud," Tradition 24:1 (fall 1988), pp. 28–37, reprinted in *Women and the Study of Torah: Essays from the Pages of Tradition,* edited by Joel B. Wolowelsky (Hoboken, N.J.: Ktav, 2001), pp. 6–12.

23. For an interesting contrast to a parallel phenomenon in contemporary Is-lamic culture, see Saba Mahmood's discussion of the women's mosque movement and its feminist implications, in "Feminist Theory, Embodiment, and the Docile Agent: Some Reflections on the Egyptian Islamic Revival," *Cultural Anthropology* 16:2 (2001), pp. 202–236.

24. For a survey of two similar educational endeavors initiated within the newly developing religious Zionist community in Palestine prior to the establishment of the State of Israel, see Lilach Rosenberg-Friedman, "The Genesis of Religious-Zionist Education for Girls," in *Women in Judaism: Discussion Papers,* no. 10, edited by Tova Cohen (Ramat Gan: Bar-Ilan University, 2002).

25. Such agreements stipulate conditions in the marriage contract, such as retroactive annulment of the marriage under certain conditions, investing power of divorce with the rabbinic courts (in Israel) or secular courts (in the Diaspora), or im-posing stiff financial sanctions on a husband reluctant to grant a divorce. The legal viability of these and other options is hotly debated in Orthodox circles. See Riskin, *Women and Jewish Divorce,* pp. 134–151; Yoram Kirsh, *Mahapeikhot Bahalakhah* (Or Yehuda: Maariv, 2002), pp. 246–264.

26. For an empathetic account of this phenomenon among Orthodox Jewish and Christian women, see Christel J. Manning, *God Gave Us the Right: Conservative Catholic, Evangelical Protestant, and Orthodox Jewish women Grapple with Femi-nism* (New Brunswick/London: Rutgers University Press, 1999).

27. Menachem Brayer, *The Jewish Woman,* 2:151.

28. Lisa Aiken, *To Be A Jewish Woman* (Northvale, N.J.: Jason Aronson, 1993), pp. 29–30.

29. All Jews who are not descended through the male line from the Levites and priests of Temple times are considered Israelites.

30. Essentialist arguments are similarly invoked by Moslem apologists. See Mu-hammad Abdul-Rauf, *The Islamic View of Women and the Family* (New York: R. Speller, 1979). They are also a prevalent theme in the writing of many Catholic apol-ogists, who contend that women's unique physiology renders them as naturally suited for more domestic roles.

31. This line of defense is especially popular with regard to the laws of family

purity. See Norman Lamm, *A Hedge of Roses: Jewish Insights into Marriage and Married Life* (New York: Feldheim, 1987); H. E. Yedidyah Ghatan, *The Invaluable Pearl: The Unique Status of Women in Judaism* (New York: Bloch Publishing, 1986); Zev Schostak, *A Guide to the Understanding and Observance of the Jewish Family Laws* (Jerusalem: Feldheim, 1971).

32. Brayer, *The Jewish Woman*, 2:147–153; Yehudah Amital, "Fundamental Problems in the Education of Women" (in Hebrew), in *Haisha Vehinukhah: Asufat Maamarim Behalakhah Ubemahshavah*, edited by Ben Zion Rosenfeld (Kfar Sabba: Amana, 1990), p. 165.

33. Mordecai Peron, "The Jewish Concept of Family" (in Hebrew), in *Mishpahot Bet Yisrael* (Jerusalem: Misrad Hahinukh, 1976), p. 275 (my translation).

34. Rabbi A. I. Kook, *Iggerot Hareayah* (Jerusalem: Machon al shem R. Zvi Yehuda Kook, 1984), 4:14, 50–53.

35. See the Aish Hatorah website at aish.com/societywork/women/rights vs. right.asp (discussion on May 10, 2001).

36. For some samples of Aristotelian influence, see Grossman, *Hassidot Umordot*, pp. 26–30.

37. Regarding Maimonides' use of this distinction as the basis for different valuing of the two sexes, see Susan Shapiro, "A Matter of Discipline: Reading for Gender in Jewish Philosophy," in *Judaism Since Gender*, edited by Miriam Peskowitz and Laura Levitt (New York: Routledge 1997), pp. 158–173.

38. See for example, *Iggeret Hakodesh*, attributed to Nachmanides, Charles Ber (Hayim) Chavel edition (Jerusalem: Mosad Harav Kook, 1963), p. 331, in which it is stated that the form of man imprints its influence on the matter of woman via his thoughts and fantasies during the act of sexual intercourse, thus establishing the nature of the new life that is conceived.

39. Aaron Soloveitchik, *Logic of the Heart, Logic of the Mind: Wisdom and Reflections on Topics of Our Times* (Jerusalem: Genesis, 1991), pp. 94–95.

40. See Shaul Lieberman, *Tosefta Ki-Fshutah*, on *Berakhot*, chap.6, pp. 38–39, s. v. "hayavot bemitzvot."

41. BT *Berakhot* 17a.

42. The Maharal still understands women's exemption from time-bound *mitzvot* to reflect their function as matter (see, for example, *Gur Aryeh* on Gen.1:23, regarding the creation of man, and in his *Hiddushei Aggadot* to *Kiddushin* 70a [s.v. "Amar Rava"], where he likens woman to the moon, which absorbs the light of the sun), but his view of matter is more benign than that of classic Aristotelianism, devoid of the wild and unruly qualities that it represented for some medievalists. He contends that women's innate passivity renders them more naturally receptive to the formative influence of Torah—as opposed to men, who require the extra control provided by such *mitzvot* to quell their turbulent nature and achieve spiritual perfection. For more extensive discussion of the Maharal's view of women, see Ben Zion Rosenfeld, "The Maharal: A Chapter in the Theory of the Soul of Man and Woman" (in Hebrew), in his *Haisha Vehinukhah*, pp. 103–123.

43. Samson Raphael Hirsch, *Commentary to Leviticus* (New York: Judaica, 1971), pp. 711–712.

44. Samson Raphael Hirsch, *Judaism Eternal*, vol. 2, chap.2, translated by Dayan Grunfeld (London: Soncino Press, 1960); reprinted in *A Torah View on Woman . . . and on Women's Lib* (Oak Park, Mich.: Rabbi A. Freedman, 1990), pp. 13–14.

45. See Rabbi A. I. Kook's defense of his objection to giving women suffrage in the first elections of the Jewish *yishuv* in 1920, in *Iggerot Hareayah*, 4:10–12, 14–15. 50–53; Z. Y. Kook, "The Power of Woman within the Human Species" (in Hebrew), *Haisha Vehinukhah*, p. 56

46. Z. Y. Kook, "The Power of Woman," p. 58.

47. Ibid., pp. 57–58.

48. Ibid., p. 58.

49. Whether women are permitted to recite "Blessed are You, O Lord, our God
. . . who has sanctified us through His *mitzvot* and *commanded* us [. . . *asher kideshanu bemitzvotav vetzivanu]* to [perform x]" if and when performing *mitzvot* voluntarily was and still is debated. The debate is ostensibly with regard to the possibility of reconciling the voluntary nature of women's performance with the literal
meaning of the blessing, which stresses the obligatory nature of the act. But the debate may also be taken in part as a reflection of the more general ambivalence regarding women's increased participation in the regimen of *mitzvot*. Those halakhic
authorities that follow the Sephardic tradition forbid recital of the blessing for fear
that this might fall under the legal category of a blessing recited in vain. In contrast,
most Ashkenazic authorities promote women's recital of the blessing. For a summary of the legal principles involved in this debate, see Noa Jesselsohn, "Women and
the Fulfillment of Positive Time-Bound Commandments," *JOFA Journal* (fall 1999),
pp. 2–6.

50. Emanuel Rackman, "Arrogance or Humility in Prayer," *Tradition* 1:1 (fall
1958), p. 17; Lamm, *A Hedge of Roses*, p. 76.

51. S. R. Hirsch on Lev. 23:23, in *The Pentateuch: Translation and Commentary*
(London: Judaica , 1967).

52. This is quite simply stated in the *Tosefta* on *Berakhot* 6 (see above chapter 1,
notes 39 and 40). This stance may also have initially evolved out of a polemical opposition to Christianity, which abolished the distinction between slave, woman, and
heathen. Paul, in his Letter to the Galatians (3:28), declares that under Christ,
"There is neither Jew nor Greek, there is neither bond nor free, there is neither male
nor female." See Joseph Tabori, "The Blessings of Self-Identity and the Changing
Status of Women and of Orthodoxy," *Kenishta* (2001), pp. 107–138. See also Yitzhak Elbogen, *Hatefilla BeYisrael Behitpathutah Hahistorit* (Jerusalem, 1972),
p. 70. According to the above hypothesis, the original formulation of the benediction
is evidence of a rabbinic wish to keep these distinctions alive. Paul's statement may
indirectly reflect Christianity's denial of the role of sexuality in human life, as opposed to the rabbinic emphasis on the power of the sexual drive and the consequent
necessity of keeping it under control.

53. David ben Yosef Abudraham, *Siddur shel Hol* (Jerusalem: 1963), pp. 39–40.
This explanation was previously given by an earlier authority, R. Jacob ben Asher, in
the *Tur, Orah Hayim* 46.

54. Rayna Batya's husband was Rabbi Naftali Zvi Yehuda Berlin (one of the
leading Lithuanian rabbis of the nineteenth century, better known as the Natziv, who
headed the yeshiva of Volozhin for forty years), and her grandfather was R. Hayyim
of Volozhin (founder of that famous yeshiva).

55. R. Boruch Epsztejn [Epstein], *Mekor Barukh,* part four, chap. 46, sec. 3
(Vilna: Rom, 1928), p. 981. The significance of this memoir is discussed in Don See-
man, "The Silence of Rayna Batya: Torah, Suffering, and Rabbi Barukh Epstein's
'Wisdom of Women,'" *Torah Umadda Journal* 6 (1995–96), pp. 91–128; idem, "Like
One of the Whole Men," *Nashim* 2 (1999), pp. 52–94. It is worth noting that the
chapter devoted to Rayna Batya in Epsztein's book was heavily censored in the re-
vised English edition, *My Uncle the Netziv* (Brooklyn: Mesorah/Jerusalem: Artscroll,
1988), translated by Moshe Dombey and N. T. Erline, omitting her protest against
the blessing of "shelo asani isha" and all other expressions of bitterness against the
ideological priority given to study and performance of *mitzvoth* by males in rabbinic
Jewish circles of her day.

56. See his commentary to the prayer book: *Olat Reiyah* I (Jerusalem: Mosad Harav Kook, 1985), pp. 71–72.

57. S. R. Hirsch, *Judaism Eternal* (London: Soncino, 1960), 2:49–96; E. Munk, *Olam Hatefillot* (Jerusalem: Mosad Harav Kook, 1978), 1:36; A. Soloveitchik, "The Torah's View of the Role of the Woman," in *Logic of the Heart, Logic of the Mind: Wisdom and Reflections on Topics of our Times* (Jerusalem: Genesis, 1991), pp. 92–97.

58. Z. Y. Kook, "The Power of Woman, p. 57.

59. See his commentary to Genesis 1. Abarbanel nevertheless emphasizes that Eve was created from Adam's rib, and not his feet, nor his head, so as not to appear either as the servant or as the mistress of the household.

60. R. Avraham ben R. David (the Ravad), *Baalei Hanefesh,* edited by Y. Kapach (Jerusalem, 1965), pp. 14–15; R. Levi ben Gershom (Gersonides, otherwise known as the Ralbag) in his commentary to the Torah in Genesis, *Mikraot Gedolot* edition (Jerusalem: Keter, 1997), p. 45. For further sources in this vein, see Grossman, *Hassidot Umordot,* pp. 26–31.

61. For further elaboration of this position and sources, see Avi Weinrott, *Feminism Veyahadut* (Tel Aviv: Yedioth Aharonoth 2001), pp. 31–42.

62. Levinas understands the second opinion brought in the Talmud—that *tzella* means rib—as referring only to sexual relations, in which woman is subordinate. Because "real humanity does not allow for an abstract equality, without some subordination of terms," there had to be some form of hierarchy between the sexes, but this does not affect the basic equity between them. Emmanuel Levinas, "And God Created Woman," in *Nine Talmudic Readings,* translated by Annette Aronowicz (Bloomington: Indiana University Press, 1994), p. 173. See also his essay, "Judaism and the Feminine," *Difficult Freedom: Essays in Judaism,* translated by Sean Hand (Baltimore: Johns Hopkins University Press, 1990), pp. 30–38. For similar accounts in Christianity and Islam, see *Eve and Adam: Jewish, Christian and Moslem Readings on Genesis and Gender,* edited by Kvam Kristen et al. (Bloomington: Indiana University Press, 1999).

63. Z. Y. Kook, "The Power of Woman within the Human Species," p. 57.

64. The following is a partial list of sources for this principle in the writings of R. Shneur Zalman of Lyadi, the founder of Chabad Hassidism: *Torah Or* (Zhytomir: Hananya Lifa, 1862), pp. 30, 43–44, 72–73, 93–94; *Likkutei Torah* (Vilna: Ylm"z, 1884) *Leviticus,* pp. 34, 37–38; *Numbers,* pp. 6, 70, 72–73, 81–82; *Deuteronomy,* pp. 25–27, 35, 74–76; *Song of Songs,* pp. 9–11, 14–17.

65. The notion of the future reversal of women's status features prominently in the prayer books of the Kabbalists in the context of what intentions (*kavvanot*) are called for when blessing the new moon. See, for example, R. Shneur Zalman of Liady, *Likkutei Torah* (Zitomir, 1843), on Shir Hashirim, p. 19, third column; idem, *Torah Or* (Brooklyn, N.Y., 1948), end of *Parshat Vayigash,* beginning with the words: *uletosefet biur bema shelamadnu al pi vayigash,* etc. See also R. Zaddok Hacohen, *Kometz Haminha,* part 2, simman 68.

66. R. Kalonymous Kalamish Shapiro, *Esh Kodesh* (Jerusalem, 1960), p. 183. For a more exhaustive discussion of the relationship to women in Hassidic thought, and further sources, see Nehemia Polen, "Miriam's Dance: Radical Egalitarianism in Hassidic Thought," *Modern Judaism* 12:1 (1992), pp. 1–21. These ideas may reflect an aftermath of Sabbatian influence. See Ada Rapaport-Albert's massive essay, "On the Position of Women in Sabbatianism" (in Hebrew), in *Hehalom veshivro: Hatenuah Hashabbetait Usheluhoteha: Meshihiyut, Shabbetaut uFrankism* (Jerusalem: Hebrew University Institute of Jewish Studies, 2001), 1: 143–329.

67. Rabbi Kalonymous Kalman Epstein, *Maor Vashemesh* (on *Shemot* 15, *Shirat Hayam*), third *drasha*. Compare with R. Tzaddok Hacohen, *Tzidkat Hatzaddik* (Jerusalem, 1968), 213–215, beginning with "beyadua deyesh iggulim veyosher."

68. Rabbi A. I. Kook, *Orot Hakodesh* (Jerusalem: Mosad Harav Kook, 1985), 1: 143–144.

69. See, for example, T. Frankiel, *The Voice of Sarah: Feminine Spirituality and Traditional Judaism* (New York: Biblio, 1990); Tehilla Abramov. *The Secret of Jewish Femininity: Insights into the Practice of Taharat Hamishpachah* (translated from the Hebrew) (Southfield, Mich.: Targum/Feldheim, 1988); *The Modern Jewish Woman: A Unique Perspective* (Brooklyn, N.Y.: Lubavitch Educational Foundation for Jewish Marriage Enrichment, 1981); Alyse Fisher Roller, *The Literary Imagination of Ultra-Orthodox Jewish Women: An Assessment of a Writing Community* (Jefferson, N.C.: McFarland, 1999).

70. See Debra Renee Kaufman, *Rachel's Daughters: Newly Orthodox Jewish Women* (New Brunswick/London: Rutgers University Press, 1991), and Lynn Davidman, *Tradition in a Rootless World: Women Turn to Orthodox Judaism* (Berkeley and Los Angeles: University of California Press, 1991). Both studies demonstrate that many secular women are drawn to Orthodoxy not primarily because of religious belief, but because it gives them "space" and respect for bearing and raising children. While feminism has given them great expectations for what they could achieve, in an untransformed society these expectations are not met.

71. Mishnah *Shabbat* 2:6.

72. According to Jewish law, sexual relations and all physical contact between husband and wife are forbidden during the course of her menstrual flow and for seven "clean" days following, after which she must immerse herself in a ritual bath before resuming normal conjugal relations.

73. Tehilla Abramov, *Two Halves of a Whole: Torah Guidelines for Marriage* (Jerusalem: Targum/Feldheim, 1994), p. 51.

74. Jody Myers and Jane Rachel Litman, "The Secret of Jewish Femininity: Hiddenness, Power and Physicality in the Theology of Orthodox Women in the Contemporary World," in *Gender and Judaism: The Transformation of Tradition*, edited by Tamar Rudavsky (New York: New York University Press, 1995), pp. 51–77. Most of my account here is a digest of their findings.

75. Myers and Litman, "The Secret," p. 70.

76. In Lurianic Kabbalah as appropriated by Hassidic thought, creation begins with the establishing of boundaries in an act of self-contraction and separation, which is subsequently annihilated by a remerging with the infinite divine reality.

77. Myers and Litman, "The Secret," p. 53.

78. Ibid., pp. 58–61.

79. For further insights on the constructive potential of apologetics, as well as some interesting ramifications upon women's issues illustrated by incorrect application of apologetics, see Shaul Magid, "Walking Softly On/With the Law: Apologetic Thinking and the Orthodox/Conservative Debate," *Conservative Judaism* (2002), pp. 29–52.

80. See the literature listed in Susan Okin, "Women and the Making of the Sentimental Family," *Philosophy and Public Affairs*, 11 (1982), p. 72 n.18.

81. Lawrence Stone, *The Family, Sex and Marriage in England, 1500–1800* (New York: Harper and Row, 1977), chap. 8; Randolph Trumbach, *The Rise of the Egalitarian Family* (New York: Academic Press, 1978), chap. 3. Feminist critics, however, doubt whether the ideal of the sentimental family ever really bore the intention of changing the hierarchical structure within the family. In actuality, it merely provided fresh justification for the subordination of women by dividing between the

spheres of the family and the general community more strictly than ever before, and associating women primarily with the home. See Okin, "Women and the Making of the Sentimental Family," pp. 73–88.

82. Adler, "The Jew Who Wasn't There," p. 12.

83. Myers and Litman, "The Secret," p. 64.

84. Ibid., p. 66.

85. Adler, "The Jew Who Wasn't There," pp. 12–18. For a similar critique of conservative apologetics, pungently expressed in the form of "role reversal fantasy," see Rita Gross, "Steps toward Feminine Imagery of Deity in Jewish Theology," in Heschel, ed., *On Being a Jewish Feminist,* pp. 238–240.

86. Taped excerpt from her talk, "Inviting Men (and Women) into the Orthodox Feminist Experience," at the third international conference on Feminism and Orthodoxy (February 2000).

3. Exploring Halakhic Malleability and Its Limits (pp. 49–59)

1. Michael Berger, *Rabbinic Authority* (New York: Oxford University Press, 1998), p. 9.

2. Ibid., pp. 8–9.

3. The example brought by Maimonides in his classic definition of such rulings is the infliction of flagellation and other punishments, even in cases where such penalties are not warranted by the law, if—in the court's opinion—religion will thereby be strengthened. This law cannot bind future generations. The same may be said for temporary abrogation of a positive or negative command of the Torah, in order to bring the multitudes back to Torah observance. See *MT, Hilkhot Mamrim* 2:4.

4. Belonging to this category are directives for mourning the destruction of the Temple or for improving the lot of socially disadvantaged groups, such as orphans, divorcees, and debtors.

5. For example, the legal category called *muktzeh,* applied to objects whose normal use is forbidden on the Sabbath; since they may not be moved, virtually all contact with them is also forbidden on that day.

6. One example of this was the tolerance by *poskim* of medieval Ashkenaz for women's practice of donning jewelry on the Sabbath, despite the fact that this conflicted with their ruling that as a form of carrying it was prohibited. Leniency in this and other cases may have involved recognition on the part of the rabbis that community practice often reflected alternative mores established in the Palestinian Talmud, even though these conflicted with rulings in the superseding Babylonian tradition. See Yisrael Ta-Shema, *Halakhah, Minhag Umeziyut BeAshkenaz, 1000–1359* (Jerusalem, 1996), especially the introduction. A more extreme example was the condoning by some leading tosafists of parents slaughtering their children (for the sake of sanctifying God's name) rather than allowing them to fall into the hands of the Crusaders. See Haym Soloveitchik, "Religious Law and Change: The Medieval Ashkenazic Example," *AJS Review: The Journal of the Association for Jewish Studies* 12:8 (fall 1987), esp. pp. 200–209.

7. See BT *Pesahim* 66a.

8. For an exemplary illustration of this dynamic, see Jacob Katz, *Exclusiveness and Tolerance: Studies in Jewish-Gentile Relations in Medieval and Modern Times* (New York: Schocken, 1973); idem, *The "Shabbes Goy": A Study in Halakhic Flexibility* (Philadelphia: Jewish Publication Society, 1989).

9. See Joel B. Wolowelsky's summary of these issues in *Women, Jewish Law and Modernity: New Opportunities in a Post-Feminist Age* (Hoboken, N.J.: Ktav, 1997),

pp. 34–42 (grace after meals), pp. 32–34 (*kiddush*), pp. 29–31 (*mayim aharonim*). See also Ari Z. Zivotofsky and Naomi T. S. Zivotofsky, "What's Right with Women and *Zimmun*," *Judaism* 168:42:4 (fall 1993), pp. 453–463.

10. See chapter 2 above, note 49, p. 263.

11. Even at cost of overriding a general ban on playing musical instruments on religious festivals for this purpose.

12. For further references regarding this issue, see chapter 2 above, note 19, p. 260.

13. See his *Mayim Hayim*, vol. 1 (Tel Aviv: 1991), responsum 28, p. 128.

14. As defined by the fourteenth-century Manoah of Narbonne, author of the *Sefer Manoah*, and quoted by R. Joseph Caro in his commentary to *MT, Kesef Mishneh* (*hametz umatzah*) 7:8, an important woman is one who has no husband whom she must serve; is the head of her household; is creative and productive; is the daughter of the generation's leading scholar; or has maids and servants who relieve her from the duties of preparing and serving the meal, which would otherwise take precedence over her duty to recline.

15. See Rashbam's commentary on BT *Pesahim* 108a.

16. Halevi, *Mayim Hayim*, responsum 28, p. 128.

17. See Ovadiah Yosef, *Yehaveh Daat* (Jerusalem, 1981), vol. 3, *simman* 51 and vol. 4, *simman* 15. For a halakhic survey of the question of *kol isha*, see Saul Berman, "Kol Isha," in *Rabbi Joseph H. Lookstein Memorial Volume*, edited by Leo Landman (New York: Ktav, 1980), pp. 45–66.

18. See Yehiel Yaakov Weinberg, *Seridei Esh*, vol. 2 (Jerusalem: Mosad Harav Kook, 1977), responsum 8, pp. 13–17.

19. See Ben-Zion Uziel, *Mishpetei Uziel Bepiskei Hazman* (Jerusalem: Mosad Harav Kook, 1977), no. 44, pp. 228–234.

20. Menahem M. Schneersohn, "Women's Obligation in the Study of Torah and Education" (in Hebrew) speech delivered on Lag Baomer (April 13, 1990); published in *Kfar Habad Newsletter* 430 (Iyar 5750) (April 21, 1990), pp. 5–7.

21. See the celebrated but very controversial decision of R. Moshe Feinstein in his *Iggerot Moshe*, part one, *Even Haezer* 10 and 71. For a radical extension of the opportunity afforded by this decision to the case of unmarried women, see Dvora Ross, "Artificial Insemination in Single Women" (in Hebrew), in *Jewish Legal Writings by Women*, edited by Micah Halpern and Chana Safrai (Jerusalem: Urim, 1998), pp. 45–72.

22. For one version of this proposal, see Shlomo Riskin, *Women and Jewish Divorce* (Hoboken, N.J.: Ktav, 1989), pp. 134–142. In the first edition of this book, the proposal is attributed (on p. 140) to J. David Bleich, who is generally opposed to halakhic innovation.

23. An appraisement procedure appears in *halakhah* and is applied by Maimonides (in *MT, Hilkhot Sanhedrin* 24:1) to monetary matters: A judge, he says, may come to a decision by relying on those—including women—whom he deems trustworthy. For further discussion of this issue, see Emanuel B. Quint, "The Role of Women in the Beth Din System," in his *A Restatement of Rabbinic Civil Law* (Northvale, N.J: 1993), 1:4–17.

24. See Joel Roth, *The Halakhic Process: A Systemic Analysis* (New York: Jewish Theological Seminary, 1986), pp. 231–315.

25. These senses of the term have become popularized in the legal theory of Ronald Dworkin. See his "The Model of Rules," *University of Chicago Law Review* 14 (1967), p. 35.

26. For more detailed discussion of the meaning of this principle and examples of the manner in which it and others like it were invoked as rationale for abrogating even biblical law, see Roth, *The Halakhic Process*, pp. 169–204.

27. For a survey of legal principles invoked by rabbinic authorities in order to overcome distinctions between Jew and Gentile for the practicing physician, see M. Farbowitz, "The Responsibility of the Jewish Physician in Jewish Law," *The Pharos* 2 (1994), pp. 28–33.

28. R. Aaron ben Avraham of Worms, *Meorei Or (Shabbat, Berakhot, Eruvin = Be-er Sheva)* (Metz: n.p., 1819), 4:20a. The suggestion that this blessing be recited silently has resurfaced in recent years (see Joel Wolowelsky, *Women, Jewish Law and Modernity,* pp. 75–84); idem, "Who Has Not Made Me a Woman: A Quiet Berkha," *Tradition* 29/4 (1995), pp. 61–68 and the response of Emanuel Feldman, "An Articulate Berakha," op. cit, pp. 69–74.

29. Weinberg, *Seridei Esh,* vol. 2, responsum 8.

30. Israel Meir Hakohen (Kagan), *Likutei Halakhot; Sotah* 20b.

31. Maimonides, *MT, Hilkhot Talmud Torah* 2:4.

32. Moshe Sternbuch, *Emunah VeTorah* (Bnei Brak: Agudat Netivot HaTorah Vehahessed, 1979), p. 72. For a contrasting and more positive reaction to present-day violation of this *halakhah* as it appears in the *Shulhan Arukh, Yoreh Deah,* 245: 20–21, see Hayim Hirschensohn's stand in *Sefer Malki Bakodesh* (St. Louis: Moynester, 1919), part 2, responsum 5, pp. 16–17, and Eliezer Schweid's discussion of Hirschensohn's views in his *Demokratiyah Vehalakhah: Pirkei Iyun Bemishnato shel Harav Hayim Hirschensohn* (Jerusalem: Magnes, 1978), pp. 96–98.

33. For an exposition of the various views and references to their sources, see Avi Sagi, *Elu Ve'elu: Mashmauto shel Hasiah Hahilkhati: Iyun Besifrut Yisrael* (Tel Aviv: Hakibbutz Hameuhad, 1996); Yohanan Silman, "The Divine Torah That 'Is Not in Heaven'—A Typological Analysis" (in Hebrew), *Bar-Ilan Yearbook* 22–23 (Ramat Gan: Bar-Ilan University, 1987), pp. 261–287; Yohanan Silman, *Kol Gadol Velo Yasef: Torat Yisrael bein Shelemut Lehishtalmut* (Jerusalem: Magnes, 1999); Aaron Kirshenbaum, "Subjectivity in Rabbinic Decision-Making," in Sokol, ed., *Rabbinic Authority and Personal Autonomy;* David Weiss-Halivni, "On Man's Role in Revelation," in *From Ancient Israel to Modern Judaism: Intellect in Quest of Understanding—Essays in Honor of Marvin Fox,* vol. 2, edited by J. Neusner, Ernest S. Frerichs, and Nahum Sarna (Atlanta, Ga.: Scholar's Press, 1989).

34. As pointed out by Silman, *Kol Gadol Velo Yasef,* p. 263.

35. In the same vein, consider the radically antispiritualist statement of the Rabbis that since the destruction of the Temple, God has nothing in His world beyond the four cubits of *halakhah.* This is not meant as rival to the many halakhic deliberations that take into account various extralegal considerations; rather, it should be read as the attempt to establish the primacy and stability of the legal system, in the face of the dangers of disintegration with the loss of political power at the time.

36. Jay Michael Harris has written a masterly historical survey of this dynamic: *How Do We Know This? Midrash and the Fragmentation of Modern Judaism* (Albany: State University of New York Press, 1995).

37. Regarding the cause and implications of the relative absence of Orthodoxy among Sephardic Jewry, see, however, the exchange between Zvi Zohar and Benjamin Brown, in *Akdamot* 10 and 11 (Jerusalem: Bet Morasha, 2000, 2001). While Zohar considers a more relaxed attitude to *halakhah* inherent to the Sephardic halakhic tradition and indicative of possible alternative reactions to the threat of modernity, Brown sees in it no more than the lack of exposure to this threat. He concludes that once such exposure intensifies, some form of Orthodoxy becomes inevitable.

38. Michael Silber, "The Emergence of Ultra-Orthodoxy: The Invention of a Tradition," in *The Uses of Tradition: Jewish Continuity in the Modern Era,* edited by Jack Wertheimer (New York: Jewish Theological Seminary, 1994), p. 26 n.4; see also chapter 1 above, note 115, p. 259.

39. Bleich, *Contemporary Halakhic Problems* (New York.: Ktav, 1977), 1:83.
40. Ibid.

4. The Meta-Halakhic Solutions of Modern Orthodoxy
(pp. 60–70)

1. Michael Silber, "The Emergence of Ultra-Orthodoxy: The Invention of a Tradition," in *The Uses of Tradition: Jewish Continuity in the Modern Era*, edited by Jack Wertheimer (New York: Jewish Theological Seminary, 1994), pp. 50–59.

2. Ibid., pp. 25–26.

3. See *Shulḥan Arukh, Oraḥ Hayim* 62:2; 101:4.

4. See R. Yehiel Michal Epstein, *Arukh Hashulhan, simman* 62:4.

5. Silber, "The Emergence of Ultra-Orthodoxy," p. 24. But see also Benjamin Brown, "A Typology of Five Classes of Stringency in Modern Times: The Hatam Sofer; R. Zvi Elimelekh of Dinnov; R. Yosef Yozel Horwitz of Nevardehok; R. Yitzhak Zev Soloveitchik of Brisk; The Hazon Ish" (in Hebrew), in *Iyyunei Halakhah Umishpat, Lichvod Professor Aaron Kirschenbaum (Dinnei Yisrael 20–21 [2000–2001])*, pp. 123–237, and especially pp. 176–177, where Brown takes issue with the tendency of some scholars to overrate the novelty of such tendencies to stringency, seeing in them merely a difference in degree and not in kind.

6. Silber, "The Emergence of Ultra-Orthodoxy," p. 57.

7. This slogan is a clever wordplay on a talmudic ruling. The word translated as "innovation" (*ḥadash*) refers in the talmudic context to the new seasonal crop of wheat, which is forbidden by the Torah until the first *omer* offering has been brought to the Temple on the second night of Passover (see Lev. 23:12).

8. For a sample of popular exposition of this approach in response to feminist demands, see Yissocher Frand, "Where There's a Rabbinic Will, There's a Halakhic Way—Fact or Fiction?" in *Home and Heart: Reflections of the World of the Jewish Woman—Collected from the Pages of the Jewish Observer*, edited by Sarah Schapiro (New York: Artscroll/Mesorah, 1993), pp. 138–160.

9. See R. Moshe Feinstein's introduction to his *Iggerot Moshe* (New York: Moriah, 1959), in which he overcomes his anxiety about the possibility of erring in his halakhic decision-making as whatever the halakhic authority decides is ipso facto Torah, even when it falls short of the truth. The same notion is expressed by R. Menahem Hameiri in the introduction to *Bet Habehira* on BT *Berakhot*, edited by S. Dickman, p. 23; by Rabbenu Nissim of Gerona in *Drashot Haran*, no. 7; by Rabbi Aryeh Leib Heller in the introduction to his *Ktzot Hahoshen*; and by R. Moshe Sofer in *Torat Moshe* on Deuteronomy 17:11.

10. BT *Niddah*, 20b; *Sanhedrin* 6b; *Baba Batra* 130b.

11. Jackson draws attention to biblical accounts of the adjudication of both kings and the judges appointed by them, which stress direct divine inspiration rather than recourse to a divine text. Pursuing this line of argument, Jackson suggests that the notion of the divinely inspired judge did not disappear with the constraints imposed by a written text. See Bernard Jackson, "*Mishpat Ivri*, *Halakhah* and Legal Philosophy: Agunah and the Theory of 'Legal Sources,'" *JSLI—Jewish Studies, An Internet Journal* (www.biu.ac.il/JS/USLJ/I-2002/Jackson.pdf), pp. 24–27. Relying upon evidence cited by Hanina Ben Menachem in *Judicial Deviation in Talmudic Law: Governed by Men, Not by Rules* (London: Harwood Academic Publishers, 1991), Jackson (p. 25) considers approximately thirty instances where the talmudic judge decided a case "not in accordance with the *halakhah*" as testimony to survival of the conception of the judicial role as based upon direct divine inspiration rather written texts.

12. See Ben Menachem, *Judicial Deviation*, "Postscript: The Judicial Process and the Nature of Jewish Law," in *The History and Sources of Jewish Law*, edited by N. S. Hecht et al. (Oxford: Clarendon, 1996), pp. 421–437, concluding at 434f. that "we are justified in doubting the sufficiency of the modern, Western concept of law for the purposes of describing the *halakhah*."

13. As Jackson acutely observes, one may argue that the lack of formal incorporation of this policy of relying on charismatic rather than rational authority "is precisely in line with its very nature." *"Mishpat Ivri,"* p. 25.

14. For an extensive discussion of the concept of *da'at Torah* as a tool of anti-modernism, see Lawrence Kaplan, *"Daas Torah:* A Modern Conception of Rabbinic Authority," in Sokol, ed., *Rabbinic Authority and Personal Autonomy*, pp. 1–61.

15. For further exposition, see Aharon Lichtenstein, "Does Jewish Tradition Recognize an Ethic Independent of Halakhah?" in *Modern Jewish Ethics: Theory and Practice*, edited by Marvin Fox (Columbus: Ohio State University Press, 1975), pp. 62–63 and corresponding note 2 on pp. 83–84; reprint, in *Contemporary Jewish Ethics*, edited by M. Kellner (New York: Sanhedrin, 1978).

16. For one suggestion, see David Hartman, *Maimonides: Torah and Philosophic Quest* (Jewish Publication Society, 1976), pp. 102–138. It is worth noting that Maimonides himself most likely regarded this distinction as a pragmatic rather than historical truth. He was no doubt aware that nearly every instance of law that he attributes to Moses, and that ipso facto should be free of debate for this reason, was known to be contested. See Jacob Levinger, *Darkhei Hamahshava Hahilkhatit shel HaRambam* (Jerusalem: Magnes, 1965), chapter 2, and especially p. 65.

17. S. R. Hirsch was one of the first to make the distinction between Torah and *derekh eretz* clearly in the nineteenth century; the latter referred to the particular culture of the surrounding society. Hirsch's main thesis was that the Torah can adjust itself to any positive cultural system into which Jews are thrust.

18. For more extensive discussion of this debate and its implications, see Aaron Lichtenstein, "Does Jewish Tradition Recognize an Ethic Independent of *Halakhah?*" pp. 62–68.

19. For some of the classic expositions of legal positivism, see John Austin, *The Province of Jurisprudence Determined* (New York: Noonday, 1954); H. Kelsen, *General Theory of Law and State* (New York: Russell and Russell, 1961); H. L. A. Hart, *The Concept of Law* (Oxford: Clarendon, 1961).

20. In theory, it certainly is possible to combine positivist or nonpositivist theories regarding the source of law with formalist or nonformalist theories regarding legal procedure. Nevertheless, in Anglo-American legal theory, positivism has usually been construed broadly, so as to appropriate some of the assumptions of formalism as well. For greater clarification of these terms and their legal usage, see Yair Lorberbaum and Hayim Shapiro, "Maimonides' 'Epistle on Martyrdom': The Hartman-Soloveitchik Debate in the Light of Legal Philosophy" (in Hebrew), *Al Olamo Vehaguto shel David Hartman: Mehuyavut Yehudit Mithadeshet*, edited by Avi Sagi and Zvi Zohar (Tel Aviv: Hakibbutz Hameuhad, 2001), 1:357–364.

21. In *The Halakhic Process: A Systemic Analysis* (New York: Jewish Theological Seminary, 1986), p. 234 n.7, Joel Roth takes the position that overarching principles are, strictly speaking, extralegal inasmuch as they are not among the systemic principles—those which govern the process by which the system works. The debate between the formalists and the nonformalists reflects similar differences of opinion in the past regarding the talmudic notion of "beyond the letter of the law" (*lifnim meshurat hadin*). Is this notion to be regarded as merely a complementary standard outside the bounds of *halakhah*, or as a necessary addition to an insufficient standard, which is sometimes normatively binding? For further reference to these debates in the history of

Jewish thought and support of a nonformalist view, see Moshe Halbertal, *Mahapek-hot Parshaniyot Behithavutan: Arakhim Keshikulim Parshaniyim Bemidrashei Hala-khah* (Jerusalem: Magnes, 1997). See also Lorberbaum and Shapiro, "Maimonides' 'Epistle on Martyrdom,'" for further illustration of the implications of this debate.

22. A few *poskim*, most notably—but not exclusively—Sephardic ones, have tended toward greater leniency in the modern period, viewing the practice of women's hair covering as dependent on context and the mores of the surrounding society. For a listing and discussion of some of the relevant sources, see Lynne Shrei-ber, "What Is Hair?" in *Hide and Seek: Jewish Women and Hair Covering,* edited by Lynne Shreiber (New York/Jerusalem: Urim Publications, 2003), pp. 27–33; Erica Brown, "'A Crown of Thorns':Orthodox Women Who Chose Not to Cover Their Hair," ibid., pp. 183–195.

23. For details regarding the finer gradations of piety denoted by various modes of covering, see Barbara Goldman Carrel, "Hasidic Women's Head-Covering: A Fe-minized System of Hasidic Distinction," in *Religion, Dress and the Body,* edited by Linda B. Arthur (Oxford: 1999), pp. 163–180.

24. Leila Leah Bronner, "From Veil to Wig: Jewish Women's Hair Covering," *Ju-daism* 42:4 (fall 1993), pp. 465–478.

25. For illustration of the impact of such considerations on halakhic ruling, see Norma Baumel Joseph, "Hair Distractions: Women and Worship in the Responsa of Rabbi Moshe Feinstein," *Jewish Legal Writings by Women,* edited by Micah D. Hal-pern and Chana Safrai (Jerusalem: Urim Publications, 1998), pp. 9–22; Rivkah Slo-nim, "Blessings from Above and Blessings from Below: The Lubavitcher Rebbe on *Kisui Rosh,*" in Schreiber, *Hide and Seek,* pp. 164–177. For further discussion of the debate surrounding this issue, see Ariel Pikar, "The Decisions of R. Ovadya Yosef in Light of Changing Dress Norms" (in Hebrew), *Tarbut Yehudit Be'ein Hasearah: Sefer Yovel Lichvod Yosef Ahituv,* edited by Avi Sagi and Nahem Ilan (Hakibbutz Hameuhad, 2002), pp. 592–625, and especially pp. 605–619.

26. For more extensive discussion of R. Soloveitchik's view of halakhah, see Lawrence Kaplan, "Rabbi Joseph B. Soloveitchik's Philosophy of Halakhah," *Jewish Law Annual* 7 (1998), pp. 139–197.

27. Joseph B. Soloveitchik, *Halakhic Man* (Philadelphia: Jewish Publication Soci-ety, 1983).

28. This distinction between the teaching of the Rav and its subsequent develop-ment by several of his disciples was drawn by Eli Holzer in a lecture delivered at the third international conference on Feminism and Orthodoxy, in New York (February 2000).

29. Moshe Meiselman, "The Rav, Feminism and Public Policy: An Insider's Overview," *Tradition* 33:1 (1998), pp. 7–8.

30. Haym Soloveitchik, "Religious Law and Change," *AJS Review: The Journal of the Association for Jewish Studies* 12:8 (fall 1987), p. 205.

31. The distinction between purely technical halakhic applications and those that are not value-free was not invented by the formalists of Modern Orthodoxy. A similar observation was already made by R. Salanter, founding father of the *musar* movement, who distinguished between the elements of erudition (*bekiut*) and acuity (*harifut*), and that of judgment (*shikkul daat*), all of which enter into the process of halakhic deliberation. See his "Essay on the Clarification of Character Traits" (in He-brew), in *Kitvei R. Yisrael Salanter,* edited by Mordechai Pachter (Jerusalem: Mosad Bialik, 1972), pp. 144–145, and Hillel Goldberg's exhaustive analysis in *Israel Sa-lanter: Text, Structure, Idea* (New York: Ktav, 1982), pp. 118–129. R. Salanter be-lieved that one can neutralize the subjective element in judgment for straight techni-cal questions; for moral issues that involve one's powers of the soul, however,

subjectivity cannot be avoided. Thus decisions about moral affairs are necessarily relative and do not always reveal the original intent of the text. Accordingly, the followers of *musar,* as the ultra-Orthodox Hassidim before them, invoke the principle of faith in the sages (*emunat hakhamim*) and rabbinic consensus (*da'at Torah*) in order to encourage reliance upon the judicial discretion of the halakhic authorities. But in their call for clearly distinguishing between pure halakhic decisions and public policy decisions, many contemporary formalists seem to be interested in the opposite: in militating against a totally unbridled position of legal realism that imposes no limits on the judicial powers of the *posek.*

32. See Maimonides' famous line of defense for the Torah's acceptance of sacrifice as an acceptable form of religious worship, in his *Guide for the Perplexed* III:32.

33. Rabbi Saul Berman, in his taped lecture at the third international conference on Feminism and Orthodoxy (February 2003): Power, Authority, and Rabbinic Persuasion. See also his contribution: "Reshut: Individual Discretion in *Halakhah,*" *JOFA Journal* 2:4 (winter 2001), pp. 4–5, for his description of the latitude provided to women by discretionary areas of *halakhah.*

5. Does Positivism Work? (71–99)

1. For additional reference to differences between the original learning revolution initiated by Sarah Schenirer and the Beth Jacob educational system and the more recent innovations, see Shoshana Pantel Zolty, *"And All Your Children Shall Be Learned": Women and the Study of Torah in Jewish Law and History* (Northvale, N.J.: Jason Aronson, 1997), pp. 263–309; Naomi G. Cohen, "Women and the Study of Talmud," *Tradition* 24:1 (fall 1988), pp. 28–37, reprinted in *Women and the Study of Torah: Essays from the Pages of Tradition,* edited by Joel B. Wolowelsky (Hoboken, N.J.: Ktav, 2001), pp. 6–12.

2. For a fairly updated listing and brief characterization of those institutions that cater to Israelis, see Tamar El-Or, *BaPesach Haba: Nashim Veoreyanut Batziyonut Hadatit* (Tel Aviv: Am Oved, 1998), pp. 28–29, forthcoming in English translation: *Next Year I Will Know More: Literacy and Identity Among Young Orthodox Women in Israel* (Detroit: Wayne State University Press).

3. See Avraham Grossman, *Hassidot Umordot: Nashim Yehudiyot BeEiropa Biyemei Habeinayim* (Jerusalem: Mercaz Shazar, 2001), pp. 312–315; Zolty, *"And All Your Children,"* pp. 174–175.

4. For further discussion of this phenomenon, its halakhic aspects, and historical development, see Ailene Cohen Nusbacher, "Efforts at Change in a Traditional Denomination: The Case of Orthodox Women's Prayer Groups," *Nashim* 2 (1999), pp. 95–112; Rivka Haut, "Women's Prayer Groups and the Orthodox Synagogue," in *Daughters of the King* (Philadelphia: Jewish Publication Society, 1992), pp. 135–157; Avraham Weiss, *Women at Prayer: A Halakhic Analysis of Women's Prayer Groups* (Hoboken, N.J: Ktav, 1990).

5. Maimonides High School, founded by Rabbi Soloveitchik in Boston, conducted coed Torah studies. In a letter to Rabbi Leonard Rosenfeld on May 27th, 1953, Rabbi Soloveitchik writes: "As to your question with regard to a curriculum in a coeducational school, I expressed my opinion to you long ago that it would be a very regrettable oversight on our part if we were to arrange separate Hebrew courses for girls. Not only is the teaching of Torah she be-al peh to girls permissible but it is nowadays an absolute imperative. This policy of discrimination between the sexes as to subject matter and method of instruction which is still advocated by certain groups within our Orthodox community has contributed greatly to the downfall of

traditional Judaism. Boys and girls alike should be introduced into the inner halls of Torah she be-al peh." My thanks to Joel Wolowelsky for alerting my attention to this missive, and to Ezra Rosenfeld for sharing it with me.

6. Maimonides High School, founded by Rabbi Soloveitchik in Boston, conducted coed Torah studies.

7. Abba Bronspigl, "Women-Only Minyanim" (in Hebrew), *Hadarom* 54 (Sivan 5745 [1985]), *Orah Hayim*, responsum 56, p. 246; Hershel Schacter, "With Regard to Synagogue Matters" (in Hebrew), *Or Hamizrach* (Tishrei 5746 [1985]), pp. 328–332; idem, "Go Forth in the Footsteps of the Sheep" (in Hebrew), *Beit Yitzhak* (5745 [1985]), pp. 118–134.

8. As reported by E. J. Kessler, "Who's Afraid of Orthodox Feminism?" *Forward* (February 25, 2000).

9. Mayer Twersky, "Halakhic Values and Halakhic Decisions: Rav Soloveitchik's Pesak Regarding Women's Prayer Groups," *Tradition* 32:3 (spring 1998), pp. 6–9.

10. Ibid., pp. 8 and 10–13.

11. Ibid., p. 13. A more nuanced formula for spreading the net of *halakhah* over lacunae, while still remaining within a formalist conception of law, is suggested by Rabbi Aaron Lichtenstein. In "Does Jewish Tradition Recognize an Ethic Independent of *Halakhah*?" he contends that despite the distinction between *halakhah* (which works according to clear-cut rules that are operative in all situations) and morality (which works according to principles that are much looser and more contextual), the *halakhah* itself demands application of moral principles in areas that are beyond its direct and explicit jurisdiction. This demand effectively eliminates the possibility of neutral areas beyond the realm of halakhic determination.

12. Moshe Meiselman, "The Rav, Feminism and Public Policy," *Tradition* (fall 1998), p. 9.

13. Ibid., p. 20.

14. Ibid., pp. 26–28.

15. Mayer Twersky, "A Glimpse of the Rav," *Tradition* 30:4 (summer 1996), pp. 98–99; reprinted in Wolowelsky, *Women and the Study of Torah.*

16. Moshe Meiselman, *Jewish Women in Jewish Law* (New York: Ktav/Yeshiva University Press, 1978), p. 40.

17. For one account of this controversy, see Lawrence J. Kaplan, "Revisionism and the Rav: The Struggle for the Soul of Modern Orthodoxy," *Judaism* 48:3 (1999), pp. 290–311; idem, "The Multi-Faceted Legacy of the Rav: A Critical Analysis of R. Hershel Schachter's '*Nefesh ha-Rav,*'" *BDD* 7 (1998), pp. 51–85.

18. Aryeh and Dov Frimer, "Women's Prayer Services: Theory and Practice," *Tradition* 32:2 (1998), pp. 5–118.

19. Ibid., pp. 37–39.

20. See Aaron Lichtenstein, "Fundamental Problems in the Education of Women" (in Hebrew), in *HaIsha Vehinucha: Asufat Maamarim Behalakhah Ubemahshavah,* edited by Ben Zion Rosenfeld (Kfar Sabba: Amana, 1990), pp. 158–160; Yehiel Weinberg, *Seridei Esh,* vol. 2, responsum 8.

21. It should be noted that although Leibowitz is using well-known halakhic terms, he is not using them in the precise sense in which they are employed in the classical literature. For my critique of Leibowitz regarding this point, see Tamar Ross, "The Status of Woman in Judaism: Several Reservations Regarding the Stance of Leibowitz" (in Hebrew), in *Yeshayahu Leibowitz: Olamo Vehaguto,* edited by Avi Sagi (Jerusalem: Keter, 1995), p. 151.

22. Here Leibowitz turns on its head Kant's castigation of Judaism as heteronomously motivated law for a canonical community, celebrating this as Judaism's greatest religious virtue.

23. Leibowitz, "The Status of Women: Halakhah and Meta-Halakhah," in *Judaism, Human Values, and the Jewish State,* edited and translated by Eliezer Goldman et al. (Cambridge. Mass.: Harvard University Press, 1995), pp. 128–129.

24. Leibowitz's opinion (as Meiselman's) could be based on a questionable extension of Maimonides' notion that a gentile may not observe a *mitzvah* such as the Sabbath, even if his observance of it falls on another day of the week. For, as Maimonides says, "One does not allow him to innovate a religion and perform commandments for himself" *(MT, Hilkhot Melakhim* 10:9).

25. Yeshayahu Leibowitz, "The Status of Women," p. 129.

26. Eliezer Berkovits, *Jewish Women in Time and Torah* (Hoboken, N.J.: Ktav, 1990).

27. Ibid., p. 76.

28. Berkovits, *Jewish Women,* pp. 88–92. See also Joel Wolowelsky's treatment of the halakhic issues involved in *Women, Jewish Law and Modernity* (Hoboken, N.J.: Ktav, 1997), pp. 34–42; and Rochelle Millen, "Social Attitudes disguised as Halakhah: *Zila Milta, Ein Havrutan Na'ah, Kevod Hatzibbur,*" *Nashim* 4 (fall 2001), pp. 183–188.

29. Berkovits, *Jewish Women,* p. 80. See also R. Yehiel Weinberg, *Seridei Esh,* vol. 3 (Jerusalem: Mosad Harav Kook, 1977), responsum 93, p. 297.

30. Appraisement procedure appears in *halakhah* and is applied by Maimonides (in *Laws of Sanhedrin,* chap. 24, para. 1) to monetary matters, regarding which a judge may—in Maimonides' opinion—make up his mind by relying on persons he deems trustworthy, including women. For further discussion of this issue, see Emanuel B. Quint, "The Role of Women in the Bet Din System," in *A Restatement of Rabbinic Civil Law* (Northvale, N.J.: Jason Aronson, 1993), 1:4–17.

31. Berkovits, *Jewish Women,* pp. 65–67.

32. Ibid., pp. 111–124. See also his *Tenai Benissuin Uveget* (Jerusalem: Mosad Harav Kook, 1967).

33. For one version of this proposal, see Rabbi Shlomo Riskin, *Women and Jewish Divorce* (Hoboken, N.J.: Ktav, 5788/1989), pp. 134–142. In the first edition of this book, the proposal is attributed to Rabbi J. David Bleich; see p. 140.

34. Berkovits, *Jewish Women,* pp. 59–60.

35. Saul Berman, "The Status of Women in Halakhic Judaism," *Tradition* 14 (fall 1973), pp. 5–28.

36. Ibid., p. 20.

37. BT *Hagigah* 16b; *Sifra Vayikra,* parshetah 2.

38. In a lecture delivered at the joint Edah-Lavi conference in Jerusalem during Sukkot 2002.

39. See above, note 21, p. 273.

40. For further elaboration, see my "The Status of Women in Judaism," in Sagi, ed., *Yeshayahu Leibowitz,* pp. 148–162.

41. As Rabbi Menachem M. Schneerson seems to do. See his *Likkutei Sihot, Parshat Emor, Erev Lag BaOmer* (1990), "On the Obligation of Jewish Women in Education and Study of Torah," pp. 171–175. For further elaboration of R. Schneerson's advocacy of women's Torah study, see Susan Handelman, "Women and the Study of Torah in the Thought of the Lubavitcher Rebbe," in *Jewish Legal Writings by Women,* edited by Micah Halpern and Chana Safrai (Jerusalem: Urim, 1998), pp. 143–179. For further discussion of Schneerson's position, and of similar distinctions introduced by modern *poskim* so as to expand halakhic latitude for women's learning, see Zolty, *"And All Your Children,"* pp. 81–95.

42. Wolowelsky, *Women, Jewish Law and Modernity,* p. 85. For a more general review of this issue in a manner sympathetic to Orthodox women's interests, see pp. 84–90.

43. See *Eshnav Lehayehen shel Nashim Behevrot Yehudiyot,* edited by Yael Atzmon (Jerusalem: Mercaz Shazar, 1995), pp. 21–22.

44. For some discussion of this anomaly, see Zolty, *"And All Your Children,"* pp. 23–30.

45. In her taped lecture, "Rabbinic Backlash Against Women's Prayer Groups: The Use and Abuses of Meta-Halakhah," at the third international conference on Feminism and Orthodoxy (February 2000).

46. Ibid.

47. The phenomenon of wives supporting their husbands' learning is not unknown in Jewish tradition, but in the past this was reserved for exceptional cases rather than being the norm.

48. BT *Kiddushin* 35a.

49. BT *Megillah* 23b. Some women have wryly suggested that according to this textual logic perhaps only *evil* men should be included. It is also of interest to note the commentary of the Keli Yakar (by Ephraim Solomon ben Aaron of Luntshits) to the passage in Numbers 13:2 ("Send *thee* men to scout the land"), in which he cites a midrash stating that God bowed to Moses' opinion on this score against His better judgment. According to this midrash, God recognized that it would have been preferable to send women to spy on Canaan, who had already demonstrated through the words of the daughters of Tzelofhad that the land was dear to their hearts.

50. Aryeh A. Frimer, "Women and Minyan," *Tradition* 23:4 (summer 1988), p. 60.

51. BT *Kiddushin* 29b.

52. BT *Kiddushin* 36a.

53. For further instances, see Chana Safrai and Avital Hochstein's forthcoming work, *"Ein Li Ela Ish*: Inclusive and Exclusionary Readings in Tannaitic *Mishnah"* (in Hebrew).

54. For a fuller discussion of this issue, see Maya Leibowitz, "Be Fruitful and Multiply and Fill the Land" (in Hebrew), in *Barukh Sheasani Isha? Ha'isha Bayahadut—MehaTanakh vead Yameinu,* edited by David Ariel, Maya Leibowitz, and Yoram Mazor (Tel Aviv: Yedioth Aharonoth, 1999), pp. 129–137.

55. Mishnah 6:6.

56. See chapter 1 above, note 60, p. 256.

57. As established in Mishnah *Kiddushin* 1:7.

58. BT *Eruvin* 27a; BT *Kiddushin* 33b–34a.

59. See chapter 1 above, notes 45 and 46.

60. BT *Eruvin* 27a; BT *Kiddushin* 33b–34a.

61. Deuteronomy 17:14 and the commentary of the *Sifrei.*

62. For classical rationalizations of the acceptance of Devorah the prophetess as judge, see Tosafot *Baba Kama* 15a; Tosafot *Shavuot* 29b. See also BT *Megillah* 14b, for an example of rabbinic discomfort with the authority granted to her and the prophetess Huldah.

63. See chapter 1, note 57, p. 256.

64. For further discussion regarding the exclusionary function of *kevod hatzibbur, zila milta,* and *ein havrutan na'ah,* see Rochelle Millen, "Social Attitudes Disguised as Halakhah," pp. 178–197. This analysis of three social principles is accompanied by a more profound critique of their anachronistic or generally unwarranted halakhic application.

65. This example was brought by Debby Koren in a lecture at the third international Feminism and Orthodoxy conference. On purely formal grounds, if a woman has not recited the *maariv* service for Sabbath evening (which she is not obligated to do), then her obligation to recite *kiddush* is, contrary to popular opinion, greater than that of her husband who has already done so in the evening service. Therefore,

it is actually halakhically preferable that she recite *kiddush* for herself and all others participating in the meal. Acknowledgment of this appears in the halakhic compendium of Rabbi Yehoshua Y. Neuwirth, *Shemirat Shabbat: A Guide to the Practical Observance of the Sabbath,* vol. 2, translated from the second edition of the Hebrew by W. Grangewood (Jerusalem: Feldheim, 1984–2000), chapter 47:39; women are advised to recite the *maariv* prayer in order to avoid this situation.

66. Whether or not the *mitzvah* of *tefillin* is time-bound has been questioned. Scripture indicates that the main object of this *mitzvah* is to serve as a general reminder of God's commands, with no reference to any particular time (Deut. 11:18). Moreover, though *tefillin* are usually donned in the morning, talmudic tradition allows for the possibility of observing this *mitzvah* throughout the day. The argument that it is a time-bound *mitzvah,* due to the fact that there are certain days and hours when donning *tefillin* is prohibited (night, Shabbat, and festivals) has been debated since the tannaitic period. If including *tefillin* in the category of time-bound *mitzvot* is problematic, then so is excluding women from the obligation on the basis of this categorization. For a more expansive discussion of the applicability of this *mitzvah* to women, see Aliza Berger, "Wrapped Attention: May Women Wear Tefillin?" in Halpern and Safrai, eds., *Jewish Legal Writings by Women,* pp. 75–119.

67. Bet Yosef, *Orah Hayim,* section 38.

68. Although the aspect of ritual impurity involved in women's menstrual flow does not appear to be the issue (see Weiss, *Women at Prayer,* pp. 87–98), the question whether this is the cause for halakhic concern regarding women's ability to maintain bodily cleanliness in the ordinary physical sense is a matter of debate. For arguments discounting of the equation between menstruation and uncleanliness, particularly in today's hygienic conditions, see Aliza Berger, "Wrapped Attention: May Women Wear Tefillin?" in Halpern and Safrai, eds., *Jewish Legal Writings by Women,* pp. 91–93.

69. For more extensive discussion of this argument and the reasoning offered in objection, see Berger, ibid., pp. 104–113.

70. The notion of *misahum yoharah* applies particularly in the case of *tzitzit:* since men's obligation to wear *tzitzit* is already voluntary (given the fact that they could refrain from wearing a four-cornerd garment), women who assume this time-bound *mitzvah* essentially take on a double option. In spite of this objection, it is noteworthy that Rabbi Moshe Feinstein offered a qualified ruling permitting women to wear a *tallit* during prayer, on condition that their motives are pure. See his *Iggerot Moshe, Orah Hayim,* part 4, responsum 49.

71. Meiselman, "The Rav, Feminism, and Public Policy," pp. 9–10.

72. Aryeh and Dov Frimer, "Women's Prayer Services," p. 41.

73. Meiselman and the Frimers cite this story to illustrate that the opposition to women's prayer groups is based on the suspicion that the drive behind them is primarily the wish to score feminist points rather than bona fide religious zeal. (In contrast is R. Weinberg's ruling allowing the innovation of *bat mitzvah* celebrations based on the more charitable assumption that the impetus is for the sake of *mitzvah* [*l'shem mitzvah*]. See Wolowelsky, *Women, Jewish Law and Modernity,* pp. 51–52.)

74. David Bleich, *Contemporary Halakhic Problems* (New York: Ktav, 1977), 1: 83, regarding moves by the Conservative movement to change the status of women in the synagogue.

75. Haym Soloveitchik, "Rupture and Reconstruction: The Transformation of Contemporary Orthodoxy," *Tradition* 28:4 (1994), pp. 64–129.

76. As one WTN participant queried, would he have responded in like manner if the woman had asked to take on the optional *mitzvah* of reciting a blessing on a cit-

ron (*etrog*) during Sukkot? Would he *then* have suggested that she first bless over a ritually blemished fruit three times before being allowed to bless over a genuinely kosher one?

77. See Aaron Lichtenstein's example, in "The Human and Social Factor in Halakha" *Tradition* 36:1 (2002), p. 8, of a major sixteenth-century *posek* who protested Rabbi Joseph Caro's decision not to allow blind men *aliyot* to the Torah. A similar example is recounted in BT *Kiddushin* 31a.

78. Maimonides rules, in *MT, Hikhot Talmud Torah* 1:13, that a woman who studies Torah merits reward, although not one equal to that of a man, because of the principle that he who is commanded merits greater reward.

79. Yeshayahu Leibowitz, "The Status of Women," p. 128.

80. Quoted by Wolowelsky in *Women, Jewish Law, and Modernity*, p. 31.

81. As does Meiselman, in the name of Rabbi Soloveitchik, particularly in the area of prayer; see "The Rav, Feminism, and Public Policy," pp. 11–18.

82. I have heard the same complaint voiced by Palestinian feminists. When their female pleaders encourage Arab women to appeal to the Israeli secular courts in matters of personal status, their opponents contend that such recourse is politically damaging to the Islamic cause. As the feminists see it, the first to be sacrificed on the altar of Arab nationalism are the women.

83. A classic example of rabbinic ingenuity in the effort to overcome the morally intolerable consequences of dry application of the law is the well-known story in the Palestinian Talmud of the man who went to sea for a year and returned to find his wife pregnant (cited by the Rosh in his commentary on *Kiddushin* 4:7, in the name of the author of *Halakhot Gedolot*). In order to clear the infant of the stigma of illegitimacy, the rabbis raised the possibility that the husband had returned to his wife during the year via theurgic use of the divine name.

84. For one expression of this view, see David Hartman, *A Heart of Many Rooms: Celebrating the Many Voices Within Judaism* (Woodstock, Vt.: Jewish Lights, 1999), pp. 20–23.

85. Louise McNay, *Foucault and Feminism* (Cambridge: Polity Press, 1992); *Feminism and Foucault*, edited by Irene Diamond and Lee Quinby (Boston: Northeastern University Press, 1988).

86. Peggy Reeves Sanday, *Female Power and Male Dominance: On the Origins of Sexual Inequality* (Cambridge: Cambridge University Press, 1981), pp. 9 and 50; Denise Carmodie, "Judaism," in *Women in World Religions*, edited by Arvind Sharma (Albany: State University of New York Press, 1987), pp. 183–206; Jacob Neusner, *Method and Meaning in Ancient Judaism*, Brown Judaica Studies, no. 10 (Missoula, Mont.: Scholars Press, 1979), pp. 96–99; Yael Atzmon, "Judaism and the Exclusion of Women from the Public Sphere" (in Hebrew)—the introduction to Atzmon. ed., *Eshnav Lehayehen shel Nashim Behevrot Yehudiyot*, pp. 13–39; Judith Romney Wegner, "Woman and the Public Domain," in *Chattel or Person? The Status of Women in the Mishnah* (New York: Oxford University Press, 1988), pp. 145–167.

87. Presented in taped lecture form at the third international Feminism and Orthodoxy conference.

88. Rochelle Millen, "Social Attitudes Disguised as Halakhah," p. 185.

89. See J. Wolowelsky's review of this issue in *Women, Jewish Law and Modernity*, pp. 84–90, where he quotes Rabbi Aaron Soloveitchik's plea for leniency: "Nowadays, when there are Jews fighting for equality for men and women in matters such as *aliyot*, if Orthodox rabbis prevent women from saying Kaddish when there is a possibility for allowing it, it will strengthen the influence of Reform and Conservative rabbis. It is therefore forbidden to prevent daughters from saying Kaddish." See also

R. Aaron Soloveitchik, *Od Yisrael Yosef Beni Hai* 32 (Chicago: Yeshivas Brisk, 1993), p. 100.

90. R. Yair Hayim Bachrach, *Havvot Yair,* responsum 222.

91. R. Shlomo Halevi Wahrman, *Sh'erit Yosef* (New York: Balsham, 1981), 2: 299f.; R. Israel Meir Lau, *Yahel Yisrael,* vol. 2 (Jerusalem, 5752 [1992]), responsum 90, p. 479.

92. R. Moshe Halevi Steinberg, *Mishberei Yam* (5752 [1992]), responsum 85, p. 96.

93. R. Menashe Klein, *Mishneh Halakhot,* vol. 1, *Tinyana* (5752 [1992]), responsum 650, p. 467. According to a minority opinion, women may even be included in a male *minyan* for the purposes of *megillah* reading. See Rachel Biale, *Women and Jewish Law: An Explanation of Women's Issues in Jewish Sources* (New York: Schocken, 1984), pp. 23–24; Wolowelsky, *Women, Jewish Law and Modernity,* pp. 94–98; Aryeh A. Frimer, "Women and Minyan," pp. 59–60.

94. Twersky, "Halakhic Values and Halakhic Decisions," p. 14.

95. See chapter 3 above, note 18, p. 267.

96. Mendel Shapiro, "*Qeri'at ha-Torah* by Women: A Halakhic Analysis," *The Edah Journal* 1:2 (Sivan, 2001) (www. Edah.org), p. 3.

97. See BT *Megillah* 23a and the commentary of R. David Fardo, *Hasdei David,* on Tosefta *Megillah,* chapter 3, *halakhah* 5.

98. In a taped lecture, "*Kevod Hatzibbur* (The dignity of the congregation): *Halakhah* and Public Policy," delivered at the fourth international Feminism and Orthodoxy conference (November, 2002).

99. A *baraita* in BT *Megillah* 23a may indicate reaction to a once prevalent practice: "Everyone goes up to read among the seven who read from the Torah, even a woman, even a minor. But the sages said: a woman may not read from the Torah [in public] because of *kevod hatzibbur.*" Another intimation is a thirteenth-century ruling by Rabbi Meir of Rotenburg that in a town made up entirely of priests (*kohanim*) with not a single Israelite, a priest will read two of the seven portions of the Torah and then women will read the rest (for it casts doubts upon the bona fide nature of *kohanim's* status if they are seen reading what is normally read only by non-priests). See Biale, *Women and Jewish Law,* pp. 27–28.

100. For exposition of feminist suspicions of this sort, see Mary Daly, *Beyond God the Father* (Boston: Beacon, 1973); Daphne Hampson, "Women, Ordination, and the Christian Church," in *Speaking of Faith: Cross-Cultural Perspectives on Women, Religion and Social Change,* edited by Diana Eck and Devakl Jain (New Delhi: Kali for Women, 1986), pp. 134–136.

101. Hartman Halbertal, in her taped lecture, "Rabbinic Backlash against Women's Prayer Groups."

102. Ibid.

6. Sociological and Historical Revisionism (pp. 103–124)

1. See, for example, Avraham Grossman, *Hassidot Umordot* (Jerusalem: Mercaz Shazar, 2002), pp. 206–207 and 496–497.

2. Judith Antonelli, *In the Image of God: A Feminist Commentary on the Torah* (Northvale, N.J.: Jason Aronson, 1997), p. xxviii.

3. Cynthia Ozick, "Notes Toward Finding the Right Question," in *On Being a Jewish Feminist,* edited by Susannah Heschel (New York: Schocken, 1983; 2d ed., 1995), p. 123.

4. For a fuller description of this trend in feminist thought, see Tova Hartman Halbertal, "Between Tradition and Change: The Meeting Between the Woman's

Voice and Authoritative Jewish Sources" (in Hebrew), *Rav-Goni* 3 (Jerusalem: Van Leer Institute, 2001), pp. 44–50.

5. See chapter 2 above, note 52, p. 263.

6. On this reading, Paul's statement in his Letter to the Galatians (3:28) is fundamental to the Christian outlook. Scholars who maintain that the original Christian intent was to grant women full participation in the Church also base their conclusion on the passage in Luke in which Jesus invites women together with men to learn and teach his gospel.

7. Leila Ahmed, *Women and Gender in Islam* (New Haven: Yale University Press, 1992); Aziza al-Hibri, "Women's Self-Identity in the Quran and Islamic Law," in *Windows of Faith: Muslim Women Scholar-Activists in North America,* edited by Gisela Webb (Syracuse, N.Y.: Syracuse University Press, 2000).

8. See Blu Greenberg, *On Women and Tradition* (Philadelphia: Jewish Publication Society, 1981; reprint, 1986), pp. 42–43.

9. Cynthia Ozick, "Notes Toward Finding the Right Question," pp. 142–151.

10. Notable is Chava Weissler's groundbreaking work on the spirituality of Ashkenazi women in the seventeenth and eighteenth centuries in central and eastern Europe as reflected by the *tkhines,* or petitionary prayers written for and by them; see her *Voices of the Matriarchs: Listening to the Prayers of Early Modern Jewish Women* (Boston: Beacon Press, 1998). More recently, Abraham Grossman's monumental *Hassidot Umordot* portrays the life of Jewish women in medieval times as straddling the fine line between greater piety and rebellion against traditional norms. And Ada Rapaport-Albert's research on the position of women in Sabbatianism reveals the surprising degree of female empowerment in the Sabbatian movement, most likely facilitated by its departure from the halakhic framework ("On the Position of Women in Sabbatianism" [in Hebrew], in *Hehalom Veshivro: Hatenuah Hashabbetait Usheluhoteha—Meshihiyut, Shabtaut Ufrankism* [Jerusalem: The Institute of Jewish Studies of Hebrew University, 2001], 1:143–329).

11. In Christianity, for example, Paul is sometimes regarded as the villain of the story: His pragmatic concern was that the church, still insecure in a pagan world, would cause scandal if it departed too far from the prevailing Greek-Roman social conventions; thus, overwilling to compromise the church's principles, he excluded women from positions of leadership and sacrificed their interests on the altar of his missionary zeal. Others discover historical layers even within Paulist teachings, claiming that certain nonegalitarian motifs to be found there are really later interpolations. Thus, some Christians will contend that the Corinthians passage in which Paul appears to speak of male hegemony, and in which it is said that women should be silent, was falsely attributed to him precisely in order to lend such ideas legitimacy.

12. Daniel Boyarin, *Carnal Israel: Reading Sex in Talmudic Culture* (Berkeley and Los Angeles: University of California Press, 1993), p. 9.

13. Daniel Boyarin, *Unheroic Conduct: The Rise of Heterosexuality and the Invention of the Jewish Man* (Berkeley and Los Angeles: University of California Press, 1997).

14. Judith Hauptman, "Feminist Perspectives on Rabbinic Texts," in *Feminist Perspectives on Jewish Studies,* edited by Lynn Davidman and Shelly Tenenbaum (New Haven: Yale University Press:, 1994), pp. 40–62; idem, *Rereading the Rabbis: A Woman's Voice* (Boulder, Colo.: Westview, 1998).

15. Neusner, in his latest book on this issue, *How the Rabbis Liberated Women* (Atlanta, Ga.: Scholars Press, 1998), reneges from the conclusions reached in his previous work, *Method and Meaning in Ancient Judaism,* Brown Judaica Studies, no. 10 (Missoula, Mont.: Scholars Press, 1979).

16. Hauptman is sympathetic to the findings of Christian feminist scholar, Elizabeth Schussler-Fiorenza, who suggests that Jesus' move away from the andocentric

focus of the Old Testament is merely the continuation of a more benevolent tendency and sympathetic attitude toward women developing in rabbinic Judaism; see Elizabeth Schussler-Fiorenza, *In Memory of Her: A Feminist Theological Reconstruction of Christian Origins* (New York: Crossroad, 1983; London: SCM Press, 1983). Hauptman believes, however, that owing to the popularity of Neusner's less charitable views of Mishnaic thinking, Schussler-Fiorenza failed to see to what degree Jesus' notions had already found expression in the Mishnah's legislative enactments, "which although not egalitarian, were certainly aimed at improving women's lives."

17. Hauptman, "Feminist Perspectives," p. 45.

18. Mekhilta to Exodus 19. 3. See also Uri Ehrlich, "'They Too Were Witness to That Miracle: The Evolution of an Egalitarian Argument in the World of *Halakhah*" (in Hebrew), in *Ayin Tova: Du-Siah Vepulmus Betarbut Yisrael—Sefer Hayovel le-Tova Ilan,* edited by Nahem Ilan (Hakibbutz Hameuchad: Neemanei Torah veAvoda, 1999), pp. 142–160.

19. Amnon Shapira, "On the Equal Status of Women in the Bible" (in Hebrew), *Bet Mikra* 159:44 (1999), pp. 309–337.

20. Theodore Friedman, "The Shifting Role of Women, From the Bible to Talmud," *Judaism* 36:4 (1987), p. 480.

21. Ibid., pp. 480–481.

22. Alongside other scholars, Friedman cites one piece of evidence for the beginnings of this regressive process in a *mishnah* that obviously predates the destruction of the Second Temple. According to *Sukkah* 5:2, "At the end of the first day of the Festival [Sukkot] they went down to the courtyard of the women and made a great improvement." Apparently the women's section, which had originally been open to the men's section and was situated just outside of it, was then enclosed with a partition. A *baraita* adds that eventually the women's section was moved above so as to prevent "levity" between the sexes. See ibid., p. 481. See also Shmuel Safrai, "Was There a Women's Gallery in the Synagogues of Antiquity?" (in Hebrew), *Tarbitz* 32 (1963), pp. 329–338; Shaye. J. D. Cohen, "Women in the Synagogues of Antiquity," *Conservative Judaism* 34:2 (1980), pp. 23–29; B. Brooten, *Women Leaders in the Ancient Synagogue* (Chico, Calif.: Scholars Press, 1982), pp. 103–138.

23. See Tikva Frymer-Kensky, "The Bible and Women's Studies," in *Feminist Perspectives on Jewish Studies,* edited by Lynn Davidman and Shelly Tenenbaum (New Haven: Yale University Press, 1994), pp. 23–24.

24. For a somewhat different and more detailed typology and critique of such exegetical strategies as developed by Christian feminist Bible scholars, see Heather A. McKay, "On the Future of Feminist Biblical Criticism," in *A Feminist Companion to Reading the Bible: Approaches, Methods and Strategies,* edited by Athalya Brenner and Carole Fontaine (Sheffield: Sheffield Academic Press, 1997), pp. 67–83.

25. Daphne Hampson, *Theology and Feminism* (Oxford: Basil Blackwell, 1990), pp. 25–29.

26. Antonelli, *In the Image of God.*

27. Phyllis Trible, *God and the Rhetoric of Sexuality* (Philadelphia: Fortress, 1978).

28. See Riffat Hassan, "The Issue of Gender Equality in the Context of Creation in Islam," in *Women's and Men's Liberation: Testimonies of Spirit,* edited by Leonard Grab, Hayim Gordon, and Riffat Hassan (New York: Greenwood, 1991).

29. Ilana Pardes, *Countertraditions in the Bible: A Feminist Approach* (Cambridge, Mass.: Harvard University Press, 1992)

30. Thus, for example, Boyarin understands two incidents recorded in the Tosefta, in which Beruria's halakhic opinion is validated by an important rabbinic authority, as against a male who disagrees with her, as records of some men's opposition to

women's exclusion from Torah study. See his "Rabbinic Resistance to Male Domination: A Case Study in Talmudic Cultural Poetics," in *Critical Jewish Hermeneutics*, edited by Steven Kepnes (New York: New York University Press, 1993), pp. 124–126.

31. For further examples of this technique, see Shulamit Valler, *Nashim Besifrut Hazal: HaTalmud HaBavli* (Tel Aviv: Hakibbutz Hameuhad, 1993).

32. Chana Safrai does this by comparing the development of variant readings of talmudic accounts of women. See "Women in the Bet Midrash: Challenge and Dispute" (in Hebrew), in *Ayin Tova*, pp. 160–179.

33. *Zohar Hadash*, Sulam edition, p. 78b, toward end; *Zohar, Vayera*, pp. 109a-111a. The same idea is developed by R. Moshe Hayim Luzzato; see *Kinat Hashem Tzvaot* (Warsaw, 1888), p. 17, where the redemptive value to be found in occasional breaking of sexual norms is specifically linked to women, as they are "the ground of the world." According to Luzzato, other types of halakhic transgressions may occasionally serve as redemptive even when committed by men, so long as they are recognized as emergency measures. For further discussion of this theme in Luzzato and his attempt to purge it of its antinomistic Sabbatian roots, see Isaiah Tishby, *Netivei Emunah Uminut: Massot Umehkarim Besifrut Hakabbalah VehaShabtaut* (Ramat Gan: Massada, 1964), pp. 169–185. Some sources view such transgressions, though necessary, as sinful in and of themselves; their merit is only because divine providence uses them to good effect. Others, however, attribute merit to the acts themselves, and to their agents when propelled by a prophetic vision of their redemptive value. The interest of feminist restorativists in such sources is not to build upon their antinomistic conclusions, but rather to highlight a preexisting appreciation in Jewish tradition for the corrective value of female insight precisely because of its connectedness to real life and the tension it reflects with the inadequacies of strictly formal halakhic norms.

34. See BT *Berakhot* 34b, which is only one of a cluster of *aggadot* dealing with this theme. For further discussion and sources, see Boyarin, *Carnal Israel;* Judith Abrahams, *The Women of the Talmud* (Northvale, N.J.: Jason Aronson, 1995); Valler, *Nashim Besifrut Hazal;* C. Safrai, "Women in the Bet Midrash."

35. BT *Taanit* 23b-24a; *Baba Batra* 74a; *Ketubot* 67b.

36. Daniel Boyarin is particularly candid about this. See, for example, the preamble in his introduction to *Carnal Israel*, pp. 18–23, or at the outset of "Rabbinic Resistance to Male Domination," pp. 118–119.

37. This term for the approach is coined by Daphne Hampson. See her *Theology and Feminism*, pp. 29–32.

38. W. V. O. Quine, *Word and Object* (Cambridge, Mass: MIT Press, 1960), pp. 58–59; see also Ronald Dworkin, *Law's Empire* (Cambridge, Mass: Harvard University Press, 1986), p. 53; G. Wilson, "Substance without Substrata," *Review of Metaphysics* 12 (1959), pp. 521–539.

39. This illustration is brought by Moshe Halbertal, *Mahapeikhot Parshaniyot* (Jerusalem: Magnes, 1997), p. 186, in the context of his discussion of the principle of charity.

40. Ozick, "Notes Toward Finding the Right Question," p. 150.

41. Ibid., p. 124.

42. See Rochelle Millen, "An Analysis of Rabbinic Hermeneutics: BT *Kiddushin* 34a," in *Gender and Judaism: The Transformation of Tradition*, edited by Tamar Rudavsky (New York: New York University Press, 1995), p. 35.

43. Daphne Hampson, *After Christianity* (London: SCM Press, 1996), p. 124.

44. Catherine Keller, *From a Broken Web: Separation, Sexism and Self* (Boston: Beacon Press, 1986), p. 42.

45. Ibid., p. 187.

282   Notes

46. Daphne Hampson, "Women, Ordination, and the Christian Church," in *Speaking of Faith: Cross-Cultural Perspectives on Women, Religion and Social Change*, edited by Diana Eck and Devakl Jain (New Delhi: Kali for Women, 1986), pp. 66–71.

47. Mary Daly, *Beyond God the Father: Toward a Philosophy of Women's Liberation* (Boston: Beacon, Press, 1985), pp. 11–12.

48. For a delightful feminist perspective on the biblical rendition, see the *midrash* written by feminist Quaker Marion McNaughton and cited by Daphne Hampson in *After Christianity*, pp. 138–140. For a few parallel symptoms of protest attributed to Sarah by Jewish *midrash*, see Yehudah Gellman, "And Sarah Died," *Tradition* 32 (1997), pp. 57–67.

49. Judith Plaskow, "Jewish Theology in a Feminist Perspective," in *Feminist Perspectives on Jewish Studies*, edited by Lynn Davidman and Shelly Tenenbaum (New Haven: Yale University Press, 1994), p. 76.

50. Clifford Geertz, "Religion as a Cultural System," in *Reader in Comparative Religion: An Anthropological Approach*, edited by William Lessa and Evon Vogt (New York: Harper and Row, 1965), pp. 205, 207, and 213. See also *Womanspirit Rising: A Feminist Reader in Religion*, edited by Carol P. Christ and Judith Plaskow (San Francisco, Calif.: Harper and Row, 1979), pp. 2–3; Judith Plaskow, "The Right Question is Theological," in Heschel, ed., *On Being a Jewish Feminist*, pp. 227–228.

51. Corroboration for this view is found particularly in the imagery used by the prophet Hosea. God likens Israel to a whoring woman, humiliates her with incessant rebukes, demands proof of her absolute loyalty in the fulfillment of inhuman requests, and does not allow her any avenue of escape, employing threats and bullying her so that she remains bound to him, even against her will. See Vicky Campo, "The Lamb of God—A Wolf in Sheep's Clothing: A Feminist Exegesis of the Love of God," prepublication paper for Laud International Symposium, Linguistic Agency University, GH Essen, Germany (1999); Naomi Graetz, *Silence is Deadly: Judaism Confronts Wifebeating* (Northvale, N.J.: Jason Aronson, 1991).

52. Yishai Rosen-Zvi and Dror Yinon, "Men's Ornaments—Women's Ornaments: A New Look at Women's Religious Obligations in the Thought of Hazal" (in Hebrew), forthcoming in *Af Hen Hayn Be'otah Haderekh*, an anthology edited by Chana Safrai.

53. Ruhama Weiss Goldman, "'I Want to Bind You in *Tefillin*': Women Adopting *Mitzvot* of Men" (in Hebrew), in *Barukh Sheasani Isha? Haisha Bayahadut: Meha Tanach vead Yameinu*, edited by David Ariel, Maya Leibowitz, and Yoram Mazor (Yedioth Aharonoth, 1999), pp. 105–121.

54. Judith Ochshorn, *The Female Experience and the Nature of the Divine* (Bloomington: Indiana University Press, 1981). Ochshorn claims that the integral connection between monotheism and patriarchy explains both why none of the monotheistic religions that are based on the notion of God as transcendent could entertain the notion of female priests and their strong taboos concerning women's biological functions. Recently some scholars have concluded that even among the ancient Hebrews, dissemination of the monotheistic message originally met with greater opposition than previously imagined. These scholars seek to reveal traces of resistance to this message and its social implications, especially among women still attached to their own polytheistic traditions who were brought to the Israelite kingdom in order to marry Jewish men . See Raphael Patai, *The Hebrew Goddess* (Detroit, Mich.: Wayne State University Press, 1990); Esther Fuchs, "The Literary Characterization of Mothers and Sexual Politics in the Hebrew Bible," in *Feminist Perspectives on Biblical Scholarship*, edited by Adela Yarbro Collins (Chico, Calif.:

Scholars Press, 1985), pp. 117–136; idem, "Who is Hiding the Truth? Deceptive Women and Biblical Androcentrism," in ibid., pp. 137–144.

55. For a brief description of this trend and some useful references, see Susannah Heschel's preface to *On Being a Jewish Feminist*, pp. xviii–xx (2d ed., 1995).

56. Adrienne Rich, *Of Women Born: Motherhood as Experience and Institution* (New York: Norton, 1976), pp. 149–150.

57. See, for example, Meryll Stone, *When God Was a Woman* (San Diego, Calif.: Harcourt Brace, 1976); Riane Eisler, *The Chalice and the Blade: Our History, Our Future* (San Francisco, Calif.: Harper and Row, 1987).

58. See Daphne Hampson, *Theology and Feminism*; idem, *After Christianity*; and Mary Daly, *Beyond God the Father*; idem, *Gyn/ecology: The Metaethics of Radical Feminism* (Boston: Beacon, 1978, 1990).

59. Daphne Hampson, *After Christianity*, pp. 254–285.

60. Ozick, "Notes Toward Finding the Right Question," pp. 133–138.

61. Plaskow, "The Right Question is Theological," p. 223.

62. Ibid., p. 224.

63. Ibid., p. 227.

64. Ibid. p. 228.

65. Ibid., pp. 231–232.

66. Judith Plaskow, "Standing Again at Sinai: Jewish Memory from a Feminist Perspective," *Tikkun* 1:2, pp. 28–29.

67. Marcia Falk, "Notes on Composing New Blessings: Towards a Feminist Jewish Reconstruction of Prayer," *Journal of Feminist Studies in Religion* 3 (spring 1987), p. 41; Janet Berkenfield, "Meditation on the *Shema*" (© 1987) in *Siddur Birkat Shalom* (Somerville, Mass.: Havurat Shalom Siddur Project, n.d.).

68. For a brief survey of some of the issues raised, see Annette Daum, "Language and Liturgy," in *Daughters of the King*, pp. 183–202; Jules Harlow, "Feminist Linguistics and Jewish Liturgy," *Conservative Judaism* 49:2 (1997), pp. 3–25.

69. Falk has done pioneering work in this direction. In transfiguring traditional blessings, Falk begins with "N'vareykh et eyn hahayim"—("Let us bless the source of life") rather than the conventional "Barukh ata Hashem Elokeinu Melekh Haolam"—("Blessed art Thou . . . King of the Universe"). See *The Book of Blessings* (San Francisco, Calif.: Harper, 1996).

70. Rita Gross, "Steps Toward a Feminine Imagery of Deity in Jewish Theology," in *On Being a Jewish Feminist*, pp. 234–247.

71. Plaskow, "The Wife/Sister Stories: Dilemmas of the Jewish Feminist," in Eck and Jain, eds., *Speaking of Faith*, pp. 118.

72. Ibid., pp. 119.

73. Plaskow, "The Jewish Feminist: Conflict in Identities," in *The Jewish Woman: New Perspectives*, edited by Elizabeth Koltun (New York: Schocken, 1976), pp. 8–10.

74. "Standing Again at Sinai: Jewish Memory from a Feminist Perspective," *Tikkun* 1:2, pp. 32–33.

75. See Tamar Ross, "Can We Still Pray to our Father in Heaven?" (in Hebrew), in *Ayin Tova*, pp. 264–278.

76. For a partial survey of ceremonial innovations on the part of Jewish feminists at large, see Shulamit S. Magnus, "Re-Inventing Miriam's Well: Feminist Jewish Ceremonials," in *The Uses of Tradition: Jewish Continuity in the Modern Era*, edited by Jack Wertheimer (Cambridge, Mass.: Jewish Theological Seminary, 1992), pp. 331–349.

77. For further elaboration, see Jody Myers,"The Midrashic Enterprise of Contemporary Jewish Women," in *Jews and Gender: The Challenge to Hierarchy*, edited by Jonathan Frankel (Oxford University Press, 2000), pp. 124–128.

78. Ibid.

79. A prime source for such examples is the feminist commentary to the weekly Torah reading produced by the Israeli Orthodox women's lobby, Kolech, and distributed in Modern Orthodox synagogues throughout the country. See also Rivka Lubitch, "Feminist Midrashim" (in Hebrew), in *Ayin Tova*, pp. 302–310; idem, "The Midrash of Dinah" (in Hebrew), in *Tarbut Yehudit Be'ein Hasearah*, edited by Avi Sagi and Nahem Ilan (Hakibbutz Hameuhad, 2002), pp. 742–754.

80. Jenny Kien, *Reinstating the Divine Woman in Judaism* (Universal Publishers/uPublish.com, 2000).

81. The contributing factors that Kien ascribes to the demise of matricentric culture include creating a role for men entering the clan of their wives in marriage, advancement of men to technological trades, the development of warlike culture, and the very emphasis on women's motherly powers, which led from reverence for their bodies to using them; see ibid., pp. 9–11. Another factor cited as a possible contributor to the affinity between patriarchy and Judaism (aside from its monotheistic theology) is the ethnic nature of the religion. See Denise Carmody, "Judaism," in *Women in World Religions*, edited by Arvind Sharma (Albany: State University of New York Press, 1987), pp. 183–184. The fact that Judaism is defined as a covenant between the Jewish people and God necessitates preservation and stability of the family in order to ensure the continuity of the biological lineage. This preserving required control of woman's sexuality, and the notion that authority over her passed directly from father to husband, without viewing her as a morally independent agent. It also led to defining women mainly in terms of their reproductive function.

82. Kien, *Reinstating the Divine Woman*, p. 204; for more favorable attitudes, see Judith Plaskow, *Standing Again at Sinai: Judaism from a Feminist Perspective* (San Francisco, Calif.: Harper, 1990), chapter 4; and Rachel Adler, *Engendering Judaism: An Inclusive Theology and Ethics* (Philadelphia: Jewish Publication Society, 1998), chapter 3.

83. Kien, *Reinstating the Divine Woman*, p. 199.

84. Ibid., p. 215.

85. Ilana Pardes, *Countertraditions in the Bible: A Feminist Approach* (Cambridge, Mass.: Harvard University Press, 1992); Carol Meyers, *Discovering Eve* (Oxford: Oxford University Press, 1988); idem, "Roots of Restriction: Women in Early Israel," *Biblical Archeology* 41:3 (1978), pp. 91–103; idem "Of Drums and Damsels: Women's Performance in Ancient Israel," *Biblical Archeology* 54:1 (1991), pp. 16–27.

86. Kien, *Reinstating the Divine Woman*, p. 164.

87. Ibid., pp. 200–201.

7. Evaluating Revisionism (pp. 125–144)

1. Mary Daly, "Post-Christian Theology: Some Connections Between Idolatry and Methodolatry, Between Deicide and Methodicide" (address given at the annual meeting of the American Academy of Religion, 1973), as reported by Judith Plaskow in *Standing Again at Sinai: Judaism from a Feminist Perspective* (San Francisco, Calif.: Harper, 1990), p. 14.

2. It is instructive to note the highly conflicting notions about women to be derived from the creation story: Ozick finds the one significant biblical assertion of equality there whereas Frymer-Kensky views it as a notable exception to the rule of a biblical gender blindness more favorable to women. As already noted (see chapter 2, pp. 38–39), the contradictory messages have supplied traditional biblical commentators much room for interpretive activity.

3. Hinduism, for example, venerates powerful goddesses, yet Indian society is patriarchal. See Katherine Young's introduction in *Women in World Religions,* edited by Arvind Sharma (Albany: State University of New York Press, 1987), p. 28.

4. For more detailed discussion of the interaction of such factors in the formative stages of the world religions, see ibid., pp. 1–36.

5. Tikva Frymer-Kensky, "The Bible and Women's Studies," in *Feminist Perspectives on Jewish Studies,* edited by Lynn Davidman and Shelly Tenenbaum (New Haven: Yale University Press, 1994), p. 18.

6. Jenny Kien, *Reinstating the Divine Woman in Judaism* (Universal Publishers/uPublish.com, 2000), pp. 97–98; Plaskow, *Standing Again at Sinai,* p. 150.

7. It appears that even in the polytheistic religions, the goddesses demanded female sacrifices, while the gods demanded the sacrifice of male children. See *The Encyclopedia of Religion,* edited by Mircea Eliade (New York: Macmillan, 1987), s.v. "goddess worship."

8. Even if anthropologists discover a correlation between the adoption of Islam by some African societies and the hierarchical structure of those societies, as opposed to other societies that remained with their original African beliefs, might not the very attraction to Islam on the part of the former societies be the reflection of an already established social system? Daphne Hampson, despite her castigation of monotheism as conducive to patriarchy, raises this question—as illustration of the inconclusive nature of evidence of a correlation between ultimate beliefs and the social order—but then proceeds to ignore it. See *After Christianity* (London: SCM Press, 1996), pp. 126–127.

9. One of the legends told of the Soloveitchik family—known for its strong women—concerns Lipsha, the wife of Rabbi Yehiel Michel Feinstein, who was known as "the iron woman of Brisk" and ruled his Tel Aviv court with a powerful hand. Her zealous protection of his time and energy was the source of much resentment among his congregants. When confronted, she responded demurely by punning on the double meaning of the Hebrew verb *osah:* "But are we not taught by the Rabbis that a good wife *osah* (does/creates) her husband's will?"

10. Young, in *Women in World Religions,* pp. 32–34.

11. See Anita Diamant's best-selling novel, *The Red Tent* (New York: St. Martin's, 1997), depicting the world of the biblical Dinah and the four wives of Jacob through this prism.

12. For a survey of diverse theories of menstrual symbolism and their anthropological function, see *Blood Magic: The Anthropology of Menstruation,* edited by Thomas Buckeley and Alma Gottlieb (Berkeley and Los Angeles: University of California Press, 1989).

13. Mary Douglas, *Purity and Danger: An Analysis of Concepts of Pollution and Taboo* (London: Routledge and Kegan Paul, 1966); idem, "Self-Evidence—The Henry Meyers Lecture," in *Proceedings of the Royal Anthropological Institute* (1972), pp. 27–43; reprinted in M. Douglas, *Implicit Meanings* (London: Routledge and Kegan Paul, 1975), pp. 276–318.

14. Maurie Sacks, "An Anthropological and Postmodernist Critique of Jewish Feminist Theory," in *Gender and Judaism: The Transformation of Tradition,* edited by Tamar Rudavsky (New York: New York University Press, 1995), p. 298.

15. BT *Megillah* 29a; *Sifri,* end of parshat *Masaei.*

16. BT *Baba Metzia* 59b. This is only one of a number of interpretations engendered by the epilogue recounting Rabbi Gamliel's death. Another views it as expression of the cosmic tension between divine and human truth.

17. Professor Moshe Idel has called my attention to this connection as it appears in Neumann's writings. See *The Great Mother: An Analysis of the Archetype* (Princeton: Princeton University Press, 1972).

18. Arthur Green recommends capitalizing on the *Shekhinah* imagery of Kabbalah as a promising beginning for expanding the language of prayer. He cautions, however, that such imagery is insufficient on its own. Because it reflects only a male view of what femininity represents, emphasizing frailty, weakness, and loss, this legacy will require embellishment incorporating the creative fruits of women's experience. See his "Bride, Spouse, Daughter: Images of the Feminine in Classical Jewish Sources," in *On Being a Jewish Feminist,* edited by Susannah Heschel (New York: Schocken, 1983), pp. 248–260.

19. See above chapter 2, pp. 39–40.

20. Many passages in R. Kook's writings are devoted to this theme. For references, see Tamar Ross, "The Concept of God in the Thought of R. Kook" (in Hebrew), part one, *Daat* 8 (Bar-Ilan University) (summer 1982), pp. 109–128; part two, *Daat* 9 (winter 1983), pp. 39–70.

21. *Arpelei Tohar* (Jerusalem: Hamakhon al shem Harav Zvi Yehudah Kook, 1983), pp. 32–33.

22. See, for example, *Orot Hakodesh* (Jerusalem: Mosad Harav Kook, 1985), 2: 283–285; *Arpelei Tohar,* pp. 2–3.

23. *Iggerot Hareayah* (Jerusalem: Mosad Harav Kook, 1985), 1:48, translated by Tzvi Feldman in *Rav A. Y. Kook: Selected Letters* (Maaleh Adumim: Maliyot Publications, 1986), pp. 93–94.

24. See *Orot Hakodesh* (Jerusalem: Mosad Harav Kook, 1985), 2:403, where his phraseology remarkably parallels Marcia Falk's language: "an embracing unity of a multiplicity of images." Compare her "Notes on Composing New Blessings: Toward a Feminist Jewish Reconstruction of Prayer," *Journal of Feminist Studies in Religion* 3 (spring 1987), pp. 39–53. .

25. On this view, the world comes, paradoxically, to compensate for God's lack of deficiency, which is the unavoidable "drawback" of His fully realized perfection. See *Orot Hakodesh,* 2:532–533; 549.

26. It should be noted, however, that even this favored formulation is, according to Kook, valid only from a human point of view; ultimately the belief in the existence of anything outside of God is only a false human perception. If man could only conquer his illusory sense of self, contends R. Kook, he would overcome all sense of detachment from his Creator, and enjoy the supreme bliss of true unity with the Divine. He then, however, adds the wise caveat: "Truly this is not as simple as we would picture. Escape from the prison of the imagination is no less difficult than the release from any real prison." See *Orot Hakodesh* (Jerusalem: Mosad Harav Kook, 1985), 2:399–401.

27. See Sheila Davaney, ed., *Feminism and Process Thought: The Harvard Divinity School/Claremont Center for Process Studies Symposium Papers* (New York and Toronto: Edwin Mellen, 1981); Catherine Keller, *From a Broken Web: Separation, Sexism and Self* (Boston: Beacon, 1988), pp. 7–46. Two prominent versions of this theology have been formulated by the French Catholic theologian Pierre Teilhard de Chardin and by the British-born mathematician and philosopher Alfred North Whitehead. Their point of contact with R. Kook is in viewing an interrelatedness and unbroken connectedness between all elements of reality, rather than identifying the essence of all objects in isolation. This connectedness also entails a kind of reciprocity between God and humankind.

28. For further discussion of the "feminine" aspects of R. Kook's thought and possible explanations for the disparity between his theology and his attitudes on the practical halakhic level, see my forthcoming article, "Feminist Aspects of Rabbi A. I. Kook's Theology" (in Hebrew), in a jubilee volume for Eliezer Schweid, edited by Aviezer Ravitzky and Yehoyada Amir, to be published in Jerusalem by the Institute of Jewish Studies of Hebrew University.

29. Jenny Kien, *Reinstating the Divine Woman,* pp. 203.

30. Plaskow, *Standing Again at Sinai,* pp. 148–149.

31. Ibid., pp. 149–150.

32. Ibid., p. 147.

33. Ibid., p. 150.

34. According to Kien, the major difference between Judaism and polytheistic religions is indeed the way in which holiness is approached: in Judaism through study of words; in polytheistic religions through study of visual symbols that may be verbalized as songs and hymns. Equating idolatry of the word and idolatry of an image, Kien suggests that addition of the goddess to Judaism can only enrich it, as the tension arising between verbal and nonverbal modes of symbolism could help prevent current Jewish practice from slipping into idolatrous veneration of the Torah scroll itself, rather than what can be achieved through its teachings.

35. Kien, *Reinstating the Divine Woman,* p. 84. Kien also strives to combat the argument that polytheism is no longer Jewish by maintaining that any solution that avoids polytheism by splitting the deity into aspects (such as the Kabbalah) is essentially polytheistic. If we are serious about our anthropomorphic imagery, she claims, we will always be imagining two images that merge into Oneness at a higher level.

36. Ozick, "Notes Toward Finding the Right Question," in Heschel, ed., *On Being A Jewish Feminist,* p. 121.

37. Gilla Rosen, "God of My Teachers: Learning with Rav Soloveitchik," in *Torah of the Mothers: Contemporary Jewish Women Read Classical Jewish Texts,* edited by Ora Wiskind-Alper and Susan Handelman (New York and Jerusalem: Urim, 2000), pp. 17–18.

38. For an illuminating account of the transformation that the rationale for this body of laws has undergone over the generations, see Jonah Steinberg, "From a 'Pot of Filth' to a 'Hedge of Roses' (and Back): Changing Theorizations of Menstruation in Judaism," *Journal of Feminist Studies in Religion* 13:2 (fall 1997), pp. 3–26.

39. Notwithstanding Hampson's protestations to the contrary. See *After Christianity,* p. 240.

40. This is equally true of Kien's description of the divine goddess. For more on the issue of realism and nonrealism in feminist goddess thealogy, see the exchange between Beverly Clack ("'The Many-Named Queen of All': Thealogy and the Concept of the Goddess") and Melissa Raphael ("Monotheism in Contemporary Feminist Goddess Religion: A Betrayal of Early Thealogical Non-Realism?") in *Is There a Future for Feminist Theology?* edited by Deborah F. Sawyer and Diane M. Collier (Sheffield: Sheffield Academic Press, 1999).

41. For further discussion of this question, see Tamar Ross, "The Meaning of Religious Statements in a Post-Modern Age" (in Hebrew), in *Tarbut Yehudit Be'ein Hasearah,* edited by Avi Sagi and Nahem Ilan (Hakibbutz Hameuhad, 2002), pp. 459–484, and especially 477–483. See also Edward Henderson, "Theistic Reductionism and the Practice of Worship," *International Journal for Philosophy of Religion* 10:1 (1979), pp. 25–40; Kevin Schilbrack, "Myths and Metaphysics," *International Journal for Philosophy of Religion* 48 (2000), pp. 65–80.

42. For an illuminating illustration of the role of tradition in establishing identity, see John Kekes's penetrating analysis of the concept of decency in *Moral Tradition and Individuality* (Princeton: Princeton University Press, 1989), pp. 71–84. Kekes distinguishes between a more superficial type of decency he terms "rule-following" and the deeper level of decency he describes as "identity-conferring" because it is an indispensable part of our concept of self.

43. See "Monotheism" in *The Encyclopedia of Religion,* 10:70, for evidence of monotheism in Egyptian religion and in Zoroastrianism.

44. Yoseph Ahitov, "Some Comments on the Use of the Concept of *Halakhah* in Orthodox Discourse" (in Hebrew), *Al Olamo Vehaguto shel David Hartman: Mehuyavut Yehudit Mithadeshet*, edited by Avi Sagi and Zvi Zohar (Tel Aviv: Hakibbutz Hameuhad, 2001), 2:553–597; Shay Akavia Wozner, "The Meaning of Faithfulness to *Halakhah*" (in Hebrew), in *Masa el Hahalakhah: Iyunim Bein-Tehumiyim Beolam Hahok Hayehudi*, edited by Amichai Berholz (Jerusalem: Yedioth Aharonoth; 2003), pp. 83–102; Itzchak Geiger, "The New Religious Zionism—Survey, Study and Critique" (in Hebrew), *Akdamot* 11 (Jerusalem: Bet-Morasha, October 2001), pp. 51–79, especially pp. 63–70.

45. For a survey of such attempts, see Arnold M. Eisen, *Rethinking Modern Judaism: Ritual, Commandment, Community* (Chicago: University of Chicago Press, 1997).

46. Current rates of assimilation within the various religious denominations of the Jewish population (which appear to grow in *inverse* proportion to the degree of their halakhic commitment) support the suspicion that contemporary attempts on the part of individuals or communities to live out their Jewish lives while discarding *halakhah* as a central medium of religious expression are not destined to last for more than a generation or two. The latest demographic census conducted by the UJC (United Jewish Communities) reveals that as opposed to the 5.5 million who were counted in the last census of 1990, U.S. Jews today number only 5.2 million. Admittedly, statistics regarding intermarriage could complicate analysis of the statistical evidence. Questions regarding the religious upbringing of the offspring of such marriages, or even whether to include in the survey such children who count themselves as Jews, yet were not raised or educated as Jews, lead back to the old question: How does one define who is a Jew?

47. See chapter 6 above, p. 138.

48. Judith Antonelli, *In the Image of God: A Feminist Commentary on the Torah* (Northvale, N.J.: Jason Aronson, 1997), pp. xxxiv–xxxv.

49. Similar formulations of some of these questions appear in Frymer-Kensky, "The Bible and Women's Studies," p. 18, and in Susannah Heschel's entry "Feminism" (in Hebrew) in *Lexicon Hatarbut Hayehudit Bizmanenu: Musagim, Tnuot, Emunot*, edited by Arthur Cohen and Paul Mendes-Flohr (Hebrew editor, Avraham Shapiro) (Tel Aviv: Am Oved, 1993), p. 391.

50. Cynthia Ozick, "Notes Toward Finding the Right Question," in Heschel, ed., *On Being a Jewish Feminist*, p. 144.

51. Judith Plaskow, "The Right Question is Theological," in Heschel, ed., *On Being a Jewish Feminist*, p. 223.

52. Plaskow, *Standing Again at Sinai: Judaism from a Feminist Perspective*, p. 32.

53. Judith Plaskow, "Standing Again at Sinai: Jewish Memory from a Feminist Perspective," *Tikkun* 1:2, pp. 28–34. Others are Frymer-Kensky and Heschel. See above, note 49.

54. Rachel Adler, *Engendering Judaism: An Inclusive Theology and Ethics* (Philadelphia: Jewish Publication Society, 1998), p. 46.

55. Plaskow, *Standing Again at Sinai: Judaism from a Feminist Perspective*, p. 60.

56. Ibid., pp. 60–74.

57. Judith Plaskow, "The Wife/Sister Stories: Dilemmas of the Jewish Feminist," in *Speaking of Faith: Cross-Cultural Perspectives on Women, Religion and Social Change*, edited by Diana Eck and Devaki Jain (New Delhi: Kali for Women, 1986), pp. 116–117. This recognition is shared to a certain extent by Adler herself, who in her later work emphasizes more clearly that when women enter the halakhic process, it will lead not only to new answers, but also to new questions. Contrast Rachel Adler, "I've Had Nothing Yet, so I Can't Take More," *Moment* 8:8 (September

1983), p. 24, and *Engendering Judaism*, to "The Jew Who Wasn't There," *Davka* (summer 1972), pp. 7–11, reprinted in Heschel, ed., *On Being A Jewish Feminist*, pp. 12–18, which was written in her earlier, Orthodox phase.

58. Plaskow, "The Right Question is Theological," pp. 230–231.

59. Plaskow, *Standing Again at Sinai*, pp. 67–72.

60. Ibid., p. 71.

61. Ibid., pp. 73–74.

62. Adler, *Engendering Judaism*, pp. 27–28.

63. Adler, Ibid., pp. xxii–xiii.

64. Ibid., p. 21.

8. Halakhic Proactivism (pp. 145–161)

1. Ronald M. Dworkin, "Is Law a System of Rules?" in *The Philosophy of Law,* edited by Ronald. M. Dworkin (London: Oxford University Press, 1977), p. 45.

2. See, for example, Dworkin's discussion of slavery in *Law's Empire* (Cambridge, Mass.: Harvard University Press, 1986), pp. 80–81, and in *A Matter of Principle* (Cambridge, Mass.: Harvard University Press, 1985), pp. 172–173.

3. As defined by Dworkin, in appropriating Quine: "Roughly, constructive interpretation is a matter of imposing purpose on an object or practice in order to make of it the best possible example of the form or genre to which it is taken to belong." See Dworkin, *Law's Empire,* p. 42.

4. See above chapter 6, pp. 109–110.

5. See, for example, Aaron Kirschenbaum, "Subjectivity in Rabbinic Decision-Making," in *Rabbinic Authority and Personal Autonomy,* edited by Moshe Z. Sokol (Northvale, N.J.: Jason Aronson, 1992), p. 88; Jonathan Sacks, "Creativity and Innovation in Halakhah," in ibid., pp. 134–135, 147–149, and 152.

6. Stanley Fish, *Is There A Text in This Class? The Authority of Interpretive Communities* (Cambridge, Mass.: Harvard University Press, 1980), p. 350; Michael Berger, *Rabbinic Authority* (New York: Oxford University Press, 1998), pp. 137–140.

7. David Kairys, introduction to *The Politics of Law: A Progressive Critique* (New York: Pantheon, 1990), p. 6.

8. Sacks, "Creativity and Innovation in Halakhah," pp. 123–169.

9. Ibid., pp. 158–162.

10. Sacks begins with an attempt to clarify what rabbinic ordination entails. The Hatam Sofer distinguishes between two categories of office referred to by Maimonides in *MT*: the crown of priesthood and the crown of Torah; as Sacks understands it, R. Sofer views the former, denied to women, as inherent to the role of the rabbi. But, as Joshua Amaru has pointed out in a detailed and unpublished critique, there is room for other readings. Although Sacks is correct that a "good" interpretation is one that we accept because it "fits without strain" (p. 149), this lack of strain is not because the interpretation was "always there," but because we have managed to be absolutely persuaded that this method, along with its preliminary assumptions and beliefs, is the correct way to understand the text. One may assume that Joel Roth of the Conservative movement sincerely believes that his halakhic responsum is faithful to the halakhic tradition. According to the Conservative position, the *halakhah* always adapted itself to moral and social conditions of the time. On this view, it might not only be possible but even incumbent upon us to declare that the ordination of women to the rabbinate is a natural continuation of the halakhic enterprise. All this does not come to take any particular side in this debate, or to defend Roth's position.

It merely comes to point out that the question of coherence and continuity with the past or change and innovation is itself a matter of interpretation.

11. Ibid., pp. 126–127.

12. See, for example, Owen M. Fiss, "What is Feminism?" (translation of a taped lecture in Hebrew), in *Iyunnei Mishpat* 18 (1993), pp. 5–17. Cover's approach has also attracted the attention of at least one theoretician of the Reform movement in Judaism; see David Ellenson, "Conservative Halakhah in Israel: A Review Essay," *Modern Judaism* 13 (1993), pp. 191–204.

13. Thomas Ross, "Despair and Redemption in the Feminist Nomos," *Indiana Law Journal* 69 (1993), pp. 101–136.

14. Robin West, "Jurisprudence and Gender," in *Feminist Legal Theory: Readings in Law and Gender,* edited by Katherine T. Bartlett and Rosanne Kennedy (Boulder, Colo.: Westview, 1991), pp. 201–234; reprinted from *Chicago University Law Review* (1988), pp. 1–23.

15. For some expositions and discussion of this trend, see Moshe Halbertal, *Mahapeikhot Parshaiyot Behithavutan: Arakhim Keshikulim Parshaniyim Bemidrashei Halakhah* (Jerusalem: Magnes, 1997), pp. 202–203; Steven Kepnes, ed., *Interpreting Judaism in a Postmodern Age* (New York: New York University Press, 1996); Susan Handelman, *The Slayers of Moses: The Emergence of Rabbinic Interpretation in Modern Literary Theory* (Albany: State University of New York Press, 1982); David Weiss-Halivni, *Peshat and Drash* (New York: Oxford University Press, 1991), pp. 158–162; David Kraemer, *The Mind of the Talmudian Intellectual History of the Bavli* (New York: Oxford University Press, 1990). For a concise summary of postmodernist thinking as it affects law, see Litowitz, *Postmodernist Philosophy and Law* (Lawrence: University Press of Kansas, 1997), pp. 7–17. For more detailed studies of postmodernism in general, see R. Bernstein, *"The New Constellation": The Ethical-Political Horizons of Modernity/Postmodernity* (Cambridge, Mass.: MIT Press, 1986); D. Harvey, *The Condition of Postmodernity: An Enquiry into the Origins of Cultural Change* (Cambridge, Mass., and Oxford: Blackwell 1989).

16. BT *Baba Metzia* 59b.

17. *Bamidbar Rabbah* (Vilna edition), parsha 13.

18. The classical source of this statement appears in BT *Eruvin* 13b. For further elaboration upon this approach, see Avi Sagi, *Eilu Ve'eilu: Mashmauto shel Hasiah Hahilkhati: Iyun Besifrut Yisrael* (Tel Aviv: Hakibbutz Hameuhad, 1996).

19. The legitimacy of rival positions alongside God's revealed will is, of course, a paradox that generates several theological problems. For example: how can there be room—in the face of God's revelation—for several conflicting opinions? Among the solutions offered: generalities were revealed but not particulars; any of a *range* of legitimate opinions are equally acceptable; determination of God's will took place in phases. Another question—if God already takes the trouble of revealing His will, why leave us with ambiguities altogether?—is countered by appreciation of the limitations of human understanding or of the value attached to partnership between God and His human disciples in determining the truth of Torah. For greater elaboration of the nature of such dilemmas and possible methods of resolving them, see Yohanan Silman, *Kol Gadol velo Yasef: Torat Yisrael bein Shelemut Lehishtalmut* (Jerusalem: Magnes, 1999), pp. 102–116; Susan Stone, "In Pursuit of the Countertext: The Turn to the Jewish Legal Model in Contemporary American Legal Theory," *Harvard Law Review* 106:4 (February 1993), pp. 849–865; Berger, *Rabbinic Authority,* pp. 88–96. Further methods of resolution will be discussed in chapter 11.

20. See David Stern's critical review of Handelman's book: "Moses-cide: Midrash and Contemporary Literary Criticism," *Prooftexts* 4 (May 1984), pp. 193–204, and Handelman's rejoinder: "Fragments of the Rock: Contemporary Literary

Theory and the Study of Rabbinic Texts—A Response to David Stern," *Prooftexts* 5 (1985), pp. 75–95; see also David Weiss-Halivni, "Midrash and Modern Literary Theories," appendix II in *Peshat and Drash* (pp. 158–162), for commonalities and differences between *midrash* and modern emphasis on the crucial role of reader response in the determination of textual meaning.

21. See Susan Stone's weighty essay, "In Pursuit of the Countertext," pp. 813–894, which focuses its critique specifically on Cover; Michael Rosenzweig ("Eilu Ve'eilu Divrei Elohim Hayyim: Halakhic Pluralism and Theories of Controversy," in Sokol, ed., *Rabbinic Authority and Personal Autonomy*, pp. 93–123) and Weiss-Halivni (*Peshat and Drash*, appendix II) also express reservations about any comparison between the application of rabbinic notions of pluralism to *halakhah* and postmodernist assumptions of truth.

22. BT *Hagigah* 3b.

23. See his *Peshat and Drash*, pp. 159–160.

24. Some traditionalists have distinguished between two categories of halakhic truth: one that is a legitimate expression of Torah and one that is established on the basis of formal halakhic procedure. See Michael Rosensweig, "Eilu Ve'eilu," p. 111ff.

25. Weiss-Halivni, *Peshat and Drash*, p. 160.

26. Cover, "The Supreme Court, 1982 Term—Foreword: Nomos and Narrative," 97 *Harvard Law Review* 4 (1983), pp. 4–68.

27. This connotation has also been preserved in the Hebrew variation: *nimus*. See BT *Megillah* 12b; *Gittin* 62b.

28. Cover, "Nomos and Narrative," pp. 19–25.

29. This same understanding is encapsulated in a parable likening the role of the halakhist vis-à-vis the community to that of the sighted individual who provides the blind man with a proper cane. The community points to the direction in which it would like to go, and the halakhic authority helps it to get there, if at all possible, without stumbling into unexpected pitfalls along the way. See Yisrael Ta-Shma, *Halakhah, Minhag, Umetziut BeAshkenaz, 1000–1350* (Jerusalem: Magnes, 1996), p. 28.

30. Robert Garet, "Comparative Normative Hermeneutics: Scripture, Literature, Constitution," *Southern California Law Review* 58:1 (1985), p. 62.

31. "Nomos and Narrative," pp. 37–40.

32. "Nomos and Narrative," pp. 26–35.

33. Slaughtered by the thousands in sixteenth-century Europe, the Mennonites searched for a place to live that would grant them religious liberty. Thus they view the guarantee of this freedom to be one of the Constitution's greatest virtues. Understanding Scripture as enjoining them to respect and obey the secular governments under which they live, they are committed, for that reason alone, without threat of punitive action, to being completely law-abiding. However, they add: "Our religious beliefs are very deeply held. When these beliefs collide with the demands of society, our highest allegiance must be toward God."

34. Rachel Adler, *Engendering Judaism: An Inclusive Theology and Ethics* (Philadephia: Jewish Publication Society, 1998), pp. xiv, xxvi.

35. Adler, *Engendering Judaism*, p. 26.

36. Ibid., pp. 34–37.

37. Ibid., p. 27.

38. It should be noted, however, that Maimonides understands the influence of the community's willingness to accept a ruling upon the degree of its normative authority as extending only to the realm of the "edicts, decrees, and customs" of the talmudic sages, rather than to interpretation of the law received from Moses. Furthermore,

such willingness serves only as a prior condition for the validation of these rulings, still leaving the source of their authority with the rabbinic court. In other words, although the power of the court's decision does initially derive from its position as representative of the communal will, it is subsequently accorded independent authority that cannot be revoked merely by changes of that will. See Berger, *Rabbinic Authority*, pp. 101–105.

Another view, favored particularly (although not exclusively) by medievalists of a mystic bent, does view the organic body of Israel as an ultimate source of legitimate Jewish thought and practice. Adopted in modern times in various guises by Solomon Schechter, by A. I. Kook, and by Louis Jacobs, the rationale for this view is that the Torah-observing community reflects God's voice. This view may come closer to the contemporary one of the importance of community in establishing law: not so much in providing the source of its authority, but in embodying a way of life to which a particular interpretation is linked. This view applies especially to R. Kook, who was confident that if a particular moral intuition reflecting the divine will achieves widespread popularity, it will no doubt enable the halakhic authorities to find genuine textual basis for their new understanding. See *Iggerot Hareayah* (Jerusalem: Mosad Harav Kook, 1985), 1:103–104. R. Kook's conviction might be regarded as a religious application of Cover's and Adler's understanding of the crucial linkage between meaning and practice.

39. Adler, *Engendering Judaism*, p. 132.

40. Robert Cover, "The Folktales of Justice: Tales of Jurisdiction," *Capital University Law Review* 14 (1985), p. 181.

41. Cover, "Nomos and Narrative," p. 11.

42. This is not to say that there is no possibility of change in these rules and conventions, but that such changes as well are accepted only in accordance with criteria established by the internal tradition.

43. Ibid., p. 39.

44. Ibid., p. 203.

45. Ibid., p. xiv–xv.

46. Ibid., p. xxi.

47. Ibid., p. 27.

48. Ibid., p. xxv.

49. Martin S. Jaffee, "'Halakhah as Primordial Tradition': A Gadamerian Dialogue with Early Rabbinic Memory and Jurisprudence," in Kepnes, ed., *Interpreting Judaism in a Postmodern Age*, pp. 108–109.

9. Halakhah Contextualized (pp. 165–183)

1. For a brief overview of the issues at stake in the "foundations of knowledge" debate, see William C. Placher, *Unapologetic Theology: A Christian Voice in a Pluralistic Conversation* (Louisville, Ky.: Westminster/John Knox Press, 1989), pp. 24–38, and John E. Thiel, *Nonfoundationalism* (Minneapolis: Fortress Press, 1991), pp. 1–38. Also see Richard Rorty's groundbreaking *Philosophy and the Mirror of Nature* (Princeton: Princeton University Press, 1979).

2. For example, Richard Rorty (who prefers to define himself as a nonfoundationalist) expresses confidence that this position does not preclude the notion of positive criteria for legal judgment: "The question about whether the judges of the higher courts explain what the law already is, or instead make new law, is as idle as the philosophical question about whether literary criticism produces knowledge or opinion. But recognizing the idleness of the first question does not make these philosophers, or

the rest of us, value the ideal of a free and independent judiciary any the less. Nor does it make us less capable of telling good judges from bad judges, any more than our lack of an epistemology of literary criticism makes us less capable of telling good critics from bad critics, boring pedants from original minds." *Truth and Progress* (Cambridge: Cambridge University Press, 1998), p. 70.

3. Ernest Sosa, "The Raft and the Pyramid: Coherence versus Foundations in the Theory of Knowledge," *Midwest Studies in Philosophy* 5 (1980), pp. 3–25.

4. Rorty, *Truth and Progress*, p. 63.

5. Fred D'Agostino, "Transcendence and Conversation: Two Conceptions of Objectivity," *American Philosophical Quarterly* 30:2 (April 1993), pp. 87–108.

6. Hilary Putnam, *Representation and Reality* (Cambridge, Mass.: MIT Press, 1988), p. 109.

7. This is not to say that all standpoint feminists are nonfoundationalists. While rejecting the possibility of ever achieving perceptions independent of the interpreter's input, some adherents of standpoint theory nevertheless remain close to conventional epistemology. Accepting the existence of a firm and predetermined truth, they see the function of amassing perspectives simply as bringing us increasingly closer to correspondence with this truth. See, for example, Louise Antony, "Quine as Feminist: The Radical Import of Naturalized Epistemology," in *A Mind of One's Own,* edited by Louise M. Antony and Charlotte Witt (Boulder, Colo.: Westview, 1993), pp. 185–225. Antony does not regard women's knowledge claims as just another orientation to be added to a diverse kitty of options, leaving all others intact. Instead, she views the encounter as mandating a dialectic interplay of perspectives in order to arrive at a more accurate understanding of what really is. The skepticism of other standpoint theorists regarding the existence of stable truths *altogether* leads them closer to what is generally characterized as a postmodernist view (although not all its adherents would equate the two, by any means). Most standpoint feminists would dissociate from a postmodernism that regards women's knowledge claims as just one more perspective among others that are all equally valid, given the lack of a neutral vantage point against which they could be checked and evaluated. For a sample formulation of some of their reservations, see Susan Strickland, "Feminism, Postmodernism and Difference," in *Knowing the Difference: Feminist Perspective in Epistemology,* edited by Kathleen Lennon and Margaret Whitford (London: Routledge, 1994), pp. 265–274.

8. For an illustration of this technique as employed in anthropology, see Tamar El-Or, *Bapesach Haba: Nashim Veoreyanut Batziyonut Hadatit* (Tel Aviv: Am Oved, 1998), chapter 4; forthcoming in English translation: *Next Year I Will Know More: Literacy and Identity Among Young Orthodox Women* (Detroit, Mich.: Wayne State University Press). El-Or uses this method in order to resolve tensions between cultural commonalties and differences, between the stance of the disinterested scientist and that of the involved researcher who sees it as his task to intervene and impose the practical applications of his study, and between the conception of literacy as a universal tool of empowerment and the view that it is a tool of surveillance and manipulation in the hands of the ruling class.

9. Douglas Litowitz, *Postmodern Philosophy and Law* (Lawrence: University of Kansas Press, 1997), pp. 166–179.

10. Rachel Adler, *Engendering Judaism: An Inclusive Theology and Ethics* (Philadephia: Jewish Publication Society, 1998), p. xxiii.

11. Ibid., p. 27.

12. As Moshe Halbertal has observed. See his *Mahapeikhot Parshaniyot Behithavutan: Arakhim Keshikulim Parshaniyim Bemidrashei Halakhah* (Jerusalem: Magnes, 1997), p. 180.

13. I make this case despite Robert Cover's disparaging comments about Gadamer's "disappointingly provincial" understanding of legal hermeneutics in "The Supreme Court, 1982 Term—Foreword: Nomos and Narrative," *Harvard Law Review* 4 (1983), p. 6 n.11. Cover criticizes Gadamer for regarding law as a special and narrow case to which the normal problems of interpretation do not apply.

14. Hans G. Gadamer, *Truth and Method* (New York: Seabury, 1975); Stanley Fish, *Is There a Text in This Class? The Authority of Interpretive Communities* (Cambridge, Mass.: Harvard University Press, 1980).

15. For further discussion of this insight as developed in the *musar* movement, see Tamar Ross, "The *Musar* Movement and the Hermeneutic Problem in the Study of Torah" (in Hebrew), *Tarbitz* 59:1–2 (1990), pp. 191–214, and especially p. 203ff. For another attempt, similar to mine, to appropriate Gadamar's ideas to traditional Jewish views of the Oral Law, see Martin S. Jaffee, "Halakhah as Primordial Tradition: A Gadamerian Dialogue with Early Rabbinic Memory and Jurisprudence," in *Interpreting Judaism in a Postmodern Age,* edited by Steven Kepnes (New York: New York University Press, 1996), pp. 85–117.

16. A similar approach has been extended to Christianity by a group of nonfoundationalist theologians who describe themselves as postliberals and their method as compatible with what has come to be known as "intratextualism." See, for example, John E. Thiel, *Nonfoundationalism;* George Lindbeck, *The Nature of Doctrine: Religion and Theology in a Postliberal Age* (Philadelphia: Westminster, 1984); Bruce D. Marshall, ed., *Theology and Dialogue: Essays in Conversation with George Lindbeck* (Notre Dame, Ind.: University of Notre Dame Press, 1990); Kathryn Tanner, *Theories of Culture: A New Agenda for Theology* (Minneapolis, Minn.: Fortress, 1997).

17. For an account of vigorous objection to this development on the part of R. Avraham Karelitz, see Larry Kaplan, "The Hazon Ish: Haredi Critic of Traditional Orthodoxy," in *The Uses of Tradition: Jewish Continuity in the Modern Era,* edited by Jack Wertheimer (New York: Jewish Theological Seminary, 1992), pp. 164–165.

18. *MT, Hilkhot Ishut* 13:11.

19. Jonathan Sacks, "Creativity and Innovation in Halakhah," in *Rabbinic Authority and Personal Autonomy,* edited by Moshe Z. Sokol (Northvale, N.J.: Jason Aronson, 1992), pp. 149–155. This solution, offered by R. Nachum Rabinowitch, his teacher and *posek* at the time, is to say the blessing of *hatov vehametiv* on the birth of a girl, despite the *baraita* (quoted in BT *Berakhot* 59b) that states explicitly that this expression of thanks to God for His beneficence applies only to the birth of a boy. Rabinowitch sees the fact that this *halakhah* is not codified by Maimonides as the latter's admission—based on BT *Baba Batra* 16b and 141a—that the blessing could apply to a daughter's birth as well.

20. Ibid., pp. 165–166.

21. For a similar defense of the legitimacy of "external" influences upon the development of Jewish tradition, see R. Kook's defense of Maimonides and his introduction of Aristotelian ideas into the body of Jewish thought, in "Maamar Meyuhad (Leumat Shitat R. Zeev Yaavetz Zatza"l Besifro Toldot Yisrael)," *Maamarei Reayah* (Jerusalem, 1984), 1:105–112. Kook establishes that just as there are many opinions in *halakhah* and we are obliged to hear them all, so too in matters of belief that have been held by various sages of the nation. We have no right to dismiss any of them as "external." Various viewpoints work differently for different individuals, but as long as any opinion leads to God and His Torah and the path of holiness, that is its justification.

22. My observations here draw on a similar analysis of the power of feminist legal scholars functioning as a lawmaking community. See Thomas Ross, "Despair

and Redemption in the Feminist Nomos," *Indiana Law Journal* 69 (1993), pp. 101–136.

23. See chapter 3 above, p. 53.

24. Lynne Schreiber, *Hide and Seek: Jewish Women and Hair Covering* (New York/Jerusalem: Urim Publications, 2003), p. 25.

25. Adler, *Engendering Judaism*, p. 26.

26. Robert Cover, "Nomos and Narrative," pp. 67–68.

27. Mendel Shapiro, "Qeri'at ha-Torah by Women: A Halakhic Analysis," *The Edah Journal* 1:2 (Sivan 2001) (www. Edah.org), p. 3.

28. Abe Katz, July 29, 2001, under "Reader Responses" in *The Edah Journal*.

29. Yehuda Henkin, *Equality Lost: Essays in Torah Commentary, Halakha, and Jewish Thought* (Jerusalem: Urim Publications, 1999), pp. 42 and 54.

30. Ibid., chapter 6 on *kaddish*, pp. 50–51.

31. Henkin continues: "This employs many principles Halakha itself provides, such as the difference between ruling *lechatchilah*, 'initially' and *bedi'eved*, 'after the fact.' Or, *sha'at hadchak*, 'pressing circumstances.' Or the obligation to keep quiet, in certain cases, when one knows one won't be listened to or when the ruling is likely to be misunderstood or misused." These remarks are made in the context of a responsum regarding women reading the Purim *megillah* for other women. See *Equality Lost*, p. 54.

32. See Henkin's response, published alongside Shapiro's article in the *Edah Journal* 1:2.

33. See chapter 11 below, p. 220.

34. Under circumstances that pose no threat of communal rift, Shapiro sees no reason why permission should not be extended to public religious space as well.

35. Henkin himself finds halakhic basis for approving these developments. See his *Equality Lost*, pp. 54–60. Note also Feinstein's change of policy within three years over the question of bat mitzvah celebrations in the synagogue: In a responsum dated Shevat 1956, it is absolutely forbidden *(Iggrot Moshe, Orah Hayim,* part 1 [New York: Moriah, 1959], *simman* 104), whereas a responsum dated Sivan 1959 allows such a celebration on synagogue premises in the form of a *kiddush* and not a ceremonial meal *(seudat mitzvah)* (ibid., part 4, *simman* 36).

36. Two responsa regarding women's suffrage in pre-state Israel display the same dynamic. Rabbi Ben-Zion Uziel invoked a type of "no taxation without representation" argument in support of giving women the right to vote. "So how can we give them obligations without the right to vote?. . . Did you ever hear of appointing guardians over a grown woman, without her consent?" *Mishpetei Uziel Bepiskei Hazman* (Jerusalem: Mosad Harav Kook, 1977), responsum 44, p. 229. See also chapter 3, circa note 19. Uziel felt he was addressing a religiously committed community that could readily internalize the new attitudes represented by his rulings. Yet he only published the responsum forty years after it had originally been written. "I wrote this responsum at the time in order to clarify *halakhah* for myself. . . . But now, as the question has resolved itself, I found it a good idea to make it public, in order to aggrandize Torah." His final criterion for distinguishing a legitimate from a questionable ruling, then, was the living nomic reality as it unfolded within the halakhic community. Rabbi Yehiel Weinberg, in similar fashion, remarked, "time, not logical debate, will eventually settle the controversy." *(Seridei Esh,* vol. 3, responsum 105, p. 322).

37. See chapter 10 below, pp. 205–206.

38. As one member of a more egalitarian Orthodox congregation confessed to me, "Although I have no doubt that our more inclusive form of prayer is morally superior, I am not as sure that we are not forfeiting some valuable element of 'fear of Heaven' in the process. When I pray on Yom Kippur, what concerns me is not

only what people do *in* the synagogue, but also their manner as they approach it, how they dress, what they talk about, how they have prepared for the Day of Judgment, and the extent to which they are capable of passing this tradition on to their children."

10. The Word of God Contextualized (pp. 184–212)

1. Maimonides, *Guide for the Perplexed* II, chapter 25.

2. Maimonides built here upon the rabbinic pronouncement that "the Torah is written in human language" in a manner almost directly contrary to its original intent. R. Ishmael, the talmudic sage who originally made this statement (see *Sifre* on *Shlach Lecha,* sect. 12), intended merely to assert that the Torah contains some expressions and literary flourishes that should be taken at face value and understood as colloquialisms. In contrast, his protagonist, R. Akiva, believed that "mounds and mounds" of *halakhot* were embedded in every biblical "jot and tittle." (For a discussion of this debate, see Abraham Joshua Heschel, *Torah min Hashamayim Baaspaklaria shel Hadorot* [London: Soncino Press, 1965], 1:3–23.) Maimonides extends R. Ishmael's statement far beyond its original application in order to assert that one must distinguish between the form of Torah and its content. This was identified then with the notion of "divine accommodation" (adjustment to human limitations). See Stephen D. Benin, *The Footprints of God* (Albany: State University of New York Press, 1993).

3. See chapter 6 above, p. 113.

4. Mordecai Kaplan, *The Future of the American Jew* (New York: Macmillan, 1958; Philadelphia: Reconstructionist Press, 1967).

5. Neil Gillman, *Sacred Fragments: Recovering Theology for the Modern Jew* (Philadelphia: Jewish Publication Society, 1990), p. 21.

6. For a schematic survey of contemporary Jewish views on revelation, see the symposium "The Condition of Jewish Belief," compiled by the editors of *Commentary* magazine and published in *Commentary* 42:2 (August 1966) and then in book form by Macmillan, also in 1966, and by Jason Aronson, in 1989. See also Gillman, *Sacred Fragments,* chapter 1, for a discussion of various Jewish views on revelation and the issues at stake.

7. Franz Rosenzweig, *Star of Redemption* (New York: Holt, Rinehart and Winston, 1971), translated from the second edition of 1930 by William W. Hallo. See also Rosenzweig's exchange of letters with Buber, "Revelation and Law: Martin Buber and Franz Rosenzweig," in *On Jewish Learning,* edited by N. N. Glatzer (New York: Schocken, 1955; republished 1987), pp. 119–124; Abraham Joshua Heschel, *God in Search of Man,* part two (Jewish Publication Society, 1956; Harper Torchbooks, 1969), particularly chapters 19 and 27; idem, *Torah min Hashamayim,* especially part II on revelation. For a systematic study of the philosophical assumptions in Heschel's work on revelation, see Lawrence Perlman, *Abraham Heschel's Idea of Revelation* (Atlanta, Ga.: Scholars, 1989), and the works of Louis Jacobs: *We Have Reason to Believe: Some Aspects of Jewish Theology examined in the Light of Modern Thought* (London: Vallentine-Mitchell, 1962, republished 1995); *Principles of the Jewish Faith* (London: Valletine-Mitchell, 1964), pp. 216–301; *A Jewish Theology* (New York: Beacon, 1973), pp. 199–210; "Torah as Divine Revelation: Is the Doctrine Still Acceptable to Moderns?" in *God, Torah, Israel: Traditionalism without Fundamentalism* (West Orange, N.J.: Hebrew Union College Press, 1990), pp. 21–55; *A Tree of Life: Diversity, Flexibility and Creativity in Jewish Law* (Oxford: Oxford University Press, for the Littman Library, 1984), pp. 236–247.

8. See Judith Plaskow, "Jewish Theology in Feminist Perspective," in *Feminist Perspectives on Jewish Studies,* edited by Lynn Davidman and Shelly Tenenbaum (New Haven: Yale University Press, 1994), p. 78.

9. Judith Plaskow, *Standing Again at Sinai: Judaism from a Feminist Perspective* (San Francisco, Calif.: Harper, 1990), p. 33.

10. Ibid. See also "Jewish Theology in Feminist Perspective," pp. 78–79.

11. Louis Jacobs, *Beyond Reasonable Doubt* (London: Littman Library of Jewish Civilization, 1999), pp. 50–51. This is an improvement upon Jacobs's original exposition, written as if one could go through the Pentateuch and tick off such passages as the commandment to wipe out the Amalekites as a human and not a divine element.

12. Jacobs, *Beyond Reasonable Doubt,* p. 51.

13. BT *Sanhedrin* 99a.

14. For some indication of the state of Orthodox confrontation with the higher biblical criticism, see *Modern Scholarship in the Study of Torah: Contributions and Limitations,* edited by Shalom Carmy (Northvale, N.J.: Jason Aronson, 1996); Steven Shaw, "Orthodox Reactions to the Challenge of Biblical Criticism," *Tradition* 10:3 (spring 1969), pp. 61–85. Although the article was written decades ago, not much has changed since in terms of theological responses.

15. For a fuller discussion of modernism and an account of the debate as to whether postmodernism is a continuation or departure from it, see R. Bernstein, *"The New Constellation": The Ethical-Political Horizons of Modernity/Postmodernity* (Cambridge, Mass.: MIT Press, 1986), p. 11, and D. Harvey, *The Condition of Postmodernity: An Enquiry into the Origins of Cultural Change* (Cambridge, Mass.: Blackwell 1989), p. 7.

16. See Shalom Carmy, "Introducing Rabbi Breuer," in *Modern Scholarship in the Study of Torah,* pp. 147–158; Shnayer Z. Leiman, "Response to Rabbi Breuer," in ibid., pp. 181–187.

17. Mordechai Breuer, "The Study of Bible and the Primacy of the Fear of Heaven: Compatibility or Contradiction?" in *Modern Scholarship in the Study of Torah,* p. 161.

18. See Marc B. Shapiro, "Maimonides' Thirteen Principles: The Last Word in Jewish Theology," *Torah U-Madda Journal* 4 (New York: Yeshiva University, 1993), particularly pp. 197–207; B. Barry Levy, "The State and Directions of Orthodox Bible Study," in *Modern Scholarship in the Study of Torah,* particularly pp. 63–65.

19. See, for example, *Mekhilta deRabbi Yishmael, Yitro, masekhet debehodesh Yitro, parsha* 3, that speaks of Moses reading to the Israelites ancient material ranging from the time of Adam to the giving of the Torah at Sinai, pending their acceptance. See also *Mekhilta deRabbi Shimon ben Rabbi Yohai,* 24:4, suggesting that the laws of sacrifice preceded transmission of the Decalogue. For further sources referring to the existence of pre-Mosaic texts eventually incorporated in the Torah, which the Israelites and Moses himself consulted for their own enlightenment, see Menahem M. Kasher, *Humash Torah Shelemah* vol 20 (Jerusalem: Torah Shelemah, 1992), supplement 33, *Monograph Regarding the Writing of the Torah* (in Hebrew), chapter 5, p. 356. In addition to written texts, many other midrashim speak of beliefs and practices appearing in the Torah that reflect pre-Mosaic traditions.

20. For a concentrated list and discussion of some of these sources, see Shapiro, ibid.

21. Zvi Werblowsky, "The Scientific Study of Bible as a Religious Problem" (in Hebrew), *Molad* (May 1960); see also the comments of Meir Weiss, Uri Simon, Jacob Katz, Joseph Heinemann, Abraham Halperin, and Jacob Zidman in *Deot* 13 (Jerusalem; spring 1960).

22. A similar methodological point was made by Spinoza in his critique of Yehudah Alfakhar (see his *Tractatus Theologico-Politicus,* chapter 15). Alfakhar criticized Maimonides' use of allegory, stating that instead of relying on reason to decide when allegory is warranted in interpretation of the Torah, one can only rely on the testimony of the Torah itself; only when it "speaks in two voices" is allegory called for. Spinoza's rejoinder was that the very identification of two voices, as well as which voice should be taken literally, involves prior subjective biases, as does the assumption that the Torah cannot contain contradictions. See Jacob J. Ross, "Spinoza and the Interpretation of the Bible in our Day" (in Hebrew) in *Baruch Spinoza: Kovetz Maamarim al Mishnato,* edited by Menachem Brinker, Marcelo Dascal, and Dan Nesher (Tel Aviv: Tel Aviv University, 1979), pp. 116–128.

23. See Moshe Lichtenstein's weekly commentary on the internet journal of Yeshivat Har Etzion, www.vbm-torah.ord/dk851mamar.htm.

24. David Weiss-Halivni, *Peshat and Drash* (New York: Oxford University Press, 1991), pp. 89–154; idem, *Revelation Restored: Divine Writ and Critical Responses* (Boulder, Colo.: Westview, 1997). Weiss-Halivni is of interest to Jewish feminists on other grounds, having resigned from his position at the Conservative movement's Jewish Theological Seminary over the issue of women's ordination to the rabbinate, which he opposed. He then went on to found the traditionalist movement, which places itself somewhere between the Orthodox commitment to traditional dogma and halakhic process and the Conservative acceptance of the findings of critical historical scholarship and their contribution to the understanding of sacred religious texts.

25. Weiss-Halivni, *Revelation Restored,* p. 89.

26. See Avi Sagi's review essay, "Between *Peshat* and *Drash*" (in Hebrew), *Tarbitz* 61 (1992), pp. 583–592.

27. *Iggerot Hareayah,* 1:164. R. Kook's remarks refer to the need to reconcile the theory of evolution and Darwinism with the literal import of the Genesis story.

28. Ludwig Wittgenstein, "Lectures on Religious Belief," in *L. Wittgenstein: Lectures and Conversations on Aesthetics, Psychology, and Religious Belief,* translated and edited by Cyril Barrett (Berkeley and Los Angeles: University of California Press, 1966). Other varieties of this response can be found in the writings of twentieth-century theologians who have developed a new appreciation of the mythic dimensions of religious language. See, for example, Paul Tillich, *The Dynamics of Faith* (New York: HarperCollins, 1957). For further discussion of the various trends, their strengths and weaknesses, see *Language, Truth, and Religious Belief: Studies in Twentieth-Century Theory and Method in Religion,* edited by Nancy Frankenberry and Hans Penner (Atlanta, Ga.: Scholars Press, 1999).

29. Hartman, Goldman, and Leibowitz have been influenced by the trend engendered by Wittgenstein to minimize religion's appeal to metaphysical claims of an absolute nature. For further description of this trend and some of its current Jewish applications, see Tamar Ross, "The Meaning of Religious Statements in a Postmodern Age" (in Hebrew), in *Tarbut Yehudit Be'ein Hasearah—A Jubilee Volume In Honor of Yosef Ahituv,* edited by Avi Sagi and Nahem Ilan (Ein Tzurim: Hakibbutz Hameuhad, 2002), pp. 450–484.

30. The solution of the mystics is to recognize the metaphysical inadequacy of religious truth claims, acknowledging their partial or illusory nature as descriptions of reality. See Tamar Ross, "Two Interpretations of the Doctrine of *Tzimtzum:* R. Hayim of Volozhin and R. Shneur Zalman of Lyadi" (in Hebrew), in *Mehkarei Yerushalayim Lemachshevet Yisrael* (Jerusalem: Deptartment of Jewish Thought, Hebrew University/ Magnes Press, 1981), pp. 153–169.

31. See, for example, Aaron Lichtenstein, "The Human and Social Factor in Halakha," *Tradition* 36:1 (2002), especially pp. 16–20. Religious considerations prompt

him to reject the possibility that halakhic change could be ascribed to the refined sensibility of innovators or that the judgment of the sages "was diverted or warped by extraneous factors." As this leading rabbinic authority asserts: "We trust that they (the Sages) were fully aware of what they were doing. The last thing we want to do is presume to understand them better than they understood themselves; to contend that while they may have thought they were pursuing one course, impelled by a given impetus, we, firmly ensconced in our social-scientific panopticon, know it was really another. The claim to superior retrospective insight is not uncommon in other contexts; but as to the critical transmitters—artificers of Torah she-be-al peh (the Oral Law), we shall have no truck with it. We shall impugn neither the wisdom nor the integrity of Hazal."

As a manifest of dogmatic religious commitment, a statement of ultimate loyalty to the sages is perfectly in place, but this statement takes ideology and dresses it up as history. This conflation raises serious doubts about the extent to which some exponents of Modern Orthodoxy have truly confronted the challenges of modernity and historicism. A similar confusion is evident in Judah L. Golding's attempt to locate the predefined limits of acceptable biblical exegesis. See his "On the Limits of Non-Literal Interpretation of Scripture from an Orthodox Perspective," Torah Umadda Journal 10 (October 2001), pp. 37–59.

32. A. I. Kook, Orot Ha'emunah (Brooklyn: Langsam Associates, 1985), pp. 101–102.

33. Ethics of the Fathers (Pirkei Avot) 6:2.

34. Isaiah ben Avraham Halevi Horowitz, Shnei Luhot Habrit (Amsterdam, 1649), Bet Hokhmah, p. 25b. See also Hayim Hillel ben Sasson's commentary on this view in Hagut Vehanhagah: Hashkafoteihem Hahevratiyot shel Yehudei Polin Beshalhei Yemei Habenayim (Jerusalem: Mosad Bialik, 1959), pp. 19–21.

35. See, for example, Saadya Gaon, The Book of Doctrines and Beliefs, chap. 2, sect. 10; Maimonides, Guide for the Perplexed II, chap. 33.

36. See Shalom Rosenberg, "Continuous Revelation: Three Directions" (in Hebrew), in Hitgalut, Emunah, Tevunah, edited by Moshe Halamish and Moshe Shwartz (Ramat Gan: Bar-Ilan University, 1976), pp. 131–143.

37. This is not to say that all of the material presented under the heading of hiddushim is new or advocates change. Most of the commentary on the Talmud is given this label even when the author is merely recording the accepted interpretation. Nevertheless, the fact remains that there is much that is innovative in this literature, and a particularly convincing "hiddush" has the ability to change the accepted consensus as to the meaning of a law. The history of halakhah is overflowing with examples of influential interpretations, such as the hiddushim of Rabbenu Tam and the Ramban.

38. Michael Berger, Rabbinic Authority (New York: Oxford University Press, 1998), p. 91.

39. See Daphne Hampson's account and disparaging dismissal of this concept in Theology and Feminism (Oxford: Basil Blackwell, 1990), pp. 22–24.

40. Bereshit Rabbah 1:1.

41. According to some of the sages, Moses—as opposed to the other prophets—referred to himself in the third person in the Pentateuch because what he wrote was copied from that Torah which preceded the creation of the world and, obviously, his own birth. See Bereshit Rabbah 8:2.

42. Zohar III, Behaalotkha, 152a.

43. Shmot Rabbah, parsha 6:1, on Exodus 20:2; Shmot Rabbah, parsha 9:4, on Exodus 20:15—whereby pregnant women, interestingly enough, constitute a separate category of those who hear "according to their strength." See also Midrash Hagadol on Exodus 19:19.

44. JT *Shekalim* 6:1, end.

45. See Rabbi Nathan T. Lopes Cardozo's description of the significance of this mystic tradition in *Between Silence and Speech* (Northvale, N.J.: Jason Aronson, 1995), pp. 119–159; much of what I say here is merely a summary. Although I agree with his analysis, my view of revelation is probably less committed to the metaphysical details of the mystic tradition; neither do I share his conviction that belief in the divine origins of the Torah requires dismissal of biblical criticism (see ibid., pp. 171–193).

46. *Sefer Yetzirah,* chap. 2. There are several variant texts of this classic mystic work. All of them are included in the edition that was republished by Rabbi Mordechai Attiya (Jerusalem, 1972).

47. Ravad, *Hilkhot Sukkah Velulav,* chapter 8, *halakhah* 5. See also Haviva Pedaya, who writes of the identification made by Kabbalists of the thirteenth century between the *Bet Midrash* and the Temple: *Hashem Vehamikdash Bemishnat R. Yitzhak Segi-Nahor: Iyun Mashveh Bekitvei Rishonei Hamekubalim* (Jerusalem: Magnes, 2001).

48. Kook, *Iggerot Hareayah* (Jerusalem: Mosad Harav Kook, 1985), 1:123–124. See also his essay: "The Sage is More Important than the Prophet" (in Hebrew), *Orot* (Jerusalem: Mosad Harav Kook, 1985), pp. 120–121; translated into English in *Abraham Isaac Kook—The Lights of Penitence, the Moral Principles, Lights of Holiness, Essays, Letters, and Poems,* translation and introduction by Ben Zion Bokser (New York: Paulist Press, 1978), pp. 253–255.

49. Nachmanides, *Introduction to Commentary on the Torah,* edited by Chaim Dov Chavel (Jerusalem: Mosad Harav Kook, 1973), pp. 6–7.

50. See, for example, the exhortation of Ben Bag-Bag, the first-century Palestinian sage, to delve continuously in Torah, for all is in it (*Pirkei Avot* 5:22).

51. This is commonly expressed as the difference between the nature of the Torah before Adam's fall in the Garden of Eden or in the Messianic age, and the manner in which it is read today. See Rabbi Avrahm Azulai, *Hessed leAvraham* (Sulzbach, 1685), 2:11; ibid., 2:27. These ideas are presented in the name of Azulai's teacher, R. Moshe Cordovero (quoted in translation and explained by Lopes-Cadozo, *Between Silence and Speech,* pp. 133–138.

52. This may explain why, according to R. Hayim of Volozhin, the forefathers allowed themselves to perform acts that violated the *mitzvot* as we know them today. It is possible that he viewed the souls of the founding fathers as remnants of the previous age of *hessed* whose function was to allow the world continued existence by softening the harshness of the powers of judgment that reign from the time of the giving of the Torah. See *Nefesh Hahayim,* part I, chaps. 21–22.

53. Identifying the present era with *din* suits the feminist critique of Judaism as legalistic, hierarchical, and dominated by divisions and atomistic thinking. And the idea of the emergence of *rahamim* accords nicely with the feminist call for nonhierarchical, nonatomistic thinking.

54. *Shemot Rabbah,* sec. 47, on the verse: "*Zehu me'at meharbeh.*"

55. See Rashi ad loc.

56. See also Nachmanides' explanation ad loc., reflecting *Midrash Shir Hashirim Rabbah.*

57. See Rashi reflecting *Midrash Sifre* on Numbers, sec. 133.

58. BT *Gittin* 6b. See R. Hayim of Volozhin's treatment of this in *Nefesh Hahayim,* part 4, chap. 6.

59. See Rabbi Israel Porat in his introduction to BT *Ketubot.* Similarly, Rabbi David Bernstein, the Hassidic Rebbe of Sukhachov (1875–1943) suggests that the settling of Palestine has been transformed into a special *mitzvah* in our times owing

to the outburst of desire on the part of the Jewish masses to observe it. See Aryeh Strikovsky, *Am veAretz, Yeud ve'etgar* (Jerusalem: Misrad Hahinukh Vetarbut/ Mahlaka Letarbut Toranit, 1992), p. 176.

60. Rabbi Yosef Eliyahu Henkin, "The End of Days" (in Hebrew), *Hadarom* 10 (Elul 1959), pp. 5–9.

61. R. Kook, *Iggerot Hareayah* 1:19–21. For further discussion of this idea, see Tamar Ross, "Between Metaphysical and Liberal Pluralism: A Reappraisal of Rabbi A. I. Kook's Espousal of Toleration," *AJS* [Association for Jewish Studies] *Review* 2: 1 (1996), pp. 81–82.

62. This idea has its source in the statement of the Mishnah that "long ago Senaherib, king of Assyria, came up and confused all the nations," implying that since the original nations are now commingled, the *mitzvah* can no longer be performed. See Mishnah *Yadayim* 4:4.

63. *Arpelei Tohar,* 1st ed. (Jaffa, 1914), p. 11. For a more exhaustive discussion of this passage and the censorship it underwent, see Tamar Ross, "Can the Demand for Change in the Status of Women be Halakhically Legitimated?" *Judaism* 42:4 (fall 1993), p. 490 n.20.

64. *Iggerot Hareayah* (Jerusalem: Mosad Harav Kook, 1985), 1:103–104. This letter appears in full in *Rav A. Y. Kook: Selected Letters,* translated and annotated by Tzvi Feldman (Maaleh Adumim: Ma'aliot Publications, 1986), pp. 183–188.

65. A. Y. Kook, *Iggerot Hareayah,* 1:103.

66. Ibid., p. 106; This letter appears in full in *Rav A. Y. Kook: Selected Letters,* pp. 3–10.

67. Indeed, this avenue has already been exploited at least once. See Daniel Shalit, *Or Shivat Yamim* (Tvai, 1998). Although Shalit, a returnee to Orthodox observance, hardly mentions R. Kook explicitly, the intricate historic scheme that lies at the heart of his thesis reveals the pervasive influence of Kook's mystic ideas and their applications to feminism. He assumes that the Torah is a dynamic entity and that its ultimate import is gradually revealed via a dialectic relationship between the moral state of the nations of the world and the Jews' religious expression of this morality. This gradual revelation is also embodied in a dialectic interaction between circular (feminine) and linear (masculine) modes of being that constitute necessary stages in the process of building up the fully developed Godhead. The ebbs and eddies in the revelation of the divine light are reflected in the state of repair of the world and humanity in general, but particularly in the status of women, which is a kind of seismograph indicating the progress of this revelation. Shalit concludes that the feminist movement cannot be viewed as a foreign import that threatens to defile Judaism. It is rather a testimony of the response of divine providence to the progress of human civilization, and the Torah community is now obliged to incorporate it in order to bring the process to full fruition. Although Shalit's work is an illuminating example of how a cumulativist approach might be applied to enable an appropriation of feminism within the framework of traditional Jewish premises, I cannot identify with it in full; I find his detailed historical scheme to be an over literal application of metaphysical statements.

68. A. I. Kook, *Eder ha-Yakar* (Jerusalem: Mosad Harav Kook, 1982), pp. 42–43.

69. A. I. Kook, *Orot Haemunah* (Brooklyn, N.Y.: Langsam Associates, 1985), pp. 48 and 74–75.

70. Plaskow, *Standing Again at Sinai,* pp. 34–36.

71. See chapter 7, pp. 130–131.

72. The notion of primary conceptions as necessary stepping-stones to more sophisticated understandings is central to R. Kook's gradualist philosophy. Thus, when discussing the relationship between monotheism and pantheism, he describes the

former as an indispensable "vessel and vestibule" for the latter, which is in some way closer to the truth. See *Orot Hakodesh* (Jerusalem: Mosad Harav Kook, 1985), 2: 399–401.

73. R. Tzadok Hacohen, *Resisei Leilah,* p. 13. Similar ideas can be found in the thought of Rav A. I. Kook; see, for example, his commentary to the Passsover Haggadah in *Olat Reiyah* (Jerusalem: Mosad Harav Kook, 1985), 2:261; *Orot Haemunah,* pp. 3–4. For further sources and discussion see Tamar Ross, "The Elite and the Masses in the Prism of Metaphysics and History: Harav Kook on the Nature of Religious Belief," *Journal of Jewish Thought and Philosophy* 8 (1999), particularly pp. 364–366.

74. See Jacob Joshua Ross, *The Virtues of the Family* (New York: Free Press, 1994). Several anthropological studies have documented the disastrous psychological effects of kibbutz experiments in breaking down gender distinctions in child-rearing.

75. Janet Radcliffe Richards, *The Sceptical Feminist : A Philosophical Enquiry* (Middlesex, Eng.: Pelican, 1980), p. 187.

76. Ibid.

77. Daphne Hampson, *After Christianity* (London: SCM Press, 1996), pp. 281–282.

11. Some Theological Remarks for the More Philosophically Inclined (pp. 213–224)

1. See Ruether's *Sexism and God-Talk: Toward a Feminist Theology* (Boston: Beacon, 1983; London: SCM Press, 1983), p. 71.

2. Ibid., p. 72.

3. Daphne Hampson, *Feminism and Theology,* pp. 28–29.

4. Ibid., p. 29.

5. Daphne Hampson, *After Christianity* (London: SCM Press, 1996), p. 134.

6. Rachel Adler, *Engendering Judaism: An Inclusive Theology and Ethics* (Philadelphia: Jewish Publication Society, 1998), p. 32.

7. See Alfred North Whitehead, *Process and Reality: An Essay in Cosmology* (New York: Free Press, 1978). For the relationship of feminism to process thought, see Sheila G. Davaney, ed., *Feminism and Process Thought: The Harvard Divinity School—Claremont Center for Process Studies Symposium Papers* (New York: Edwin Mellen, 1980).

8. Mary Ellen Ross, "Feminism and the Problem of Moral Character," *Journal of Feminist Studies in Religion* 5:2 (fall 1989), pp. 63–64.

9. See for example, Kook, *Orot Hakodesh* (Jerusalem: Mosad Harav Kook, 1985), 2:395–396, 397–398, 399–401.

10. For another exposition of an antitheodicy approach based on an interpretation of Job, see Howard Wettstein, "Against Theodicy," in *Judaism* 50:3 (2001), pp. 341–350.

11. This approach is reminiscent of one of the classical moves used in justifying why "bad things happen to good people": asserting that the present iniquity will be redressed in the world to come. Yet if God is indeed good and all-powerful, could He not have overcome even the illusion of injustice and temporary suffering? The usual theistic response to this is that in the given historical context, the norm being replaced was not viewed as wrong. God works with human beings, so that only when human society has reached a certain stage of development does it become appropriate for a new sensibility or norm to be revealed.

12. Michael Walzer, *Spheres of Justice* (New York: Basic Books, 1983), pp. 312–313.

13. Hampson, *Theology and Feminism,* pp. 28–29.

14. See R. Leiner's interpretation of the binding of Isaac in *Mei Hashiloah* (Jerusalem, 1976), I:16; ibid., II:12. For further sources, see Jerome Gellman, "A Hassidic Interpretation of the Binding of Isaac," in *Dat Umusar,* edited by Danny Statman and Avi Sagi (Ramat Gan: Bar-Ilan University, 1993), xxiii-vii.

15. Kathryn Tanner, *Theories of Culture: A New Agenda for Theology* (Minneapolis, Minn.: Fortress, 1997), p. 81.

16. See Mendel Shapiro, "Concluding Responses to *Queri'at ha-Torah* for Women," *The Edah Journal* 1:2 (Sivan 2001) (www.Edah.org), p. 2.

17. A version of this objection to my position was presented forcefully to me by Rabbi Joshua Amaru, to whom I am indebted for the stimulation of this debate. My summary includes verbatim some of his arguments, originally expressed in private communication.

18. Such as Saadya Gaon, as well as the author of the *Halakhot Gedolot.*

19. See Maimonides' general introduction to his commentary to the Mishnah (Jerusalem: Mosad Harav Kook, 1961), chap. 2.

20. This more open-ended understanding of Torah need not be equated with rejection of heteronomous authority, any more than a view of accumulating revelation deserves to be equated with mindless passivity. Nonetheless, some contemporary theologians who are driven by a Kantian concern for human autonomy are attracted to this approach precisely because they see its rejection of the appeal to metaphysics affording a more autonomous view of human activity. See Arnold Eisen's survey of this trend in "Jewish Theology in North America: Notes on Two Decades," in *American Jewish Year Book, 1991,* pp. 9–17. For an exposition of one of its chief spokesmen, see David Hartman, *A Living Covenant: The Innovative Spirit in Traditional Judaism* (New York: Free Press, 1985); idem, *Maimonides: Torah and Philosophic Quest* (Philadelphia: Jewish Publication Society, 1976).

21. Maimonides, *Guide for the Perplexed,* part III, chap. 32.

12. Visions for the Future (pp. 227–249)

1. Lauren B. Granite, "Tradition as a Modality of Religious Change: Talmud Study in the Lives of Orthodox Jewish Women" (Ph.D. diss., Drew University, 1995).

2. Tamar El-Or, *BaPesah Haba: Nashim Veoreyanut Batziyonut Hadatit* (Tel Aviv: Am Oved, 1998); forthcoming in English translation. See also my review of this book: "Between Anthropology, Women and Tradition" (in Hebrew), *Badad 9* (Bar-Ilan University; summer 1999), pp. 67–76. Although I believe that El-Or's conclusions are not unfounded, the *midrasha* at Bar-Ilan is not representative of this feminist avant-garde; therefore I regard them as educated guesses that have little to do with the ethnographic material she cites as evidence.

3. El-Or, *BaPesah Haba,* p. 31.

4. BT *Yevamot* 118b.

5. Because the term *rabbanit* is generally employed to designate the rabbi's wife, non-Orthodox denominations, which now accept women rabbis, prefer to grant them the title of *Rabbah.*

6. See El-Or, *BaPesach Haba* regarding the interface among religious women, Torah literacy, and active participation.

7. See chapter 1 above, p. 16.

8. *Jewish Legal Writings by Women,* edited by Micah D. Halpern and Chana Safrai (Jerusalem: Urim Publications, 1998), is a collection of contemporary original articles on Jewish law by religious women from around the world. While much of

the book tends to historical survey rather than purely legal discussion, and it is only a first step toward women's mastery of highly technical halakhic material, one can already discern the novel contribution of women to the field, a precursor of things to come.

9. See, in this connection, Rabbi Yehuda Henkin's remarks in "The New 'Poseks': Orthodox Women," by Michele Chabin, *Jewish Week* (New York), October 8, 1999; Chana Henkin, "Women and the Issuing of Halakhic Rulings," in *Jewish Legal Writings,* pp. 285–286.

10. R. Israel Meir Hacohen (Kagan), *Likkutei Halakhiot,* Sotah 20b.

11. I refer, for example, to the project of Rabbi Abraham J. Twerski, author of *The Shame Borne in Silence: Spouse Abuse in the Jewish Community* (Pittsburgh, Pa.: Mikrov Publications, 1996) , which has been carried into American yeshiva high schools by organizations such as Project SARAH (Stop Abusive Relationships at Home) and the Israeli Crisis Center for Religious Women, founded by psychologist Debbie Gross.

12. On Bin-Nun's understanding, the category of independent women did exist in biblical times. Moreover, postbiblical *halakhah* recognizes a progressive scale of independence among women; the category of an "important woman" *(isha hashuvah)* comes closest to the liberated status of many women today. Initially, Bin-Nun assumed that women no longer bound by the needs of others should be regarded as obligated to perform all the optional *mitzvot.* Confronted with a general reluctance by women to assume men's roles, however, he altered his position, concluding that modern women who are not bound to the yoke of family responsibilities should also be left free to choose which of the optional *mitzvot* they will adopt.

13. Bin-Nun specifically excludes the status of women in marriage. While accepting that a bride's monetary rights can be made equal to those of her husband by use of a suitable prenuptial agreement, he does not envisage the possibility that the other aspect of the contract, whereby her husband acquires exclusive right to her sexual services, can be annulled. He suggests, however, that even such asymmetry can be overcome by voluntary commitment of the husband (even on oath) to the same sexual constraints. Linkage between contemporary women's liberated status and their right to greater obligation of *mitzvah* performance is alluded to in a somewhat different manner by Noam Zohar ("Women, Men and Religious Status: Deciphering a Chapter in Mishnah," in *Approaches to Ancient Judaism,* edited by Herbert Basser and Simha Fishbane, vol. 5 [Atlanta: Scholars, 1003], chap. 2), envisaging eventual reformulation of the marriage contract.

14. *Magen Avraham, Hilkhot Sefirat Haomer, simman* 489, *seif katan* 1.

15. Bin-Nun's line of argument bears some similarity to that pursued by R. Shlomo Goren; in one of his responsa Israel's late Ashkenazi chief rabbi defended women's right to carry out a full prayer service, including all those rituals and texts that normally require a *minyan,* on strength of the special dispensation granted women by Rabbenu Tam in the twelfth century, allowing them to recite blessings upon performing voluntarily adopted obligations. Goren's position (which he himself subsequently qualified) has so far been rejected by the overwhelming majority of Orthodox halakhic authorities. See Aryeh and Dov Frimer, "Women's Prayer Services—Theory and Practice," *Tradition* 32:2 (1998), pp. 7–14.

16. This formulation from a paper submitted by David Feldman to the Committee on Jewish Law and Standards of the Conservative movement's Rabbinical Assembly, supporting the traditional Orthodox ruling that women are not to be counted as part of a *minyan,* is quoted approvingly by David Bleich in *Contemporary Halakhic Problems* (New York: Ktav, 1977), pp. 81–82.

17. Ibid.

18. For a more nuanced and context-related approach to this issue, see Rabbi Hayim Hirschensohn, *Malki Bakodesh* (St. Louis, Mo.: Moynester, 1919–1928), 2: 193–202.

19. See Haym Soloveitchik, *Halakhah, Kalkalah, Vedimui Azmi: Hamashkonaut Bimei Havenayim* (Jerusalem, 1985).

20. An example of this is the dispensation for an *eruv*, a symbolic enclosure, nowadays usually constructed out of wire and poles. It serves as a legal device that allows for the carrying of objects on the Sabbath within an area (*carmelit*) that has been forbidden by the Rabbis (*reshut harabbim miderabbanan*) even though it falls short of the specifications defining public domain according to biblical law (*reshut harabbim mideoraita*). One of the disputed specifications referring to a biblical public domain is whether such an area requires that 600,000 people pass simultaneously within that area during the Sabbath. If so, according to some scholars, even a modern metropolis the size of Manhattan may be transformed, via an *eruv*, into an area with the status of a courtyard where carrying is permitted. In spite of their strenuous opposition to its use in such circumstances, *poskim* have often been pressured by public demand into allowing for an *eruv* even in such disputed areas. It is obvious in this case that social need has overridden strict conformance with formal legal considerations.

21. For a fuller account of use of this principle as a tool for bridging gaps between *halakhah* and reality, see Neriah Gotel, "'The Changing of Nature': A Halakhic, Doctrinal or Naturalistic Response to 'Conflicts' between *Halakhah* and Reality?" (in Hebrew) *Badad* 7 (summer 1998), pp. 33–47; idem, *Hishtanut Hatevaim Behalakhah* (Jerusalem: Yahdav, 1998).

22. This statement was made in a public lecture at Pelekh high school (Jerusalem, 2001). A related formulation of this difference, as phrased by Rabbi Benny Lau ("The Halakhah Lost its Way: An Introduction to the Conservative Movement via Study of the Writings of the 'Vaad Hahalakh,'" [in Hebrew], *Deot* 6 [December 1999], pp. 22–26), is that while decisions of the Conservative rabbinate are addressed to a constituency of halakhically apathetic followers, the authoritative force of changes within Orthodoxy draws from the fact that such changes already reflect the genuine struggles of a halakhically committed laity.

23. A women's *bet midrash* can now schedule a lecture on *halakhah* and intimacy conducted jointly by a sex therapist and mainstream rabbi, and draw a packed audience—a possibility that would have been most unlikely in this context a decade ago. It is also noteworthy that the 2002 international conference on Feminism and Orthodoxy was entitled "Discovering/Uncovering/Recovering Women in Judaism."

24. Thus, *halakhah* stipulates that when a man is ill and has no one to help him, his wife may do so even if she is in the state of *niddah*, provided she takes care to keep physical contact to a minimum. However, according to Sephardic ruling, her husband may not do the same for her in this situation. See *Shulhan Arukh, Yoreh Deah*, chap. 195, secs. 15 and 16.

25. See, for example, R. Ovadyah Yosef, *Yabia Omer*, vol. 1, *Yoreh Deah*, sec. 15.

26. Ibid., and see Magen Avraham on *Orah Hayim* at the end of *simman* 706.

27. A documentary film entitled *Purity*, recently produced in Israel, highlights some of the problems that result from this asymmetry of perspective for religious women observing the laws of family purity. For Orthodox couples to engage in full sexual relations on their wedding night without having had any physical contact whatsoever beforehand may be tolerable in terms of male sexuality, but to a young woman the prospect is traumatic; the bleeding that accompanies the loss of her virginity means that she then faces two weeks without any further touch from her husband.

28. As Haviva Ner-David has pointed out, the very term "family purity," developed only in the twentieth century as a euphemism for the laws of *niddah* in order to reflect more favorable attitudes to these laws, may ironically be most responsible for such insidious effects. Although this terminology is generally used in conjunction with the notion that observing the laws of *niddah* is a way to improve married life, by extension ensuring the well-being of the couple's entire family, it gives the impression that it is the woman's responsibility "to protect the 'purity' of her family" through such observance—"a mistaken notion, since purity is not the primary focus of these laws today." See her forthcoming article, *"Niddah: A Case in Point of Feminist Reinterpretation,"* in *"To Be A Jewish Woman—Part B": Proceedings of the Second International Conference: Woman and Her Judaism,* edited by Margalit Shilo (Kolech—Religious Woman's Forum/Urim Publications, 2003).

29. In a talk delivered in 1999 at Kenes Lavi, a convention dedicated to issues of Israeli Modern Orthodoxy.

30. As does Rabbi Yaakov Ariel. See "The Women's *Bet Midrash*" (in Hebrew), in *Haisha,* edited by Zeev Karov (Jerusalem: El-Ami, 2000), pp. 94–95.

31. Note, for example, Avivah Zornberg's volumes on Genesis and Exodus, Susan Handelman and Ora Wiskind-Alper's *Torah of the Mothers: Contemporary Jewish Women Read Classical Jewish Texts* (New York: Urim, 2000), and most particularly the sheets of commentary on the weekly portion of the Torah produced by the Orthodox women's lobby, Kolech, and distributed in Israeli synagogues at the Sabbath service. The proliferation of such sheets by various religious organizations and the creatively imaginative use made of the biblical text for supporting widely varying and even conflicting ideologies on the contemporary scene merits a separate study.

32. Two halakhically observant women enrolled in the gender studies program of Bar-Ilan University are currently writing doctorate theses on the influence of gender assumptions on *halakhah;* Haviva Ner-David focusing on the laws of *niddah* and Ronit Ir-Shai on reproductive issues.

33. Women of the Wall, who convene once a month for prayer on the women's side at the Western Wall, also exemplify this trend; adhering to the standards of Orthodox women's prayer groups, its membership spans the denominational spectrum. The Jewish Orthodox Feminist Alliance (JOFA) has also invited Jewish feminists of other denominations to participate and address their conferences.

34. A formula prescribed and adopted in our day by some halakhically conscientious authorities of a formalistic bent. See, for example, Moshe Yaakov Weingarten, *Kol-bo Leseder Leil Pesah Bahalakhah Ubaaggadah: Otzar Dinim, Minhagim, Perushim Uremazim im Mekorot Vehearot,* part 1: *Haseder Hearukh* (Jerusalem: Weingarten, 1991), pp. 459 and 472.

35. For sample expositions of this view, see Carol Gilligan, *In a Different Voice: Psychological Theory and Women's Development* (Cambridge, Mass.: Harvard University Press, 1982); Jean Grimshaw, *Feminist Philosophers: Women's Perspectives on Philosophical Traditions* (Brighton, Sussex: Wheatsheaf Books, 1986), pp. 187–226 (also published as *Philosophy and Feminist Thinking* [Minneapolis: University of Minnesota Press, 1986]).

36. See chapter 7 above, pp. 131–137.

37. Hanina Ben Menahem, "Postscript: The Judicial Process and the Nature of Jewish Law," in *An Introduction to the History and Sources of Jewish Law,* edited by N. S. Hecht et al. (Oxford: Clarendon Press, 1996), pp. 421–437.

38. See Steven F. Friedell, "The 'Different Voice' in Jewish Law: Some Parallels to a Feminist Jureisprudence," in *Indiana Law Journal* 67 (1992), pp. 915–949; Leonard D. Gordon, "Toward a Gender-Inclusive Account of Halakhah," in *Gender and*

Judaism: The Transformation of Tradition, edited by Tamar Rudavsky (New York: New York University Press, 1995), pp. 3–12; Chana Safrai, "Feminist Theology in a Jewish Context," in *Sources and Resources of Feminist Theologies: Yearbook of the European Society of Women in Theological Research,* edited by Elisabeth Hartlieb and Charlotte Methuen (Kampen, The Netherlandds: Kok Pharos Publishing, 1997), 5:140–147.

39. Revisionist history stemming from traditional circles prefers to picture Sarah Schnirer's initial plan for establishing a school dedicated to Torah education for girls in 1918 as something the rabbis readily agreed to or even suggested themselves. Yet the language employed by the Hafetz Hayim in his initial responsum, which eventually opened the floodgates to the basic and far-reaching advances that have been made in religious education for women, indicates a rather halfhearted approval; he appears to be making the best of a bad situation, in hope that eventually things would return to "normal." (See Yisrael Meir Hacohen, *Likkutei Halakhot, Sotah* 21, and his lesserknown letter of 23 Shevat, 1933.) Although the current leader of the Hassidic dynasty of Gur at that time, Rabbi Abraham Mordekhai Alter, displayed more foresight with regard to the educational needs of Jewish women in the modern world, Rabbi A .I. Kook and other traditionalists vigorously opposed this trend.

40. See, for example, Haym Soloveitchik, "Religious Law and Change: The Medieval Ashkenazic Example," *AJS Review* 12:2 (fall 1987), pp. 205–221.

41. See chapter 2, p. 26.

42. For a poignant expression of this wish, see Sarah Idit (Susan) Schneider, "The Daughters of Tzlafchad: Towards a Methodology of Attitude Around Women's Issues," in *Torah of the Mothers: Contemporary Jewish Women Read Classical Jewish Texts,* edited by Ora Wiskind-Alper and Susan Handelman (New York: Urim, 2000), pp. 155–169.

43. See the testimony of Estie Rosenberg, in *Hinukh Habat Beyameinu* [Proceedings of the seventh annual conference of Mikhlelet Lifshitz] (Jerusalem, 2002), p. 71.

44. This idealization of uncritical submissiveness has been especially propagated in modern times in certain schools of the *musar* movement. See T. Ross, "Anti-Rationalism in the *Musar* Movement" (in Hebrew), in *Alei Shefer: Studies in Jewish Thought Presented in Honor of Rabbi Dr. A. Shafran,* edited by M. Halamish (Ramat Gan: Bar-Ilan University, 5750 [1990]), pp. 145–163. Opposition to this trend can be found in certain streams of Hassidut and in the writings of R. Kook. Eloquent expression of the disagreement is focused in various interpretations of the sacrifice of Isaac; see Jerome Gellman, *The Fear, the Trembling and the Fire: Kierkegaard and Hassidic Masters on the Binding of Isaac* (Lanham, Md.: University Press of America, 1994).

45. This real-life situation was dramatized in Yaakov Friedland's documentary film, *Sheasani Isha,* on the effects of the women's learning revolution on the lives of Israeli religious women.

Index